Global Sport Sponsorship

Sport Commerce and Culture

Series ISSN: 1741-0916

Editor:
David L. Andrews, *University of Maryland*

The impact of sporting issues on culture and commerce both locally and globally is huge. However, the power and pervasiveness of this billion-dollar industry has yet to be deeply analyzed. Sports issues shape the economy, the media and even our lifestyle choices, ultimately playing an unquestionable role in our psychology. This series examines the sociological significance of the sports industry and the sporting world in contemporary cultures around the world.

Previously published books in the series:

Sport and Corporate Nationalisms, *edited by Michael L. Silk, David Andrews & C.L. Cole*

Global Sport Sponsorship

Edited by

John Amis and T. Bettina Cornwell

Oxford • New York

English edition
First published in 2005 by
Berg
Editorial offices:
First Floor, Angel Court, 81 St Clements Street, Oxford OX4 1AW, UK
175 Fifth Avenue, New York, NY 10010, USA

Berg is the imprint of Oxford International Publishers Ltd.

Library of Congress Cataloging-in-Publication Data
Global sport sponsorship / edited by John Amis and T. Bettina Cornwell.
     p. cm. — (Sport, commerce and culture)
     Includes bibliographical references and index.
     ISBN 1-84520-081-0 (pbk.) — ISBN 1-84520-080-2 (cloth)
     1. Sports sponsorship. 2. Sports and globalization. I. Amis, John, 1968- II. Cornwell,
T. Bettina. III. Series.

     GV716.G57 2005
     796'.0698—dc22

                                                                      2005013775

British Library Cataloguing-in-Publication Data
A catalogue record for this book is available from the British Library.

ISBN-13   978 1 84520 080 0 (Cloth)
              978 1 84520 081 7 (Paper)

ISBN-10   1 84520 080 2 (Cloth)
              1 84520 081 0 (Paper)

Typeset by JS Typesetting Ltd, Porthcawl, Mid Glamorgan
Printed in the United Kingdom by Biddles Ltd, King's Lynn

www.bergpublishers.com

Contents

Contents

List of Tables and Figures

Notes on Contributors

John Amis, Associate Professor, Department of Health & Sport Sciences and Department of Management, University of Memphis, USA

David L. Andrews, Associate Professor, Department of Kinesiology, University of Maryland, USA

Colleen Bee, Assistant Professor of Marketing, School of Business Administration, University of San Diego, USA

T. Bettina Cornwell, Professor of Marketing, University of Queensland School of Business, Australia

Timothy Dewhirst, Associate Professor, Department of Management and Marketing, University of Saskatchewan, Canada

Oliver Dieterle, Program Manager, Deutsches SportFernsehen GmbH, Germany

Francis Farrelly, Senior Lecturer, School of Marketing, Monash University, Australia

James Gladden, Associate Professor, Department of Sport Management, University of Massachusetts at Amherst, USA

Andrew D. Grainger, Doctoral Candidate, Department of Kinesiology, University of Maryland, USA

Kevin Gwinner, Associate Professor, Department of Marketing, Kansas State University, USA

Janet Hoek, Professor of Marketing, Department of Marketing, Massey University, New Zealand

Shannon Jetté, Doctoral Candidate, School of Human Kinetics, University of British Columbia, Canada

Monica LaBarge, Doctoral Candidate, Lundquist College of Business, University of Oregon, USA

Helen Jefferson Lenskyj, Professor, Ontario Institute for Studies in Education, University of Toronto, Canada

Robert Madrigal, Associate Professor, Lundquist College of Business, University of Oregon, USA

Mark McDonald, Associate Professor, Department of Sport Management, University of Massachusetts at Amherst, USA

Tony Meenaghan, Professor of Marketing, Graduate School of Business at University College Dublin, Ireland

Joshua I. Newman, Assistant Professor, Department of Kinesiology, Towson University, USA

Pascale Quester, Professor of Marketing, School of Commerce, Adelaide University, Australia

Don Roy, Assistant Professor, Department of Management & Marketing, Middle Tennessee State University, USA

Amanda Schweinbenz, Doctoral Candidate, School of Human Kinetics, University of British Columbia, Canada

Sally Shaw, Lecturer, School of Physical Education, University of Otago, New Zealand

Michael Silk, Assistant Professor, Department of Kinesiology, University of Maryland, USA

Robert Sparks, Associate Professor, School of Human Kinetics, University of British Columbia, Canada

Mike Weed, Lecturer, Institute of Sport and Leisure Policy, Loughborough University, UK

Detlev Zwick, Assistant Professor of Marketing, Schulich School of Business, York University, Canada

Sport Sponsorship in a Global Age

John Amis and T. Bettina Cornwell

A dominant topic of study and conversation across the social sciences in recent years has been the extent to which our lives have become permeated by forces encapsulated under the nebulous and contested term "globalization." Contending with such forces has similarly become a prevalent consideration in the strategizing of executives at most major corporations. Difficult to define in any succinct manner, globalization has been variously examined in terms of the ideological, political, economic, technological and social changes that have become manifest in, and characteristic of, our existence. While the degree to which these various dynamics do indeed impact our lives has been questioned (e.g. Hirst & Thompson, 1999; Rugman, 2003), there is little doubt that we exist in a "global age" and thus must fundamentally revise our conceptualization of an array of previously taken for granted operating practices, organizing assumptions and modes of interaction (Albrow, 1996).

Prominent within this consideration has been the changing role of the nation-state; the increased prominence of large, private corporations engaged in cross-border trade; the spread of capitalism and neo-liberal ideologies; the technological advancements that have precipitated seemingly instantaneous communication across, and access to information from, disparate parts of the world; the creation of networks of organizations that span international boundaries; the role of supra-national institutions such as the United Nations, World Bank and European Parliament; the creation of powerful trading blocs such as the North American Free Trade Agreement, the European Union, and the most recent Free Trade Area of the Americas; the more distant, rapid and frequent travel of individuals around the world for work and leisure; and the changing emphases on traditional societal institutions such as the family, church and workplace in different countries (see, for example, Albrow, 1996; Castells, 1996; Giddens, 2002; Harvey, 1990; Held, McGrew, Goldblatt & Perraton, 1999; Parker, 1999; Segal-Horn & Faulkner, 1999; Tomlinson, 1999). Clearly, this list is neither exhaustive nor are the various manifestations independent, but together they constitute a very changed operating environment for organizations and institutions of all types.

Despite this increased level of scholarly and practical interest, attention devoted to the ways in which sport sponsorship has been affected by, and has influenced, the global corporate and social landscape has been negligible. There have been occasional descriptive studies that have sought to examine different sponsorship practices across countries (cf. Walliser, 2003); aspects of the global nature of "sport business" have also been the subject of several pieces (see, for example, Westerbeek & Smith, 2003, and various articles in trade publications such as Street & Smith's *Sport Business Journal*). However, there has been a pronounced lack of engagement with the ways in which the dynamics outlined above affect, and are affected by, sport sponsorship practices. Thus, while sport has been lauded by practitioners and scholars for its ability to both transcend national borders and achieve local resonance, the nuanced appropriation of sport properties by sponsors operating in varied contexts and with multiple objectives has scarcely been examined.

This lack of investigation into global sport sponsorship – defined as an investment in an individual, event, team or organization with the expectation of achieving certain corporate objectives in multiple countries – is problematic for a number of reasons. First, the flows of global capital to achieve such objectives have become increasingly significant. Applebaum (2004), for example, writing for *Brandweek*, recently concluded that companies spent approximately US$30 billion worldwide on sponsorship in 2003, with about 77% of that total being spent on sport. Thus, decisions made to engage in sport sponsorship agreements have become strategically much more important for corporate executives. Second, the economic, political and social issues that accompany this trend of increased investment are similarly ill-understood. Third, we are still at a nascent state of comprehension with respect to the ways in which economic, technological, ideological, social and geopolitical shifts will interact to reconstitute global sport sponsorship opportunities.

Steven Heyer, President of Coca-Cola (2003), describes business practices in the new social and economic landscape as altering with "a magnitude and urgency of change that isn't evolutionary – it's transformational." Cornwell and Drennan (2004) have also noted that research examining consumers and consumption must change radically in order to better understand the forces of globalization and fragmentation in the areas of environment, identity, well-being, market structure and policy. We similarly argue that while sport sponsorship is playing a central role in the cross-border brand positioning strategies of many firms, our understanding of the dialectical nature of such sponsorship investments on the global and local environments in which firms operate is decidedly unclear and in need of consideration.

While we contest that a lack of adequate theoretical and empirical investigation has severely hampered our understanding of the important corporate, political and social issues that accompany global sport sponsorship agreements, the rationales for entering into such arrangements are quite well documented. Sport sponsorship has been used, among other things, as a perceived mechanism for overcoming some cultural and linguistic barriers, providing direct access to local media, and providing corporate hospitality opportunities (see, for example,

Meenaghan, 1991; Mintel, 1994; Walliser, 2003; Witcher, Craigen, Culligan & Harvey, 1991). However, there has been surprisingly little research carried out on the utilization of sport sponsorship as a strategic tool (cf. Meenaghan, 1999; Walliser, 2003); inevitably, consideration of sponsorship as part of a global strategy is even scarcer. The two most cited rationales for entering into sport sponsorship agreements, increasing awareness and modifying firm or brand image (e.g. Cornwell & Maignan, 1998; Meenaghan, 1991; Mintel, 1994) have also been the topics of most scholarly examination (cf. Walliser, 2003). While these are clearly important, particularly with respect to our still very limited understanding as to how image transfer occurs from a sport property to a sponsor in different contexts (see Gwinner, 1997, and this volume), they are certainly not sufficient in terms of understanding the rationale for, and outcomes of, sport sponsorship investment.

For example, the utilization of sport sponsorship to build and enhance rela-tionships with employees, corporate partners, politicians and regulators through the use of corporate hospitality opportunities has become an increasingly visible manifestation of sponsorship at "global events" such as the Olympics, Wimbledon Tennis Championships, Ryder Cup and FIFA World Cup. Research into the strategic utilization of sponsorship in this way requires much greater analysis, particularly in terms of the ways in which such hospitality influences decision-making of those being hosted.

Further, the corporate scandals that have befallen firms such as WorldCom, Enron and Arthur Andersen have increased the steps that many firms have taken to present themselves as good corporate citizens. Thus, the role of sport sponsorship as a strategic part of a global corporate social responsibility (CSR) program needs to be investigated, both in terms of its effectiveness and the potential negative outcomes – rarely considered – that such arrangements might generate. There is evidence of such work forthcoming, but this is mainly focused on local and domestic programs (e.g. Lachowetz & Irwin, 2002). Research into more global CSR campaigns, such as King's (2001) investigation of Avon, continues to be the exception rather than the norm.

As importantly, while our understanding of global sport sponsorship processes remains underdeveloped, that work which has sought to uncover the strategic nature of such investments and their associated outcomes has been almost entirely positive and uncritical. There appears to be little thought given to some of the more problematic practices that sponsors engage in – such as dictating performance schedules, defining what constitutes (un)acceptable behaviors, and rewarding only those individuals and organizations that conform to certain preconceived notions of desirability – nor the detrimental outcomes that they may have for key publics, including athletes, supporters, sport organizations and members of society.

Consequently, our intent with this text has been to gather together a group of leading scholars able to bring a refreshing and informed perspective to global sport sponsorship from a variety of disciplinary perspectives, including marketing, management, sociology, cultural studies, gender studies and tourism. In addition to the multidisciplinary nature of the book's content, the perspectives of the authors are enhanced by their "global citizenry," encompassing eight nationalities and a multitude of transnational relocations. Each essay within this collection has been crafted with the intent of providing a "cutting-edge" perspective on some aspect of the global sport sponsorship debate. Thus, the book has been positioned to offer a detailed understanding of the theoretical debates and practical realities that: define and locate sport sponsorship within a global context; impact the development and utilization of sponsorship as a potentially valuable strategic asset; and raise a series of problematic issues that other approaches to sponsorship research have largely missed. Indeed, while the chapters have been set in a particular sequence in order to bring some coherence to the text as a whole, all inform multiple areas of these debates.

We have also asked the authors to make their work accessible, something that has been universally forthcoming. Thus, while we intend this collection to be reflective of the current state of the field and thus germane to those scholars interested in being at the forefront of important topical debates, we also intend the text to be of interest to thoughtful corporate executives and others charged with creating and managing global sport sponsorship programs. The remainder of this introduction is intended to provide additional articulation as to the development of each of these three areas and outline how we perceive the various chapters to be positioned within the associated debates.

The Global, the Local and the Multivocal: A New Sport Sponsorship Context

As we noted above, there is little doubt that we exist in a global age that evidences a political, economic, technological and social landscape much changed from even two decades ago. The expansion of regional trading blocs, furthered by neo-liberal legislation that has removed trading barriers in the European Union, North and South America, Asia and the Pacific Rim have been accompanied by the collapse of communism and the subsequent opening up of markets in the former Soviet Union and her various satellite states, a raised awareness of international terrorism, and greater commercial access to China. The adoption of the Euro by twelve countries in Europe also emanated from a desire to ease and promote trade, not just within Europe, but also to make investment from external sources, notably North America and Asia, more attractive. With increased trade in different parts of the world comes more opportunity for sport sponsorship as firms seek to ingratiate themselves in locales within which they may have no heritage or tradition. Further, the awarding of major sporting events – such as those presented to previously excluded countries China (2008 Olympics) and South Africa (2010 FIFA World Cup) – are undoubtedly influenced by the desire to help develop certain commercial opportunities for global sponsors.

Such transformations in global, sporting and corporate environments have been accompanied, and to some extent defined, by an increasingly concentrated "network society" (Castells, 1996). While social in origin and organized according to who holds power in dominant institutions, such networks are based on flows of capital and have become dramatically expanded in terms of their reach and complexity of interaction by recent rapid technological advances. The development of the Internet and satellite television have rendered national borders almost totally permeable to the distribution of images and messages, while cheaper transportation has allowed people to move more frequently – and further afield – for work or pleasure than ever before. In fact, Harvey (1990) has suggested that time and space have disappeared as meaningful dimensions when considering individual thoughts and actions. When these technological advancements are allied to the changed political economy outlined above, it becomes apparent why some commentators have argued that nation-states have become somewhat anachronistic in the global economy (Hardt & Negri, 2001); instead it has been suggested that large, private corporations are playing much more of a determining role in "the growing integration of national economies" (Frenkel, 2001, p. 531).

The impacts of such shifts on the utilization of global sport sponsorship by private firms have become apparent in a number of ways. Sport sponsorship agreements have increasingly featured in the creation and reinforcement of Castells' (1996) networks as corporations, sport organizations, media companies, and local and federal governments, among others, are brought together. While increasingly important, the impact of such networks has been rarely discussed, much less empirically examined. The pressures, overt and more subtle, that corporate sponsors exert on sport governing and organizing bodies – such as the IOC and FIFA – is another area that requires more sustained examination (notwithstanding the exposé-type investigative texts such as those produced by Simson & Jennings (1992) and Jennings & Sambrook (2000), or the more critical analyses of Sugden & Tomlinson (1999)). Such manipulations become even more likely with governing bodies that lack the profile and funds of the IOC and FIFA and thus may be more susceptible to corporate pressures.

From a corporate perspective, the political, economic and technological shifts outlined above have of course radically altered the pallet of competitive options available to corporate executives. Amis (2005) cites the Brand Manager for Guinness in Great Britain who commented on the ways in which brand positioning had to take account of changes in the global landscape:

> From a parochial point of view, for myself in Great Britain, … every time we showed an ad on satellite TV over here, that ad was also shown to everyone in Ireland who was watching satellite TV at the time, which is a fair audience. And when Ireland and ourselves had very different styles of advertising, which was only say a year ago, then that was becoming more and more of a problem: that consumers would be watching satellite one minute, see one completely different ad with a different strap line and a different idea behind it, to when they switched on to their terrestrial TV. And there are more examples of that, of media starting to cross more countries. Also, the fact that, whether or not it was just consumers in one country or consumers moving around from country to country, they would see a

slightly schizophrenic brand because in different countries you would see such a different type of positioning around it. And then thirdly, also an element of cost efficiency by the fact that ultimately we can reach the stage where we can show the same advert in different countries.

The desire to realize greater efficiencies from scale economies is a clear benefit offered by the technological advances that have eased communications across national borders. However, of greater import is the utilization of sport sponsorship to realize global and local objectives. Guinness has used a global sponsorship, the 1999 Rugby World Cup, to help present a consistent brand image across multiple global markets (Rines, 2001). Similar outcomes have been realized by firms sponsoring the European Champions League, such as Sony, Ford, MasterCard and Amstel, who are able to benefit from identical packaging of television broadcasts wherever in the world games are screened. In this respect, sport sponsorship has long been acknowledged as being a mechanism that allows firms to overcome some of the complexities of language and culture that Bartlett and Ghoshal (1989) cite as a major impediment to global trading.

Globalization has also brought pronounced alterations to the social environment that also require attention from those interested in global sport sponsorship. With the increased opportunity for virtually instant communications across various electronic media, and the ability of firms to rapidly enter multiple markets, advertising and marketing executives are frequently faced with the complex task of differentiating their firms from global competitors while simultaneously having to overcome the inherent advantages held by locally established firms. It is of little surprise, therefore, that those charged with such a task seek to imbricate their firms with local consumers by drawing on elements of local culture and nostalgia (Morley & Robins, 1995). The need for such an approach becomes more acute when we consider that individuals in, particularly, most western societies, are inundated with a plethora of what are often very similar commercial messages. Concomitantly, those societal structures – such as extended families, the church, and long-term sites of employment – have become less stable and prominent in the lives of many individuals (see, for example, Giddens, 2002). The increased transience and ephemerality of much of society has left a void that marketers have rushed to fill. Tradition in this case becomes produced and marketed "as an image, a simulacrum, a pastiche" (Harvey, 1990). In other words, drained of context and heavily commercialized, traditions are reconceptualized and repackaged, leading Giddens to suggest that as a society we are "living after the end of tradition" (Giddens 2002, p. 43). This reimagining of tradition is a clear objective of many global sport sponsors. For example, adidas' sponsorship of the New Zealand "All Blacks" rugby team was an overt attempt to craft an artificial heritage within New Zealand society, particularly through associations with famous national rugby teams of the past (Jackson, Batty & Scherer, 2001).

Guinness has also sought to use sport sponsorship to invoke meaningful attachments to local people and places to help overcome the "disjuncture" (Appadurai,

1990) between global processes and local cultures, notably through investments in rugby and horseracing in Great Britain, soccer in Africa and hurling in Ireland (Amis, 2003). In fact, the effective utilization of sport sponsorship by those at Guinness to realize certain objectives highlights how our understanding of sport sponsorship needs to be realized within a theoretically informed understanding of the changed global dynamics that shape executive decision-making.

The global shifts discussed above form the backdrop for this text. In particular, the theoretical engagement with, and reconstitution of, a changed global sponsorship context is developed in the next five chapters. In chapter 2, Bob Sparks, Tim Dewhirst, Shannon Jette and Amanda Schweinbenz bring a comprehensive historical location for global sport sponsorship with their analyses of the tobacco and alcohol industries, traditionally viewed as drivers of sport sponsorship as a form of marketing communication. The case study that Sparks and his colleagues provide well illustrates the changed political economy of global sport sponsorship set against the involvement of what have become highly regulated tobacco and alcohol firms. While exploring the moral and political issues that are inextricably intertwined with both industries, Sparks et al.'s analysis also considers the wider implications for organizations – and governments – involved in this facet of the sponsorship industry as regulations curtailing sponsorship become more stringent, particularly for tobacco firms, around the world. Clearly, while we can continue to debate whether sport organizations should be involved with tobacco and alcohol firms, much less consideration has been given to the ways in which decision-making in a governing body is impacted by sponsors, something that is potentially much more important from a wider critical understanding of sport sponsorship processes.

The work of Mike Silk and David Andrews in chapter 3 provides a useful complement to that of Sparks and his colleagues by broadening out the theoretical consideration of transnational corporatism and associated sponsorship strategies. In particular, they assess the ways in which changes in the role of the nation in global economic systems have led to an alteration in the perceived logics of capital accumulation. From this theoretical base, they go on to examine the "cola wars," and notably the ways in which Coke executives have utilized cricket and their sponsorship of the Indian cricket team as part of a sophisticated market penetration strategy. In chapter 4, Andy Grainger, Josh Newman and David Andrews also base their work in a consideration of recent shifts in the global context to elaborate on the multiple ways in which sponsors utilize sporting celebrities to promote particular products and services. Drawing on three exemplary celebrities sponsored by adidas, Grainger and his colleagues discuss the differing conceptualization and utilization of "the transnational celebrity," exemplified by English soccer player David Beckham, "the global-local," personified by Australian swimmer Ian Thorpe, and "the exotic local," New Zealand rugby player Jonah Lomu. This, they suggest, provides a categorization of the differing ways in which sponsoring firms use sporting celebrities – as "global idol, local luminary, or foreign enigma" – in differing contexts, presenting a new theoretical lens through which to engage with the sponsorship of sporting celebrities.

The necessity of understanding the ways in which technological shifts have resulted in increased flows of people around the globe is illustrated by Mike Weed in chapter 5. Extending the theoretical scope of the book, Weed explores the ways in which sport sponsorship and sport tourism are reciprocally linked by drawing on contemporary notions of globalization and the realization of tourism through the provision of sporting events, from the small and local to the Olympics and the Ryder Cup.

In chapter 6, Detlev Zwick and Oliver Dieterle examine flows of a different type in their assessment of the impact of the shifting global landscape, the advent of the Internet and associated electronic networks, and the creation of what they term "(e)-sponsorship ... a promotional tool *par excellence* for the fragmented, 'glocalized' marketplace of the twenty-first century." In so doing, they open up a new line of inquiry for those interested in the development of global sport sponsorship, an area of theoretical and empirical study – and to some degree practical exploitation – that has yet to materialize despite the rapid development of the technology on which it is based.

These opening chapters present, in varying ways, persuasive arguments as to how the changed global environment in which commercial transactions take place has resulted in an entirely new conceptualization of the global-sport-sponsorship nexus. The next section, in the context of this book, builds on these opening chapters through a series of investigations that provide insight into the multi-contoured strategic realities of developing, managing, activating and evaluating global sport sponsorship agreements.

The Strategic Realization of Sport Sponsorship

While work on the strategic nature of sport sponsorship has started to emerge, there is little doubt that our understanding of the strategic conceptualization, execution and evaluation of sport sponsorship agreements is distinctly underdeveloped (Meenaghan, 1999; Walliser, 2003). Understanding the role that sport sponsorship can play in the strategic positioning of a firm or brand has assumed greater importance as the level of expenditures has increased, and the duration of agreements has risen – from a 4.2 year average for the top fifty sponsorships in 2001 to 6.7 years in 2002 and 7.6 years in 2003 (Applebaum, 2004). While the relationship between international diversification and firm performance may be decidedly mixed (Hitt, Hoskisson & Kim, 1997; Vermeulen & Barkema, 2002), there is little doubt that there is an apparent belief among many corporate executives as to the capability of sport sponsorship to realize certain transnational advantages.

Some insight into how sport sponsorship can be utilized as a route to a sustainable competitive advantage (SCA) becomes apparent when an actual or potential sport sponsorship opportunity is considered a strategic resource and evaluated accordingly. Adopting this approach, and drawing on the resource-based view of the firm literature (e.g. Barney, 1991, 2001; Peteraf, 1993; Wernerfelt, 1984) Amis, Pant and Slack (1997) assessed the sponsorship initiatives of two firms, and illustrated that sport sponsorship, if treated as a potentially valuable resource – with the appropriate consideration given to heterogeneous distribution, inimitability, lack of mobility and the inevitable *ex ante* limits to competition – can indeed be utilized as an effective marketing tool. This is achieved primarily through the enhancement of the key intangible resources of image and reputation (Amis, 2003). By contrast, agreements that are not managed with a view to their development as strategic resources will almost certainly fail to realize a useful return on investment.

Further support for the potential strategic impact of sport sponsorship comes from a consideration of its ability to contribute to brand equity. For example, Cornwell, Roy and Steinard (2001) found that management practices contributed to the ability of a sponsorship to differentiate a brand from its competitors and to add financial value to the firm. Thus, the need for marketing and advertising executives – those who occupy the critical symbolic production space between a firm and its consumers – to develop a "distinctive competence" (Amis, Slack & Berrett, 1999) in the recognition and development of useful sport sponsorship agreements can be considered both vital and in need of future investigation. Don Roy, in chapter 7, develops this strategic conception of sponsorship with his examination as to how it can fit into the strategic planning of a firm engaged in international trade. While Roy examines the notion of sport sponsorship as a resource, he provides a broader strategic analysis by considering the utilization of sponsorship as a key component of a firm's marketing communications program. More specifically, he discusses the utility that sponsorship can have in strategies designed to facilitate market penetration, brand positioning and improved market share.

While it may be useful to consider global sport sponsorship agreements as resources capable of affecting brand image and reputation, it is necessary that further work is carried out that investigates the ways in which global sport sponsorship has an impact on actual and potential consumers. Kevin Gwinner, in chapter 8, investigates the most elemental aspect of this with a discussion of various contingencies that affect the transfer of image from a sponsored property to a particular brand. An underdeveloped concept, particularly from a transnational standpoint, the theoretical ideals and practical realities of "image transfer" present a useful starting point from which to consider the rationales for and outcomes of global sporting investments. The two sporting events with the largest global significance, and that to have a significant potential for image transfer, are the Olympic Games and the FIFA World Cup. In chapter 9, Bob Madrigal, Colleen Bee and Monica LaBarge provide a useful examination of these global events through a contrasting of the strategic initiatives of Visa's sponsorship of the Olympics and MasterCard's support of the World Cup. As

Madrigal and his colleagues point out, these events present unequaled means of leveraging secondary associations with sport properties across international borders, exemplified by the cumulative television audiences of 40 billion for the 2004 Olympics and 28.8 billion for the 2002 World Cup, each spread across more than 200 countries.

In contrast to the traditional and well-established properties examined in chapter 9, perhaps the most interesting – and ill-understood – aspect of sport sponsorship centers on the use of "action sports" as a way to infiltrate the life-styles of the increasingly influential 10–24 year old age bracket. In chapter 10, Jay Gladden and Mark McDonald provide an informed assessment of the strategies involved in reaching this segment of the population through a medium that "combines sport, music and fashion into a lifestyle receptive to interactive branding." However, they caution that there is a need for particular care with educating key members of the circuit of cultural production as to the nuances of these non-traditional sports and target groups, particularly as this group is extremely sensitive to the perceived over-commercialization of their sports.

Irrespective of the type of sponsorship, it has become apparent in recent years, particularly as rights fees have escalated, that a major problem for rights holders and official sponsors are the behaviors of so-called "ambush" marketers. Inevitably at each major sporting event, there are multiple examples of the efforts of marketers to ambush their "official" rivals. While there has been some discussion regarding what ambush marketing is, and whether it should be considered immoral or good strategic practice, Janet Hoek reframes the debate, in chapter 11, to a potentially more useful consideration of how and when ambush marketing can be considered illegal. She also assesses how greater coordination between media and event owners may be a vital step in obviating the efforts of ambush marketers, and how the existence of multiple rights levels, while ostensibly useful in opening up additional categories of sponsorship, may ultimately contribute to the undermining of the value of sponsorship rights because of the increased ambushing opportunities.

Of course, opportunities for ambush marketing can be reduced if the rights holder and the "official" sponsor develop a close working relationship. Reconsidering the sponsor–sponsored dyad as a strategic alliance can precipitate a number of benefits for both parties. Francis Farrelly and Pascale Quester, in chapter 12, explore the development of such alliances through the creation of shared objectives, the establishment of mutual trust, and the realization of a shared commitment to the alliance from both parties. They suggest that the establishment of such alliances can be particularly beneficial for firms engaged in sponsorship agreements that span multiple markets.

While each of the topics for this book have been selected on the basis of their perceived importance, there is perhaps a most pronounced need for work that allows the development of effective methods, and measures, of evaluation. Meenaghan (1999) described this as the "Holy Grail" of sponsorship research, and while the potential difficulties in developing suitable tools have been widely acknowledged (e.g. Currie, 2004; Meenaghan, 1999), the accompanying advancement to the industry would be immense. Most work to date that has purported to be evaluation-type analysis has reported quantitatively expressed exposure times, awareness levels and recall rates. These are of limited utility because there is no clearly demonstrated link between, for example, the ability of an individual to recall a sponsor of an event and his/her propensity to make a purchase decision based on this information. Meenaghan extends this debate in chapter 13 by considering the versatility of global sport sponsorship, and suggesting that this versatility creates (surmountable) "hurdles" for evaluation. He argues that while there has been a reluctance of sponsors to engage in measurable evaluation that has in turn resulted in a lack of consistency and coherence with respect to evaluation among sponsors and agencies, there is a need to consider the range of publics that are targeted by the sponsorship and the range of objectives capable of being pursued. There is little doubt that as levels of expenditure rise, so too will the demand for more appropriate evaluative tools.

Towards a Critical Understanding of Sport Sponsorship

As we noted above, the political, economic and technological shifts that have become apparent in recent years have been accompanied by pronounced alterations to the societal structures that have traditionally formed the linchpins of our lives. More transient work places, a reduced emphasis for the church in many countries, variations in the make-up of the family unit, and a changing role for the nation state are characteristics of our "global age" (e.g. Giddens, 2002). It has been argued that this has led to a fundamental transformation of the mechanisms through which many of us define who and what we are. Parker (1999), for example, has posited that "global" firms fill a void by serving as conduits for the establishment of alternate values and norms. This challenge to our traditional anchors of existence can come through direct influence of firms on our decision-making, as in the array of products that we are pressured to purchase, exposure to co-workers from other countries, or a need to turn a profit in an increasingly competitive market (Parker, 1999). Alternatively, we can be exposed to mediated experiences that cause us to accept without question particular norms, such as our belief in the free market or the presence of sponsors at major sporting events. While this in and of itself is not necessarily bad, what is apparent is that executives of "global" firms have the ability to exert considerable influence on the ways in which we think and act. Consider, for example, the influence that those at Microsoft and News Corporation have on us through their seemingly limitless appetite for vertical and horizontal expansion of the media outlets that we draw upon every day, from newspapers to news channels, Internet service providers to web browsers, publishers to filmmakers, and so on (see, for example, Andrews, 2003; McGaughey & Liesch, 2002; Thompson, 2003).

Within the context of sport sponsorship, it is also important that we consider the wider impact that sport sponsors have. We must get beyond the conceptualization of sponsorship as simply a neutral exchange process but instead more critically assess some of the broader outcomes that accompany such agreements (Slack & Amis, 2004). For example, to what degree does a sponsorship agreement allow a sponsor access to local cultural traditions and norms? The appropriation and manipulation of Mäori cultural imagery by cultural intermediaries at adidas to augment their sponsorship of the New Zealand Rugby (NZRU) Union caused widespread offence among certain groups in New Zealand because of a perceived lack of concern for those who had originally produced the cultural images that were being used (Jackson et al., 2001). As Jackson and Hokowhitu (2002) subsequently pointed out, while new technologies have allowed global communication among like-minded, marginalized groups – such as indigenous peoples – and permitted such groups to draw attention to various issues, so it has also contributed to the exploitation of their interests by avaricious marketers keen to maximize the returns on their investments.

A second issue that has become increasingly apparent concerns what constitutes acceptable sponsorship activity. The sport sponsorship industry was, to a large degree, launched by the desire of tobacco and alcohol executives to overcome marketing constraints by using various sports as legitimate conduits for their marketing messages (Cornwell, 1997). Debate has been widespread as to the appropriateness of sport organizations accepting money from such firms, culminating in the current ban on alcohol sponsorship in France and tobacco sponsorship in Canada, and the curtailing of tobacco sponsorship in the United Kingdom and the USA from 2006 (Currie, 2004; Dewhirst, 2004; Sparks et al., chapter 2). Sport organizations have predominantly responded to such legislation by finding alternative, often less lucrative, sources of funding. By contrast, Formula One (F1) motor racing executives, still heavily dependent on cigarette manufacturers – indeed, as Sparks and his colleagues point out in chapter 2, the five private firms that dominate global cigarette production are all involved in sponsorship of F1 teams – have altered their race schedule to avoid those countries where legislation is more extreme and accommodate countries in which tobacco advertising laws are more relaxed. This illustrates the inherently political nature of global sport sponsorship and the need for research that strips the veneer from sponsorship decisions to allow us to access the norms and values that dictate such arrangements.

Such influences are apparent in the ways in which sponsors have pressured governing bodies for new, more television-friendly versions of games. The launch of "Twenty20" cricket and Monday Night Football in England, floodlit "head-to-head" golf matches in the USA, and beach volleyball at the Olympics can all be attributed to the desire of governing and organizing bodies to satisfy commercial sponsors and broadcasters in order to maximize income. What is often not considered are the impacts on athletes forced to follow an exacting schedule and yet still perform at an optimal level, fans who must travel great distances at inconvenient times to support their teams, and local residents living near event venues who must put up with late-night, floodlit sporting events with the accompanying traffic disruption and noise. Slack and Amis (2004) also noted the ways in which sponsors are able to secure most, if not all, prime seating for major events further disadvantaging the economically less powerful individual fan.

It is not just in major, high-profile events that the seemingly inexorable power of global sponsors is being realized. A debate that is gathering strength in a number of countries, including the USA, UK and Australia, concerns the sponsorship of school sporting (and other) activities, particularly by purveyors of so-called 'junk food' (Currie, 2004; 'Hain attacks minister over chocolate scheme', 2004). With legislators in the USA and UK exhibiting increasing concern at the high levels of obesity and Type 2 diabetes by calling for a limit in the sale of junk food and soft drinks in schools and use of celebrities to promote such products (e.g. Associated Press, 2004; Cozens, 2004), it is apposite that we consider the ethical dimension of school sport sponsorship by global purveyors – and indeed local firms – of all product types. It can be argued that such arrangements bring much needed revenue into underfunded schools and thus allow the provision of sporting activities that would otherwise be denied. However, we need to examine the impact that overt marketing messages, positioned in environments of learning in which information that is provided is typically accepted without question, have on vulnerable children.

A final point that we wish to make concerns the inherent inequities involved in global sport sponsorship arrangements and the overt and covert power that sponsors wield. Silk and Andrews, in chapter 3, note the widespread variation in beneficiaries both across and within countries based, in particular, on economic attractiveness to sponsors. A similar consideration needs to be accorded to the differential distribution among athletes and sports, and the associated pressures exerted on athletes, and by extension other members of society, to conform to certain idealized norms. Males and, more particularly, females are expected to exhibit particular body images, dress in certain ways and engage in "conventional" behaviors deemed acceptable and desirable by western corporate executives (predominantly of course, white middle-class males). For those that conform to these stereotypes – such as Anna Kournikova, Martina Hingis, and Venus and Serena Williams – the rewards from sponsors keen to craft and exploit particular images on a global scale can be enormous. Serena Williams, for example, has recently signed a five-year contract with Nike that will pay her up to US$60 million (Applebaum, 2004). By contrast, as Sally Shaw notes in chapter 14, those athletes – and sports – that do not conform to such idealized norms are often marginalized and excluded. For example, tennis professional Amelie Mauresmo, very open about her homosexuality, was warned by the Women's Tennis Association (WTA) – the governing body of the international women's tennis tour – to limit public displays of affection with her partner Sylvie Bourdon in case it negatively affected sponsors' perceptions of the WTA. Shaw argues that this differentiation is based on an unquestioned and problematic philosophy of sponsors aligning with sport properties that are perceived to superficially "fit" a desired image. Instead of this politic of exclusion, Shaw calls for a more equitable process based on Bauman's (2001) "ethic of moral sensitivity." Such an approach would not only benefit a wider range of sporting institutions and individuals, but, she suggests, would still allow sponsors to achieve their corporate objectives.

Helen Lenskyj, in chapter 15, also considers a traditionally marginalized group in her assessment of the development of the Gay Games. In discussing the contrasting pressures to "hetero-normalize" the event and the contested definitions and strategies opined by more radical and liberal groups, Lenskyj presents a critical account of the changed role of sport sponsorship in the development of the event as private corporations have sought to become increasingly involved.

The types of critical issues raised here are important in allowing us to gain a more holistic understanding of the wider rationales for, and outcomes of, various sponsors' activities. It is thus important that we go beyond descriptive accounts and simplistic explanations to engage more fully with the wider dynamics and underlying motivations of global sport sponsorship relationships. With this in mind, in chapter 16 we look to the future by following current trajectories with regard to sport, sponsorship measurement, audiences and the further intensification of global forces.

Conclusion

There is little doubt that firm executives are exposed to a multitude of rapidly changing pressures. Organizations are expected to become increasingly efficient and socially responsible, able to accommodate homogeneity and heterogeneity across functional areas, and reduce perceived inequities while enhancing returns to shareholders (Parker, 1999). Within this revised global corporatism, it is apparent that our conceptualization of how sport sponsorship agreements are configured and managed must also be scrutinized. We need to understand how changed global operating conditions and more complex strategic requirements are reciprocally related to the practices of, in particular, those executives responsible for the crafting and execution of sport sponsorships. Further, it is incumbent upon us to take a more critical view of the impact that sponsors have on both the immediate sporting context and the wider society. In so doing, we should heed previously articulated cautions of an overreliance on positivist cross-sectional research designs carried out on convenience samples of university students (e.g. Slack & Amis, 2004; Walliser, 2003). Instead, as we embrace a variety of theoretical perspectives with which to underpin research and practice, so we argue for engagement with a wider range of epistemologies and methods – including interviewing, participant and non-participant observation, semiotic and discourse analyses, and ethnography – that will allow us to access the nuanced data required to advance the field. In sum, we hope that this text provides some of the theoretical and practical insights required to allow us to significantly develop our understanding of global sport sponsorship.

References

Albrow, M. (1996) *The Global Age: State and Society Beyond Modernity*, Stanford, CA: Stanford University Press.

Amis, J. (2003) "'Good Things Come to Those Who Wait': The Strategic Management of Image and Reputation at Guinness," *European Sport Management Quarterly*, 3: 189–214.

Amis, J. (2005) "Beyond Sport: Imaging and Re-imaging a Transnational Brand," in M. Silk, D. Andrews and C. Cole (eds) *Sport and Corporate Nationalisms*. Oxford: Berg, pp. 143–165.

Amis, J., Pant, N., and Slack, T. (1997) "Achieving a sustainable competitive advantage: A resource-based view of sport sponsorship." *Journal of Sport Management,* 11: 80–96.

Amis, J., Slack, T., and Berrett, T. (1999) "Sport sponsorship as distinctive competence," *European Journal of Marketing*, 33: 250–273.

Andrews, D.L. (2003) "Sport and the transnationalizing media corporation," *The Journal of Media Economics*, 16: 235–251.

Appadurai, A. (1990) "Disjuncture and Difference in the Global Cultural Economy," *Theory, Culture & Society*, 7: 295–310.

Applebaum, M. (2004) "Sponsorship holds steady." *Brandweek.Com*. http://www. brandweek.com (accessed April 3, 2004).

Associated Press (2004) "Senate sends governor bill limiting school junk sales." http:// www.wkrn.com/Global/story.asp?S=1846401&nav=1ugFMu71 (accessed May 17, 2004).

Barney J. B. (1991) "Firm resources and sustained competitive advantage." *Journal of Management*, 17: 88–120.

Barney, J. B. (2001) "Resource-Based Theories of Competitive Advantage: A Ten-Year Retrospective on the Resource-Based View," *Journal of Management*, 27: 643–650.

Bartlett, C. A. and Ghoshal, S. (1989) *Managing Across Borders: The Transnational Solution*, Boston, MA: Harvard Business School Press.

Bauman, Z. (2001) *Conversations with Zygmunt Bauman/Zygmunt Bauman and Keith Tester*, Cambridge: Polity Press.

Castells, M. (1996) *The Rise of the Network Society*, Oxford: Blackwell.

Cornwell, T. B. (1997) "The Use of Sponsorship-Linked Marketing by Tobacco Firms: International Public Policy Issues," *Journal of Consumer Affairs*, 31: 238–254.

Cornwell, T. B. and Drennan, J. (2004) "Cross-Cultural Consumer/Consumption Research: Dealing with Issues Emerging from Globalization and Fragmentation," *Journal of Macromarketing*, forthcoming.

Cornwell, T. B. and Maignan, I. (1998) "An International Review of Sponsorship Research," *Journal of Advertising*, 27 (1): 1–21.

Cornwell, T. B., Roy, D. P. and Steinard, E. A. (2001) "Exploring Managers' Perceptions of the Impact of Sponsorship on Brand Equity," *Journal of Advertising*, 30: 41–51.

Cozens, C. (2004, 9 March) "Stars should fight child obesity, says FSA," *The Guardian*, http://www.guardian.co.uk (accessed May 28, 2004).

Currie, N. (2004) "Interview with Nigel Currie, Joint Chairman, European Sponsorship Association" (with Simon Rines). *International Journal of Sports Marketing & Sponsorship*, 5: (4) 246–252.

Dewhirst, T. (2004) "'Smoke and ashes': Tobacco sponsorship of sports and regulatory issues in Canada," in L. R. Kahle and C. Riley *Sports Marketing and the Psychology of Marketing Communication*. Mahwah, NJ: Lawrence Erlbaum Associates.

Frenkel, S. J. (2001) "Globalization, athletic footwear commodity chains and employment relations in China," *Organization Studies*, 22: 531–562.

Giddens, A. (2002) *Runaway World: How Globalisation is Reshaping our Lives* (2nd edn). London: Routledge.

Gwinner, K. P. (1997) "A Model of Image Creation and Image Transfer in Event Sponsorship," *International Marketing Review*, 14 (3): 145–158.

"Hain attacks minister over chocolate scheme" (2004, 28 May) *The Guardian*. http://www.guardian.co.uk (accessed May 28, 2004).

Hardt, M. and Negri, A. (2001) *Empire*, Cambridge: MA: Harvard University Press.

Harvey, D. (1990) *The Condition of Postmodernity: An Enquiry into the Origins of Cultural Change*, Oxford: Blackwell.

Held, D., McGrew, A., Goldblatt, D. and Perraton, J. (1999) *Global transformations: Politics, economics and culture*. Stanford, CA: Stanford University Press.

Heyer, S. J. (2003) "Steve Heyer's Manifesto for a New Age of Marketing: Madison and Vine Explained as Coca-Cola's Global Master Plan," AdAdge.com. (http://www.adage.com/news.cms.cms?newsId-37076).

Hirst, P. and Thompson, G. (1999) *Globalization in Question* (2nd edn). Cambridge: Polity Press.

Hitt, M. A., Hoskisson, R. E. and Kim, H. (1997) "International Diversification: Effects on Innovation and Firm Performance in Product-Diversified Firms," *Academy of Management Journal*, 40: 767–798.

Jackson, S. J. and Hokowhitu, B. (2002) "Sport, tribes and technology: The New Zealand All Blacks *Haka* and the politics of identity," *Journal of Sport & Social Issues*, 26: 125–139.

Jackson, S. J., Batty, R. and Scherer, J. (2001) "Transnational sport marketing at the global/local nexus: The Adidasification of the New Zealand All Blacks," *International Journal of Sports Marketing & Sponsorship*, 3: 185–201.

Jennings, P. and Sambrook, C. (2000) *The Great Olympic Swindle: When the World Wanted its Games Back*, New York: Simon and Schuster.

King, S. (2001) "Marketing generosity: Avon's women's health programs and new trends in global community relations," *International Journal of Sports Marketing & Sponsorship*, 3: 267–289.

Lachowetz, T. and Irwin, R. (2002) "FedEx and the St Jude Classic: An application of a cause-related marketing program (CRMP)," *Sport Marketing Quarterly*, 11 (2): 114–116.

McGaughey, S. L. and Liesch, P. W. (2002) "The global sports-media nexus: Reflections on the 'Super League saga' in Australia." *Journal of Management Studies*, 39: 383–416.

Meenaghan, T. (1991) "The role of sponsorship in the marketing communications mix," *International Journal of Advertising*, 10: 35–47.

Meenaghan, T. (1999) "Commercial sponsorship: The development of understanding," *International Journal of Sports Marketing & Sponsorship*, 1: 19–31.

Mintel (1994) *Sports Sponsorship*, London: Mintel International Group Limited.

Morley, D. and Robins, K. (1995) *Spaces of Identity: Global Media, Electronic Landscapes and Cultural Boundaries*, London: Routledge.

Parker, B. (1999) "Evolution and Revolution: From International Business to Globalization," in S. R. Clegg, C. Hardy and W. R. Nord (eds) *Managing Organizations: Current Issues*, Thousand Oaks, CA: Sage, pp. 234–256.

Peteraf, M. A. (1993) "The cornerstones of competitive advantage: A resource-based view," *Strategic Management Journal*, 14: 179–191.

Rines, S. (2001) "Guinness' Rugby World Cup sponsorship; A global platform for meeting business objectives," *International Journal of Sports Marketing & Sponsorship*, 3: 449–465.

Rugman, A. M. (2003) "Regional strategy and the demise of globalization," *Journal of International Management*, 9: 409–417.

Segal-Horn, S. and Faulkner, D. (1999) *The Dynamics of International Strategy*. London: International Thomson Business Press.

Simson, V. and Jennings, P. (1992) *The Lords of the Rings*. New York: Simon and Schuster.

Slack, T. and Amis, J. (2004) "'Money for nothing and your cheques for free?' A critical perspective on sport sponsorship," in T. Slack (ed.) *The Commercialisation of Sport*. London: Frank Cass, pp. 269–286.

Sugden, J. and Tomlinson, A. (1999) *Great balls of fire: How big money is hijacking world football*. Edinburgh: Mainstream Publishing

Thompson, D.N. (2003) "AOL Time Warner, Terra Lycos, Vivendi, and the transformation of marketing," *Journal of Business Research*, 56: 861–866.

Tomlinson, J. (1999) *Globalization and Culture*. Cambridge: Polity.

Vermeulen, F. and Barkema, H. (2002) "Pace, rhythm, and scope: Process dependence in building a profitable multinational corporation," *Strategic Management Journal*, 23: 637–653.

Walliser, B. (2003) "An international review of sponsorship research: Extension and update," *International Journal of Advertising*, 22: 5–40.

Wernerfelt, B. (1984) "A resource-based view of the firm," *Strategic Management Journal*, 5: 171–180.

Westerbeek, H. and Smith, A. (2003) *Sport Business in the Global Marketplace*. New York: Palgrave MacMillan.

Witcher, B., Craigen, J. G., Culligan, D. and Harvey, A. (1991) "The links between objectives and function in organizational sponsorship," *International Journal of Advertising*, 10: 13–33.

2

Historical Hangovers or Burning Possibilities

Regulation and adaptation in global tobacco and alcohol sponsorship

Robert Sparks, Timothy Dewhirst, Shannon Jette and
Amanda Schweinbenz

This chapter provides a brief but critical account of global trends in the tobacco and alcohol industries and the effects of these trends on tobacco and alcohol sponsorship of sports. Tobacco and alcohol firms have long been at the forefront of sport sponsorship innovations, and examining their activities is useful not only for understanding sponsorship activities in these sectors, but also for gaining insight into the global economic and political dynamics of sport sponsorship more generally. The chapter focuses on the market and regulatory conditions affecting these two industries and their use of sponsorship as a means to respond to these conditions. This approach positions the chapter as a case study in the political economy of global sponsorship and affords an opportunity to examine how, in an emerging global marketplace, some corporations (typically transnational corporations or TNCs) are able to achieve competitive advantage not only through corporate integration and enhanced productive capacities (economies of scale), but also by making comparatively better use of global marketing opportunities available to them, including sponsorship. This analysis, in turn, also affords an opportunity to comment on how the success of these strategies impacts upon the health and livelihood of the national and international populations who end up being the targets of these marketing initiatives. Tobacco and alcohol are unique industries on many fronts. For one, they are highly regulated sectors that require corporations to be strategic and innovative in order to maintain profitability. This in its own right is an important, if sometimes overlooked, fact and helps to account for why so many marketing innovations, including the use of sports and related images for product lifestyle associations, can be traced back to these two industries. Whether or not tobacco and alcohol companies invented these practices, several companies (Philip Morris, the Miller Brewing Company and Anheuser-Busch are recent examples) raised the level of sophistication in their use, as will be demonstrated below. A second and less endearing way in which they are unique is in terms of their health consequences. According to World Health Organization (WHO) statistics, tobacco use is the single greatest cause of preventable death (including accidents and all other chronic diseases) in developed nations (Roemer, 1993). Alcohol consumption, by comparison, is a health burden in both the developed and developing world, and constitutes a greater collective burden at this time than tobacco (behind malnutrition, poor water, sanitation and hygiene, but on a par with unsafe sex in terms of number of years of life lost to death and disability) (WHO, 1999). Nevertheless, the rising rates of smoking in the developing world mean that tobacco will become a greater health burden than alcohol over the long term. Estimates are that global tobacco-related deaths will rise to 10 million a year (from 4.8 million a year at present) by 2025 unless measures are taken to curb tobacco use (Roemer, 1993; Ezzati & Lopez, 2003).

These realities raise moral as well as political questions about the use of sport sponsorship by TNCs to enter global markets, and they also help to explain why protective measures in many countries have been undertaken through health legislation under health ministerial authority rather than through industrial and trade legislation alone. On June 16, 2003, twenty-eight countries and the European Community signed the WHO's new Framework Convention on Tobacco Control (FCTC) that identifies comprehensive measures for the regulation and control of tobacco products among member states. Article 36 of the FCTC stipulates that the convention would come into force on the ninetieth day after the fortieth country ratified it. On November 29, 2004, Armenia and Ghana both ratified the convention, and brought the count of assenting countries to forty. As a result, the FCTC officially came into force for ratifying nations on February 27, 2005, less than two years after it was approved by the World Health Assembly on May 21, 2003. At this writing 61 countries have ratified the convention (Micronesia became the sixty-first country on March 18, 2005), and 168 countries are signatories (see www.who.int/tobacco/framework/countrylist/en/, 2005). While no similar convention yet exists for alcohol, the WHO has established monitoring and alcohol control criteria and published the *Global Status Report on Alcohol* (1999) and the *Global Status Report: Alcohol Policy* (2004) that point the way towards developing stricter international guidelines for alcohol-related health legislation in member states. At present there are clear signs, therefore, that in addition to the market pressures and competitive exigencies of the emerging global economy, tobacco and alcohol companies will face increasing regulatory pressures in the future. The question is how will they respond to these conditions and how will their responses affect the global sponsorship of sport? To answer these questions, we have endeavored to map out how these two industries have reacted to market and regulatory conditions in the past, and to use these trends as guidelines for how they might respond in the future. The chapter is organized in four sections. We begin with a brief retrospective look at the early use of sports to market tobacco and alcohol brands. Next, we examine the changing market conditions in the two industries and the emergence of a global imperative in tobacco and alcohol marketing. Third, we assess the changing regulatory context of the two industries. Lastly, we discuss the future of tobacco and alcohol sponsorship in light of the industries' past responses to global market trends and regulation.

Background: Early Use of Sport Sponsorship

The tobacco and alcohol industries both have a long history of involvement with sports, although alcohol sponsorship, as such, predates that of tobacco. In the early 1700s, pub owners in Great Britain and North America capitalized on the popularity of sports among their patrons and promoted events such as cricket, wrestling, tennis, boxing and cockfighting (Collins & Vamplew, 2002; Gorn & Goldstein, 1993). By the mid-1800s, brewery owners also became involved and provided financial support for amateur sports groups. For instance, C. F. Tetley played an important role in the establishment of Headingley as a major rugby and cricket stadium in England, while George Sleeman provided both moral and financial support for the Guelph Maple Leafs, members of an amateur North American baseball league (Collins & Vamplew, 2002; Sneath, 2001). With the formation of the Football League in England in 1888, many clubs needed financial backing to improve their facilities, and breweries capitalized on this need as an opportunity to promote their brands. In return for financial support, the name of a sponsoring brewer was painted in large letters across the roof of event stands, as was the case with Aston Villa that had "'Mitchells & Butlers Good Honest Beer' running around the overhanging lip of a stand roof" (Collins & Vamplew, 2002, p. 46). By the late 1890s, most rugby and football match-day programs carried advertisements for the local brewer, and advertising in sports handbooks became commonplace, as demonstrated by the Hull Brewery advertisement in the 1895/96 guide for the Hull and District Rugby Union (Collins & Vamplew, 2002).

This was also the period during which tobacco companies became interested in sports. In 1875 Allen & Ginter began to package their cigarette brands with sports cards to stiffen the pack and offer their customers a premium. The popular cards featured a range of famous sports personalities including rowers, boxers, wrestlers, baseball, pool and billiard players (gfg.com/baseball/ginter. shtml, 2004; www.tobacco.org, 2004). W. T. Blackwell used outdoor signage to advertise their "Bull" Durham brand, and by the early 1900s, the bull sign was a regular feature in Major League Baseball parks in the USA. Players who hit the sign with a batted ball won $50 and players who hit a home run "won 72 packs of smoking tobacco" (Miller, 1991). The bull sign is credited with giving rise to the term "bull pen" to designate the area where pitchers warm up (scriptorium.lib.duke.edu, 2004; Crompton, 1993; McGowan, 1995). In Australia, W.D. & H.O. Wills sponsored an English golfer's tour in 1919, in one of the earliest commercial sponsorships of sport in that country (Furlong, 1994). Camel (R. J. Reynolds) and Fatima cigarettes (Liggett & Myers) were advertised using sports images in the 1920s, a practice that anticipated the development of lifestyle-themed advertising (see *The New Yorker* magazine, April 3, 1926 and September 14, 1929, for examples). Chesterfield (Liggett & Myers) sponsored scorecards and game programs for high school football in the USA (Hilts, 1996), and Pollay (1989) notes that prominent professional athletes became common endorsers of US cigarette brands from the 1930s through the 1960s. Tobacco companies actively sponsored radio and television programs as these media developed, and R. J. Reynolds sponsored a number of popular sports programs in the USA, including American Football League (AFL) football games, "American Sportsman," and American Broadcasting Corporation (ABC) "Wide World of Sports" (Miles, 1982).

Changing Market Conditions and a New Global Imperative

Despite these early involvements, the more highly integrated relationship between the tobacco and alcohol industries and sports, seen today, did not develop until the latter part of the twentieth century, and this is the period that has greatest relevance for present-day sport sponsorship and helps to identify future trends.

Lifestyles, Sports and Beer: 1970s and Beyond

The alcohol industry divides into three main sectors based on products, production technologies and product markets: distilled spirits, wine and beer. Although all three sectors are involved in sponsorship, by far the largest amount of sport sponsorship activity has been, and continues to be, conducted in the beer category. The reason for this is that sports fans tend to overlap closely with the core market of beer consumers, young to middle-aged men (generally 18–35 years of age, depending on the legal age for drinking). Of course, the demographics of sports vary, and some sports like golf support a broader fan base by age that includes older males that are attracted to distilled spirit brands like Johnnie Walker (e.g. "Johnnie Walker Classic" is a European PGA Tour event in Bangkok, Thailand and an Australasian PGA Tour event in Perth, Australia) (www.golf.web.com, 2003). Other distilled spirits brands like Jose Cuervo Gold target a young adult segment of active men and women, and use sponsorship of beach volleyball tournaments to reach their core consumer groups (www.volleyball.org/cuervo, 2003). For brevity, we have focused our analysis in this chapter on the beer sector both because it is the most active in sports sponsorship and because it exemplifies the activities of the alcohol industry more generally. Breweries have responded to many of the same market forces and conditions as the other two sectors, and in doing so they have led the industry in their use of sports.

Present trends of globalization in the beer category have their origins in the 1970s during a watershed period that saw significant industry consolidation, the rise of sport marketing, and the emergence of a new imperative to exploit national and international markets. Cavanagh and Clairmonte (1985) explain that rising inflation, high interest rates, and a global recession in the early 1970s exacerbated an earlier trend of industry consolidation by making increased integration of production and exploitation of national and, eventually, international markets desirable as a means to sustain profitability and maintain shareholder confidence. Between 1960 and 1980, the number of breweries in most developed countries fell sharply as a result of mergers, acquisitions and failures (e.g. from 57 to 9 in Sweden, 15 to 5 in Finland, 247 to 81 in the UK, 38 to 14 in the Netherlands, and 171 to 43 in the USA). The trend towards industry consolidation has continued to the present day, although some markets have seen a rise in small, localized breweries that sell "craft" beers. The "microbrewery" phenomenon aside, most markets are decidedly oligopolistic. In North America, for example, four companies – Anheuser-Busch, Miller, Coors and Pabst – now control 86% of the US market.

Implementing a mass media and mass market strategy in most product categories puts a premium on marketing communications, but this is particularly true in the beer category, because beer preferences tend to be highly regionalized (Standard & Poor's, 2003). By most accounts, beer advertising prior to the 1970s was not sophisticated, and tended to rely on a copy strategy that emphasized product attributes, jingles and mascots. What changed this picture in North America was the acquisition of Miller Brewing in 1970 by Philip Morris, an event that ended up revolutionizing beer marketing in North America and contributing to a global shift in the industry, as sport and lifestyle marketing became increasingly identified as core strategies for positioning beer products. According to Robert Weinberg, a former vice president at Anheuser-Busch, the acquisition brought immediate and irrevocable changes to the beer industry:

> In the '50s and '60s most of the beer ad campaigns on [North American] television either were silly comic things like Hamm's beer bear or they were deadly serious ego trips for the brewer that pontificated about excellence and fineness and quality. It was not until Philip Morris bought Miller that really sophisticated marketing programs for beer came into being. Nothing has been the same in the beer business since. (Quoted in Johnson, 1988, p. 73)

Philip Morris was an early innovator in the tobacco industry, and between 1932 and 1965 had maneuvered from the number six position in the US cigarette market to number two behind R. J. Reynolds through product innovation and astute marketing (Miles, 1982; Cavanagh & Clairmonte, 1985). This same approach was applied to Miller. As well as increasing the brewery's productive capacity and efficiency, the new Philip Morris management introduced "Lite Beer," a reduced calorie brand (this innovation drew in part on the firm's leadership in introducing "light," "reduced tar" cigarettes), and increased the marketing budget for the brewery to three times that of its nearest competitor. Miller invested heavily in market segmentation, target marketing and image-oriented advertising and by the late 1970s commanded more than half of all beer-related commercial air time on network sports programs in the USA (Johnson,

1988). McCann-Erickson, Miller's advertising agency at the time, used retired sports personalities like former New York Met Matt Snell to endorse Lite Beer when it came on the market in 1973 in order to give the brand an acceptable masculine image (Van Munching, 1997). As a result of these strategies, between 1970 and 1977 Miller moved from seventh position to second in the US market behind Anheuser-Busch, in a dramatic change of market share (4% to 15%) that demonstrated, inter alia, the lifestyle segmentation and communications value of television sports properties and personalities (Miles, 1982). Anheuser-Busch responded to the Miller threat in the late 1970s by more than tripling its own marketing budget (from US$30 million to US$100 million in 1978) and was able to thwart Miller's challenge and maintain market share, in no small part by increasing its sports media-related holdings and sponsorship contracts, an act which further dramatized the value of sports media properties (Van Munching, 1997; Johnson, 1988). By 1981, Anheuser-Busch sponsored ninety-eight professional and 310 university sports events (Cavanagh & Clairmonte, 1985).

Similar results were experienced using sports in other countries, but the market strategies and outcomes varied according to national cultures and the size and structure of the markets. In Canada, for example, the rights to television sports were bid for by two national broadcast networks, CTV and CBC, and the three major breweries of the day, Labatt, Carling O'Keefe and Molson, bought commercial time from the networks. This was the same pattern of bidding and brokering that prevailed in the USA, however, the Canadian market was one-tenth the size of that in the USA and by the late 1970s the breweries were themselves sufficiently capitalized to bid directly for media properties. Labatt was an early leader in this strategy and acquired the Canadian broadcast rights to Major League Baseball in the early 1980s. During 1984 to 1988, Labatt consolidated its interests in media sports properties by acquiring full ownership of the Toronto Blue Jays (a Major League Baseball franchise), incorporating and starting up The Sports Network (TSN, an English-language all-sports cable television channel in Canada), contributing to the start-up (50% ownership) of "Le Réseau des sports" (RDS, a French-language all-sports channel), and acquiring Dome Productions, the televisual production facility in Toronto's SkyDome, the home of the Blue Jays (Sparks, 1992). This was a classic vertical integration strategy in marketing communications that was prescient in the market environment of the day, and enabled Labatt to move well ahead of its two major competitors, Molson and Carling O'Keefe. Through these holdings, Labatt was able to profit from the direct revenue production of each unit and from the integration of its marketing functions for the sport properties and the brewery that resulted. Carling O'Keefe struggled in the changed environment and in 1987 was acquired by IXL Elders, an Australian brewery. In 1989, Elders merged Carling O'Keefe with Molson, the other competitor to Labatt, to create a new company, Molson Breweries Canada that was 40% owned by Elders and commanded 53% of the Canadian market (Sneath, 2001). Molson Breweries Canada, in turn, acquired the rights to a number of different sports properties (some already owned by Molson

Breweries Ltd before the merger) including the Molson Centre in Montreal, Championship Auto Racing Teams (CART) events in Toronto and Vancouver (and eventually Montreal), and Molstar Entertainment, a televisual production unit. In this new market relationship, Molson Breweries Canada and Labatt vied for sponsorship contracts over valuable properties like Olympic broadcast sponsorships in Canada and the celebrated "Hockey Night in Canada" broadcast, as well as commercial air-time during national and regional sports telecasts.

The same market imperatives of market share, profitability and growth that propelled these developments in domestic markets, led breweries to seek out international markets as sites for new growth, particularly in cases where their own markets were mature and the prospects for increasing market share were costly. During this period, large breweries such as Anheuser-Busch and Miller in the USA, Kirin and Sapporo in Japan, Heineken in the Netherlands, Brahma in Brazil, Molson and Labatt in Canada, and Bass, Allied-Lyons and Whitbread in the UK, began entering foreign markets in what for many became a three-stage process of exploitation starting with exporting their most popular brands, followed by licensing agreements for local production and ultimately by acquisition of local breweries and distribution networks (Cavanagh & Clairmonte, 1985; Standard & Poor's, 2003). Here again, sports sponsorship played an important role. In 1989, for example, Labatt acquired two Italian breweries, Moretti and Prince Brau, and in 1991–1992 sponsored the drivers' uniforms for the Canon-Williams Formula One (F1) racing team (this included the series winner in 1992, Nigel Mansell), as part of a bold undertaking to enter the European Union market. In 1995, after experiencing success in Europe and Mexico, Labatt was purchased in a friendly takeover by the Belgium brewing conglomerate, Interbrew, in a new phase of consolidation that is decidedly global in scope (Sneath, 2001). Ironically, Interbrew follows a single-line (horizontal) strategy of integration and divested itself of Labatt's media holdings in the late 1990s, although Labatt Canada continues to sponsor sports and Labatt products continue to be advertised on TSN, RDS and Sportsnet, a new all-sports channel.

In August 2004, Interbrew combined assets with Ambev, the Brazilian brewing conglomerate, to form InBev, which at this writing is the world's largest producer of beer by volume with 13% share of the global market (161 million barrels a year). Anheuser-Busch is the largest in terms of revenue (US$13.8 billion versus InBev's US$11.3 billion, 2003 figures) and second largest by volume (130 million barrels a year) with an estimated 11% share of the worldwide market in 2002 compared with SABMiller's 9% (South African Breweries purchased Miller Brewing in 2002, however, Philip Morris, reincorporated as Altria, retains 36% interest in the new company), and Heineken NV's 7% (Tomlinson, 2004; Standard and Poor's, 2003). As a result of this recent consolidation, 40% of the world's beer production is now controlled by these four major brewery conglomerates. InBev operates in thirty-two countries with a portfolio of 200 local and international brands that are sold in over 120 nations, including Stella Artois, Brahma, Beck's and Bass. The majority of Anheuser-Busch's business is in the USA, but it also operates breweries in China and the UK, has licensed operations in seven additional countries, and sells beer in more than eighty countries including the number one and number two brands in the world by volume, Bud Light and Budweiser (Tomlinson, 2004; www.anheuser-busch, 2005). Anheuser-Busch, more than any other brewery, promotes its brands by sponsoring premier sports events, such as the 2002 and 2006 International Association Football Federation (FIFA) World Cup, the 2006 Olympic Winter Games, and the 2008 Beijing Summer Games. In North America, Anheuser-Busch sponsors the Ladies Professional Golf Association (LPGA), Major League Baseball, the National Basketball Association (NBA), the National Football League (NFL), the National Hockey League (NHL), Major League Soccer, the Women's National Basketball Association (WNBA), the Professional Golf Association (PGA) Tour, the Association of Volleyball Professionals, National Association for Stock Car Auto Racing (NASCAR), National Hot Rod Association (NHRA), boxing, hydroplane racing, lacrosse, and snowboarding (Anheuser-Busch, 2002) as well as numerous university sports. Anheuser-Busch is the second highest ranked company in the USA by sponsorship investment (behind PepsiCo, Inc.), and the highest ranked brewery, having spent US$260–265 million in 2004. Miller Brewing Co. spent US$160–164 million, which made it sixth overall and second among breweries. Coors Brewing Co. spent US$45–50 million for twentieth position and third among breweries in terms of sponsorship investment (IEG Inc., 2004).

Cigarettes, Public Health and Tobacco Marketing Innovation

Tobacco products commonly divide into five major categories: cigarettes, cigars and cigarillos, smoking tobacco (pipe and roll your own), chewing tobacco and snuff. Although some national markets have major sub-categories (e.g. bidis and kreteks – hand-rolled, flavored cigarettes produced in India and Indonesia, respectively), the largest category in terms of overall consumption and sport sponsorship is machine-manufactured cigarettes. US per capita consumption in 2001 for individuals 18 years and over, for example, was 2,051 cigarettes (male and female) versus 39.6 cigars and cigarillos (male only) (Standard & Poor's, 2003). Chewing tobacco, snuff and smoking tobacco are only a fraction of cigarette sales. While some smokeless tobacco brands such as Skoal and Copenhagen have sponsored motor sports and rodeo events, we have focused our analysis on cigarette manufacturers because they have been the major investors and innovators in sport sponsorship.

The cigarette industry faced a different set of market imperatives during this period than the breweries, but their foray into sports ultimately has followed a similar path as that just described, in part because of the lifestyle marketing benefits they could achieve and in part because sports sponsorships afforded them on-air exposure at a time when they faced increasing restrictions on advertising. What is different in the tobacco case is that the emphasis on marketing innovation started nearly twenty years earlier in response to mounting health concerns surrounding smoking. When investigators at the Sloan-Kettering Institute for Cancer Research in the USA linked smoking with cancer in monumental studies published in 1950 and 1953, it forced the tobacco industry to reassess its marketing strategies from the ground up. Although research dating back to 1939 had shown a smoking and cancer connection, the coauthored studies by Ernst Wynder and Evarts Graham were well publicized and reinforced a pre-existing downward trend in consumption. Two national reports followed, one by the Royal College of Physicians in London in 1962 and one by the US Surgeon General in 1964, which further elevated public concerns and mobilized governments to consider stiffer tobacco marketing regulations. Miles (1982) characterizes the industry's response to this "threat" as involving three essential strategies: domain defense, domain offense and domain creation. All three of these are pertinent to present-day strategies the industry is using to protect its interests, including its investments in sport marketing, and are worth briefly reviewing here. A key point that will be demonstrated is that global sport sponsorship today is part of a comprehensive strategy of global domain creation that started in the early 1950s. Much of the early action played out in the USA and this can serve as an illustration of the broader case.

After the release of the two Sloan-Kettering studies, the "big six" tobacco manu-facturers in the USA – R. J. Reynolds, Liggett & Myers, American, Lorillard, Brown & Williamson, and Philip Morris – collaborated in a domain defensive strategy to counter the negative public reaction that ensued. In 1954, five of the companies founded the Tobacco Industry Research Committee (later renamed the Council for Tobacco Research) with a mandate to fund scientific research on the health effects of smoking. While primarily a public relations vehicle to demonstrate their supposed concern for public health, the Council also gave them "first to know" access to new research data, and enabled them to stay ahead of public regulators (Miles, 1982; Dewhirst, 2005). In 1958, they created the Tobacco Institute, Inc., a collaborative lobbying agency. Among the Institute's objectives was to redirect and undermine the health debate by emphasizing "the inconclusiveness of the research evidence, the contribution of tobacco products to the national economy, and the individual rights of smokers" (Miles, 1982, p. 67). When the Federal Trade Commission (FTC) sought to restrict cigarette advertising and mandate warning labels on cigarette packages in 1963, the Institute questioned the rights of the FTC to set rules, hoping to force the issue to go to the Congress (it eventually did), which was more sympathetic to the industry's position (Miles, 1982). In support of this strategy, the "big six" created a third joint venture in 1964, the Cigarette Advertising Code, Inc., whose mandate was to develop and oversee a "self-policing," voluntary advertising code. The benefits of a self-administered standard of practice over government measures were several, including minimizing government interference in the industry's affairs, staving off further government controls, and contributing to a public image of the industry as concerned and responsible. Ironically, the first companies to capitalize on this were not in the USA. Tobacco manufacturers in Canada instituted their own code in 1964 several months before their US counterparts (Cunningham, 1996). According to the Canadian code, tobacco advertising on television was restricted until after 9.00 p.m., a condition that prevailed until 1972 when the industry agreed to stop advertising cigarettes on radio and television altogether (the Canadian Broadcasting Company had already stopped accepting tobacco ads in 1969). Broadcast tobacco advertising was banned through legislation in the UK in 1965, in the USA in 1971 and in Australia in 1976 (Walker, 1991; Warner, 1986; Winstanley, Woodward, & Walker, 1995).

These new regulatory conditions led the tobacco manufacturers in all four countries to invest in televised sports and cultural events as part of a strategy to compensate for lost brand advertising (Dewhirst, 2004). Major tobacco companies such as Philip Morris, R. J. Reynolds, British American Tobacco (BAT), and Imperial Tobacco sought out sponsorship opportunities that would enable them to preserve their brand positioning strategies while extending the image and exposure of the sponsoring brands. Maintaining television coverage was an important part of this strategy, but sports events also facilitated promotional extensions, such as onsite advertising, product sales and corporate hospitality, that complemented the mass media strategies. F1 auto racing was to become a major site for tobacco brand sponsorship (including, over the years, such major brands as Camel, West, John Player Special, Marlboro, Mild Seven, Rothmans, Benson & Hedges, and Sobranie), but the first cigarette brand to sponsor F1 was Player's Gold Leaf (UK), the sponsor for Team Lotus in 1968, three years after the ban (Donaldson, 2002; Noble and Hughes, 2004). In Canada, Player's brand began sponsoring motor racing events in 1961 (Dewhirst & Sparks, 2003), and went on to become a major sponsor of CART racing as did Marlboro, Kool, Hollywood, Skoal and Copenhagen (snuff). Winston began sponsoring NASCAR racing in 1971, the same year the USA imposed the broadcast ban (King, 2003).

At the same time that the US tobacco manufacturers engaged in a collaborative strategy of domain defense, they competed with each other head-on with product modifications and marketing campaigns for filter and "reduced tar" cigarettes (machine measured) as part of a domain offense strategy. Each of the "big six" introduced filter cigarettes between 1953 and 1954, and by 1959 filter-tipped brand sales surpassed non-filter sales. As well as reassuring the public about the "safety" of smoking, filter cigarettes were more profitable because they contained about one third less tobacco than non-filter brands owing to a shorter column, a new freeze dry "puffing" process and greater use of reconstituted tobacco sheet (Miles, 1982; Pollay & Dewhirst, 2002). A key strategy for marketing the new brands was to target health-concerned smokers with reassuring images and ad copy, an approach that eventually became increasingly visual and exploited active lifestyle imagery and sports. In 1955, Philip Morris reintroduced Marlboro as a filter brand for men (with two important packaging innovations – the "flip-top" box and red tear-tape, see Miles, 1982, p. 103 and Kluger, 1997, pp. 176–182), and positioned the brand with masculine imagery, initially using a tattooed male model, but switching over to its now famous cowboy advertising strategy in the late 1950s (Hilts, 1996) and eventually to sport sponsorships including motor bike racing and CART, Indy Racing League (IRL) and F1 auto racing. Ellen Merlo, vice president of marketing services at Philip Morris, explains that the company saw F1 and CART racing as adding "a modern-day dimension to the Marlboro Man" (The Business of Racing, 1989, p. 5A). It is noteworthy that all of the brands identified above as sponsoring auto racing are filter-tipped. Recent Euromonitor figures for the UK (Jones, 2003) demonstrate the continued importance of the filter-tipped product strategy for developed countries where smokers are health conscious and knowledgeable about smoking risks. Mid, low and ultra low tar brands experienced 23% growth in retail sales volume from 1998 to 2003 and are forecast to see increased growth (98% projected) to 2007, despite the fact that overall cigarette sales in the UK are declining (18% from 1998 to 2003 and 8% projected to 2007). What accounts for the difference (decline in overall volume versus growth in low tar) is that the high tar product category is being squeezed out of the market (36% decline from 1998 to 2003, and nil forecast for 2007).

The third core strategy of domain creation involved moving overseas into regions with opportunities for growth. Here again, Philip Morris was an early innovator among the "big six," setting up a purchasing company in Syria in 1953 and a manufacturing company in Australia in 1954, the first of the "big six" to locate operations offshore (Miles, 1982). By 1955, Philip Morris consolidated its overseas operations in an international division that pursued rapid expansion. By 1961, the company was selling cigarettes in 104 countries, and by 1971, it marketed 140 brands in 162 countries. Its premium brand, Marlboro, became the number one selling cigarette in the world in 1972. Philip Morris had effectively outflanked the rest of the "big six" and even its major international competitor BAT. In 1975, Philip Morris owned holdings (subsidiaries and license agreements) in 43 countries versus 39 countries for BAT, 24 for R. J. Reynolds, 22 for Lorillard, 17 for Liggett & Myers, and 2 for American Brands (owned by BAT).

As an integral part of domain creation, the tobacco companies also sought out opportunities to vertically integrate their operations and to diversify into complementary industries. Philip Morris again was an early mover and made the first external acquisition, purchasing Milprint, a packaging company, in 1957 to support its filter-tip cigarette manufacturing. The Liggett Group was the first to invest in an alcohol company, and acquired the Paddington Corporation (maker of J. & B. scotch) and Carillon Importers Ltd (licensee for US sales of Grand Marnier) in 1966 (Miles, 1982). Alcohol production was a complementary industry, considering that alcohol and tobacco are often consumed together, and by the early 1980s most of the major tobacco companies owned interests in alcohol companies including Philip Morris and Miller, R. J. Reynolds and Heublein, the Imperial Group and Courage, American Brands and Jim Beam, and the Rembrandt/Rothmans Group that owned inter alia Rembrandt KWV (wines) and Rothmans of Pall Mall Canada that owned Carling O'Keefe Breweries in Canada, which owned two sports teams (Cavanagh & Clairmonte, 1985). The Liggett Group itself was acquired by Grand Metropolitan in 1980 (Miles, 1982).

Recent consolidation in both the tobacco and alcohol industries has seen a return to more line-specific holdings with greater integration (both vertical and horizontal) and less conglomeration, as demonstrated in the Interbrew case. The global tobacco industry is now dominated by five major corporations (disregarding China National Tobacco Corporation, which is a monopoly), all of which presently sponsor F1 racing: Altria Group, Inc., which includes Philip Morris USA and Philip Morris International (Marlboro, Ferrari), British American Tobacco PLC (Lucky Strike, BAR Honda), Japan Tobacco Incorporated (Mild Seven, Renault F1), Imperial Tobacco Group PLC (West, McLaren Mercedes), and Gallaher Group PLC (Sobranie, Jordan Grand Prix). The appeal of F1 for these companies is not only the global television reach and glamour of the race series, but the fact that the race organizers have managed to limit the impact of tobacco control legislation by expanding the series into countries with either limited tobacco sponsorship restrictions or formal exemptions for F1, and pulling out of countries with prohibitions (Dewhirst & Hunter, 2002). This raises the issue of sponsorship regulation and of how the alcohol and tobacco industries are responding to regulatory changes that are underway globally. The greatest single threat to both industries is the mounting legislation to control their brand promotional activities, including sport sponsorship.

The Changing Regulatory Context of Alcohol and Tobacco Sponsorship

Although the alcohol and tobacco industries have followed similar strategies of using sport sponsorship to support overseas expansion and to market their international and domestic brands, the regulatory conditions they have faced have differed in severity and type. These differences are seen in government regulations and international sport federation restrictions on alcohol and tobacco sponsorship. We discuss each of these in turn.

National Regulation of Alcohol and Tobacco Sponsorship

Tables 2.1 and 2.2 summarize national restrictions on alcohol and tobacco sponsorship and help to illustrate the different regulatory circumstances of the two industries. Compared with tobacco manufacturers, alcohol producers face relatively fewer sponsorship restrictions, and these vary by product category as reflected in the alcohol-by-volume designations (ABV) and category listings. For example, Table 2.1 shows that 41 countries presently restrict beer sponsorship – 32 via legislation, 8 via industry self-regulation (voluntary agreement) and 1 via a combination of voluntary industry code and legislation (Denmark) – whereas 52 countries restrict wine and spirit sponsorship, the 41 just noted plus an additional 11. By comparison, 83 countries impose some form of restrictions

Table 2.1 *Countries with restrictions on alcohol sponsorship of sports*[1]

Country/Region	Sponsorship[2]	Advertising[3]	Sale @ venue/event[4]	Drinking @ venue/event
African Region				
Algeria	L(P) [5] (beer/wine/spirit)	L(P)(tv/radio/print/bb)		L(P)(sprt & leis evnts)
Benin	No restrictions	No restrictions		L(P)(sprt evnt) Nr(leis evnt)
Cape Verde		L(R)(tv/radio/print)(bb-ua)		L(P)(sprt evnt) Nr(leis evnt)
Central African Republic	VA(beer/wine)(spirit-ua)	VA(beer/wine-tv/radio) L(P)(spirit-tv/radio) Nr(print/bb)		L(R)(sprt evnt) Nr(leis evnt)
Eritrea	L(P)(beer/wine/spirit)	L(P)(tv/radio) Nr(print/bb)		L(P)(sprt & leis evnts)
Gabon	L(R)(beer)(wine/spirit-ua)	L(R)(tv/radio) Nr(print/bb)		VA(sprt evnt) Nr(leis evnt)
Gambia	Nr(beer/wine) L(P)(spirit)	L(P)(tv/radio)VA(print/bb)		L(P)(sprt evnt) VA(leis evnt)
Ghana	VA(beer/wine/spirit)	VA(tv/radio/print/bb)		L(R)(sprt & leis evnts)
Guinea	No restrictions	(tv/radio-ua) Nr(print/bb)		L(P)(sprt & leis evnts)
Malawi	No restrictions	No restrictions		L(P)(sprt evnt) Nr(leis evnt)
Mauritius	L(P)(details ua)	L(R)(tv/radio) Nr(print/bb)		L(P)(sprt & leis evnts)
Mozambique				L(R)(sprt & leis evnts)
Namibia	No restrictions	VA(tv/radio/print)L(P)(bb)		L(R)(sprt & leis evnts)
Niger	L(R)(beer/wine/spirit)	No restrictions		VA(sprt evnt) R(leis evnt)
Nigeria	No restrictions	L(R)(tv/radio) Nr(print/bb)		L(P)(sprt evnt) Nr(leis evnt)
Seychelles	No restrictions	L(R)(tv) P(radio/bb) VA(print)		L(P)(sprt & leis evnts)
Togo	No restrictions	No restrictions		VA(sprt & leis evnts)
UR Tanzania	No restrictions	No restrictions		L(R)(sprt evnt) Nr(leis evnt)
Zambia	No restrictions	No restrictions		L(R)(sprt evnt) Nr(leis evnt)
Eastern Mediterranean Region				
Egypt		L(P)(all advert banned, except print: beer-Nr, wine-R)		L(P)(sprt & leis evnts)
Islamic Republic of Iran	L(P)(beer/wine/spirit)	L(P)(tv/radio/print/bb)		L(P)(sprt & leis evnts)

Table 2.1 (*continued*)

Country/Region	Sponsorship[2]	Advertising[3]	Sale @ venue/event[4]	Drinking @ venue/event
Jordan	L(P)(beer/wine/spirit)	L(P)(tv/radio/bb) R(print)		VA(sprt evnt) Nr(leis evnt)
European Region				
Armenia	No restrictions	No restrictions		VA(sprt & leis evnts)
Austria	No restrictions	VA(tv/radio/print/bb)		VA(sprt evnt) Nr(leis evnt)
Azerbaijan	L(R)(evnts id w/ brand)	L(R)(all advert restricted except beer: Nr-tv/radio/bb; print-ua)		L(P)(sprt evnts) R(leis evnts)
Belarus	No restrictions	Nr(beer) L(wine/spirit: P-radio/print/bb; R-tv)		L(P)(sprt evnt) R(leis evnts)
Belgium	Nr(beer) VA(wine/spirit) (evnts id w/ brand)	L(beer/wine: R-tv/radio, VA-print) VA(spirit-tv/radio/print)		L(R)(sprt & leis events)
Bosnia & Herzegovina	L(R)(beer/wine) P(spirit)	No restrictions		L(R)(sprt evnts) Nr(leis evnts)
Bulgaria	L(R)(evnts id w/ brand)	L(P)(advert that attributes beneficial properties to alcohol)	L(P)(entertainment events, sports fixtures intended for youth)	L(R)(sprt evnt) VA(leis evnts))
Croatia	L(R)(beer) P(wine/spirit) (evnts id w/ brand)	Nr(beer) L(P)(wine/spirit-tv/radio/print /bb)		L(R)(sprt & leis evnts)
Czech Republic	No restrictions	Nr(tv/radio/print) L(R)(bb)		L(R)(sprt evnts) Nr(leis evnts)
Denmark	C(P)(ABV ≥ 2.8%)	L(P)(tv/radio) VA(print/bb)		L(R)(sprt evnts) Nr(leis evnts)
Finland	L(R)(beer/wine) (P)(spirit) (evnts id w/ brand)	L(ABV ≥ 22%) P(direct/indirect advert-tv/radio/print/bb)		L(R)(sprt & leis events)
France	L(P)(object/purpose direct or indirect advert of brand or trade mark)	L(ABV > 1%) P(sport grounds, stadia, swim pools) P(tv) R((radio/print) Nr(bb)		L(R)(sprt evnts) VA(leis evnts)
Georgia	Nr(beer)(wine/spirit-ua)	Nr(beer) L(R)(wine/spirit-tv/radio) Nr(bb)		VA(sprt & leis events)
Germany	VA(beer/wine/spirit) (evnts id w/ brand)	VA(tv/radio/print/bb)		L(R)(sprt evnts) Nr(leis evnts)

Country/Region	Sponsorship[2]	Advertising[3]	Sale @ venue/event[4]	Drinking @ venue/event
Greece	No restrictions	No restrictions		L(R)(sprt evnts) Nr(leis evnts)
Hungary	Nr(beer) R(wine/spirit)	VA(all advert except: wine: P-tv; spirit: P-radio)		No restrictions
Iceland	L(P)(evnts id w/ brand)	L(P)(tv/radio/bb) R(print)		VA(sprt & leis evnts)
Ireland	No restrictions	C(spirits) L(R)(ad before tv/radio sports progs)		L(R)(sprt & leis evnts)
Italy	VA(beer) R(wine) L(P)(spirit) (evnts id w/ brand)	C(tv/radio/print/bb)	L(P)(ABV ≥ 21%) sport venues/gatherings)	VA(sprt & leis evnts)
Kazakhstan	(beer/wine-ua) L(R)(spirit)	Nr(beer-tv) Nr(print/bb) L(R)(wine/spirit-tv/radio)		L(R)(sprt & leis evnts)
Kyrgyzstan	No restrictions	L(R)(tv/radio/print/bb)		VA(sprt evnts) Nr(leis evnts)
Latvia	Nr(beer) L(R)(wine/spirit) (sprt sponsorship may not contain references to alcoholic beverages)	L(P)(spirit-tv/radio) (may not associate alcohol with sports activities) Nr(beer/wine-tv/radio/print/bb)		VA(sprt & leis evnts)
Lithuania	L(R)(evnts id w/ brand)	Nr(beer/wine-tv/radio/bb) L(R) (spirit) (print)		L(R)(sprt & leis evnts)
Luxembourg	No restrictions	L(R)(tv & radio advert showing sportsmen) Nr(print/bb) VA(tv/radio)		VA(sprt & leis evnts)
Netherlands	VA(evnts id w/ brand)	L(R)(tv)VA(radio/print/bb)		L(R)(sprt evnts) Nr(leis evnts)
Norway	L(P)(evnts id w/ brand)	L(P)(tv/radio/print/bb) (P)(cross-promotion in ads for other products)		L(R)(sprt & leis evnts)
Poland	L(R)(beer/wine) P(spirit) (evnts id w/ brand)	L(P)(wine/spirit-tv/radio/print/bb) (R)(beer)		L(P)(sprt evnts) VA(leis evnts)
Portugal	L(R)(evnts id w/ brand)	L(R)(tv/radio) Nr(print/bb)		VA(sprt evnts) Nr(leis evnts)
Republic of Moldova	No restrictions	Nr(beer)		L(R)(sprt & leis evnts)
Romania	No restrictions	No restrictions		L(P)(sprt evnts) UA(leis evnts)
Russian Federation	VA(beer) L(P) (wine/ spirit) (evnts id w/ brand)	Nr(beer) L(wine/spirit: P-tv/radio, R-bb) (wine: Nr-print) (spirit: R-print)		L(P)(sprt evnts) R(leis evnts)
Slovakia	VA(evnts id w/ brand)	Nr(beer) L(wine/spirit: P-tv, R-radio)		L(R)(sprt evnts) VA(leis evnts)

Table 2.1 (*continued*)

Country/Region	Sponsorship[2]	Advertising[3]	Sale @ venue/event[4]	Drinking @ venue/event
Slovenia	Nr(beer) VA(wine/spirit)	L(tv/radio/print: R-beer/wine, P-spirit) P(bb))		No restrictions
Spain	No restrictions	L(R)(tv/radio/print/bb, except spirit: P-tv) P(sport centres)		L(P)(sprt evnts) VA(leis evnts)
Sweden	No restrictions	L(P)(tv/radio/print/bb, excpt beer: R-print)		L(R)(sprt & leis evnts)
Switzerland	Nr(beer/wine) L(R)(spirit) (evnts id w/ brand)	L(P)(tv/radio) R(print/bb) (P)(sport fields/events)		No restrictions
The former Yugoslav Republic of Macedonia	No restrictions	No restrictions		Nr(sprt evnts) L(R)(leis evnts)
Turkey	Nr(beer) L(P)(wine/spirit)	L(R)(tv/radio/print/bb, excpt beer: Nr-print, R-bb)		L(P)(sprt evnts) Nr(leis evnts
Turkmenistan	VA(beer/wine/spirit)	VA(tv/radio/print/bb)		L(P)(sprt & leis evnts)
Ukraine	Nr(beer) L(R)(wine/spirit) (evnts id w/ brand)	L(P)(wine/spirit-tv/radio) R(print/bb, excpt beer: Nr-tv/radio/bb, R-print)		L(R)(sprt evnts) VA(leis evnts)
United Kingdom	No restrictions	VA(tv/radio/print/bb)		L(R)(sprt evnts) VA(leis evnts)
Uzbekistan		L(R)(tv/radio/print)		L(P)(sprt evnts) L(R)(leis evnts)
Region of the Americas				
Argentina	L(R)(beer/wine/spirit)	L(R)(tv/radio/print/bb)		L(P)(sprt & leis evnts)
Belize		L(R)(tv/radio/print/bb)		L(R)(sprt & leis evnts)
Bolivia	L(R)(beer/wine/spirit)	L(R)(tv/radio/print/bb)		Nr(sprt evnts) R(leis evnts)
Brazil	L(R)(ABV ≥ 13%)(mark or slogan allowed; can't suggest consumption)	L(ABV ≥ 13%) P(allowed tv/radio 9pm-6am; nor Olympic sports & championships)		No restrictions
Canada	L(R)(spnsr ads of motor vehicle events must have responsble use message)	L(P)(athletic achievement)		R(sprt & leis evnts)
Chile	No restrictions	L(R)(tv/bb) VA(radio) Nr(print)		L(P)(sprt evnts) UA(leis evnts)

34

Country/Region	Sponsorship[2]	Advertising[3]	Sale @ venue/event[4]	Drinking @ venue/event
Colombia	L(R)(beer/wine/spirit)	L(R)(tv/radio/print/bb)		L(P)(sprt & leis evnts)
Costa Rica	L(P)(beer/wine/spirit)	L(R)(tv/radio/print/bb)		L(P)(sprt & leis evnts)
Dominican Republic	L(R)(beer/wine/spirit)	L(R)(tv/radio/print/bb)		No restrictions
Ecuador	L(R)(beer/wine/spirit)	L(P)(name or picture of juvenile sport star via posters, films, records)		L(P)(sprt & leis evnts)
El Salvador	No restrictions	No restrictions		VA(sprt & leis evnts)
Guatemala	L(P)(beer/wine/spirit)	L(R)(tv/radio/print/bb)		L(P)(sprt & leis evnts)
Guyana	No restrictions	No restrictions		VA(sprt & leis evnts)
Honduras	No restrictions	L(P)(sports) (R)(tv/radio/print/bb)	P(sports centres)	L(P)(sports centres) VA(sprt & leis evnts)
Mexico	L(R)(beer/wine/spirit)	L(P)(sports activities) L(R)(tv) Nr(radio/print/bb)		VA(sprt & leis evnts)
Paraguay	L(P)(ABV ≥ 4%)(sports or athletic activities; clothing, luggage, bags; excluded: car, mtrcycle, boating evnts restricted to brand or product)	L(ABV ≥ 4%) R(ads in sports facilities limited to brand name w/ 10% ad space warning) (R)(tv/radio/print/bb)		L(P)(sprt & leis evnts)
Trinidad and Tobago	No restrictions	No restrictions		L(R)(sprt & leis evnts)
United States	No restrictions	VA(tv/radio/print/bb)		VA(sprt evnts) L(R)(leis evnts)
Uruguay	No restrictions	No restrictions		No restrictions
Venezuela	L(R)(beer/wine/spirit)	L(P)(tv/radio)(R)(print/bb)		L(P)(sprt & leis evnts)
South East Asia Region				
India	L(P)(beer/wine/spirit)	L(P)(tv/radio/print/bb) (allowed at sport evnts)		VA(sprt & leis evnts)
Indonesia	L(P)(beer/wine/spirit)	L(P)(tv/radio/print/bb)		L(P)(sprt & leis evnts)
Nepal	L(P)(beer/wine/spirit)	L(P)(tv/radio) Nr(print/bb)		VA(sprt evnts) Nr(leis evnts)

Table 2.1 *(continued)*

Country/Region	Sponsorship[2]	Advertising[3]	Sale @ venue/event[4]	Drinking @ venue/event
Western Pacific Region				
Australia	No restrictions	VA(tv/radio/print/bb)		VA(sprt evnts) L(R)(leis evnts)
China	No restrictions	No restrictions		VA(sprt evnts) Nr(leis evnts)
French Polynesia	No restrictions	L(P)(tv/radio) Nr(print/bb)		UA(sprt evnts) P(leis evnts)
Lao PDR	No restrictions	L(R)(tv/radio) Nr(print/bb)		Nr(sprt evnts) L(R)(leis evnts)
Malaysia	L(R)(beer/wine/spirit)	L(P)(tv/radio) R(print/bb)		No restrictions
Mongolia	No restrictions	L(P)(tv/radio/print,bb-ua)		L(P)(sprt & leis evnts)
Netherlands Antilles		L(R)(allowed tv 10 pm-6am)		
New Zealand	No restrictions	L(R)(allowed tv 9 pm-6am)(ad content restrict) Nr (radio/print/bb)		L(R)(sprt & leis evnts)
Palau	No restrictions	No restrictions		L(R)(sprt & leis evnts)
Papua New Guinea		L(P)(print)(restricted to licensed premises, sanctioned sponsorshp of sport evnts & teams)		
Philippines	No restrictions	L(R)(tv/radio/print/bb)		VA(sprt & leis evnts)
Republic of Korea	No restrictions	L(P)(spirit-tv/radio) Nr(beer) Nr(wine/spirit-print/bb)		VA(sprt evnts) Nr(leis evnts)
Vietnam	Nr(beer) VA(wine) L(R)(spirit)	L(P)(spirit-tv/radio) Nr(beer-tv/radio/print, VA-bb) (R)(wine-tv/radio)		VA(sprt evnts) Nr(leis evnts)
Other Countries [6]				

Notes:

[1] This Table has been compiled using legislative listings in the *International Digest of Health Legislation* (WHO, 1970-2004, excluding 1997); the *Global Status Report on Alcohol* (WHO, 1999); the *Global Status Report: Alcohol Policy* (WHO, 2004); the Eurocare Website accessed during July, 2003 (www.eurocare.org); *Self-Regulation of Beverage Alcohol Advertising* (ICAP, January 2001); and the WHO EU Alcohol Control Database accessed during January, 2004 (data.euro.who.int/alcohol/). Unless otherwise indicated, the information is for all alcohol product sponsorships (beer, wine, spirits).

[2] The sponsorship column lists restrictions on sport sponsorship, and includes sport-specific information where available (e.g., see Paraguay).

[3] The advertising column lists restrictions on traditional forms of advertising that have a sport theme or image or that depict an athlete, sport celebrity, sports event or sports activity. This column includes restrictions on product advertisements at sports facilities, centres, fields or events, as designated, as well as broader restrictions that we interpreted to cover sports (even though sport was not mentioned). For example, Algeria has a complete ban on television, radio, print and billboard advertising for all alcohol products.

[4] Little summary information was available on the regulation of alcohol sales at sports events and venues. The drinking @ venue/event column is therefore a more accurate reflection of sales restrictions.

[5] L (legislation) refers to legislated restrictions, VA (voluntary agreement) refers to restrictions that are the result of industry self-regulation, C (combination) refers to restrictions that are the combined result of legislation and industry self-regulation, ABV (alcohol by volume) refers to percent of pure alcohol, P (prohibited) is used in cases of outright bans, R (restricted) is used in cases of partial restrictions, (evnts id w/ brand) means a restriction on sponsored events identified with an alcohol product brand name, "ua" (unavailable) or a blank space mean that no information was available, Nr or "No restrictions" indicates information was available and no restrictions were found.

[6] Twenty additional countries may have alcohol sponsorship restrictions due to religious orientation, however, legislation could not be found to confirm this. The countries are: Afghanistan, Bahrain, Bangladesh, Djibouti, Egypt, Iraq, Kuwait, Maldives, Morocco, Oman, Pakistan, Qatar, Saudi Arabia, Senegal, Sudan, Syria, Syrian Arab Republic, Tunisia, United Arab Emirates, and Yemen.

Table 2.2 *Countries with restrictions on tobacco sponsorship of sports*[1]

Region/Country	Sponsorship[2]	Advertising[3]	Sales @ sport facilities and events	Smoking @ sport facilities and events[4]
African Region				
Algeria	L(P)[5]			
Cameroon	VA(sponsorship targeting minors)	VA(football stadiums)		
Mauritius	L(sponsorship in relation to tobac products, trade names, & assoc. brands)			L(swimming pools, gymnasiums, public sport halls)
Niger	L(TIF-events/aud & ads)			
Senegal	L(TIF-events/aud & ads)			
South Africa	L(tobac product adv & promo in relation to sponsored events)			
Eastern Mediterranean Region				
Bahrain	L(P)(sporting events)	L(tobac product adv by sport event sponsors)		
Cyprus	VA(spnsr adv of events)	L(sporting events)		
Djibouti	L(P)(sporting events)			
Egypt	L(TIF-events/aud & ads)			
Iran (Islamic Republic of)	L(TIF-events/aud & ads)			
Jordan	L(P)(sporting events)			
Kuwait	L(TIF-events/aud & ads)			L(public sports arenas)
Libyan Arab Jamahiriya	L(P)(sporting events)			
Morocco	L(P-sponsorship of social events)(sponsor ads of sporting events)			L(enclosed places where sports held)

Region/Country	Sponsorship[2]	Advertising[3]	Sales @ sport facilities and events	Smoking @ sport facilities and events[4]
Oman	L(P)(sporting events)			
Qatar	L(P)(sporting events)			
Saudi Arabia	L(P)(sporting events) (TIF-event ads)			
Sudan	L(P)(sporting events)			
Syrian Arab Republic	L(P)(sporting events)			
Tunisia	L(sporting events & events with young audience)(TIF-event ads)			L(covered sports halls)
West Bank and Gaza Strip	L(P)(sporting events)			
European Region				
Austria	L(sports personalities) (assoc of tobac names & logos w/ spnsrd events)	L(P)(tv, radio) (R)(print/bb) (P)(sportsmen)		
Azerbaijan	L(P)(brand name)	L(P)(tv/radio/print/bb) L(100 m. proximity to sporting institutions) (sportsmen, success)		
Belarus	L(R)(brand name)	L(R)(tv/radio/print/bb)		
Belgium	L(P)(brand name)	L(tobac adv except POP; incl. extensions)		L(sports arenas)
Bosnia and Herzegovina	L(P)(brand name)	L(R)(tv/radio/print/bb)		
Bulgaria	L(P)(all forms)	L(P)(tv/radio/print/bb)		L(sports premises)
Croatia	L(TIF-event ads)	L(P)(tv/radio/print/bb)		L(parts of buildings used for sports/rec, excpt designated areas)
Czech Republic	L(R)(brand name)	L(P)(tv/radio/print/bb)		L(arenas)
Denmark	L(P)(tobac goods spnsr)	L(P)(tv/radio/print/bb)		
Estonia	L(TIF-event ads)			

39

Table 2.2 (continued)

Region/Country	Sponsorship[2]	Advertising[3]	Sales @ sport facilities and events	Smoking @ sport facilities and events[4]
VA(non-adult events)	L(P)(tv/radio/print/bb)	L(sports establishments)	L(sports buildings &, facilities)	
European Community	L(P)(Oct 1 2006)	L(P)		
Finland	L(P)	L(P)(tv/radio/print/bb)		
France	L(all sponsorship, in so far as object/effect = direct/ indirect tobac prod advert or propaganda	L(P)(tv/radio/print/bb)		
Georgia	L(R)(brand name)	L(P)(tv/rad)(R)prt/bb)		
Hungary	L(R)(brand name)	L(P)(tv/radio/print/bb)		
Iceland	L(TIF-events/aud & ads)	L(P)(tv/radio/print/bb)		
Ireland	L(sports events <18 yr olds) (adv: basic event info allowed, no tobac prdct mention or picture)	L(P)(tv/radio/print/bb)		
Israel	L(R)(brand name)	L(P)(tv/rad/bb)(R)(prt)		
Italy	L(R)(brand name)	L(P)(tv/radio/print/bb)		
Kazakhstan	L(R)(brand name)	L(P)(tv/rad/bb)(R)(prt)		
Kyrgyzstan	No restriction	L(R)(tv/radio/print)		
L(sports orgs & 100 m. proximity) (physical fitness, sport success)				
Latvia	No restriction	L(R)(tv/rad/prt)(P)(bb)	L(sports institutions)	
Lithuania	L(events <18 yr olds)	L(P)(tv/radio/print/bb)		
Luxembourg	L(events-child/adolescn) (no spnsr ads during events except sign or vehicle of prod name)	L(P)(tv/rad)(R)(prt/bb)		

Region/Country	Sponsorship[2]	Advertising[3]	Sales @ sport facilities and events	Smoking @ sport facilities and events[4]
Netherlands	L(P)(brand name)	L(P)(tv/radio/print/bb) L(sports)	L(sports establishments)	
Norway	L(use of name or logo in spnsrshp of sport events)	L(P)(tv/radio/print/bb)		
Poland	L(TIF-events/aud & ads)	L(P)(tv/radio/print/bb)	L(sports/rec grounds)	L(designated smoke areas req'd in sport/leisure facilities)
Portugal	L(TIF-events/aud & ads)	L(P)(tv/radio/print/bb)		L(arenas/sports facilities)
Romania	L(R)(brand name)	L(P)(tv/rad)(R)(prt/bb)		
Russian Federation	No restriction	L(P)(tv)(R)(radio/print)	L(sports facilities & 100 m. proximity)	
Slovakia	No restriction	L(P)(tv/radio/print/bb)		L(sporting venues)
Slovenia	L(direct/indirect advert via sports sponsorship)	L(P)(tv/rad/prt)(R)(bb) L(inside sports arenas)		
Sweden	L(by tobac brands)	L(P)(tv/rad/prt)(R)(bb)		
Switzerland	L(events targeted at <18 yr olds)	L(P)(tv/rad)(R)(prt/bb)		
The former Yugoslav Republic of Macedonia	L(R)(brand name)	L(P)(tv/radio/print/bb)		
Turkey	L(TIF-events/aud) VA(brand name)	L(P)(tv/radio/print/bb)		
Turkmenistan				
Ukraine	L(events <18 yr olds & if name/image used)	L(athletic success)	L(sports grounds)	
UK	L(P)(sponsorship agreements)(Global events have until 2005)			
VA(events <18 yr olds)	L(P)(tv/rad)(R)(prt/bb)			
Uzbekistan	L(R)(brand name)	L(P)(tv/rad/bb)(R)(prt)		

41

Table 2.2 *(continued)*

Region/Country	Sponsorship[2]	Advertising[3]	Sales @ sport facilities and events	Smoking @ sport facilities and events[4]
Region of the Americas				
Argentina	L(marketing or promo activities restricted only if directed at minors)	L(assoc tobac prod with physical activities such as sports)		
Barbados	VA(spnsr adv of events)			
Bolivia	L(TIF-event ads)	L(sporting activities)		
Brazil	L(allowed until 2002; F1 exempt from ban) (TIF-event ads; only name & logo; not in program)			
Canada	L(P)(events)(Oct 1 2003)	L(lifestyle)		
Costa Rica	L(TIF-events/aud, ads)	L(sports publications, billboards near sporting facilities		
Dominican Republic	L(TIF-event ads)			
Ecuador	L(TIF-event ads)	L(billboards/posters near sports facilities) (sport stars/celebs)		
Guatemala		L(500 m. proximity to sports complexes) (sports athletes)	L(samples @ events)	
Guyana	L(TIF-event ads)			
Honduras	L(events spnrd by tobac company where brand name used req'd to display health warning)	L(sports)		
Mexico		L(stadiums, sports centres)(advert ideas or images must not assoc with sports)	L(stadiums, sports centres)	
Nicaragua	L(TIF-events/aud, ads)			
Panama	L(TIF-event ads)			

42

Region/Country	Sponsorship[2]	Advertising[3]	Sales @ sport facilities and events	Smoking @ sport facilities and events[4]
Paraguay	L(TIF-event ads)	L(assoc of tobac with sports)		L(enclosed stadiums excpt in special areas)
Trinidad and Tobago				
United States of America		L(tobac promo to children prohibited) VA(sport figures)		
Venezuela	L(TIF-event ads)	L(sports facilities)		L(sports arenas)
South East Asia Region				
Bangladesh	L(P)(sporting events)			
India				L(govt-run stadiums)
Maldives		L(billboard adv in some sporting grounds)		L(sports arenas & 100 m. proximity)
Sri Lanka	L(spnsrshp &/or promo obtained from agency promoting tobac prohibit in govt buildings)		L(school events such as sports meets)	
Thailand	L(P)			L(smoking restricted to private rooms in indoor sports arenas)
Western Pacific Region				
Australia	L(certain int. sporting events exempt until Oct 1 2006)(print adv permit for exempt's)			
China	L(TIF-event ads)	L(stadiums, gymnasiums)		
Fiji	L(events attended by < 18 yr olds)(exempt events: ads contain only brand name/trade mark, must not encourage use; health warning 20% of area, not on handed out printed matter, only on perimeter or ground)			

Table 2.2 (continued)

Region/Country	Sponsorship[2]	Advertising[3]	Sales @ sport facilities and events	Smoking @ sport facilities and events[4]
Hong Kong				
Malaysia		L(athletes)		
New Zealand	L(specified events permitted: multi-nat. with 3 country min part.)			L(sports complexes)
Republic of Korea	VA(sponsored events must not be directed at women or children)	VA(ads shall not depict smoking by anyone participating in events requiring physical stamina)		
Singapore	L(specified events exempt provided ads do not directly/ indirectly promote smoking)			L(sports arenas)
Solomon Islands	L(P)(use of brand name/trade mark in public representation that promotes sporting org, activity, event; that acknowl contribution by manuf. or importer of tobac prod)			
Taiwan	L(P)(sports events under tobac brand name)			
Tonga				L(sports stand when open to public)
Viet Nam	L(tobac companies to display names on spnsrshp materials)		L(sporting centres)	

44

Notes:

[1] These figures have been compiled using legislative summaries in *Tobacco Control Country Profiles* (WHO, 2003; see also Shafey O, Dolwick S, Guindon, 2003) accessed via UICC GLOBALink during August, 2003 (www.globalink.org/), recent legislative listings in the *International Digest for Health Legislation* (WHO, 1998-2004), the WHO EU Tobacco Control Database accessed during January, 2004 (data.euro.who.int/tobacco/), and Hoek and Sparks (2000).

[2] The sponsorship column lists restrictions on sport sponsorship-related marketing and communications. To be included in this category, the restrictions had to specifically identify "sponsorship" as a related condition.

[3] The advertising column lists restrictions on traditional forms of advertising that have a sport theme or image or that depict an athlete, sport celebrity, sports event or sports activity. This category includes restrictions on product advertisements at sports facilities, centres, fields or events, as well as broader restrictions that we interpreted to cover sports. For example, Bulgaria prohibits television, radio, print and billboard advertising of tobacco products.

[4] It is possible that additional countries prohibit smoking in sport arenas under a general prohibition of smoking in 'enclosed public places', but only the countries which specified a smoking prohibition in sports venues were included in this table.

[5] L (legislation) refers to legislated restrictions, VA (voluntary agreement) refers to restrictions that are the result of industry self-regulation, C (combination) refers to restrictions that are the combined result of legislation and industry self-regulation, (P) (prohibited) is used in cases of outright bans, (R) (restricted) is used in cases of partial restrictions, (TIF) (tobacco identifying information) refers to all identifying elements including brand name, trade mark, logo, and slogans, (events/aud) means a restriction on displaying TIF at events sponsored for certain (typically under-aged) audiences, (event/ad) means a restriction on TIF in advertisements for events sponsored by tobacco companies.

on tobacco sponsorship (78 of these via legislation and 5 via voluntary industry codes), and the restrictions do not distinguish product categories such as "light" cigarettes, cigars, pipes or snuff, or levels of nicotine or tar. The latter might seem a minor point, but it means that tobacco manufacturers do not have the same opportunities as alcohol producers to utilize a "light" category strategy (e.g. low alcohol beer, wine coolers, pre-mixed spirit drinks) to get around sponsorship restrictions.

A second observation is that several of the alcohol regulations allow product sponsorship under some circumstances, whereas the tobacco regulations are more restrictive. For example, Brazil allows alcohol sponsorship of events not related to routine television or radio programs, provided only a product mark or slogan is used without any suggestion of consumption. Canada allows alcohol sponsorship but requires advertisements for events involving motorized vehicles to include a "responsible use" message about drinking and driving. Paraguay prohibits advertising alcoholic beverages in relation to sports or athletic activities, but exempts sponsorships of motor sports (car, motorcycle, boating events). Athletes and athletic support staff in Paraguay are prohibited from using clothing, luggage, bags or other objects containing advertisements for alcoholic beverages during a sports competition, unless they are associated with motor sport events (drivers, cars, crew). By comparison, the majority of tobacco sponsorship regulations (n = 55, 66%) are undertaken specifically to prohibit the use of brand names and other "tobacco-identifying information" (TIF) in relation to sponsored events or associated advertising, albeit a small group of countries still allow tobacco sponsorship of exempted events (Brazil, Australia, Singapore, New Zealand) or allow sponsorship under restricted conditions such as displaying a health warning (Honduras) or if the event does not target children or youth (n = 23 countries). A third comparison of Tables 2.1 and 2.2 is that there are relatively more restrictions on drinking alcoholic beverages at sports events and venues (n = 87) than there are restrictions on smoking (n = 20). This difference is perhaps a consequence of the spectator management issues that arise with alcohol consumption, but taken together (n = 107) these restrictions speak to the issues of product placement, demonstration, sales and sampling for both tobacco and alcohol sponsors, that otherwise would be a normal expectation of a sponsorship contract.

Although these observations help to identify some of the unique regulatory constraints for alcohol and tobacco sponsorship, there are several limitations to Tables 2.1 and 2.2 that need to be emphasized. First, the information in the two tables was obtained by searching secondary sources produced by major health and industry associations such as the WHO and the International Center for Alcohol Policies (ICAP, an industry group). These sources were focused mainly on national-level policies and regulations, and it is possible that in some countries alcohol and tobacco regulation might be a sub-national (regional, provincial, municipal) responsibility and therefore not reflected in the tables. Second, the information was summarized in different ways by different organizations and although this afforded an opportunity to cross-check some listings, it means that the tables themselves contain information that was coded using different descriptive taxonomies. As well, the amount of information varied by geographic region, with some areas, particularly Europe, having more complete records. Comparisons of data, within as well as between tables, should be done with caution, therefore, as details about the relevant legislation and voluntary agreements were oftentimes lacking. Third, Table 2.1 may underreport the incidence of regulatory constraints on alcohol sponsorship and advertising as well as prohibitions on alcohol sales. As discussed in note 6 of Table 2.1, it seems likely that countries with religious prohibitions against alcohol consumption would also prohibit alcohol sponsorship and certainly alcohol sales and drinking at sports venues and events. This would potentially add twenty countries to Table 2.1, however, we did not find legislative information to confirm this. In addition, the WHO European Area database provided summary information on alcohol consumption restrictions, but did not have a separate category for sales. Because a prohibition on consumption logically assumes a related prohibition on sales, the drinking restrictions are a better indication of sales restrictions at sports venues and events than is the sales column.

As a final observation, a more useful way to compare Tables 2.1 and 2.2 might be to see them as reflecting different temporal realities. The regulatory framework for alcohol, one might argue, is similar today to that for tobacco fifteen years ago when very few countries had regulations that explicitly governed tobacco sponsorship. Findings by Hoek and Sparks (2000) indicate that, before 1990, only eleven countries had legislation that restricted tobacco sponsorship. The rise in tobacco regulations globally that has occurred since then has been the result of systematic efforts by organizations such as the WHO to reign in the global epidemic of tobacco-related diseases. While there is no authoritative account yet published of the history of tobacco regulation, Roemer (1993) reported steady increases in the number of countries with tobacco control legislation in each of the three years she carried out legislative surveys: 1982, 57 countries; 1986, 72 countries; 1993, 91 countries. Hoek and Sparks (2000) put the number at 98 countries in 1998, 88 of which had regulations restricting tobacco advertising and 26 of which had regulations limiting or prohibiting tobacco sponsorship. This raises important questions. Allowing for the differences in the two products, are alcohol control regulations likely to follow the same pattern as tobacco? Will tobacco regulations themselves continue to intensify and spread globally? If there are increased control measures, will these encompass sponsorship generally, and sport sponsorship particularly?

The answer to these questions appears to be affirmative. As noted in the introduction to this chapter, the WHO is already collecting epidemiological and social cost data on alcohol-use, and in 1999 published the *Global Status Report on Alcohol*, followed in 2004 by the *Global Status Report: Alcohol Policy*. These are only the most recent undertakings in a long line of alcohol-related research dating back to 1975 when *Alcohol Control Policies in Public Health Perspective* was first published (Bruun, Edwards & Lumio, 1975, cited in WHO, 1999).

In 1979, the World Health Assembly (WHA), the governing body for the WHO, passed Resolution WHA32.40 asking WHO member states to "take all appropriate measures to reduce the consumption of alcohol among all sectors of the population" (WHO, 1999, p. 48). This kind of integrated approach to policy research and implementation is similar to that taken by the WHO and other health agencies such as the International Union Against Cancer (UICC) with respect to smoking and tobacco use prior to initiating the Framework Convention on Tobacco Control (FCTC) in 2003 (see WHO, 1976; Roemer, 1993). While alcohol control measures do not yet place the same emphasis on promotion and sponsorship as the tobacco control measures, they certainly could in the near future. If successful, the FCTC could readily serve as a template for a similar treaty on alcohol control. Either way, however, indications are that the WHO is preparing to take action on alcohol marketing. The WHO Executive Board approved a draft resolution at its meeting on January 20, 2004 that identifies alcohol as a priority and targets media messages about alcohol, "including marketing and advertising" (www.eurocare.org, 2004). According to Eurocare, this is the first time in twenty years that the issue of alcohol has been raised as a primary concern of the WHO's highest executive.

Recent evidence suggests that the FCTC itself is gaining momentum, and that its restrictions on sponsorship are likely to have a profound effect on countries that follow the convention. Even though only a relatively small group of nations (61) have ratified the FCTC at this time and the treaty is legally binding only in those that ratify it, the fact that an additional 107 countries (168 in total) are already signatories speaks to the treaty's potential impact (see www.who.int/tobacco/framework/en, 2004). The 168 countries collectively represent 91.4% of the world's population (Cunningham, 2005), and the treaty's statutes themselves are far-reaching. The FCTC defines sponsorship broadly as "any form of contribution to any event, activity or individual with the aim, effect or likely effect of promoting a tobacco product or tobacco use either directly or indirectly" (WHA56.1, 2003, p. 6). This sweeping definition is matched in Article 13, Clause 2 by a condition for each ratifying country, "in accordance with its constitution or constitutional principles, (to) undertake a comprehensive ban of all tobacco advertising, promotion and sponsorship" (p. 11). While it is still early to predict the policy changes the FCTC will bring about, it seems likely based on present evidence that the convention will have greater reach and impact than previous initiatives. For example, FCTC Article 8, Clause 2 enjoins countries to adopt and implement legislation "providing for protection from exposure to tobacco smoke in indoor workplaces, public transport, indoor public places, and, as appropriate, other public places" (WHA56.1, 2003, p. 9). This condition supports making sports events smoke-free as well as tobacco sponsorship-free, and will help solve the inconsistency of prohibiting tobacco sponsorship while allowing tobacco sales and consumption. If alcohol control regulations follow this same legislative path, then opportunities for sport sponsorship will become much more constricted for both industries.

International Sport Federation Restrictions

Despite the fact that some organizations such as the International Automobile Federation (FIA), the governing body for F1, continue to cater to tobacco and alcohol companies, a number of major sports federations have moved to restrict alcohol sponsorship, particularly of spirit alcohol, and to prohibit tobacco sponsorship altogether. The International Olympic Committee (IOC), for example, prohibits tobacco and spirit alcohol sponsorship for Olympic Games, but allows beer and wine sponsorship, dependent on local legislation and advertising practices (IOC, 2001). As one would expect, the federations that represent the thirty-five Olympic sports mainly follow suit, and as a minimum follow the IOC guidelines. In a survey we conducted of Olympic sports via email during July–August 2003, using an initial contact with four follow-ups, none of the respondents (n = 26, 74% response rate) had tobacco sponsors at the time and most indicated either that tobacco sponsorship was banned outright (n = 8) or that they followed IOC (n = 10) or national regulations (n = 5). Spirit alcohol sponsorship was prohibited, but beer and wine sponsorship was allowed where not restricted under national regulations. Only the International Archery Federation (FITA) indicated that alcohol sponsorship was banned, and this was because alcohol is a banned substance in archery. The International Shooting Sport Federation (ISSF) had no official policy on tobacco or alcohol sponsorship, but indicated there was not a need, as they had no sponsors in these categories. Six federations had alcohol sponsors at the time: International Association Football Federation (FIFA, Budweiser), International Judo Federation (IJF, Doosan), International Triathlon Union (ITU, Heineken), International Volleyball Federation (FIVB, Molson Dry), International Biathlon Union (IBU, Krombacher) and International Ski Federation (FIS, Warsteiner). The IBU explained that Krombacher makes energy drinks and mineral water as well as beer and non-alcoholized beer, and that the basis of the sponsorship was the energy drinks and water. Doosan makes beer, soju, wine and rice wine.

The evidence we found suggests that most sports federations (amateur and professional) will fall in line with the policies and regulations of the countries in which they operate and will not follow the path taken by F1 of moving into less restrictive regions. For example, the British Darts Organization (BDO) in the UK and NASCAR in the USA that have both had longstanding tobacco sponsorship contracts (with Embassy and Winston, respectively) have already begun to move away from tobacco sponsorship in anticipation of the coming regulatory changes (interestingly, BDO is also attempting to separate itself from its close association with alcohol in order to "target families") (BDO to clean up UK darts' image, 2002; Glick, 2003). FIFA was forced to overturn Anheuser-Busch's rights to perimeter board advertising when France proclaimed a complete ban on advertising of alcohol beverages at sports events in 1998. Anheuser-Busch had paid £20 million to purchase the sponsorship rights from FIFA, and its Budweiser brand was an official sponsor of the FIFA World Cup held that year in France. The football federation was powerless when the European Commission refused to overturn the French ruling just prior to the World Cup, and Anheuser-Busch ended up selling its hoardings to Casio (Brand power, 1998). These examples suggest that the spreading alcohol and tobacco control legislation discussed above will have a substantial impact on these industries' sport sponsorship programs.

One of the main principles driving this legislation is the understanding that the active association of alcohol and tobacco products with athletes, sports teams and sports events makes consumption of these products attractive, and thereby contributes to start up, maintenance, and social acceptability of their use. This is to say that sports sponsorship functions as an implicit form of social marketing that attributes socially desirable qualities to the actions of drinking and smoking themselves, not simply to brands. Youth are thought to be particularly vulnerable to these messages (see Sparks, 1999), a point that helps to explain why sport sponsorship and sponsorship of cultural events that target youth have been singled out for restrictions, even in countries such as Portugal and Switzerland where alcohol and tobacco sponsorship are not yet banned outright. In this respect, sport sponsorship is likely to draw increasing attention, not less, over the next while. This, finally, raises the question of how the alcohol and tobacco industries might respond to these challenges, and what impacts their responses will have on sport sponsorship.

Alcohol and Tobacco Industry Response to Global Regulatory Conditions

Based on the evidence presented above, the most probable response is that both industries will carry on as they have previously, but the alcohol industry will start to undertake measures similar to those adopted by the tobacco industry if alcohol control restrictions continue to intensify, that is, of collaborating in domain defensive strategies against sponsorship restrictions and competing head-to-head in domain offensive and domain creative strategies over sponsorship properties and global brand marketing. The net result will be that tobacco and alcohol sponsorship of sports will continue over the near term, but the precise form and execution (including program components, use of media, event locations) will change to accommodate the shifting regulatory context. The long-term picture is less clear, and will depend on the success of the FCTC and similar treaties that the WHO might undertake with respect to alcohol control.

There is already evidence of domain defensive strategies for both industries. During the recent development of the FCTC, the tobacco TNCs, in a throwback to earlier times, joined forces and lobbied to soften the convention's provisions as well as to discredit the WHO position on issues such as second-hand smoke. The alcohol TNCs are also collaborating. A group of major corporations, including Allied Domecq PLC, Asahi Breweries Ltd, Bacardi-Martini, Brown-Forman Corporation, Coors Brewing Company, Diageo PLC, Foster's Group Ltd, Heineken NV, SABMiller and Molson, have joined together to sponsor the

International Center for Alcohol Policies (ICAP) which inter alia studies alcohol control policies and lobbies for the industry. In official terms, ICAP's mission is to (1) "help reduce the abuse of alcohol worldwide and promote understanding of the role of alcohol in society" and (2) "encourage dialogue and pursue partnerships involving the beverage alcohol industry, the public health community and others interested in alcohol policy" (www.icap.org, 2004). However, in functional terms the organization is very similar to previous tobacco research and lobby groups. It has already published several reports on alcohol consumption and alcohol control policies, including *Drinking Patterns & Their Consequences* (Grant & Litvak, 1998) and *ICAP Report 9, Self-Regulation of Beverage Alcohol Advertising* (ICAP, 2001), which it presented to the WHO as part of a discussion paper on beverage alcohol advertising and youth. ICAP, like the tobacco manufacturers' council, appears to be intended as a first line of domain defense against increased regulation. This strategy may not ultimately prove effective if the WHO develops a framework convention on alcohol marketing, but even in the face of mounting global restrictions, there are still a number of domain defensive, offensive and creative strategies that alcohol and tobacco companies can undertake with respect to their sport marketing and sponsorship properties. In some cases these strategies may converge around particular sport series and entities that cater to alcohol and tobacco sponsorship like F1, while in other cases they may entail independent initiatives. We briefly discuss both of these possibilities below.

Competitive Strategy Convergence: The Special Case of Formula One

F1 has already been mentioned several times in this chapter, but as one of the last remaining global sponsorship properties for tobacco TNCs, it warrants special attention. Some of the major yachting competitions such as the Volvo Ocean Race (formerly the Whitbread Round the World Race) and the America's Cup have accommodated tobacco sponsorship through legislative exemptions for international events (for example, in New Zealand and Australia) similar to those enjoyed by F1. Other transnational events, such as the India-New Zealand cricket series (sponsored by Wills in India) (Vaidya, Naik & Vaidya, 1996) and CART (Australia, South Korea, Mexico) have capitalized on similar exemptions. None of these, however, have the global television audience of F1. In fact, no series or event, including World Cup Soccer or the Olympics, comes close, and this makes F1 a critical property for TNCs, and especially the tobacco TNCs. During the period from 1995 to 1999, for example, F1 averaged an aggregate annual global audience of 49.9 billion viewers in 202 countries (Deutsche Banc Alex. Brown, 2000). In 1999, the aggregate audience was 57.7 billion in 206 countries, a figure that is equal to ten times the world population. Auto racing is not invulnerable to the competitive exigencies of television, and in 2002 these rates fell 9% and stayed soft (1% increase) in 2003, mainly as a result of the uncontested success of Ferrari and its top driver Michael Schumacher (Jones, 2002b; Beached buggies, 2003; Formula 1 turns off TV viewers, 2003). As with most televised sports, when outcomes are predictable, events become boring to watch and audiences simply tune out. In addition to these issues, national identity also mediates interest (see Jones, 2002b for European figures) and national viewing rates for F1 are affected by race locations as well as team and drivers' standings. Despite this variance, however, the high aggregate audience figures and level of frequency and reach that they represent are unrivalled by any other sport, and as a result, F1 has unique strategic value as a global communications platform.

F1 is an example of strategy convergence in a sports property, as demonstrated in the fact that the tobacco TNCs are collectively using FIA and F1 to counter legislative restrictions and exploit loopholes, but at the same time they are directly competing with each other for consumer awareness and global market share (not unlike the racing teams they support) and they are endeavoring to use F1 to open up new markets. The tobacco sponsors have supported the series' growth into countries with exemptions or less stringent legislation, including Malaysia, Bahrain, China and Japan where they have expansionist interests, and they have helped FIA to pressure national governments to protect the promotional rights of the tobacco sponsors (Australia, Spain, Brazil) or to compensate them for lost promotional value. The Grand Prix of Canada, for example, was saved from being cancelled from the 2004 schedule when the Quebec and Canadian governments each put up $CAN6 million to help compensate tobacco-sponsored race teams participating in the event for the next three years (Marowits, 2003). One can expect that this kind of domain defensive activity will continue. FIA is an umbrella organization for approximately 150 national automobile clubs, associations, touring clubs and motor-sport groups in 117 countries (Deutsche Banc Alex. Brown, 2000), and wields a lot of political power.

Most of the domain offensive activities in F1 have followed well-established brand positioning strategies of associating the tobacco brands as closely as possible with the sponsored drivers and the teams. Felt (2002) for example notes how, with the advent of tobacco sponsorship in 1968, corporate colors began to replace the traditional national color schemes of F1 cars, drivers and crew, specifically, white for Germany, red for Italy, green for Great Britain and blue for France. The Gold Leaf logo was stenciled in gold on a red and white background in 1968 and the John Player Special logo likewise was in gold but on a solid black background during the mid 1970s, even though these were both British teams (Donaldson, 2002). As further regulation comes to bear, it is likely that brand colors will become increasingly important as a means of associating a tobacco brand with a sponsored entity (see Sparks, 1997a), albeit in some markets trademarked colors are considered brand elements and are banned. Most tobacco TNCs have undertaken conventional sponsorship contracts with F1 teams regarding licensing rights for names and trademarks. The exception is British American Tobacco (BAT), which purchased the Tyrrell team outright in 1999 and operates under the moniker of British American Racing (BAR) (Wilson, 1999). Benetton, the international clothing manufacturer, similarly purchased a team ten years earlier in 1989, and found ownership to be a more effective means for leveraging brand communications than sponsorship because teams typically carry the names of their principal owners (e.g. Benetton, McLaren, Williams). Benetton was also able to obtain enough sponsors so that it no longer had to subsidize the team itself (Wilson, 1999). It is unclear whether ownership has conferred these benefits on BAR given the team's poor performance and repeated flare-ups with its (now departed) star driver, Jacques Villeneuve. It is also unclear whether ownership might have more legal purchase than sponsorship for coping with tobacco sponsorship restrictions, but this may yet prove to be the case in some national contexts.

The offensive strategic value of F1 is not limited to tobacco. Anheuser-Busch is using its five-year £50 million sponsorship of the BMW Williams team to build its profile in Europe and to re-enter South Africa where it wants to gain a foothold in the backyard of its arch-rival SABMiller (Beers change lane, 2003; Anheuser-Busch reintroduces Budweiser, 2003). Labatt, which has been without a motor sport sponsorship in Canada, is contributing $CAN5 million to sponsor the Canadian Grand Prix for three years (Marowits, 2003), which gives it an inroad on its main Canadian competitor, Molson Breweries, that until recently supported three CART events (Montreal, Toronto, Vancouver). Both of these properties are somewhat tenuous for the Canadian breweries, however. The future of the Canadian Grand Prix is uncertain beyond the present three-year contract, and CART was put into receivership in 2003 and narrowly escaped dissolution (Beamish, 2004). Vancouver no longer has a place in CART (now renamed the Champ Car World Series). By comparison, the other two main racing leagues in North America, NASCAR and the IRL (a second open-wheel series to Champ Car) are both doing well (NBC, TNT ratings up, 2002; ESPN sports poll, 2003).

These three leagues provide a useful comparison to F1 and help clarify its strengths in a global market. Founded in 1996 as a breakaway league from Champ Car, the IRL races strictly on oval tracks (like NASCAR) and has broad appeal in the central and southern states of the USA. In what became a prophetic move in hindsight (although criticized at the time, especially by Champ Car advocates), IRL organizers required teams to drive identically configured cars in order to minimize costs, even the field of competition, and heighten the uncertainty of race outcomes. The result is that IRL races, like NASCAR races, have close finishes (e.g. margins of victory of .0281, .0024 and .0932 seconds in three races in 2002) and are exciting for fans to watch (Revved up for growth, 2004). NASCAR and the IRL offer a secure sponsorship platform for the alcohol industry in North America (Champ Car's future is less certain), but opportunities for tobacco sponsorship end in 2006 as a result of the Agreement of the States' Attorneys General which will prohibit all tobacco sponsorship of sports in the USA (Glick, 2003). NASCAR is strictly a domestic series in the USA, but the IRL has one race in Japan and Champ Car has two races in Mexico, two in Canada, one each in Australia and South Korea, and plans for expanding to China in 2006 (Coffin, 2005). These out-of-country events have potential value for a tobacco TNC sponsor, even if tobacco companies are prohibited from openly sponsoring a team in the series (because they occur predominantly in the USA). Altria Group Inc., for example, could obtain domain offensive and domain creative value from sponsoring the IRL's Indy Japan 300 with its Marlboro brand and having signage at the Twin Ring Motegi track, because this is home turf for Japan Tobacco Incorporated (JTI) and its two global brands that compete with Marlboro: Mild Seven and Winston (an RJR brand to which JTI owns the international rights). Such a plan would be contingent on several factors including Philip Morris International's (PMI) respective domain offensive and creative priorities, the regulatory conditions in Japan (currently favorable), and provisions in the various national markets where Marlboro is sold against using overseas broadcasts to reach domestic consumers (so far this is not a significant factor) as well as PMI's ability to broker the deal. As successful as such a strategy might be, however, it would be limited to a one-off event in a series that is closed to tobacco sponsorship, and it would provide limited opportunities for leveraging brand awareness in Japan or in North American markets during the remainder of the season. By comparison, F1 is a far more valuable property for pursuing overseas interests as well as for penetrating domestic markets, because it operates in eighteen different countries (nineteen races) over an eight-month season, and its races are televised globally. A reasonable question to ask in the present regulatory climate, however, is how much longer will this opportunity last? The answer is, probably not long.

Unless further concessions can be worked out, F1 has a similar time frame as the auto leagues in the USA, one season before a European Union advertising ban will prohibit all tobacco sponsorship in member countries. Some commentators have wondered whether Bernie Ecclestone, the head of F1, might move the series out of Europe entirely in order to maintain tobacco sponsorship (F1 attacked, 2003), and this remains a possibility (see Baird, 1997). Several factors weigh against this course of action, however. For one, communications, information technology and courier companies have awakened to the value of sports sponsorship, and are beginning to invest in major properties, bringing with them not only money but technical expertise and benefits. For example, the wireless communications company, Nextel, has taken over the title sponsorship of NASCAR's premier series (formerly the Winston Cup, now the Nextel Cup) (Glick, 2003). In 2002, Deutsche Post WorldNet subsidiary DHL, a courier company, took over the title sponsorship for Jordan Honda from Benson & Hedges (which continued in a secondary sponsorship) in a three-year contract worth £21 million per year (Jones, 2002a). Nortel Networks was a sponsor of the Williams team in 2000, and other computer companies including Compaq, Intel and Hewlett-Packard have also stepped up, although they tend to contribute technology, expertise and personnel rather than money, in a similar arrangement as the car and engine manufacturers (Newing, 2000). A second reason that makes locating outside of Europe unlikely is that Europe is home to most of the F1 teams (Baird, 1997). Most importantly, however, a third reason is that the tobacco companies themselves are already pursuing alternative sponsorship programs, as well as developing new strategies unrelated to sponsorship. This raises the issue of strategy divergence, that is, of the TNCs' pursuit of competitive advantage through independent sponsorship initiatives and alternative brand marketing programs.

Competitive Strategy Divergence: Exploiting Global Opportunities

While collaborating to preserve markets is a new reality, most sponsorship activity is undertaken by tobacco and alcohol companies to support their own brands and corporate interests. This entails independently exploiting sponsorship opportunities that give them strategic and tactical advantage over their competitors, as well as undertaking alternative brand communications programs. One such possibility is to use sponsorship to help build relations with a foreign government in order to overcome national advertising restrictions and other barriers to entry such as import restrictions, investment restrictions and duties. For example, the Marlboro Tennis Tournament organized by Philip Morris International in China in 1980 is reported to be the first sponsorship event held in that country (Wu, 1999; cited in Geng, Burton & Blakemore, 2002). Typical of Philip Morris's innovative stance, this gave them first entrant status in the Chinese marketplace with respect to sponsorship, and helped to build corporate good will at a time when they were trying to introduce Marlboro into the country.

Competing in New Markets: The Special Case of China   China is a country of keen interest for tobacco and alcohol companies alike because of its size (1.2 billion people) and market characteristics. There are 350 million smokers in China (63% of adult males and 4% of adult females smoke), who collectively consume 30% of the world's cigarettes (Dean, 1998; O'Sullivan & Chapman, 2000; Fowler, 2003a, 2003b). In addition, 61% of Chinese adults, roughly 530 million people, drink alcohol at least once yearly (WHO, 1999, p. 342). Spirits are still the principal form of alcohol consumed, but the beer market has been growing steadily at 6% per annum, and in 2002 China surpassed the USA as the "world's largest beer market" by volume, a fact that helps to explain the rising investments of Anheuser-Busch and SABMiller in Chinese breweries (Anheuser and SAB raise stakes, 2003).

Beer sponsorship of sports is increasing in China. Budweiser was an early entrant, and has sponsored the China National Basketball League since the late 1990s (Young adult beer drinkers, 1997; China football, 2003). Budweiser is also sponsoring the Budweiser University League Soccer Games, Budweiser Cup Amateur 6–on-6 Soccer Tournaments, the 2004 Chinese Olympic Team, the China Olympic Committee, the 2008 Beijing Olympic Games, and TV broadcasts in China of FIFA, NBA and the English Premier League games (www. anheuser-busch.com/overview, 2004). Heineken has sponsored the Heineken Open Shanghai from 1999 to 2004 as part of the Association of Tennis Professionals (ATP) Tour. This was the first such event to be owned and operated by a Chinese company, the Shanghai Bus Co. (Beer, tennis and bus companies,

1999). In a reversal of the usual flow of alcohol products and marketing from developed to developing countries, the US distributor for Yanjing Beer Group Corporation, Harbrew Imports, signed a five-year US$6 million contract in 2003 to sponsor the Houston Rockets where the Chinese basketball star, Yao Ming, plays. The goal of the contract is to reach consumers in China who watch NBA games as well as Chinese Americans (Khermouch, Einhorn & Roberts, 2003; Balfour, 2003).

Further to exploiting sport sponsorship to support the introduction of their premium brands in China, Anheuser-Busch and Heineken have also invested in domestic breweries. Anheuser-Busch has interests in the Budweiser International Brewing Co. Ltd in Wuhan, the Tsingtao Brewery Co. Ltd in Qingdao, and the Harbin Brewery Group Ltd in Harbin that collectively amount to more than US$1 billion. The Wuhan brewery, for example, is 97% owned by Anheuser-Busch and has capacity for 3.2 million hectoliters of beer production as a result of US$197.5 million of capital investment by Anheuser-Busch that has tripled the brewery's capacity since 1995 when it was first acquired (www.anheuser-busch.com/overview, 2004). Heineken first entered China in 1929 and began to pursue the market more vigorously in the 1980s, but only established a dedicated entity for import, marketing and distribution in May 2002. Heineken is presently the leading imported brand in China, and can be bought in major cities throughout China. Heineken owns interests in two breweries, Asia Pacific Brewery in Shanghai and Hainan, which have capacity for 223,000 and 440,000 hectoliters, respectively (www.heinekeninternational.com, 2004). While Anheuser-Busch and Heineken are exploiting "pull" and "push" strategies of creating demand through sponsorship and integrated marketing communications and meeting demand through import and domestic brewing, SABMiller appears to be focused on a domain creation strategy that emphasizes mainly a "push" strategy and use of productive and distributive capacities to gain market share. No evidence of sponsorship activity could be found (sport or otherwise), but SABMiller has invested heavily in domestic production, and owns 49% interest in China Resources Breweries Ltd, a joint SABMiller-Chinese venture that owns 32 breweries with a collective brewing capacity of 45,831 million hectoliters in an overall market in China of 241,447 million hectoliters (www.sabmiller.com, 2004). This strategy is different from the one they have used in South Africa and the USA, but it has given them a major share of the Chinese domestic beer market, albeit with a portfolio of relatively minor brands.

China signed the FCTC on November 10, 2003, but is not yet party to the agreement. Even though tobacco advertising is currently prohibited in China, domestic tobacco companies have managed to exploit legal loopholes to promote cigarettes using sponsorship. For example, Baisha Group, the largest cigarette manufacturer in China, signed the Sydney Olympics 110m hurdles gold medalist, Liu Xiang, under its Baisha Culture Propagation Co. division, which is named after Baisha, China's best-selling brand (Olympic sprint champion

Liu Xiang, 2004). Supportive advertising for the sponsorship was banned by the State Administration for Industry and Commerce in November 2004, but the contract, which is between Baisha Culture and the Market Development Department of the SSGA Track and Field Management Center, is not illegal as such (www.chinatoday.com.cn/English/e2005/e200504/p39.htm, 2005). Similarly, Yunann Hongta Group promoted its brands for a number of years by funding local sports clubs such as the "Hongta Soccer Club" (Fowler, 2003a). This is a wise choice of sport, as are Budweiser's and Yanjing Beer's selection of soccer and basketball. According to a 1999 survey, soccer, basketball, table tennis and volleyball are the four most watched sports on television in China (73.4%, 40.3%, 34.8% and 31.0% of respondents) followed by swimming, badminton, athletics, tennis and golf (28.4%, 24.6%, 18.5%, 17.0% and 9.0%, respectively) (What is Asia's favourite sport, 1999).

New Markets and the Rising Importance of New Media   A second way for a tobacco or alcohol TNC to achieve domain offensive and creative advantage over its competitors is to use sponsorship opportunities in countries with lenient regulations to leverage brand awareness and market acceptance in countries with stricter regulations. The goal of such a sponsorship program, as seen in the case of F1, is to use global media to gain recognition that is consistent with the brand's positioning internationally in the targeted countries. As regulations for broadcast media intensify, however, it will be increasingly important for sponsors to assess the value of their sports properties in terms of new media.

As valuable as F1 is as a broadcast property, it has been slow to capitalize on web highlights, web broadcasts and cell phone-based sports updates as a potential means to leverage its audience reach, and it does not appear that teams and sponsors are yet able to independently avail themselves of these opportunities (Fighting for control, 2003). Bernie Ecclestone invested £35 million in digital television technologies in 1997 anticipating that pay per view (PPV) might become a major source of revenue (Fry, 1997), and he is reported to be looking into wireless rights as well as considering launching a subscription-based web portal. From an industry standpoint, this is a move in the right direction, but it is somewhat behind the times. By comparison, Rugby Union in the UK already offers fans highlights of England and Premiership matches through broadband rights distributor Sportev, and the England and Wales Cricket Board has already licensed web streaming rights for a number of its major events, including Test series and one-day internationals. The Football Association and the Premier League were recently reported to be negotiating web and wireless rights including the rights for clubs to show highlights, archived footage and live matches on their own official websites (Fighting for control, 2003). Turner Sports Interactive, a Time Warner Company, owns NASCAR's interactive rights and has produced the series' official website since January 2001, along with a wireless service and various other multimedia features including video and audio highlights, live scoring and timing during races, and Nextel Cup practice sessions (www.nascar.com). Using these kinds of digital services in combination with portal technology could potentially enable a tobacco and alcohol sponsor to honor sponsorship restrictions in regulated countries, while still communicating with consumers in unregulated markets, by directing web visitors to different web pages and interfaces. Intrawest, the North America ski resort company, uses portal technology to direct visitors to appropriate web pages based on the region of Canada (local, out of province) and country they reside in.

Some analysts have speculated that the varied nature of sponsorship restrictions might encourage "selective sponsorships" where a restricted sponsor supports properties in countries with exemptions and another sponsor, perhaps a subsidiary or corporate partner, supports related properties in countries with bans, not unlike Budweiser was forced to do with its World Cup hoardings in France. Most evidence suggests that this second strategy for alcohol and tobacco companies is unlikely, however, as sponsors need a consistent presence in order to achieve value. Sponsors interested in a localized national presence would be more likely to look for signage packages or arrangements with a specific event than to try to coordinate a global campaign on an intermittent basis (Wilson, 1999). What might change this arrangement is the possibility of using digital technologies such as virtual signage to alter sponsorship attribution in television broadcasts according to target markets. Sparks (1997b), for example, has argued that such technologies would allow a tobacco brand sponsor such as Marlboro to be replaced by a non-tobacco brand owned by Altria Group such as a Kraft Food product in telecasts beamed into restricted markets, while the Marlboro brand could be carried in unrestricted markets, irrespective of the actual presentation of the brand logo at the live event. Virtual signage has not yet achieved widespread acceptance, however, in part because of concerns about paid spots being overwritten in international markets, and it is again not clear that this would deliver the message consistency that a tobacco and alcohol sponsor would need to justify the expense. At the end of the day sponsorship is about receiving a real return on investment (ROI). If it is not profitable, tobacco and alcohol TNCs will abandon sport sponsorship for other strategies. Some brief examples illustrate these possibilities.

Alternatives to Sport Sponsorship   As noted at the beginning of this chapter, the developing world constitutes a growth market for the global tobacco industry. Tobacco TNCs like Philip Morris International have used a variety of means to introduce their premium brands into third world markets including methods that are now prohibited in many developed countries such as brand extensions (e.g. Marlboro clothing and accessories), couponing (putting redeemable coupons in cigarette packs) and product sampling (giving away free product samples), in addition to outdoor advertising and sponsorship (INFACT, 1998). Sampling is a particularly insidious tactic, because it contributes to smoking uptake. The logic of giving away free samples is to stimulate product trial by making the brand readily available, and to create a positive image for the brand based on the apparent "generosity" of the manufacturer and the attractive appearance of the people handing it out (usually young women). In North America and Australia where product giveaways are prohibited, sampling has recently been converted into a sales strategy, and cigarette girls are now making a return in licensed bars and lounges. In Canada, for example, Imperial Tobacco and Rothmans have hired DJs and organized club events where scantily clad, attractive young women circulate with trays selling cigarettes to patrons. Imperial's original program called Redseat had a dedicated website, redseat.ca, which gave prospective customers information about events. Similarly, Rothman Inc's Gold Club Series program had its own web location, goldclub.ca (Nutall-Smith, 2003). Both of these programs are now closed down, but Imperial Tobacco's bar promotions were rebranded as Definiti in September 2003 (website: definiti.ca) and managed by two subsidiaries: Rumbling Walls Entertainment, which provides integrated marketing services through magazines, the web and events, and Channel 2, which provides non-traditional product displays (www.smoke-free.ca, 2004). In Australia, Philip Morris formed a "shell" company called Wavesnet to promote its mentholated Alpine brand. The bar and fashion events program is complemented by a website (wavesnet.net) and a magazine entitled, *Waves* (Carter, 2001; Harper, 2001). Use of events and websites provides an opportunity to collect personal information from participants that can subsequently be used as part of a direct marketing and database marketing strategy. This has particular value at present, because communicating directly with customers via mail and email is still allowed in most countries and offers possibilities for undertaking one-to-one marketing. Several tobacco manufacturers have already launched lifestyle magazines that are designed to improve their brand profiles and that use direct mail distribution to reach targets in the company's database. Imperial Tobacco's magazine, *Rev*, for example, contains content that is similar to *Maxim* or *Gear*, and closely matches the psychographic dimensions of the target market for their Player's brand. *CML* (with content matching the brand imagery of the Camel brand) is published four times a year by R. J. Reynolds, while *Unlimited* is a publication by Philip Morris for its Marlboro brand.

Another strategy available to the tobacco and alcohol companies is to capitalize on legislative loopholes between countries (Cornwell, 1997). For example, although print advertising for tobacco products was banned in the UK in 2003, Gallaher ran a flight of full-page advertisements for its Mayfair brand in the Spanish edition of *The Sun*, a national tabloid newspaper, in order to target British vacationers on the Costa del Sol in Spain (Cigarette firm bypasses legislation, 2003). *The Sun's* overseas circulation is 81,560. According to British Travel Agents, 6.7 million package holidays to Spain were sold in 2001. While this opportunity was eliminated when European Union legislation came into effect in September 2004, there is little to prevent tobacco companies from exploiting these kinds of loopholes in print, poster and broadcast media in unregulated overseas markets to reach their various targets, particularly if the ad campaigns are for major international brands like Marlboro, Lucky Strike and

Mild Seven. This kind of campaign could be linked to a more "viral" approach where attractive, trend-setting people are hired to go to particular resorts or attend particular events and smoke (or drink) the client's brand. This is a more insidious version of the use of cigarette girls (and boys). All of these campaigns help to build brand image and awareness, which can then be leveraged at retail by brand exposure in behind-the-counter tobacco products display cases or in liquor stores and duty-free shops (West promotion, 2003; Selling in the dark, 2000; Sparks, 1997b). Given these possibilities, even if tobacco and alcohol sponsorship of sports is reduced globally by increasingly restrictive legislation, these industries will nonetheless be able to market to young people of a legal age, but who are still in their formative years, and therefore susceptible to peer influences. In this case, smoking and drinking will not go away, rather the initial years of uptake will simply be moved up from pre- or mid-teen to late teen or early twenties. In such a scenario, it is possible that in addition to music clubs, licensed sports bars and lounges will also become sites of sponsorship activity for alcohol and tobacco companies. Favoring this is the fact that the clientele fit the demographic profile of the industries' respective core customer groups for brands with a predominantly male market. Secondly, the sports connection would offer the same lifestyle segmentation and brand association benefits that sports properties presently achieve for their sponsors, and could be leveraged using direct marketing methods. Thirdly, sports bars often carry overseas and PPV broadcasts that are likely to be the last holdouts for tobacco and alcohol sponsorship, and the bars could also use broadband technology to carry web broadcasts. Lastly, the tobacco and alcohol companies have been using sports properties for decades and know the territory very well. Whether such an approach would ultimately prove profitable is hard to determine, but what is clear is that alcohol and tobacco TNCs will continue to explore their options and exploit the opportunities that are available to them, including any remaining chances for using sport sponsorship to enhance their corporate image, stimulate product trial and build brand equity.

Conclusion: The Global Dynamics of Sponsorship

Although this chapter has focused on two highly regulated industries that are experiencing increased restrictions on their use of sport sponsorship, the two cases amply demonstrate the strategic value of sport sponsorship in an emerging global economy. In our brief analysis we have shown that even in their early involvements with sport, tobacco and alcohol companies already had a good sense of the lifestyle association and segmentation value of different sports and were able to capitalize on the reach and appeal of celebrity athletes, sports events and symbols in their advertising and sponsorship campaigns. The more recent activities of the tobacco and alcohol TNCs, however, show that, further to image-based and lifestyle marketing, sports properties can also be used in support of essential domain defensive, offensive and creative strategies to help achieve and maintain competitive advantage in the face of increasing industry consolidation and regulation globally. In addition to capitalizing on restructuring, production efficiencies and economies of scale, industry leaders like Anheuser-Busch, Labatt (now part of InBev), Miller (now SABMiller) and Philip Morris (now Altria) have been able to build market share, in part, through innovative use of sport sponsorship to overcome advertising restrictions and compete against rival firms. They have also used sponsorships to help overcome trade barriers and gain access to new markets. The approach they have taken in the latter case has tended to follow the three-stage process described by Cavanagh and Clairmonte (1985), in this instance, of using sports to support an initial export strategy for their global brand(s), followed by licensing agreements for local production and subsequently by acquisition or start-up of local manufacturing and distribution entities. Their use of sport sponsorship to support overseas expansion nicely illustrates Kotler's (1986) conception of "mega-marketing," and situates sport sponsorship among an array of economic, political and public relations tools that corporations can exploit to help build good will and gain political cooperation and support ("political capital") in targeted national economies. Philip Morris International's sponsorship of the Marlboro Tennis Tournament in China in 1980 is a good example of this, as it gave them first entrant status with sponsorship and helped open opportunities for introducing the Marlboro brand in local markets with the intention of gaining a share of the lucrative Chinese cigarette market. The same principles can be seen in the sponsorship programs of Anheuser-Busch and Heineken in China, as in each case, they are using sponsorship to support premium brand imports at the same time that they are investing in local breweries with a long-term objective of gaining market share in the world's largest national beer market.

Another finding in the chapter is that sports properties can have inter-firm, industry-level strategic value as well as firm-specific value, and that these conditions can converge in some instances. This is demonstrated in the case of F1 where the major tobacco TNCs have worked together (and with FIA) to maintain the race series as a site for their collective sponsorship activities (collaborative domain defense), at the same time that they have competed with each other during the season for brand image and awareness (firm-specific domain offense) and for corporate image and political capital in markets where they have expansionist interests (firm-specific domain creation). Even the firm-specific functions of sport sponsorship are seen to serve an overall industry purpose, however, in the sense that they help to legitimize the right of industry members to advertise and market their brands (which contributes to the social acceptability of product use), and, in cases like F1 where a sport series expands into new markets that are of strategic importance to the sponsors (i.e. Malaysia, Bahrain, China and Japan), they offer collective opportunities for industry growth. Localized sport properties such as national or sub-national (regional, municipal) teams, venues, series, events, and personalities have similar industry and firm-specific strategic potential, albeit there is less basis for collaborative activities and strategy convergence than there is with a global series such as F1.

The very recent sponsorship activities of the tobacco and alcohol firms reviewed in the chapter also demonstrate the potential benefits for sponsors of new media and targeted communications methods such as PPV, wireless, virtual signage and the World Wide Web as well as direct, database, relationship, one-to-one, and viral marketing. While the respective research literatures on the efficacy of these technologies and methods were beyond the scope of the analysis we undertook, it is quite clear in broad terms that as the tobacco and alcohol TNCs continue to innovate, they are capitalizing on new technologies and marketing methods and taking an early adopter position in the diffusion of these practices. As a result, their sponsorship programs already demonstrate many of the practices that one assumes will eventually become more widely adopted in the industry, and now, as in the past, they are tending to lead the field. This is of course a point of irony as, in doing so, they are also contributing to a worldwide spread of tobacco and alcohol use which is following its own diffusion curve and will reach global epidemic proportions in the next two decades, as noted at the beginning of the chapter. A final point to make in conclusion, therefore, is that scholarship of global sport sponsorship needs to examine both sides of the ledger and come to terms with the social trajectories and costs of sponsorship activities as well as the benefits that they bring to corporations.

References

"Anheuser and SAB raise stakes in China." (2003) *Modern Brewery Age*, July 7, 54 (27): 1.

Anheuser-Busch. (2002) *Anheuser-Busch Companies: At a Glance*, St Louis, Missouri: Anheuser-Busch Companies, Inc., Corporate Communications Department, May.

"Anheuser-Busch reintroduces Budweiser in South Africa." (2003) *Knight-Ridder/Tribune Business News*, September 24.

Baird, R. (1997) "BAT poised to buy Tyrell F1 team in L300m deal," *Marketing Week*, November 13, 20 (33): 7.

Balfour, F. (2003) "Game plan B: Sponsors find sports marketing in China hard to learn," *Business Week*, Sep 15, 56.

"BDO to clean up UK darts' image." (2002) *Marketing Week*, May 9, 25 (13).

"Beached buggies." (2003) *Marketing Week*, October 9, 26 (41): 21.

Beamish, M. (2004) "Indy remains in Vancouver," *The Vancouver Sun*, January 29, D1.

"Beer, tennis and bus companies." (1999) *Business China*, October 25, 25 (22): 5–6.

"Beers change lane and revert to sport." (2003) *Marketing Week*, July 10, 26 (28): 14.

"Brand power." (1998) *Liquid Foods International*, February, 2 (2).

Bruun, K., Edwards, G., and Lumio, M. (1975) *Alcohol Control Policies in Public Health Perspective*, Helsinki: Finnish Foundation for Alcohol Studies, Vol. 25.

Carter, S. (2001) "Worshipping at the Alpine altar: Promoting tobacco in a world without advertising," *Tobacco Control*, 10: 391–393.

Cavanagh, J. and Clairmonte, F. (1985) *Alcoholic Beverages: Dimensions of Corporate Power*. London: Croom Helm.

"China Football hands brand job to DDB." (2003) *Media* (Hong Kong), July 25: 1.

"Cigarette firm bypasses legislation and targets UK tourist in Spain." (2003) *Marketing Week*, July 5, 26 (30).

Coffin, D. (2005) "Champ Car heading to China," Pitstop, *Monterey Herald.com*, www.montereyherald.com/mld/montereyherald/sports/11244235.htm, accessed March 27.

Collins, T., and Vamplew, W. (2002) *Mud, Sweat and Beers: A Cultural History of Sport and Alcohol.* Oxford: Berg.

Cornwell, T. B. (1997) "The use of sponsorship-linked marketing by tobacco firms: International public policy issues," *Journal of Consumer Affairs*, 31: 238–254.

Crompton, J. (1993) "Sponsorship of sport by tobacco and alcohol companies: A review of the issues," *Journal of Sport and Social Issues*, 17 (December): 148–167.

Cunningham, R. (1996) *Smoke and Mirrors: The Canadian Tobacco War*, Ottawa: International Development Research Centre.

Cunningham, R. (2005) Personal correspondence, February 25.

Dean, J. (1998) "Smoke and mirrors," *Far Eastern Economic Review*, November 26, 161 (48): 62.

Deutsche Banc Alex. Brown. (2000) Deutsche Banc Alex. Brown Europe, *Brokerage Report*, March 31.

Dewhirst, T. (2004) "Smoke and ashes: Tobacco sponsorship of sports and regulatory issues in Canada," in L.R. Kahle and C. Riley (eds), *Sports Marketing and the Psychology of Marketing Communication*, Mahwah, NJ: Lawrence Erlbaum Associates, Inc., pp. 327–352.

Dewhirst, T. (2005) "Public relations," in J. Goodman (ed.), *Tobacco in History and Culture: An Encyclopedia.* Farmington Hills, MI: Charles Scribner's Sons, pp. 473–479.

Dewhirst, T. and Hunter, A. (2002) "Tobacco sponsorship of Formula One and CART auto racing: Tobacco brand exposure and enhanced symbolic imagery through co-sponsors' third party advertising," *Tobacco Control*, 11: 146–150.

Dewhirst, T. and Sparks, R. (2003) "Intertextuality, tobacco sponsorship of sports, and adolescent male smoking culture: A selective review of tobacco industry documents," *Journal of Sport and Social Issues*, 27: 372–398.

Donaldson, J. (2002) *Formula 1: The Autobiography*, London: Weidenfeld and Nicholson.

"ESPN Sports poll shows interest in IRL has doubled in three years." (2003) *IRL Insider*, 1 (4), www.indyracing.com/insider/story.php?story_id=37, accessed March 27, 2005.

Ezzati, M., and Lopez, A.D. (2003) "Estimates of global mortality attributable to smoking in 2000," *The Lancet*, 362 (9387): 847–852.

"F1 attacked over tobacco ads U-turn." (2003) *Marketing Week*, July 10: 5.

Felt, J. (2002) "How sports sponsorship can help your brand: Corporate interests and new technology can complicate brand protection strategies in sponsorship deals," *Managing Intellectual Property*, 24, December.

"Fighting for control: With the arrival of broadband and 3G mobile networks, can football clubs face up to broadcasters and win back some of the rights to showing their matches on these platforms?" (2003) *New Media Age*, May 29, 34.

"Formula 1 turns off TV viewers." (2003) *Automotive News Europe*, September 8, 8 (17): 30.

Fowler, G. (2003a) "Treaty may snub out cigarette ads in China," *Wall Street Journal*, December 2: B1.

Fowler, G. (2003b) "Butt out: Tobacco marketers in China fret about what an anti-smoking treaty could mean for them," *Far Eastern Economic Review*, December 4, 166 (48): 35.

Fry, A. (1997) "Race relations," *Marketing*, September 11: 22–23.

Furlong, R. (1994) "Tobacco Advertising Legislation and the Sponsorship of Sport," *Australian Business Law Review*, 22 (3), 159–189.

Geng, L., Burton, R. and Blakemore, C. (2002) "Sport sponsorship in China: Transition and evolution," *Sport Marketing Quarterly*, 11 (1): 20–32.

gfg.com/baseball/ginter.shtml, November 3, 2004.

Glick, S. (2003) "Nextel replaces Winston in NASCAR," *Edmonton Journal*, Dec 5: H13.

Gorn, E. J., and Goldstein, W. J. (1993) *A Brief History of American Sports*. New York: Hill and Wang.

Grant, M. and Litvak, J. (1998) *Drinking Patterns and Their Consequences,* Washington, DC: Taylor and Francis.

Harper, T. (2001) "Marketing life after advertising bans," *Tobacco Control*, 10: 196–197.

Hilts, P. (1996) *Smoke Screen: The Truth Behind the Tobacco Industry Cover-Up*, Reading, MA: Addison-Wesley Publishing Company.

Hoek, J. and Sparks, R. (2000) "Tobacco promotion restrictions: an international regulatory impasse?" *International Marketing Review*, 17 (2-3): 216–230.

IEG, Inc. (2004) *IEG Sponsorship Report*, 23 (24) December 27: 4.

INFACT. (1998) Global Aggression: The Case for World Standards and Bold US Action Challenging Philip Morris and RJR Nabisco, *INFACT's 1998 People's Annual Report*, New York: The Apex Press.

International Center for Alcohol Policies. (2001) *ICAP Reports 9: Self-regulation of Beverage Alcohol Advertising*, January.

International Olympic Committee. (2001) *The Olympic Broadcast Handbook: Salt Lake 2002*, Lausanne: International Olympic Committee.

Johnson, W. (1988) "Sport and suds: The beer business and the sports world have brewed up a potent partnership," *Sports Illustrated*, August 8, 69 (6): 68–82.

Jones, M. C. (2002a) "Tobacco sponsorship heads for the pits as IT takes poll," *Brand Strategy*, December, 10 (2).

Jones, M. C. (2002b) "Do not believe the hype: Formula One teams are having a hard time with sponsors," *Brand Strategy*, 9, December.

Jones, M. C. (2003) "What doesn't kill you might even make you stronger," *Brand Strategy*, November, 10.

Khermouch, G., Einhorn, B. and Roberts, D. (2003) "Breaking into the name game: China's manufacturers are building their brands to go global," *Business Week*, April 7, 54.

King, B. (2003) "How NASCAR outgrew RJR's tobacco-stained image," *The Business Journal*, December 5, 6(13).

Kluger, R. (1997) *Ashes to Ashes: America's Hundred-Year Cigarette War, the Public Health, and the Unabashed Triumph of Philip Morris*, New York: Vintage Books.

Kotler, P. (1986) "Megamarketing," *Harvard Business Review*, March-April, 64 (2): 117.

Marowits, R. (2003) "F-1 deal keeps GP event in Canada," *National Post* (National edition), November 19: S4.

McGowan, R. (1995) *Business, Politics, and Cigarettes: Multiple Levels, Multiple Agendas,* Westport, CT: Quorum Books.

Miles, R. (1982) *Coffin Nails and Corporate Strategies*, Englewood Cliffs, NJ: Prentice-Hall, Inc.

Miller, R. (1991) "The baseball parks and the American Culture," in A. Hall (ed.), *Cooperstown Symposium on Baseball and the American culture* (1990), Westport, CT: Meckler in association with the State University of New York College at Oneonta, pp. 168–86.

"NBC, TNT ratings up 13 percent over last year." (2002) Associated Press, November 22.

Newing, R. (2000) "FT-IT Review: Formula One pushes technology to the limit," *Financial Times Surveys Edition*, August 2, 5.

Noble, J. and Hughes, M. (2004) *Formula One Racing for Dummies*, West Sussex, England: John Wiley and Sons.

Nutall-Smith, C. (2003) "Big tobacco brings message to club scene," *The Vancouver Sun*, September 08: D3.

"Olympic sprint champion Liu Xiang signed up to endorse China's biggest cigarette maker." (2004) Associated Press, October 21, sportsillustrated.cnn.com/2004.

O'Sullivan, B. and Chapman, S. (2000) "Eyes on the prize: Transnational tobacco companies in China 1976–1997," *Tobacco Control*, 9: 292–302.

Pollay, R. W. (1989) "Filters, flavors ... flim-flam, too! On 'health information' and policy implications in cigarette advertising," *Journal of Public Policy and Marketing*, 8: 30–39.

Pollay, R. W. and Dewhirst, T. (2002) "The dark side of marketing seemingly "Light" cigarettes: Successful images and failed fact," *Tobacco Control*, 11: i18–i31.

"Revved up for growth – Built for opportunity." (2004) *Indy Racing League Partnership Sales Brochure (PDF)*, Indy Racing League.

Roemer, R. (1993) *Legislative Action to Combat the World Tobacco Epidemic*, Geneva: World Health Organization.

scriptorium.lib.duke.edu/eaa/tobacco.html, February 24, 2004.

"Selling in the dark." (2000) *Travel Retailer International*, January.

Shafey, O., Dolwick, S. and Guindon, G. E. (eds) (2003) *Tobacco Control Country Profiles 2003*, Atlanta, Georgia: American Cancer Society.

Sneath, A. W. (2001) *Brewed in Canada: The Untold Story of Canada's 350-Year-Old Brewing Industry*. Toronto: The Dundurn Group.

Sparks, R. (1992) "'Delivering the male': Sports, Canadian television, and the making of T.S.N.," *Canadian Journal of Communication*, 17 (3): 319–342.

Sparks, R. (1997a) "Bill C-71 and tobacco sponsorship of sports," *Policy Options*, 18, 3: 22–5.

Sparks, R. (1997b) "Tobacco control legislation, public health and sport sponsorship," *Asia-Australia Journal of Marketing*, 5 (1) December: 59–70.

Sparks, R. (1999) "Youth awareness of tobacco sponsorship as a dimension of brand equity," *International Journal of Sport Marketing and Sponsorship*, 1 (3): 236–260.

Standard and Poor's. (2003) *Industry Surveys: Alcoholic Beverages & Tobacco*, January 23, 171 (4), Section 1: 1–26.

"The business of racing, Marlboro advertisement." (1989) *The New York Times Magazine*, July 9: 5A.

Tomlinson, R. (2004) "The new king of beers," *Fortune* (Europe), October 18, 150 (7): 63.

Vaidya, S. G., Naik, U. D. and Vaidya, J. S. (1996) "Effect of sport sponsorship by tobacco companies on children"s experimentation with tobacco," *British Medical Journal*, 313: 400–416.

Van Munching, P. (1997) *Beer Blast: The Inside Story of the Brewing Industry's Bizarre Battles for Your Money*, New York: Times Business.

Walker, N. (1991) "Tobacco Control Act 1990 (WA)," *Western Australia Law Review*, 21 (2): 391–398.

Warner, K. (1986) *Selling Smoke: Cigarette Advertising and Public Health*, Washington, D.C.: American Public Health Association.

"West promotion to drive growth," (2003) *Duty-Free News International*, June 1, 17 (10): 14.

"What is Asia's favourite sport?" (1999) *Marketing Week*, August 5, 30.

WHO (1970–1996) *International Digest of Health Legislation*, 21–47 (1–4).

WHO (1976) *Legislative Action to Combat Smoking Around the World: A Survey of Existing Legislation*, Geneva: WHO.

WHO (1998–2004) *International Digest of Health Legislation*, 49–55 (1–4).

WHO (1999) *Global Status Report on Alcohol*, Geneva: WHO.

WHO (2003) *Tobacco Control Country Profiles*, Geneva: WHO.

WHO (2004) *Global Status Report: Alcohol Policy*, Geneva: WHO.

Wilson, R. (1999) "Sponsors have a lot of influence in the world of motor racing, but can companies such as BAT find a way to beat the threatened worldwide ban on Formula One's tobacco sponsorship?," *Marketing Week*, January 21, 21 (45): 51.

Winstanley, M., Woodward, S., and Walker, N. (1995) *Tobacco in Australia: Facts and issues* (2nd edn), Carlton: Victorian Smoking and Health Program (Quit Victoria).

World Health Assembly. (2003) *WHO Framework Convention on Tobacco Control*, WHA56.1, May 21.

Wu, S. (1999) *The Chinese History of Sports*, Beijing, China: People's Publisher of Sports.

www.anheuser-busch.com/publications/AtaGlance03.pdf, March 27, 2005.

www.anheuser-busch.com/overview/abiichina.htm, December 12, 2004.

www.anheuser-busch.com/news/Beiing_092804.htm, December 12, 2004.

www.chinatoday.com.cn/English/e2005/e200504/p39.htm, March 28, 2005.

www.eurocare.org/who/alcohol.html, February 6, 2004.

www.golf.web.com/tournaments/europeantour/index.html, December 22, 2003.

www.globalink.org/, March 26, 2004.

www.heinekeninternational.com/search.do?query=ch, November 18, 2004

www.icap.org/about_icap/sponsors.html, February 24, 2004.

www.nascar.com/guides/about, March 24, 2004.

www.sabmiller.com/SABMiller/Our+business/Markets/china.htm, December 12, 2004.

www.smoke-free.ca/filtertips04/definiti.htm, November 1, 2004.

www.tobacco.org/resources/history/Tobacco_History19.html, February 24, 2004.

www.volleyball.org/cuervo, December 22, 2003.

www.who/int/tobacco/framework/en, October 10, 2004.

www.who.int/tobacco/framework/countrylist/en/, March 27, 2005.

"Young adult beer drinkers change global market – study." (1997) *Business World* (Manila), September 30.

3

The Spatial Logics of Global Sponsorship
Corporate capital, cola wars and cricket

Michael Silk and David L. Andrews

For many social theorists, the expanding range of information flows and the spatial reach of digital communications systems are leading to new kinds of social formations that are said to coexist, if not surpass, the political, cultural and place-based identities that characterized the era of capitalist industrialism. The essence of the argument suggests political, economic and cultural shifts in the production and consumption of goods and services has led to an international economy based on networks of corporations (and nations) linked by the flow of information and symbolism through fiber optics and satellites rather than the concrete or steel, physical or tangible systems, that characterized an earlier age. This has led to countries, especially those on the fringes of the capitalist core, attempting to connect themselves to networks through redeveloping themselves as places that can attract the right sort of firms and be a part of the information infrastructure (Castells, 1996).

There have clearly been significant shifts and transformations within late capitalism – modes of development and modes of production have, at least in many "Western" countries, been transformed from a material and labour oriented structure to those that are dependent upon information and knowledge. However, and rather than apocalyptically proclaiming the "end of the nation," it is important to critically interrogate the continued role of the nation-state and the salience of national/local specificities within the production of culture. Thus, despite a global cosmopolitanism that characterizes the global (sport) literature, "geography still matters" in a very real sense as local and national specificities continue to shape production and consumption processes in many sectors in different ways (Preston & Kerr, 2001). Within this chapter we are interested in the use of sport sponsorship within the wider dictates of corporate capital; in particular the role sport sponsorship has played in the spatial logics of transnationals seeking to engage with new and emergent marketplaces. Our focal point is the shifting "cola wars" (Pendergrast, 2000) between the PepsiCo Company and the Coca-Cola Company, wars that have been relocated from the physically bound American nation to more fluid, epistemologically construed spaces. Prior to addressing these effervescent antagonisms within emergent (corporate) sporting vernaculars, it is pertinent to outline briefly the processes and spatial logics of transnational sporting capital.

The Spatial Logics of Corporate Capital

According to Held, McGrew, Goldblatt and Perraton (1999), globalization is "a process (or set of processes) which embodies a transformation in the spatial organization of social relations and transaction – assessed in terms of their extensity, intensity, velocity and impact – generating transcontinental or interregional flows and networks of activity, interaction and the exercise of power" (p. 16). Given this logic of increased interdependence and interconnectedness, it can be argued that contemporary conditions of advanced globalization have seriously undermined the economic and political autonomy that helped constitute the modern nation. For example, the expanding range of information flows and the spatial reach of digital communications systems are argued, by some social theorists, to be leading to new kinds of social anomie, a "dissolution" of social relationships and the collapse of political, cultural and place-based identities which characterized the era of capitalist industrialism (Preston & Kerr, 2001). Further, and perhaps most important in the consideration of the spatial reach, organization and manifestation of the economics of sport sponsorship, Lash and Urry (1987) have suggested a move from organized capitalism to disorganized capitalism centered on the deconcentration of capital through globalized production, financing and distribution, a concomitant shift in the occupational structures of core and periphery economies and the growth of capitalism in the "developing" world. This process of the "the withering away of the nation" (Hannerz, 1996, p. 81) and the concomitant move towards a disorganized capitalism began in earnest during the 1970s, when the confidence in Fordist/Keynesian economic policies that had held sway in many Western economies since the end of World War II began to unravel. The demise of Pax Americana, the advances in telecommunications, flexible manufacturing and information technology, and a need to distance themselves from national accumulation and regulatory modes (Allen, 1992) meant corporations looked to rationalize and restructure.

In fleeing rigid national labor, accumulation and regulatory regimes, corporations, aided and abetted by concomitant shifts in the geopolitical landscape, became internationally mobile, operating through a globally connected communications network and a financial system with floating exchange rates (Harvey, 1989). In the wake of this crisis of economic confidence, many major corporate entities shifted from focusing on commodity production and capital accumulation within individual national economies (a strategy that largely existed within, and helped constitute, national boundaries) to a more flexible and dynamic approach within which the corporate footprint transcended national borders in the search for more rational and efficient commodity chains. Hence, the transnational corporation was born – those nomadic economic institutions (e.g. Toyota, Philips, Sony, Coca-Cola and Nike) that scour the globe for the ever cheaper labor costs and underexploited markets that would ensure expected rates of growth (Silk & Andrews, 2001a, 2001b). The branded expressions of these monolithic enterprises are centered on emotional content and inspire a loyalty among disparate consumer groups that extends beyond their *raison d'être* (du Gay, 2000; Rose, 1990). As Olins (2000, p. 63) suggests, "such brands can sweep across the world; their fiscal and emotional presence is ubiquitous; and they seem omnipresent, almost omnipotent." Working beyond national boundaries, these transnational corporations evidence the degree to which "'the nation' today is visibly in the process of losing an important part of its old functions, namely that of constituting a territorially bounded 'national economy'" (Hobsbawm, 1990, p. 173).

However, and somewhat paradoxically, *the* nation plays an increasingly important role within the machinations of transnational corporate capitalism, and the marketing, advertising and sponsorship armatures of transnational organizations are fully attuned to the continued relevance of national cultures despite the cultural threat of cosmopolitanism that has accompanied the increased transnational flow of products, images, capital and organizations. Somewhat ironically then, the very processes and organizations involved in the dissolution of nation are those that are fully aware of the continued relevance of national cultural sensibilities through which they can engage the desired populace. In this sense then, rather than using uniform and invariant global sponsorship initiatives, these organizations are aware of the necessities of engaging the peculiarities of place and thereby engage the nationalist sensibilities of local consumers (Silk & Andrews, 2001a). In this regard, and although the advancement of capitalism has always been about the overcoming of spatial constraints as a means of improving the flow of goods from producer to consumer (Hall, 1991; Morley & Robins, 1995), the intrinsically rationalizing logic of market capitalism initially came unstuck when faced by the "warm appeal of national affiliations and attachments" (Robins, 1997, p. 20). So, rather than attempting to neuter cultural difference through a strategic global uniformity, many corporations have realized that securing a profitable global presence necessitates negotiating with the local, "and by negotiate I mean it had to incorporate and partly reflect the differences it was trying to overcome" (Hall, 1991, p. 32). It is in this sense that Robins (1997) acknowledged that "globalization is, in fact, about the creation of a new *global-local* nexus" (p. 28); it is about the ability of transnational corporations to operate seamlessly within the language of the local simultaneously in multiple locations (Dirlik, 1996) – sport sponsorship has been a critical tool employed to negotiate the local/global dialectic.

Engaging the Local Sporting Vernacular

Although a somewhat vacuous research domain, a lacuna this volume and a few notable exceptions are beginning to address (see e.g. Amis, 2003; Amis, 2005; Amis & Silk, in progress, Silk & Andrews, 2001a, 2001b), sport sponsorship has been assimilated by transnational corporations in the realization of massive economies of scale to be derived from a truly global reach. Transnational corporations have operated under the assumption of, and indeed capitalized on, the stylized excitement and glamour that characterizes most contemporary, consumer-oriented sporting forms and competitions. As leading sport marketing agency ISL's Daniel Beavois has indicated, "Sport is probably the only thing that fascinates everyone in the world... Many people now feel more concerned by sport than almost anything else in their lives" (quoted in Bell & Campbell, 1999, p. 22). Although clearly an over-exaggeration – what else would one expect from an employee of one of the world's largest and most influential sport marketing agencies – such sentiment does point to the ways in which the corporate world has come to view sport sponsorship and its potential as a means of engaging and mobilizing consumers around the globe.

From humble beginnings in 1984 as a division of Racal Electronics, Vodafone (as it became known in 1985) won a tender to build and run the second UK cellular telephone network. In just twenty years, Vodafone Air Touch (renamed following the acquisition of American network Air Touch), boasts more than 95 million customers in 29 countries on 5 continents, has lucrative relationships with American communications giant, Bell Atlantic, and has established itself as a global player in the telecommunications industry (BBC News, February 4, 2000). Yet, it is not so much this remarkable rise to ascendancy that is noteworthy here; rather Vodafone is emblematic of the appropriation of sporting culture in establishing a presence within the locales in which it penetrates. Indeed, as a precursor to entering the Asian marketplace, Vodafone entered into a £30 million four-year sponsorship with Manchester United, allowing the partners to draw on each others global consumer base (Maidment, 2002). To build brand awareness and ingratiate itself within the local as part of its globalizing strategy, Vodafone has taken the annals of sport sponsorship to the extreme through establishing an array of sponsorship relationships with (supra)national sporting entities – for example the Australian Wallabies Rugby Union team, the New Zealand Warriors Rugby League team, the New Zealand Silver Ferns netball team, the Vodafone Otago NPC rugby team, the Egyptian national soccer team, the Egyptian Marathon, the Ferrari Formula One team, the English cricket team, and the Hungarian Paralympics team (Vodafone, 2003).

Vodafone's global/local sport sponsorship strategizing can be located in the rather ubiquitous, and somewhat amorphous "think globally, act locally" rhetoric pedaled by transnational entities as surmounting evidence of their spatial reach. However, and rather than champion the corporate engagement with the sporting vernacular, it is important to affirm that the local produced within this context is routinely little more than transnational corporations' commercially inspired inflections of local cultures. As such, they are liable – though certainly not preordained – to be superficial and depthless caricatures of national cultural differences. As Arif Dirlik has proposed, "the recognition of the local in marketing strategy, however, does not mean any serious recognition of the autonomy of the local, but is intended to recognize the features of the local so as to incorporate localities into the imperatives of the global" (1996, p. 34). In this regard, we can suggest that national and local (sporting) cultures are at the mercy of the broad corporate agenda as the spatial logics of corporate capital provides opportunities and encouragement for organizations to move into new foreign markets. The very cultural differences purported to be celebrated by engaging the sporting local are thereby at risk from the intrinsic logics and irresistible lure of homogenizing transnational corporate capital. This confuses and misrepresents local difference, often giving rise to commercially bound representations whose design combines elements of stereotype with principles of marketing – images generated by particular sartorial features that borrow heavily on myth and on the idea that one can step into and out of cultures and that cultural characteristics are found in commodities or in simplified representations based merely on the "ambience" of culture (Varney, 1998).

In addition to engaging sporting forms, leagues and competitions, transnational corporations are clearly ensconced in a logic centered on forming promiscuous relations with national sporting heroes, regularly appropriating sporting celebrities as mechanisms of identification. Perhaps not surprisingly, given the Western neo-liberal preoccupation with "the personal, the intimate, and the individual" (Marshall, 1997, p. xiii), the virtual intimacy created between celebrity and national audience has been capitalized upon by the sponsorship armatures of the sporting transnational. Nike, for example, as perhaps the *arbiter* of sporting celebrity has utilized various athletic personas whom act as de facto cultural shorthand delineating particular national sentiments in their attempts to engage national sensibilities (Silk & Andrews, 2001a). In Australia for example, the Nike sponsorship of Australian cricketer Shane Warne, can be seen as part of a wider effort to nurture an authentic sense of national affiliation (Hobsbawm & Ranger, 1983) for the company, which still could be perceived as something of an interloper into Australian culture. In selecting a national sporting hero and a national sporting pastime, and through attaching their commodity sign (brand identity) to these potent national cultural signifiers, Shane Warne's sponsorship provides an insight into the ways in which transnational entities seek to ingratiate a global brand (Nike) within a local context (national) through the sporting vernacular. Of course, Warne is by no means Nike's only nationally bounded sport celebrity, as evidenced by the considerable promotional work the company has put into nurturing such national sporting icons as Ian Wright (the English footballer), Jeff Wilson (the New Zealand rugby player), Christian Vieri (the Italian footballer), and Americans Tiger Woods (golf) and Lebron James (basketball). Furthermore, Nike is by no means the only organization to appropriate the sporting celebrity, national sporting culture, or indeed accrue the benefits of engagement with emergent markets. Along with Nike, and perhaps McDonald's, the Coca-Cola company is perhaps the most potent signifier of transnational capitalist expansion, as well as being one of the first truly global sport sponsors – their "partnership with the International Olympic Committee began in 1928 and has recently been extended until the 2008 games, a temporal relationship that, at least in perception, will be surpassed by their '100 year' sponsorship of the National Basketball League" (Miller, McKay & Rowe, 2001). Given this brief account of spatial logics of sporting transnationalism, the balance of this paper is concerned with the archetypal case of the Coca-Cola Company, who not only exhibit the local/global tendencies addressed above, but provide a telling insight into the shifting spatial dimensions and problematics of (sporting) corporate capital.

Coca-Colonization and the Changing Cartography of Cola Wars

The history of the Coca-Cola Company's engagement with the global marketplace could be seen as a history of transnational corporatism in and of itself. Like many in the fledgling stages of the transnational era, Coca-Cola attempted to use uniform and invariant global initiatives that negated entrenched national cultural boundaries. Epitomized as an America-flavored Coca-Colonization, a bringing of "America to the world" through Coca-Cola, Disney, McDonald's and so forth (Leslie, 1995), Coca-Cola initially strategized around the hawking of Americana (the symbols and products readily associated with American culture) – an approach that is perhaps still resonant in the efforts targeted at engaging the global youth market. Rather than the universal "giving the world a Coke" as its late 1980s campaign proclaimed, Coca-Cola, like many trans-national corporations driving the global economy clearly acknowledged the pitfalls associated with such blanket strategizing and modified their approaches accordingly. In this vein, Coca-Cola began to soften its American edge, initially by producing nationally ambiguous and thereby globally inclusive advertising campaigns such as the "I'd like to buy the world a Coke" television commercial that first aired in 1971 (Pendergrast, 2000). Whether intentionally or otherwise, this inevitably led to charges of a cultural imperialism being waged by American corporations, accused of treating the world as a single and homogenous entity. Following Theodore Levitt's provocative classic, "The Globalization of Markets", Coca-Cola was widely lambasted by academics for its all-encompassing relentless homogenization, operating "as if the entire world (or major regions of it) were a single, largely identical entity" and subsequently attempting to sell the "same things in the same way everywhere" (Levitt, 1983, p. 22).

Most organizations, like Coca-Cola, soon realized the impracticability of treating the global market as a single, homogenous entity. In response to such criticism and in an effort to seek out, and indeed capitalize upon, the realization and enduring resonance of experiences of national belonging and further distance the brand from its storied American roots, certain Coca-Cola campaigns provided a narrower focus on specific regional and national cultures. In these campaigns, sport was seen as a locally sensitive practice that could be use to represent a nation or region and thereby ingratiate the Coca-Cola brand within the local vernacular. The "Eat Football, Sleep Football, Drink Coca-Cola" advertising and sponsorship campaign is a telling example of this practice. In separate pan-North American (American football), pan-European (Association football), and pan-Australian (Australian Rules football) television advertisements, Coca-Cola was unselfconsciously conjugated with regional sporting cultures through narratives that focused on the passion, intensity, and excitement of the various football codes and, by inference, drinking Coca-Cola itself. More recently, Coca-Cola has questioned its think globally, act locally strategizing. As Kent Wertime (in Yoon, 2001) of advertising agency Ogilvy & Mather in Bangkok suggested, Coke "thought they were 'glocal' – both global and local at the same time. But now, they're realizing that that may not be possible: They need to choose one or the other. They've decided to localize more." To do so, Coca-Cola is "going native" by tailoring drinks to individual countries (Yoon, 2001). Coca-Cola's localization strategies are in part down to former CEO Douglas Daft who, as Coca-Cola Japan's country manager in the 1980s, recognized the need to break with tradition and expand the company's product line beyond carbonated drinks – Georgia canned coffee and Royal Milk Tea were fostered – to resonate with the tastes of the Japanese public (Yoon, 2001). Daft learned from the Japanese experience, and has sought to shift the focus, even in mainstay markets such as the United States, from soda to faster-growing teas, waters and juices, thereby making Coke more responsive to local markets. Daft's "think local, act local" strategy is a radical departure from the uniform strategies undertaken in early periods of transnationalization.

The strategy is also rooted in the shifting patterns of carbonated consumption – consumer choice and preference has meant increased competition for Coca-Cola from juices, waters and sports drinks. To counter these processes, Coca-Cola attempted to acquire its new competitors, however, anti-trust legislation has regulated their abilities to do so – a deal to buy Orangina was blocked in 1999 and a bid to acquire Gatorade parent company, Quaker Oats, was nixed by Coca-Cola's own board (Yoon, 2001). In response, Coca-Cola has begun to roll out a series of new drinks – Soon Soo (pure water) in Korea called Soon Soo 100; Pump and Kinley bottled waters, developed and sold in Australia and India respectively; Lift Plus, an energy drink in Australia; Qoo, a juice-drink aimed at young girls, and Sokenbicha for the "twentysomethings" both for Japanese consumption and multi-flavored juice lines Smart and Heaven and Earth in China – aimed at connecting with the sensibilities of an increasingly fragmenting market. The "think local, act local" strategy has been especially enthusiastically received by Coca-Cola's Asian country managers where carbonated drinks enjoy a far smaller share of the drinks market than in the United States. In 2001 alone then, Coca-Cola rolled out 15 new drinks in 45 Asian markets, hoping that localization will be the key to engaging the diverse, and emergent world marketplaces (Yoon, 2001).

Competition has of course not been a stranger to the Coca-Cola Company. Most famously, the company has been historically involved in battles with the PepsiCo Company, a battle that had its roots in the late 1800s following the invention of Coke and Pepsi in 1886 and 1898 respectively. A burgeoning consumerism in 1920s America, driven by the mavens of Madison Avenue, intensified the visibility of the brands that were at the forefront of the emergent cultural industries in the United States. The first Coca-Cola magazine advert appeared in *Munseys* in 1902, followed by advertisements on billboards, street cars, in newspapers and on soda glasses and Pepsi used their first celebrity endorser in 1909, automobile racing driver Barney Oldfield. Pepsi was the first to embrace radio advertising, in 1939 their first jingle was so popular it played in jukeboxes and entered the hit parade (The Cola Wars, 2003). Coca-Cola hit the radio airwaves in 1941, but was soon to realize the importance of the symbolic turn through embracing the small screen and deploying a range of tactics more familiar to the contemporary marketing world – celebrity endorsers such as Tom Jones, Connie Francis, Nancy Sinatra, the New Beats, and the Supremes, semantic slogans such as "The Real Thing," and a range of commercial campaigns that manifested the brand image (The Cola Wars, 2003). These symbolic wars took a physical turn in the 1970s with the Pepsi Challenge, a series of taste tests held at malls and other public outlets, which invited consumers to once and for all determine their cola preferences. Despite a few well documented-formulaic flops (New Coke and Crystal Pepsi are perhaps the most well-renowned) (see Pendergrast, 2000), the battle continued unabated through the symbolic realm. Through commercial platforms for their embodied branded celebrities, the Pepsi Generation (Michael Jackson, Madonna, Michael J. Fox, Billy Crystal, Lionel Ritchie, Gloria Estefan, Cindy Crawford, The Spice Girls, The Osbournes, Bob Dole, Faith Hill, and Joe Montana) and the Coca-Cola Kids (Michael Jordan, the New Kids on the Block, Aretha Franklin, Elton John, Paula Abdul, and the whole American Idol cast) have continued the carbonated crusade.

While these wars once took place within the physical confines of the United States, the spatial reach of transnational capitalism has seen a transformation in the spaces in which these rhetorical clashes have been fought (see e.g. Wagnleitner, 1994). The cola wars have thus undergone an epistemological and cartographic shift within the symbolic regimes of late capitalism. Cola wars are still taking place within various spaces within the United States, although even here the location of such battles has changed – high schools, colleges, movie sets (as in Pepsi's US$500 million sponsorship of Lucasfilm's *Star Wars* trilogy), "musical" endorsers (highly charged sexualized campaigns centered on Coke's Christina Aguilera and Pepsi's Britney Spears) even cityscapes (as in the case of Coca-Cola's sponsorship of downtown Baltimore's regeneration and their association with New York's Empire State Building) have profited from soda companies' willingness to pay for exclusivity. Indeed, the spatial reach of such battles has perhaps reached its literal nadir in Pepsi's hawking of soda pop aboard Russia's space station Mir, and Coca-Cola flying a soda fountain into space aboard the shuttle Endeavour (Halvorson, May 16, 1996). As Coca-Cola marketing spokesman Michael Myers claimed, "Our goal is to take Coca-Cola wherever humans are, whether that's the space shuttle or somewhere beyond" (in Halvorson, 1996). Yet it is the shifting cartographic location of cola wars, and the appropriation of sport within these wars, that is of most interest in this chapter. Following the spatial reach of the monolithic carbonated drink oligopolies has been an epistemological shift in the form, content and location of the cola wars. Indeed, by 1987, according to Yoffie and Seet (1999), cola wars between Pepsi and Coca-Cola had been fought in nearly every major market outside the United States. The one exception to the cartographic landscape of cola wars was India. Coca-Cola and Pepsi had "withdrawn" (perhaps a more accurate term, at least for Coca-Cola, is removed by Samata Party Leader George Fernandes, who denounced the company as a symbol of American exploitation and imperialism) from India in 1961 and 1977 respectively (Mazzarella, 2003). Returning at the outset of the 1990s the cola giants embraced the seductive, yet paradoxical Indian marketplace – a population of over 800 million, riding consumer affluence and liberal economic policies belied the per capita cola consumption of three servings (Yoffie and Seet, 1999). Given the absence of Coca-Cola and Pepsi, the carbonated drinks market in India was, well, flat, and became the newest physical stage for the latest bout of a cola battle characterized by sabotage, ambush marketing and at one Coke sponsored music event, a riot due to PepsiCo reportedly giving away free Pepsi (Yoffie & Seet, 1999). Of course, given sport's role as 'national cultural shorthand' (Silk & Andrews, 2001a), it is of no surprise that sporting forms and stars have been used as mercenaries for the cola cause. For India, cricket is the sport, bar none, at least according to the logics of the cola companies, with which to engage the local populous: "the popularity of cricket and cricketers in India transcends all boundaries of age and region" (Pepsico India Spokesperson, in Slater, March 6 2003).

Men in Blue and Red – Carbonated Mercenaries and Other Tales from India's Sporting Cola Wars

Monolithic transnational Coca-Cola CEO, Douglas Daft's somewhat paradoxical "think local, act local" strategy appears extremely well suited to the Indian marketplace. Starting in the mid-1980s, economic reform, "liberalization" and globalization bought a movement towards a new, externally oriented, consumption-oriented pathway to national prosperity – a movement that was met with political and economic turbulence and backlash (Mazzarella, 2003). Abundant in the Indian rhetoric at this time was the emergence of the term: *swadeshi* – a term that literally means one's own country and can be appropriated here as an attempt to come to terms with the ways in which globalization was heightening, rather than effacing, the importance of locality and local identity (Mazzarella, 2003). For those seeking to engage the Indian marketplace, and for those within India looking toward western investment to bolster economic prosperity, *swadeshi* was seen as a cynical marriage of convenience, an approach that is pro-globalization and pro-Indian (no matter how superficially or ephemerally), without being anti-foreign – a calibrated approach that can speak simultaneously to widely disparate constituencies (Keshavan, 1998; Mazzarella, 2003). For Coca-Cola, on its return to the Indian market following exclusion, it was faced with the popularity of the Indian cola brand, *Thums Up* manufactured by Parle – a company Coca-Cola swiftly incorporated in its brand stable. However, to engage the Indian market, and in the spirit of *swadeshi*, Coca-Cola turned to sport, particularly cricket, to engage the national populous.

According to Guha (1999), with the exception of cinema, cricket reaches more people on the Indian subcontinent than any other form of entertainment. The game is followed by hundreds of millions of spectators and the players have a truly iconic status. The game is seen in India as the game of the educated elite, a sport that crowds out football and other competitors in the nations sporting imaginary (Dimeo, 2001), a collective memory perhaps most lavishly retold in the recent Bollywood, and Oscar-nominated, motion picture, *Lagaan*, directed by Asutosh Gawarikar and produced by lead actor Aamir Khan (see Majamdar 2002). Passion for the game in India is almost unprecedented among sports throughout the world, and has often generated extreme responses from consumers – for example, an 18-year-old female from Mysore committed suicide in 1999 following news that star player Sachin Tendulkar had a career-threatening back injury; a fan in the state of Orissa stabbed and killed a shopkeeper who turned off a game between Kenya and India during the 1999 World Cup; a 65-year-old man collapsed and died in the wake of a loss to Sri Lanka in the year 2000; fans burnt effigies of players and called for a boycott of sponsors products following the World Cup final loss to Australia in February 2003 (Parmar, 2003). For sponsors, the intense passion and depth of loyalty to the game in India is exacerbated when considering the booming Indian economy. Between 1990 and 2000, India's average growth was 5.5% annually and the gross domestic product grew by 5.6% in 2002 to US$261.2 billion (Parmar, 2003). The potential to capitalize on the burgeoning economy in India was clearly realized by sporting goods firm adidas, who following association with star cricketer Sachin Tendulkar, saw their Indian sales shoot up by 200% (Parmar, 2003).

It is perhaps no surprise then that the latest, and perhaps most sophisticated, efforts to engage emergent markets has seen transnationals turn their attention to the East. The emergent markets of China and Indonesia, containing 2.4 billion people, nearly half the world's population, are the location for the latest round of cola wars. Pepsi realize that Coca-Cola's presence is growing but does not yet dominate, and has thus focused its attention on these emergent populations – both companies have realized the prime potential of the young populations, exploding incomes, and the underdeveloped soft drink demand. This "soft-drink paradise" is further compounded by a strong Muslim presence that is forbidden to drink alcohol (Going Global, August 31, 2003). The battle for India is clearly hotting up as the two international cola giants try and garner a bigger share of the nearly US$900 million market – Coca-Cola's brands make up 48% of the Indian market and Pepsi's 46% (Srivastava, 2000). Since being readmitted to India in 1993, Coca-Cola has invested nearly US$1 billion, in the year 2000 writing off US$405 million of its assets in India and to this point yet to report a profit (Orr, 2003). The very real poverty experienced by much of India's vast populace would suggest little consumer interest in a carbonated soft drink that to many would represent an unattainable luxury. Nevertheless, the sheer volume of the Indian population (approaching 1 billion) means that – although small in percentage terms of the total populace – the potential market for Coca-Cola (India's young, urban, middle and upper classes) is sizeable enough to encourage global corporations into the Indian market. This market is thereby considered attractive enough to penetrate, and following Coca-Cola's localization strategy, it is sport sponsorship that has been the cultural manifestation of the carbonated "think local, act local" strategizing. The initial sporting foray into the Indian marketplace came in 1996, as an element in the carbonated battle for the 1996 Cricket World Cup held on the Indian subcontinent.

As with the, often violent, passion demonstrated by fans during the 1996 World Cup, the carbonated warriors demonstrated little of the tradition, heritage and order of the "gentleman's game." Officially, Coca-Cola outbid Pepsi to ensure its place as the official soft drink of the tournament, a US$3.6 million honor (Karp, 1996; Mazzarella, 2003). Celebrating the official sponsorship of the event, Coke took full advantage of its rights to further its presence on the Indian subcontinent. Coca-Cola's incursion into the passion and sporting realm of Indian popular consciousness was most graphically, and indeed beautifully, realized through the series of advertisements that accompanied their sponsorship. The 1996 "Red" commercial developed by Wieden and Kennedy, Portland, depicted the vibrancy and complexity of Indian culture keying on the byline "Passion has a color" – the color in this instance being red: the red of chili drying in fields, the red of a Rajasthani man's turban, the red of the *bindis* adorning women's foreheads, the red of the *dupata* drying on river banks, the red of the cricket balls that regularly punctuate the visual narrative, and the red of the Coca-Cola brand symbolism so subtly and seamlessly inserted into this panoramic sweep of Indian culture. With the backdrop of the late Nusrat Fateh Ali Khan's hypnotic Sufi-inspired devotional "Mustt Mustt" (himself a Pakistani but with a considerable following in India), the commercial brazenly synthesizes India's passion for cricket (red ball) with a desired passion for Coca-Cola (red logo). Through this association with the cricket thematic, Coca-Cola sought to thrust itself into the mainstream of Indian culture by providing itself with a seemingly natural place within local culture and experience. The "Red" commercial and the allied cricket sponsorship is a vivid example of the way in which national sporting practices have been mobilized by the symbolic processes, and through the mediated products, associated with the transnational corporate modus operandi.

However, and in a clear case of ambush marketing (see Hoek, this volume), Pepsi attempted to hijack Coca-Cola's official sponsorship of the 1996 Cricket World Cup. Plastering major cities with posters and billboards featuring leading Indian cricketers under contract to promote the Pepsi brand (such as Sachin Tendulkar, Mohamad Azaruddin, Vinod Kambli), floating helium balloons emblazoned with the Pepsi logo over Indian stadiums (downed by Coca-Cola with the support of the police), promoting a series of television spots, and giving away free Pepsi merchandise at tournament games, Pepsi attempted to ensure their brand was ingrained within the national discourse. As Pepsi Indian spokesperson, Deepak Jolly (in Karp, 1996) articulated, "[our World Cup ads] were the talk of the town." Pepsi's "unofficial" sponsorship campaign was a clear attack on the "official" semantic. In a clear attempt to capture the Indian youth market, Pepsi's slogan "Kaha na war hai" (nothing official about it) mocked the notion of "official" as staid and boring – the result of Pepsi's market research that suggested the most disliked words among Indian youth were "official," "corruption" and "discipline" (Karp, 1996; Chatterjee & Masand, 2000). The phrase quickly became appropriated as a part of the Indian youth vernacular, capitalized on by Pepsi through strengthening its association with cricket and its star performers (Chatterjee & Masand, 2000; Srivastava, 2000).

Building on their 1996 Cricket World Cup successes, both carbonated organizations sought to develop their associations with their target market. As India's youth embrace consumerism, the Cola companies are pitching straight to their desires and hearts. As Coca-Cola India's vice president has articulated, "we want to bond with the young through their fashion and their lives" (in Taipei Times, 2003). In an effort to attract youth, Pepsi developed the slogan "Yeh Dil Maange More" (This heart demands more), again readily appropriated by India's young consumers (Kripalani, 1999). Along with the other staples of India's entertainment focused society – the Internet has become a virtual battleground within India between the cola companies, with high quality audio and video that drives relationship marketing campaigns – and the hawking of 'hipper' products targeted towards the younger Indian demographic (Pepsi Blue, Pepsi Mountain Dew, Pepsi Code Red, which outsold the traditional Coke mainstays), both global companies have cultivated an aggressive local image centered on high-profile sporting events and players (La Monica, 2002).

Not surprisingly, given cricket's status as the national sport, both companies have attempted to ingratiate themselves within the sport – above and beyond the (un)official sponsorship of the World Cup. Coca-Cola, in concert with its "official" sponsor status has consistently used cricket fans, rather than actors to promote their products. Pepsi meanwhile have looked to other cricket competitions to secure a presence in the subcontinent. Through sponsorship of the "Pepsi Cup Triangular Series," as well as the coterie of official duties performed as part of this sponsorship, such as the "Pepsi Man of the Series," and the Sahara Cup competition between India – Pakistan (associate sponsor), Pepsi is clearly attempting to become appropriated as part of the national consciousness. Not to be outdone, Coca-Cola also sought to become ingrained within the, often bitter, and deeply rooted, rivalry between India and Pakistan through title sponsorship of six one-day tournaments in Sharjah and the United Arab Emirates as well as developing in 1999, in concert with the Asian Cricket Council, the Asian Cricket Test Championship – a tournament marked in 2001 by India's boycott over Pakistan's alleged sponsorship of terrorism in Kashmir and the subsequent withdrawal of Coca-Cola's title sponsorship (Ehsan Ali, 2001; Guha, 1999).

Despite its dominance, cricket has not been the only sport capitalized upon by the cola companies in their efforts to ingratiate themselves within the national vernacular. Recognizing the popularity of pool and the Internet to India's youth, the Coca-Cola company teamed up with Hungama.com, a website specializing in e-promotions and contests – indeed, on the Hungama website, the consumer is given the chance to visit India's first virtual city, Coke City. In an effort to build the Sprite brand among the Indian youth, Coca-Cola sponsored April Fools Day through the Hungama web site. Renaming the day "April Pools Day," Coca-Cola utilized snooker champion Geet Sethi, sponsoring his tour of five popular entertainment centers including the "Super Drome" and the "Bowling Company" in Mumbai. For those not able to attend, Coca-Cola, through Hungama.com, broadcast the tour and hosted chat shows with Sethi on the site (Srinivasan, 2001). However, the crown jewel of the Indian marketplace continues to be cricket, and it is major cricket events that continue to dominate the sponsorship strategies of the cola giants.

The 1999 Cricket World Cup, held in England, provided an opportunity for Pepsi to muscle in on Coke's 1996 sponsorship. Pepsi paid the International Cricket Council (ICC) US$3.33 million to be the Global Partner of the World Cup. However, Pepsi invested three times that amount to promote the sponsorship in India; Coca-Cola of course matched Pepsi's airtime during this period (Bandopadhyay, 1999). To support its expenditure, Pepsi took the World Cup on a tour of fourteen different Indian cities prior to the outset of the tournament. Of course, to appeal to the target demographic, the tour was accompanied by a Pepsi music concert and light show (Bandopadhyay, 1999). The 2003 World Cup, held in South Africa and Zimbabwe, provided another opportunity for PepsiCo to enhance their status among the Indian (sporting) consciousness. Pepsi maintained its status as "presenting sponsor" of the World Cup, paying US$30 million to belong to the ICC's highest sponsorship tier with 12.5% of the event signage space (Parmar, 2003) and armed itself with a coterie of cricket related activities designed to garner the attention of the desired segment of the Indian populous. Designed to "connect with cricket lovers across the country" (Rajeev Bakshi, Chairman Pepsico India Holdings Pvt Ltd, in The Hindu Business Line, 2003), Pepsi's World Cup initiatives are centered on commemorative, special edition, bottles, and Pepsi Blue products designed to raise awareness of the "refreshingly cool" brand profile and a direct challenge to the previous color of Indian cricket passion – red (Indiantelevision.com, 2003a). Further, the Pepsi Predikta Jackpot was a contest that took four finalists from the promotion to the World Cup Finals, and who then played for the Predikta Jackpot live on TV. The promotion was telecast across the Sony network throughout the World Cup, with questions and bonus points being found behind Pepsi labels and under Pepsi crowns (Indiantelevision.com, 2003a). Consolidating this base and in an attempt to further ingratiate the idea that "Blue is the color of the Indian cricket team, Blue is the color of the Indian fan's passion and we all root for our Men in Blue" (Indiantelevision.com, 2003a), and thereby distance cricket's association from Coke's "Passion has a red color," in September, 2003, Pepsi, along with TVS Motors and Videocon, signed a three-year contract for sponsorship of international cricket matches in India through May, 2006.

Recognizing the logic of forming promiscuous relationships with national sporting heroes, and thereby appropriating the visual intimacy created between the celebrity, as representative subjectivity, and the national audience, the cola giants have embarked on a series of quite bitter rivalries to attract sporting mercenaries to their army of endorsers. Initially, Coca-Cola did not use celebrities in its local strategizing, preferring to use cricket fans to engage the national populous. However, and in response to Pepsi's battalion of cricketing endorsers – Sachin Tendulkar, Kapil Dev, Saurav Ganguly, Rahul Dravid, Harbhajan Singh, Zaheer Khan and Mohamad Kaif, as well as actor Amitabh Bachchan – Coca-Cola signed cricketers Saurav Ganguly (from Pepsi) and Javagal Srinath and employed a range of other popular Indian celebrity figures – Bollywood actors Hrithik Roshan, Salman Khan and Aamir Khan, and actress Aishwarya Rai – in the latest rendition of the cola wars (Chatterjee, 2002; Srivastava, 2000). Additionally, as Indian women won both the Miss Universe and Miss World pageants in the same year, Coke and Pepsi respectively signed the winners to their stables. The carbonated branding of the celebrity corporeal points to the latest chapter in the conflation between image, reputation and corporate identity – the "expressive" regimes of accumulation based around the brand (Schultz, Hatch & Larsen, 2000) manifested through the coterie of symbolic sponsorship functions performed by the embodied expressions of the cola brands.

The latest round of cola wars, reflecting the manifestation of the expressive organization, has thus been fought on the entertainment super highways, deemed so important to the Indian marketplace – sport, of course, has been fully bound with the avaricious dictates of the late capitalist symbolic economy. Within these semiotic campaigns, the cola giants have attempted to place their brand identity as part of the vernacular of Indian semanticism. Coca-Cola's initial foray featured embodied Coke celebrity, movie "heartthrob" Aamir Khan, coinciding with Khan's Oscar nomination for *Lagaan*. Khan, using the generic Indian slang term, *thanda* (cold drink), delivers the line, "cold drink means... Coca-Cola" (Taipei Times, 2002, p. 21). Pepsi quickly responded to Coke's efforts to appropriate cold drink with Coke in Indian vernacular, utilizing the popular Indian actors Rahul Khanna and Fardeen Khan. In this campaign, a young child actor buys a Pepsi for a customer-less Coke vendor who uses the *thanda* in another sense: "Cold Business means... Coca-Cola" (Taipei Times, 2002, p. 21). The "gloves were off" in a metaphorical sense following these two 2002 commercials, with Coke vice president for marketing, Shripad Nadkarni expressing concern over Pepsi's tactics, "We'd rather fight in the marketplace" (Taipei Times, 2002, p. 21). Nantoo Banjeree, director of communications for Coca-Cola pitched in on the battle, "We're twice as big as them in India .. . even though they also sell potato chips and export rice and add it all to their bottom line" (in Taipei Times, 2002, p. 21). Nadkarni's opposite number at PepsiCo, Vibha Paul Rishi called the campaign "Pepsi's little joke ... with a dose of irreverence" and dismissed the competition, in cold war rhetoric, as "the reds" (Taipei Times, 2002, p. 21). This heated war of words stimulated an all out use of celebrities as brand mercenaries. In 2003, as part of the strategizing around the 2003 World Cup Cricket sponsorship, Pepsi launched a music video, rolled out on network television, featuring entertainers Amitabh Bachchan, Kareen Kapoor, Abhishek Bachchan and its band of cricketing celebrities (Hindu Business Line, 2003), Coca-Cola responded by hiring the director of hit feature film, *Lagaan*, to make its future commercials.

The deployment of these carbonated mercenaries perhaps points to some emergent issues for global sport sponsorship. In Indian cricket at least, the endorsements that star players such as Sachin Tendulkar and Sourav Ganguly earn from their relationships with the cola giants far outweigh the salaries to be derived from the game itself (Morning Star, 2002, p. 12). This potential problem reached almost catastrophic proportions in the lead up to the 2002 ICC Champions Trophy in Sri Lanka. The global partners for this tournament were LG Electronic and Pepsi, the official sponsors being Hutch (the Indian branch of Hutchison Electronics, a global cellular phone service provider), Honda and South African Airlines. Prior to the event, players from all the nations were asked by the ICC to sign legislation designed to prevent ambush marketing and protect headline sponsors interests (Marketing Week, April 3, 2003). Clause 13 in the contract (in Banjerjee, 2003) stated:

> The squad member shall not from 30 days before the first match until 30 days after the last match in the event, directly or indirectly allow his name, voice, image, likeness or other representation to be used either (a) in any advertising or endorsement or (b) for any commercial purpose in any media whatsoever by or on behalf of a competitor of any official sponsor or global partner or official supplier.

The Indian cricket board (the BCCI) objected to clause 13, outlining that they would not be able to comply with the clause in its totality. As Indian Cricket Board President Jagmohan Dalmiyah (in Banjerjee, 2003) stated, "we can't prevent our players from not taking part in any advertisement or endorsement from 30 days before the event till 30 days after the event ... we do not interfere with such rights of players because it directly affects their fundamental rights under the constitution of India." Dalmiyah also heavily critiqued the ICC for failing to recognize that 80% of the world's cricketing revenue derives from India, and that the board should be more considerate of the pressures this places upon Indian players (Lal, 2000). Several high profile players, those associated with Coca-Cola, refused to sign the contracts, which initially led to them being dropped from the Indian team and a second eleven being prepared to compete in the tournament – a compromise was eventually reached with the players agreeing to abstain from their own endorsements for the actual period over which the tournament took place (Banjerjee, 2003; Morning Star, August 22, 2002). The team as a whole though did meet with some extremely difficult encounters, one of Indian cricket's sponsors, Indian Airline, Air Sahara, withdrew its US$13.5 million dollar sponsorship from the team after they ran onto the field without the Air Sahara logo on their shirts – Air Sahara could not be endorsed due to the tournaments official sponsorship with South African Airlines (Tribune India, September 12, 2002). The Australian and Bangladesh teams also experienced similar problems with their Ansett Airlines and Coca-Cola sponsorships respectively.

The row between official sponsors and players individual sponsors rumbled through the World Cup, resulting in ground evictions for spectators drinking Coca-Cola in the Pepsi sponsored tournament (Marketing Week, April 3, 2003). The ramifications for Indian cricket and the cola wars are perhaps more far-reaching. The ICC initially refused to give India the US$9 million held back from the BCCI due to India for allowing players to violate World Cup sponsorship contracts – the players had refused to surrender their personal endorsement and image rights in favor of official tournament sponsors. By November 3, 2003, the ICC claimed it was ready to give India the money, providing they met a series of thus far unstated conditions (India Express.com, November 3, 2003). Further, according to PepsiCo India chairman, Rajeev Bakshi, the relationship between the BCCI and Pepsi needed to be resolved – Pepsi are claiming damages from the ICC for ambush marketing and the BCII stated they would be "extremely cautious" in dealing with their World Cup sponsors following the recent sponsorship controversy (Hindu Business Line, January 25, 2003; India Express. com, November 3, 2003).

The passion of the game and the Indian public's almost religious devotion to cricket – 94 million people in India were estimated to have watched each game during the 2003 World Cup (Indiantelevision.com, 2003b) – is clearly sufficient for the cola companies willingness to engage the Indian marketplace in the face of these complexities, evidenced by Pepsi's latest deal through 2006. However, it is perhaps the ability to placate the Indian populous through its sporting and entertainment mercenaries that is most attractive to the cola giants. Early in 2002, the Indian Centre for Science and Environment (CSE) found that 12 brands of both Coca-Cola and PepsiCo contained harmful pesticides. Both companies utilize the ground waters in India of which 90% is not tested and for which there are no "normal" standards (Upadhyay, 2003). Given these conditions, the cola companies failed to carry out with diligence their own tests on the ground water that provides the main raw material for their products, a statement that in and of itself makes a mockery of a supposed homogenous global standard for Coca-Cola and Pepsi soft drinks and reveals the tensions explicit in such transnational engagement with those desirable Indian consumers and their use, or exploitation, of inadequate resources. Such an argument is of course furthered in considering the companies only reach about 10% of the Indian population – the young, urban rich – the other 90% priced out of the consumption of a soft-drink luxury and who live in rural areas are at this time untouched by the organizations promotional strategizing, except of course in the cheap labor market in which Coca-Cola has 45 bottling plants, Pepsi 44 (Taipei Times, 2002).

However, it is the lengths that the cola companies will go to ensure the dictates of their corporate agendas are met which is of most concern for global sport sponsorship – the use of respected representative subjectivities to ensure the populace of the safety of the soft drinks. According to Sunil Gupta, vice president of Coca-Cola India Ltd (in Chatterjee, 2002), the important point is driving the safety message home to consumers, a campaign strategy geared to retreat the safety standards of the company through star performers:

> It is [Bollywood actor] Aamir Khan who will win the game for Coke ... our tv and print campaigns will emphasize the safety of our products, as are our sales people who are meeting with the retailers to reassure them that Coke has always maintained safety standards. Using stars is part of this strategy to win shaky consumer confidence and strengthen the emotional bond with consumers.

Utilizing their coterie of star performers, Coca-Cola and Pepsi have clearly sought to negotiate the complexities the locale provides, and through various sport sponsorship and promotional strategizing based on cricket and entertainment, engage, and indeed reassure, the desired target market – the urban young. Cricket of course has been fundamental in these processes, and cricket is now fully bound with the complexities, and indeed problematics, of the global sport sponsorship marketplace. Many in India have decried cricket's newly secured entrenchment within the dictates of corporate capital, claiming that this ethos has led the Indian game astray and opened it to Western commercial exploitation (Slater, 2003). Indian magazine *Jaalmag* for example has claimed that events such as contest winners serving a particular brand of soft drink to the players on the field during a break in play or appearing on podiums with "man of the match" winners, the array of politicians lining up to associate with the carbonated sporting mercenaries, points to the secularization of the "national religion" and the violation of the games "sanctum sanctorum" (Jaalmag, 2002). In a slightly different sense and in a way that points to the changing of the Indian nation under the rubrics of transnational discourse, through cricket, Indian national identity becomes located in the realm of a media-centered, Western capitalist popular culture which speaks to the peculiar tensions inherent between nationalisms, decolonization and national identities (Appadurai, 1996; Madan, 2000) within the nuances and ambiguities of Indian *swadeshi*.

Coda: The New Cola Wars and the Spatial Logics of Sporting Capital

Clearly the opening up of the Indian economy in 1991 reveals the extent to which the cola wars have capitalized upon the sport of cricket, and its star performers, in an epistemological battle for the Indian marketplace. The importance of cricket, along with the entertainment industry (the two of which have become increasingly inseparable), are seen as crucial tools in this battle due to the clear statements the game can make to the (desired) local marketplace. Cricket is seen by Pepsi and Coca-Cola as de facto cultural shorthand of nation, or more accurately certain elements of the Indian nation, young urbanites with disposable income who have embraced Western capitalist discourse. In this case, and as part of the strategies of transnational localization, cricket stands (along with the Bollywood film industry) as an (albeit superficial) marker of *the* locale in the face of global political, economic and cultural homogenization. The battle between the "Men in Blue and Red" not only speaks to the spatial reconfiguration of cola wars but to the current imbalances within what the apologists of the International Monetary Fund and the World Trade Organization advocate as a global economy. Global expenditure on sponsorship may well have exceeded US$30 billion in 2003, with 77% of that being spent on sport (Applebaum, 2004), yet such expenditure points to the imbalances within this market. While some locations, such as Africa, are almost excluded from the high table of the global feast (Nguyen, 2000), sponsorship strategies such as those addressed in this chapter point to imbalance within a given nation – only those who fit the dictates of transnational corporate logics being invited to participate in the "spoils" of global capital – a process that not only impacts shifts in India's cricket culture but speaks to polarizations between 'connected' urbanites and the disconnected rural population.

Coca-Cola and Pepsi may well continue to play on the "accepted" hegemony of their key brands, yet the ontological reality of their engagement with India and other previously closed Eastern marketplaces has forced these organizations into different patterns of brand strategizing. In the face of intensified anti-Western sentiment, especially following the "response" to the events of September 11, 2001, "alternative" soft drinks have begun to emerge in the Middle East and Europe that directly challenge Western capitalist hegemony. Brands such as Mecca Cola, Zam Zam (which has been in existence since the Islamic government of Iran banned Pepsi in 1954), and Qibla Cola (recognizing the direction in which Muslims pray towards the house of Allah in Mecca) (Majidi & Passariello, 2003), playing heavily on subtle alterations to the established commodity signs of the cola giants, have become new weapons in a very different set of cola wars that speak to, and embrace, the domineering, and perhaps tyrannous, Western presence throughout the Middle East. In the wake of such oppositional tendencies, the need for global sponsors to distance themselves, at least in a symbolic sense, from their western origins and histories may well become increasingly apparent. In this sense, and in addition to the creation of new products designed to be embedded and ingrained within the specificities of the locale in question (more precisely, the particular market segments desired), sport, with its hot national symbolism, may well become an even more important mechanism for appropriating the market – the ramifications for sport, national cultures and the continued hegemony of a predominantly Western, transnational corporate capitalism, will thus be ingrained with the fortunes of the spatial logics of sporting capital.

References

Allen, J. (1992) "Post-industrialism and post-fordism." In S. Hall, D. Held, and A. McGrew (eds), *Modernity and its futures* Cambridge, UK: Polity, pp. 168–204.

Alavy, K. (2003) "Cricket sponsorship will have to adapt to survive." *Marketing Week* (April 3rd, 2003).

Amis, J. (2003) "'Good things come to those who wait:' The Strategic Management of Image and Reputation at Guinness." *European Sport Management Quarterly*, 3: 180–214.

Amis, J. (2005) "Beyond Sport: Imaging and Re-imaging a Transnational Brand," in Silk, M., Andrews, D. and Cole, C. L. (eds) *Sport and Corporate Nationalisms*. Oxford: Berg, pp. 143–165.

Amis, J. and Silk, M. (2005) "Believe: The Spatial Expression and Transnational Management of Corporate Capital." Paper presented at the 2005 Academy of Management Meeting, August 5–10, Honolulu, HI.

Appadurai, A. (1996) *Modernity at Large: Cultural Dimensions of Globalization*. Minneapolis: University of Minnesota Press.

Applebaum, M. (2004, 17 February) "Sponsorship holds steady." *Brandweek. Com.* http://www.brandweek.com (accessed April 3, 2004).

BBC News (February 4th, 2000) "The Rapid Rise of Vodafone." Available at: http://news.bbc.co.uk/1/hi/business/527754.stm (accessed November 3, 2003).

Bandopadhyay (1999) "Hockey Just Ain't Cricket." Available at: http://www.bharatiyahockey.org/index.html (accessed November 3, 2003).

Banjerjee, C. (2003) "Indian cricket board says its players can't be kept from World Cup by signing conditional ICC contracts." *Associated Press Worldstream* (January 11, 2003).

Bell, E. and Campbell, D. (1999) "For the love of money." *The Observer*, May 23, p. 22.

Castells, M. (1996) *The Rise of the Network Society: The Information Age: Economy, Society and Culture*, Vol. 1, Oxford: Blackwell Publishers.

Chatterjee, D. and Masand, R. (2000) "Kaha na war hai? Coke, Pepsi cross swords over Shah Rukh, 'Hrithik' ad." Indian Express Daily, Available at: http://www.indianexpress.com/ie/daily/20000513/ina13043.html (accessed, November 3, 2003).

Chatterjee, S. (2002) "Glitzy commercials enliven soda wars." Available at News India Times: http://www.newsindia-times.com (accessed November 3, 2003).

Cola Wars (2003) "Over a Century of Slogans, Commercials, Blunders, and Coups." Available at: http://www.geocities.com/colacentury/ (accessed November 30, 2003).

Dimeo, P. (2001) "Contemporary Developments in Indian Football." *Contemporary South Asia*, 10 (2): 251–264.

Dirlik, A. (1996) "The Global in the Local," in Wilson, R. and Dissanayake, W. (eds). *Global/Local: Cultural Production and the Transnational Imaginary*, Durham, NC and London: Duke University Press

du Gay, P. (2000) "Markets and Meanings: Re-imagining Organizational Life," in Schultz, M., Hatch, M. and Larsen, M. (eds). T*he Expressive Organization: Linking Identity, Reputation, and the Corporate Brand*, Oxford: Oxford University Press, pp. 66–74.

Ehsan Ali, R. (2001) "Asian Test Championship as Scheduled." Available at The Hindu: http://www.hindu.com/thehindu/2001/08/24/stories/07240282.htm (accessed November 3, 2003).

Going Global (August 31, 2003) "Way to our business." Available at: http://weblog.wtob.ws/archives/002120.html (accessed November 30, 2003).

Guha, R. (1999) "Batting for the Nation." *The UNESCO Courier* (April), 30–31.

Hall, S. (1991) "The local and the global: Globalization and ethnicity," in King, A. D. (ed.), *Culture, Globalization and the World-system*, London: Macmillan, pp. 19–39.

Halvorson, T. (May 16, 1996) "Coke, Pepsi take cola wars to space" http://www.floridatoday.com/space/explore/stories/1996/051696a.htm (accessed November 30, 20030.

Hannerz, U. (1996) *Transnational Connections: Culture, People, Places*. London: Comedia.

Harvey, D. (1989) *The Condition of Postmodernity*, Cambridge: Blackwell.

Held, D., McGrew, A., Goldblatt, D. and Perraton, J. (1999) *Global Transformations: Politics, Economies and Culture*, Stanford, CA: Stanford University Press

Hindu Business Line (2003) "Pepsico unveils World Cup promo." Available at: http://www.blonnet.com/2003/01/25/stories/2003012501530600.htm (accessed November 30, 2003).

Hobsbawm, E. J. (1990) *Nations and Nationalism since 1870: Programme, Myth, Reality*. Cambridge, UK: Cambridge University Press.

Hobsbawm, E. and Ranger, T. (eds). (1983) *The Invention of Tradition*. Cambridge, UK: Cambridge University Press.

India Express.com (2003) "ICC confirms stand on releasing withheld money to India." Available at: http://www.indiaexpress.com/news/sports/cricket/20031103–1.html (Accessed November 30, 2003).

Indiantelevision.com (2003a) "Will Pepsi blast leave rivals Blue?" Available at: http://www.indiantelevision.com/mam/headlines/y2k3/jan/janmam68.htm (accessed November 3, 2003).

Indiantelelvision.com (2003b) "HLL tops advertising charts for World Cup 2003– Audience movement during breaks leaves an impact on viewership across channels." Available at: http://www.indiantelevision.com/tamadex/y2k3/mar/cricbra7.htm (accessed, May 21, 2004).

Jaalmag (2002) Jaal Desi Satire. Available at Jaalmag.com: http://www.jaalmag.com/01032002/mainstory.htm (accessed November 3, 2003).

Karp, J. (1996) "Business Aside: Fizzy Wicket." *Far Eastern Economic Review*, 159 (13) (March 28), p. 62.

Keshaavan, N. (1998) "Swadeshi Goes Global." *Outlook*, April 27.

Kripalani. M. (1999) "We Want to Grab the Funky Market" *Business Week*, Available at: http://www.businessweek.com/1999/99_41/b3650018.htm (accessed November 30, 2003).

La Monica, P. (2002) "Coke vs. Pepsi: the new cola wars." Available at *CNN Money*: http://money.cnn.com/2002/05/10/pf/investing/q_cola/index.htm (accessed November 3, 2003).

Lal, K. (2000) "Dalmiya slams India's stubborn cricketers as contracts row rages." Agence Press France (August 26, 2000).

Lash, S. and Urry, J. (1987) *The End of Organized Capitalism*. Madison, WI: University of Wisconsin Press.

Leslie, D. A. (1995) "Global scan: The globalization of advertising agencies, concepts, and campaigns." *Economic Geography*, 71(4): 402–425.

Levitt, T. (1983) "The Globalization of Markets," *Harvard Business Review*, 61 (3): 92–102.

Madan, M. (2000) "'It's Not Just Cricket!' World Series Cricket: Race, Nation, and Diasporic Indian Identity." *Journal of Sport and Social Issues*, 24 (1): 24–35.

Maidment, P. (2002) "Manchester United Expands its Global Reach." Available at: http://www.forbes.com/2002/09/30/0930manchester.html (accessed November 3, 2003).

Majidi, N. and Pasariello, C. (2003) "After Iraq, Cola Wars Heat Up." Available at *Business Week*.com: http://www.businessweek.com/bwdaily/dnflash/apr2003/nf20030417_5930_db039.htm (accessed November 3, 2003).

Majumdar, B. (2002) "Cultural Resistance and Sport: Politics, Leisure and Colonialism – *Lagaan* – Invoking Lost History." *Culture, Sport, Society*, 5 (2): 29–44.

Marshall, P. (1997) *Celebrity and Power: Fame in Contemporary Culture*. Minneapolis: University of Minnesota Press.

Mazzarella, W. (2003) *Shovelling Smoke: Advertising and Globalization in Contemporary India*. Durham, NC and London: Duke University Press.

Miller, T., McKay, J. and Rowe, D. (2001) *Playing the World: Globalization and Sport*. London: Sage.

Morley, D. and Robins, K. (1995) *Spaces of Identity: Global Media, Electronic Landscapes and Cultural Boundaries*. London: Routledge.

Morning Star (August 22, 2002) "Players threaten cricket boycott."

Nguyen, T. (2000) "World Games: The U.S. Tries To Colonize Sport. Colorlines: Race, Culture," Action, 3, 2, Available at: http://www.arc.org/C_Lines/CLArchive/story3_2_05.html (accessed November 3, 2003).

Olins, W. (2000) "How Brands are Taking Over the Corporation," in M. Schultz, M. Hatch, and M. Larsen (eds). *The Expressive Organization: Linking Identity, Reputation, and the Corporate Brand*, Oxford: Oxford University Press, pp. 51–65.

Orr, D. (2003) "Big Colas Real Hitch in India." Available at Forbes Global: http://www.forbes.com/global/2003/0901/022.html (accessed November 3, 2003).

Parmar, A. (2003) "Fandemonium; Jiminy; cricket!; Sponsorship deals for the sport grow in India." *Marketing News*, March 17.

Pendergrast, M. (2000) *For God, Country and Coca-Cola: The unauthorized history of the great American soft drink and the company that makes it*. New York: Touchstone.

Preston, P. and Kerr, A. (2001) "Digital Media, Nation States and Local Cultures: The Case of Multimedia Content Production." *Media, Culture & Society*, 23 (1): 109–131.

Robins, K. (1997) "What in the world is going on?" in Du Gay, P. (ed). *Production of Culture/Cultures of Production*, London: Sage Publications, pp. 11–67.

Rose, N. (1990) *Governing the Soul*. London: Routledge

Schultz, M., Hatch, M. and Larsen, M. (eds) (2000) T*he Expressive Organization: Linking Identity, Reputation, and the Corporate Brand*, Oxford: Oxford University Press.

Silk, M. and Andrews, D. L. (2001a) "Beyond a Boundary: Sport, Transnational Advertising, and the Reiminaging of National Culture," *Journal of Sport and Social Issues*, 25 (2).

Silk, M. and Andrews, D. L. (2001b) "Understanding Globalisation: Transnational Marketing and Sponsorship." *International Journal of Sports Marketing & Sponsorship*, June/July, 2001: 11–15 (Special Issue Devoted to Transnational Marketing and Sponsorship).

Slater, J. (March 6, 2003) "Cashing in on Cricket." *Far Eastern Economic Review* (March 6, 2003).

Srinivasan, L. (2001) "Coke's April pool hungama promos to add Sprite to sales." Available at: http://www.financialexpress.com/fe/daily/20000402/fst02020.html (accessed November 3, 2003).

Srivastava, S. (2000) "Cola Row in India." Available at: http://news.bbc.co.uk/1/hi/world/south_asia/753931.stm (accessed November 30, 2003).

Taipei Times (2002) "Sassy commercials enliven soda wars in India: Battle of the Ads." Available at: http://taipeitimes.com/News/worldbiz/archives/2002/03/30/129881 (accessed November 30, 2003).

Tribune India (2002) "Sahara changes sponsorship logo." Available at: http://www.tribuneindia.com/2002/20020912/ncr3.htm (accessed November 30, 2003).

Upadhyay, V. (2003) "Beyond the Cola Wars." Available at: http://www.indiatogether.org/2003/sep/vup-cola.htm (accessed November 30, 2003).

Varney, W. (1998) "Barbie *Australis:* The Commercial Reinvention of National Culture." *Social Identities*, 4 (2): 161–176.

Vodafone (2003) "About Vodafone – Sponsorship." Available at: http://www.vodafone.com/section_article/0,3035,CATEGORY_ID%253D305%2526LANGUAGE_ID%253D0%2526CONTENT_ID%253D31022,00.html (accessed, November 3, 2003).

Wagnleitner, R. (1994) *Coca-Colonization and the Cold War: The Cultural Mission of the United States in Austria after the Second World War.* Chapel Hill and London: The University of North Carolina Press.

Yoffie, D. and Seet, R. (1999) *Internationalizing the Cola Wars (B): The Battle for India.* Ivey Publishing: Harvard Business School.

Yoon, S. (2001) "Working up a Thirst To Quench Asia." *Far Eastern Economic Review,* February 1.

4

Global adidas

Sport, celebrity and the marketing of difference

Andrew D. Grainger, Joshua I. Newman and
David L. Andrews

As the editors note in their introduction to this volume, sport sponsorship has long been lauded – by practitioners and scholars alike – as a mechanism through which aspirant multi- and trans-nationals may simultaneously achieve both global and local objectives: that is, when taken as exemplar of the "global popular" (Kellner, 1995), sport is seen to transcend national borders; conversely, its local resonance means sport is often seen as a means by which to engage national markets. The topic of global sport sponsorship therefore represents a unique opportunity to examine a debate stretching back at least as far as "The Globalization of Markets" (Levitt, 1983): global standardization versus local accommodation. However, rather than weigh the relative efficacy of each approach – the global sporting market vis-à-vis the consumer passions evoked through national sporting sentiment – and in taking up the editors' call for projects examining the multifarious ways in which sponsors, operating in multiple contexts with varied corporate objectives, have appropriated sports properties, our aim in this chapter is to develop a more nuanced understanding of the global-local nexus as it relates to the meeting of sport and the advertising industry.

We do so through examining the confluence of sport, celebrity, sponsorship and advertising in the recent promotional initiatives of the global apparel giant adidas. In particular, we aim to develop a typology of the "global sport celebrity" that accords with the "three stripes" of athlete embraced within the adidas stable of global endorsers: the "transnational" celebrity, the (nationally coded) "global-local" celebrity and, finally, the (globally viable) "exotic-local." As the adidas philosophy attests, we suggest that global marketing through celebrity endorsers is not always merely about signing up the best-known stars in the best-known sports (for instance, a number of the adidas's pantheon lack "global recognition"). Nor is the converse necessarily true, in that global presence is facilitated only by the commercial appropriation of local athletes for local markets. Rather, the global currency of a number of adidas's global endorsers appears to hinge on their ability to transcend national or ethnic borders by, paradoxically, being marked by them. Hence, adidas athletes may be global idol, local luminary or foreign enigma, yet in one way or another ultimately all engage – and indeed help to constitute – the global sport market.

Though we could perhaps be accused of indulging in academic fence-sitting, we argue that recent forays of the advertising industry into the world of sport suggest the "local" to be something simultaneously elided *and* engaged. That is, though we concur with Silk and Andrews (2001) in their belief that the nation is increasingly embraced "as a source of consumer identification," this does not necessarily presuppose the demise of "uniform and invariant global marketing and advertising initiatives that attempt to negate entrenched national cultural boundaries" (or vice versa depending on the view to which one subscribes) (Silk & Andrews, 2001, pp. 186–199). Instead, the global and local often operate simultaneously, sometimes negotiating, sometimes negating, the local, and some-times, as we propose below, neither, wherein the local takes on a global currency, a *national* chic open to *inter*national exploitation.

adidas and Corporate Transnationality

In a purely operational sense, there is little doubt that adidas is an archetypal "global" sport corporation: in 2003 its parent company, adidas-Salomon AG, had over 13,000 employees worldwide, approximately 100 subsidiaries, joint ventures and licensees, while adidas footwear, apparel, and equipment was sold in over 160 countries. From humble beginnings producing canvas training shoes in a small workshop in Herzogenaurach, Germany during the 1920s, adidas has evolved to become a major player in the global athletic footwear and apparel industry (the company's global revenue reached US$7.9 billion in 2003), eclipsed only perhaps, in symbolic and economic terms, by the Nike leviathan (which, in 2003, for the first time surpassed US$10 billion in global revenue). Arguably, this growing cultural import, though perhaps something of a by-product of the maturation of the sporting goods industry more generally, can be attributed to adidas's deployment of sport as a potent idiom through which to infuse their brand identity with meanings which are both globally resonant, yet locally inflected: that is, adidas has capitalized upon the ways in which sport may simultaneously engage multiple markets at one and the same time (witness the Olympics and the World Cup), while conversely, and somewhat paradoxically, remaining a "de facto cultural shorthand" (Silk & Andrews, 2001, p. 183) for the nation (see rugby in New Zealand or ice hockey in Canada) which permits marketers to "engage the nationalist sensibilities of local consumers" (Silk & Andrews, 2001, p. 186). Hence, adidas's moves to become an official sponsor of global sporting "mega-events" (Roche, 2000) such as the FIFA World Cup or the Olympics, while concurrently endeavoring to sign both local clubs and local athletes as a means of entrée into more nationalized sporting (consumer) publics.

Concomitant with its passage into the ranks of sporting goods producer *par excellence* has been adidas's ascension into the vanguard of the brand (Klein, 1999) – or commodity-sign (Goldman & Papson, 1996) – culture that now characterizes contemporary capitalism; indeed, the company and its attendant "cultural intermediaries" (Bourdieu, 1984) in the advertising, marketing, public relations and media industries have become key trendsetters in the world of global marketing. Its current cultural import – as well as its broad organizational footprint – however, belies the fact that for many of the company's first eighty-four years adidas's brand identity has been a much more "niched" affair; indeed, "Die Marke Mit Den 3 Streifen," has long been synonymous with its German roots, an association fostered through its lengthy sponsorship of the German soccer team, relationships with athletes such as Sepp Herberger and Franz Beckenbauer, and a "scientific" approach to product development purportedly reflective of Teutonic efficiency. Like BMW, Mercedes Benz and others, adidas has often played to assumptions of German engineering excellence, which, when combined with its early co-option of the sport of soccer – far and away the dominant Continental game – has allowed it to gain a European market preeminence. As one reporter succinctly put it, "Through much of the mid-20th century, adidas [has] owned Europe" (Herzog, 2003, p. E1). Even today "Shoppers still buy more adidas gear in Europe than any other brand" (Herzog, 2003, p. E1), with its main competitor Nike still being seen as something of an American interloper, as well as a footballing-come-lately.

In recent years, however, adidas has undertaken numerous moves to expand – though by certainly no means sever – its "European" imaged identity. Foremost among these initiatives has been the move toward globally oriented campaigns, engineered and distributed through global advertising agencies. Of particular note was the hiring of the Amsterdam-based 180 agency in 1998, a company whose "corporate mission speaks to universal traits, experiences, and emotions in a manner designed to appeal beyond the specificities of national cultural borders" (Silk & Andrews, 2001, p. 181):

> When we execute things we work hard to make sure it doesn't look like it's from one specific place… We ask, is this thing too American, too German, too Spanish. We identify what are the styles that tend to emerge out of those countries and make a conscious effort to avoid them (Hunter, 2000, p. 15).

More recently, adidas has also announced the appointment of leading US agency TBWA (whose accounts include global brands such as Sony, Apple and Nissan) to work alongside 180. According to Erich Stamminger, the member of the executive board of adidas-Salomon AG responsible for global marketing, the resultant "global agency network" represents "the next logical step in the evolution of our global brand positioning… By appointing one global agency network, we are continuing our strategy of strengthening the adidas brand worldwide" (quoted in adidas-Salomon AG, 2002).

In many ways, adidas's recent sponsorship and marketing shifts – both operational and thematic – suggest a potential waning of the "nation" as a source of identity and differentiation within the world of marketing. However, the possible emergence of a *supra*national, global marketplace has been continually undermined by what appears to be an enduring relevance of the nation as a cultural entity. Notably, during the course of the more than twenty years since Theodore Levitt's provocative dictum that emergent global markets would permit the selling of the "same things in the same way everywhere" (Levitt, 1983, p. 22), numerous marketers have found that the delivery of marketing messages, like popular culture more generally, is nonetheless highly dependent on "processes which are peculiar to particular national (and sub-national) structures" (Street, 1997, p. 81). The response of some, of course, has been to champion a new aphorism said to guarantee a profitable global presence: "think global, act local." As one article in the *International Journal of Advertising* put it: "in many circumstances local adaptation is essential due to fundamental differences in social, economic, cultural, legal, regulatory, political and media factors" (Dibb, Simkin & Yuen 1994, pp. 135–136). Rather than the "sweeping emergence of a global market" (Quelch, 2003, p. 22), advertisers have often instead found that "securing a profitable global presence necessitates negotiating with the local" (Silk & Andrews, 2001, p.187).

The archetypal transnational corporation has thus become one which can seamlessly operate within the language of the local, simultaneously, in multiple locations (Dirlik, 1996). In some instances, this has meant severing the ties of nationality to brand image through the production of "nationally ambiguous and thereby globally inclusive advertising campaigns" (Silk & Andrews, 2001, p. 192). In others, the process of "global localization" entailed the indigenization of marketing and sponsorship campaigns, and sometimes the product itself. And, finally more recent global-local promotional initiatives have also attempted to appeal to the local through "multivocal, multinationally oriented texts that attempt to engage a multitude of national markets at one and the same time" (Silk & Andrews, 2001, p. 191). In essence, sponsors and advertisers have increasingly undertaken to "incorporate localities into the imperatives of the global" (Dirlik, 1996, p. 34).

As we allude to in our introduction above, and as recent adidas marketing attests, often such reference to locality is embodied in and through locally resonant brand endorsers. Sporting celebrities, in particular, have often been used as a means "to nurture the distinctly local (national) demeanor of [a] global brand": either by deploying national sporting celebrities as "brand mercenaries" in local contexts, or, by utilizing athletes "as signifiers of national cultural difference" in "monotextual yet multivocal" campaigns (Silk & Andrews, 2001, pp. 191–196). Interestingly, however, the enduring relevance of the nation in global sport sponsorship does not necessarily deny the existence of universal, globally focused directives, nor the place of celebrity athletes within such rationalized strategies. For instance, Silk and Andrews (2001, p. 182) note the "adidas makes you do better" campaign from Amsterdam's 180 agency, which elides the nationality of featured athletes in favor of focusing on "seemingly universal moralistic and heroic traits," as a means to "[transcend] the nationality of the athlete in question and the national cultural context within which the advert is consumed." Such a strategy suggests a somewhat paradoxical engagement with the concepts of nation and national identity in contemporary advertising; either indifferent, or enthusiastic, or both. Athletic personas may therefore either be deployed as symbolic of a placeless universality or exploited as a way of giving a local accent to a global brand.

Further, beyond merely the type of campaign in which they appear, certain athletes themselves may more readily elide, or, on the contrary, be inscribed with, the markers of nationality. For instance, Giardina (2001, p. 202) proffers tennis player Martina Hingis as an example of "a flexibly global celebrity capable of adapting her identity to meet the ever-changing climate of global capitalism." He suggests Hingis as projecting divergent meanings in different settings, projecting "polymorphous media representations" (Giardina, 2001, p. 201) that allow her to appeal to localized cultural meanings and consumer desires. Conversely, it would seem that other adidas endorsers such as English rugby star Jonny Wilkinson or Australian swimmer Ian Thorpe, appeal to more specific, localized, national or consumer markets. Unlike Hingis who more readily transcends national cultural borders, Wilkinson and Thorpe are evidence of adidas's attempts to engage the local as part of a globalizing strategy.

This suggests two emergent typologies of celebrity athlete within the adidas stable of global endorsers: firstly, the flexible, or what Giardina (2001) calls the "transnational," celebrity; and, secondly, the "nationally coded" celebrity, who may be either "global-local" – that is, a "local" face making an appearance in a global campaign – or simply a local athlete for a local market. To these we would also add a third category, that of the "exotic local," whose global appeal is their very "foreign-ness." While the exotic-local may certainly resonate with a specific local market as for the global-local, they also have a more universal currency by way of their ability to appeal to global consumers in search of fresh or differential commodity-signs. In essence, the ethnic or national "otherness" of the exotic-local becomes a commodity-sign, at once demonstrative of global corporate reach and enticing to consumers attracted by the unfamiliar. An example of the exotic-local among adidas endorsers is New Zealand rugby player Jonah Lomu, an athlete playing a sport best described as marginal in North America and major markets in Western Europe, from a country few could probably locate on a map.

In sum, these typologies suggest that the adidas philosophy for global sponsorship through celebrity endorsers is not simply a case of either signing up globally resonant stars or, conversely, signing local athletes for local markets. Rather, adidas moves to address global niches through athletes who may be either global idol, local luminary, or foreign enigma. Such typologies are, of course, by no means comprehensive or exhaustive. More importantly, they must be seen as being fluid, with the characteristics of one often overlapping or bleeding into another. Nor are they mutually exclusive; for instance, an athlete may exhibit the recognition of locality, while simultaneously promoting a superficial representation of nationality or ethnicity designed to engage not national markets, but those merely coveting symbolic difference. However, such caveats aside, we now wish to examine these three typologies of adidas global endorser in greater detail. Taking the typologies in turn – the transnational celebrity, the global-local celebrity, and the exotic-local – we trace three different exemplars who best exhibit the traits of each categorization: David Beckham (who, like Hingis, exemplifies the transnational celebrity); Australian swimmer Ian Thorpe (the global-local); and the aforementioned Jonah Lomu (the exotic local). We then conclude by examining the potential effects of these corporate-inspired representations of nationality and ethnicity on contemporary understandings of cultural identity.

David Beckham: The Transnational Celebrity

He bends the ball, and we bend him like the ball.

(Peter Conrad, "Blend it Like Beckham")

In 2003, *Time* magazine suggested David Beckham to be "the world's best-known sports star" (Elliot, 2003, p. 40). Indeed, Beckham has been elsewhere – and somewhat more hyperbolically – described as a "global celebrity" (Deford, 2003), "the 21st century's first genuinely global icon" (Cashmore, 2000, p. 22), and a "planetary phenomenon" who is "as multinational as the Nike logo or Tommy Hilfiger's flags" (Conrad, 2003, p. 1). Beyond mere fame, however, Beckham is perhaps the standard bearer for the alluring convergence of sport, celebrity, and consumer capitalism. Married to a former Spice Girl, plying his trade on the Continent with one of Europe's most storied and powerful football clubs, and with a portfolio of endorsement contracts that includes the global giants Pepsi and adidas, Beckham embodies the new logics of the global sport-media-business nexus; tellingly, Beckham's first game for the Spanish club Real Madrid came against a Chinese team in Beijing, while the match was beamed to millions of television viewers around the world.

Indeed, it is likely that Real coveted Beckham, purportedly "the hottest marketing machine in the sports world since Michael Jordan" (Brownell, 2003, p. 88), as much for his marketable face as his footballing feet. Arguably, much of Beckham's appeal to both Real and corporate image-makers more generally is his ability to "negotiate various borders of the global market" (Giardina, 2001, p. 201). For instance, Real have openly admitted that Beckham provides an entrée into the lucrative Asian market – a market currently dominated by Beckham's former club Manchester United. Moreover, while Real have, in the words of their sporting director Jorge Valdano, traditionally represented "the South ... everything that is Latin" (quoted in Carlin, 2003, p. 17), they see Beckham as embodying the English-speaking world of "the North." However, while Beckham's move to Real may indeed be a "dream ticket" (as adidas CEO Herbert Hainer once described it) for the image-makers at adidas, it is unlikely that Beckham's brand value will be much affected by the neat brand symbiosis of adidas-athlete with adidas-club. Rather, Beckham has emerged as a, to use the words of one of his sponsors, "global brand" (quoted in Milmo, 2003, p. 3), not because of the fame of his clubs or the marketing power of his boot endorser (though we would not wholly dismiss either as factors), but rather his unique ability to reveal "different facets to different types of fans" (Deford, 2003).

By way of example, much has been made in recent years, about Beckham's ability to "bend" traditional male stereotypes (particularly, those surrounding the game of soccer), embracing "a complex and contradictory identity" (Cashmore & Parker, 2003, p. 224) that suggests the possibility for varying constructions of contemporary masculinity (see Cashmore & Parker, 2003; Conrad, 2003; Elliott, 2003; Whannel, 2001, 2002). Supposedly, it is this blurring of the masculine and feminine, this "androgynous blend of opposites" (Conrad, 2003, p. 1) – the sarong-wearing family man – that explains Beckham's adoration by "young and old, men and women, straight and gay" (Elliott, 2003, p. 40). Yet, we would argue that the polyvalency of Beckham extends beyond merely his sexuality. Rather, with respect to the meanings Beckham embodies in particular nationally based markets, we suggest him to be equally ecumenical. That is, we maintain that Beckham's global celebrity is attributable to an "eminent malleability of [his] mediated image, in terms of its ability to appeal to highly localized cultural meanings and desires" (Andrews & Jackson, 2001, p. 15). Hence, following Giardina (2001, p. 207), we suggest Beckham to be an exemplar of a transnational celebrity, a prototypical "flexible citizen" who: "becomes tied to the foundational characteristics of a given locality *while at the same time* operating amidst a multi-faceted global plane which transcends (inter)national boundaries."

In the initial commercial from adidas's new US$50 million "Impossible is Nothing" campaign – its first global major advertising effort in five years – Beckham, through the powers of modern computer technology, joins Muhammad Ali on one of his famous long runs. Accompanying Ali and Beckham are a number of other athletes from the adidas stable including runner Haile Gebreselassie, NBA basketballer Tim Duncan, and Australian swimmer Ian Thorpe. In many ways the commercial is an archetype of the single, multivocal, multinationally oriented texts Silk and Andrews (2001) see as emblematic of the stratagem of "cultural Toyotism": the commercial plays worldwide, with the local demeanor of the adidas brand expressed through athletes who resonate with particular national or sporting niches. With the possible exception of Ali, however, we suggest that Beckham is unique among those alongside him in this commercial. Beckham is not necessarily a mechanism by which to engage a particular locality, though he certainly may do so; rather, unlike Gebreselassie, Thorpe, and even Duncan, Beckham appeals across boundaries of nation, because he is, as one reporter for *The Guardian* put it, a "creature of infinite plasticity" (Conrad, 2003, p. 1).

In the USA, Beckham's identity plays to the glamorous trappings of international celebrity: often referred to as the "husband of Posh Spice," he recently appeared as a presenter at the *MTV Video Music Awards*, was named to *Vanity Fair*'s "Best Dressed List," and his name, though not the man himself, firmly entrenched itself at the Hollywood box-office with the surprise hit *Bend it Like Beckham*. At home in England, though undoubtedly enmeshed in similar discourses of fame, style, and commerce (see Whannel, 2001, 2002), his footballing skills also command admiration and affection: beyond mere celebrityhood, he is the "working-class-boy-made-good" excelling in a traditionally working-class game, a *national* hero playing the *nation's* game, *England's* captain, the embodiment of Tony Blair's Cool Britannia. Indeed, adidas themselves have even used Beckham in this way: in a 2001 Irish and UK campaign for adidas football, Beckham, ostensibly showing the commercial's naïve protagonist what "makes the British game unique" (adidas-Salomon AG, 2001), shows off his footballing skills to the sounds of a distinctly English soundtrack of The Jam's "That's Entertainment." Now on the Continent, however, Beckham has become the very measure of the new Europe: "not characterized by the provinciality so common among Englishmen" (Farred, 2002, p. 15), Beckham is the cosmopolitan, the envy of fashionista and football fan alike, playing alongside some of Europe's top players – Figo, Zidane, Raul et al. – in a team known in Spain as "Los Galacticos." Finally, in Asia, Beckham lends his name to products "which he would probably not touch in the West ... his portfolio of endorsement contracts bulges with deals specifically for the East Asian markets" (Cashmore, 2000, p. 22).

The meanings of Beckham are therefore very much dependent upon the locale in question. In post-structuralist terms it could be argued that Beckham is a "floating signifier": his identity plays to differing narratives specific to national context, he is an exemplar of "a free-floating celebrity commodity-sign" (Giardina, 2001, p. 205). Whannel (2002, 202) has said of Beckham's imaged identity that it is "strangely elusive anchorless ... a floating signifier that can become attached to a range of discursive elements with equal plausibility." Similarly, we suggest Beckham is the archetypal transnational celebrity, in that he "comes to inhabit the local by playing off both [his] known celebrity qualities as well as, and at the same time, appearing as a *tabula rasa* on which local meanings and desires are inscribed" (Giardina, 2001, p. 204). Thus Beckham becomes a brand unto himself, his appeal as well as his imaged identity malleable, transcending the strictures of the country in which he plays or the club to which he is signed; and, something realized by adidas, as Jan Runau, the head of global public relations for adidas, puts it as rumors of Beckham's return to England continue to abound: "He is a great athlete and a great icon for us and would be for whichever big European club he will play for" (quoted in Talbot & Scott, 2004, p. 4).

Ian Thorpe: The Global-Local

While teen-sensation Michael Phelps dominated the headlines of America's sports pages during the 2004 Athens Olympics, the undoubted international face of swimming is still a 22-year-old from Sydney, Australia. Known simply as the "Thorpedo," Ian Thorpe has been described as "one of the hottest properties in the sports marketing business" (Thomson, 2002, p. 54). And, it would also seem prudent for potential sponsors with any global aspirations to take note of Thorpe's "growing profile in other countries" (Thomson, 2002, p. 54) outside of his native Australia. Indeed, in the past four years Thorpe has appeared on the *Tonight Show with Jay Leno* in the United States, was spotted in the front row at the launch of Giorgio Armani's Spring-Summer 2003 collection in Milan, and in 2002 was voted the most popular athlete in China by readers of the *China Sports Daily* newspaper (Thomson, 2002).

The extent of Thorpe's global celebrity, and consequently his global corporate appeal, is also illustrated in a recent study by an Australian consultancy specializing in valuing sponsorships that suggested him to be "as close as you are going to get to being the complete marketing package. He is good looking, he is well spoken, his profile is building internationally as well" (cited in McGuire, 2003, p. 3). The public relations manager for Audi Australia, one of Thorpe's sponsors, has also described him as "Australia's most high-profile sportsman around the world" (quoted in Thomson, 2002, p. 54). And, in 2003 Thorpe was rated Australia's "'most valuable' sporting commercial property, ahead of tennis players Lleyton Hewitt and the retired Pat Rafter" (McGuire, 2003, p. 3). Currently, Thorpe has twelve main sponsorship and marketing deals with a range of Australian and foreign companies, including telecommunications company Telstra and Qantas Airlines. His most lucrative deal, however, is with adidas which pays him "an estimated $1 million a year to promote the brand" by wearing adidas clothes and swimming gear, appearing at special events, and "appearing in adidas's international marketing campaigns" (Thomson, 2002, p. 54).

Since donning his signature adidas "Fullbody Swimsuit" in 1999 Thorpe has won three Olympic gold medals and nine world titles, breaking numerous world records along the way. In the process he has become one of the company's most marketable stars. In Australia, Thorpe is seen as adidas's key to marketing their swimming products to the swimming public (see Jeffery, 2002), while his popularity in Asia, particularly in Japan where he is "revered like royalty" (Yeaman, 2002, p. 35), provides adidas with a passport to one of the world's more lucrative consumer markets. Unsurprisingly, in both Asia and Australia Thorpe is also the cornerstone of the "Impossible is Nothing" campaign. Significantly, and dispelling any doubts of what adidas see as his global cache, he also appears alongside Ali in the globally disseminated "Long Run" commercial from this campaign, and which we describe in our discussion of David Beckham above. However, though they may both appear in the same commercial, unlike Beckham we argue that, while Thorpe certainly has an international celebrity presence, and though he is obviously recognized throughout the world as a star athletic performer, he does not exhibit the same national flexibility with regard to his celebrityhood: rather, Thorpe should be understood primarily through Australian narratives and a celebrity identity that marks him as Australian (Giardina, 2001, p. 207).

It could therefore be argued that Thorpe is exemplar of what we term a global-local; a globally viable, yet nonetheless nationally coded athletic body.

For instance, though "deified" (Weaver, 2002) in countries like China and Japan, Thorpe is nonetheless undoubtedly "the face of Australia" (McGuire, 2004, p. 23) in Asia. In the first instance, his Australian-ness is nurtured through his role as a "holiday ambassador" for the Australian Tourist Commission, while, secondly, much of his fame has come through his successes as a member of the Australian team in international nation-based competition (as opposed to Beckham whose imaged identity arguably allies more closely with club than country on the international scene). Arguably much of Thorpe's global celebrity is predicated upon such nationally based rivalries. Most notably, Thorpe's celebrityhood, both in Australia and beyond, has been largely nurtured at major international events such as the Olympics, where it is nation versus nation battles that most often take center stage. For instance, at the Athens Games it was the "Australia-America" rivalry in the pool that dominated the Games opening days. Likewise, at the 2000 Sydney Olympics, Thorpe was a key figure in a similar nation-based contest, a celebrity deeply enmeshed in the discourses of Australian nationalism and anti-American enmity:

Still just 17, Thorpe won the 400 free and lowered his own world record. Less than an hour later, he anchored Australia in the 400 freestyle relay, in which the previous seven gold medals had gone to the United States. When Thorpe out-dueled Gary Hall Jr., chests puffed out even more than normal. (McMullen, 2003, p. 1E)

Such nationally coded antagonisms are also played out in the way Thorpe's imaged identity was defined, in both the lead-up to, as well as during, the Games at Athens, in contradistinction to Phelps. While a recent article in *The Baltimore Sun* highlighted what it saw as "uncanny similarities" between Thorpe and Phelps, the popular press has generally played to their purported differences. For instance, at the 2003 World Swimming Championships one reporter summed the two up thus: "Phelps, an all-American boy with a rigidly cut fringe and a slightly brash turn of phrase, is not the worldly young man Thorpe was at the same age" (Saltau, 2003a, p. 66). Though it is a rivalry Thorpe seems loathe to acknowledge, much was also made of Phelps swimming in Thorpe's favorite 200 meters and 400 meters freestyle events in Athens. As Peter Mitchell (2003) claimed prior to Athens, "Phelps, 18, going head-to-head with Thorpe in his strongest races would be the battle of the Olympics." Certainly, this was also the way the 200 and 400 rivalry was billed during the Games themselves, and given the global media interest in both events – the hotly contested 200 meters in particular – Thorpe's subsequent victories only seem likely add to his celebrity status both at home and abroad, especially in markets where he is already a recognizable (Australian) icon.

Though it would undoubtedly be an overstatement to suggest swimming to have the global recognition of sports such as soccer or basketball, his popularity in key global markets – Asia in particular – thus suggest that Ian Thorpe is nonetheless "an international force in marketing" (Saltau, 2003, p. 4). Further, unlike Phelps, whose appeal is largely limited to the US, Thorpe appears to enjoy an "altogether more worldly appeal" (Saltau, 2003b, p. 4). Yet though he is a global celebrity, we would also argue that Thorpe's identity nevertheless plays to and reinforces both difference and nationality. Though during Athens Thorpe was primarily mediated as "Australian" via his rivalry with Phelps, he is further "localized" or "nationalized" through traditional narratives and stereotypes of Australian culture. For instance, reporter Paul McMullen posits Thorpe's status as an Australian "national hero," and implicitly his athletic success, as being a product of a nation in which water sports are prevalent, and in which "90 percent of Australians live within six miles of surf, and parents who don't teach their children to swim are considered negligent" (McMullen, 2003, p. 1E). Such descriptions, common in media discourse about him, position Thorpe as the product of an "Australian lifestyle"; a national cultural embodiment. That is, Thorpe's identity both globally and locally, plays to traditional narratives of Australian culture, and in essence he becomes a "representative figure implicated in national fantasies of origin, organization, character" (Cole & King, 1998, p. 56); and, it is this mix of global fame and embodied national difference that makes Thorpe an exemplary global-local. In Australia, Thorpe "is a national hero who has been swimming for himself and his country since he could walk and doing it with class" (Mitchell, 2004, p. 19).

Jonah Lomu: Exoticizing the Local

In all likelihood, there are few outside the rugby-playing world who could place the name Jonah Lomu. Yet, as anyone with even a fleeting familiarity with the sport would tell you, he is probably rugby's most identifiable face. As a reporter for London's *The Times* has put it, while Lomu's playing career may be indefinitely on hold, walk any other player down a street with him "and you know he is the one they instantly recognise" (O'Connor, 2003, p. 36). Indeed, though his celebrity may have waned in recent years, he nonetheless remains rugby's "first true global icon" (O'Connor, 2003, p. 36). During the height of his fame in the mid-to-late 1990s Lomu was an imposing presence on the field, while becoming the highest paid player off it. And, today, despite being sidelined by a serious kidney ailment Lomu still remains third in a current list of the game's top earners.

Much of that paycheck comes from a recently renewed contract with adidas. Though the size of both his deal (rumored to be in the vicinity of US$700,000) – and perhaps his fame – may be dwarfed by counterparts such as David Beckham or Tracy McGrady, Lomu is among the twenty-two athletes to feature in adidas's "Impossible is Nothing" campaign. In fact Lomu was even due to appear in the "Long Run" commercial featuring Ali, Beckham and Thorpe until being forced to withdraw owing to the demands of kidney dialysis. Moreover, despite not even playing at the most recent Rugby World Cup in October–November 2003, Lomu nonetheless featured prominently in adidas's promotional initiatives during the tournament: among the posters of "paint-splattered portraits of individual players in motion" (see Gardner, 2003) developed by 180 and TBWA for the campaign there is one of Lomu accompanied by the tagline "He's the speed, you're the bump"; while the sidelined Lomu also became something of a roving "adidas ambassador" through a number of guest appearances and speaking engagements during the World Cup. While his adidas contemporaries may be names like Kournikova, Beckham and Zidane, in the words of one adidas executive Lomu is "right up there... He features in our global advertising programmes, that's how highly adidas rates him" (Kayes, 2002, p. 15).

Though the contract with Lomu would initially appear to be an obvious example of adidas's attempts to engage a particular national or sporting market, it nonetheless seems curious that the company would choose Lomu as a candidate to feature in their global campaigns; what precisely then does adidas see in Lomu? It is our contention that the signing of Lomu by adidas is not simply a matter the company's efforts to engage either the New Zealand, or wider rugby-playing, market. Though Lomu may indeed be a mechanism of identification for such consumers, he actually has a wider global appeal borne of the fact that he is largely unknown in major global markets such as Western Europe and North America. In particular, we suggest that his "foreign-ness," his "exoticism," appeals to global consumers explicitly looking for commodity-signs that embody difference and otherness. As Goldman and Papson (1996) have noted, in a world inundated with media messages, it has become increasingly difficult for advertisers to arrest consumer attention as well as differentiate their corporate commodity-signs, brands, and images. Thus:

> the pressure is on to find fresher, more desirable, and more spectacular images to enhance the value of products... As sign value competitions intensify, advertisers invent new strategies and push into fresh cultural territory, looking for "uncut" and "untouched" signs. (Goldman & Papson, 1996, p. v)

One response has been the global parade of images of particularity and ethnic otherness. Hence, Lomu, the amorphous other playing a sport on the global sporting fringes, who at once appeals to the rugby fan and the consumer in search of the next marker of contemporary popular cultural hipness.

Of course, at this juncture we should note that the issue of race cannot be divorced from discussion of Lomu's otherness. In particular, though we suggest Lomu to be representative of a broader commercialization of otherness, his marketability must be situated within a long history of the "commodification of the black athletic body" (Carrington, 2001/2002, p. 109). Through this commodification, "black bodies function as racialised symbols of cultural difference" (Carrington, 2001/2002, p. 108). As Ben Carrington has noted, within the contemporary sign economy of ads, brands, and images, "blackness," and the black body (and particularly the black sporting body) "have become highly valued commodities" (Carrington, 2001/2002, p. 104). Through the processes of the global spectacle of mass-mediated sexualization and objectification black bodies "have been transformed into commodity-signs to be bought and sold throughout the globalised media market" (Carrington, 2001/2002, p. 104).

This commodification of blackness, or the exotic more generally, is not simply indicative of attempts by advertisers to reach black or minority markets. Rather, though not to suggest that marketers ignore black and minority consumers, this trading in otherness has been largely the provenance of white producers and audiences. According to Carrington (2001/2002) there has been a "centring of blackness as an object of desire, prestige and 'cool'" (p. 108) among white consumers, with "the black athlete, above all, [occupying] pride of place in the fetishised desire for blackness" (p. 104). Significantly, in demonstrating both the national and black exoticism we have heretofore suggested as been characteristic of his brand identity, it has been elsewhere argued that Lomu enjoyed his greatest popularity among white middle-class consumers outside New Zealand (see Mirams, 2004).

We also suggest that there are at least two further elements that contribute to Lomu's commercially viable exoticism: black sexuality and Polynesian descent. With regard to the former, Carrington (2001/2002, p. 98) proposes that "the black male torso as object of visual desire is *everywhere.*" Stuart Hall (1997, p. 274) has likewise noted the "erotic dimensions" of popular media representations of the black body; and, the black male sporting body has become a particular object of desire and envy. As Carrington continues:

> Currently, the muscled black male torso as a commodity-sign has achieved almost iconic status within the Western media, within both popular cultural and high art spaces, in replaying, at the connotative level, colonial fantasies and desires about the perceived sexual excesses of black masculinity. (2001/2002, pp. 97–98)

In such a context, we suggest that part of the consumer appeal of Lomu can be explained by the way his identity plays to this commercially inspired sexualization of the black athletic body.

In many ways the commodification of otherness and the sexualization of the black body also intersect with a third element of Lomu's exoticism: his Polynesian origins. Indeed, the marketing of Lomu can be set against the backdrop of a long history of representations of the South Pacific Islands which play to images of the exotic. From Gauguin's forays in Tahiti to the tales of Robert Louis Stevenson, from Hollywood films like *Moana of the South Seas* to the "Tiki culture" of the 1950s and 60s, Western culture has long traded in images of Polynesian otherness. Interestingly, a number of recent transnational marketing campaigns have also appropriated elements of indigenous Polynesian culture. For instance, Danish toy manufacturer Lego named the figurines from one of its recent *Bionicle* lines after the gods of New Zealand's indigenous Mäori. And, pertinent to our discussion of Lomu, adidas's sponsorship of the New Zealand All Blacks rugby team included a global campaign which centered on a Mäori *haka*, as well as "stereotypes of Mäori" (Jackson & Hokowhitu, 2002, p. 133) more generally. We argue that Lomu's appeal must therefore be situated within the context of this global promotion of Pacifica exotica; indeed, his brand identity both exploits and contributes to this exploitation of Pacific Island culture by transnational corporate capitalism.

In sum, rather than being a global icon, Jonah Lomu could perhaps be best described as an exotic local. Though he may play a sport funded and watched in the main by the white middle classes, as well as be a largely unknown quantity outside the realm of rugby, his black (sexual) exoticism allows Lomu to cross both cultural and consumer divides. In particular, and in a global sense, we argue that Lomu exudes a commercially exploitable ethnic chic which appeals to consumers even if they may know little about either him or the sport he plays.

Coda

According to Smith (1999, p. 89) "trading in the Other" has become "the first truly global commercial enterprise." Certainly, while "globalization" has oftentimes been appropriated as an empty metaphor, a bland descriptor of the "flattening out of cultural difference in postorganized capitalism" (Williams, 1994, p. 378), it is our contention that images of ethnic and national difference have instead moved to the forefront of global capitalism. In the first instance, difference is often embraced as a source of brand *differentiation* and consumer *identification*: hence, the incorporation of, and adaptation to, local cultural tastes and interests, in this case perhaps best exhibited in adidas's signing of local endorsers or the customization of its marketing messages. However, we should also not ignore how 'the local' has increasingly filtered back into the imperatives of the global: that is, the ways in which difference has been incorporated into transnational marketing strategies. For instance, as we suggest above, the value of adidas's endorsers such as Ian Thorpe or Jonah Lomu appears to hinge on their ability to transcend national or ethnic borders precisely by being inscribed by such markers of difference. Thus, while sport sponsorship is playing a central role in transnational brand positioning, the local and the global should not be seen as mutually exclusive, but rather dialectically constitutive of the sponsorship environment in which firms operate.

In this chapter we have argued that recent adidas sponsorship initiatives provide an exemplar of this global-local market dialectic: adidas's global sporting celebrities increasingly conflate boundaries between global and local, their mediation paradoxically emblematic of both economies of scale and the integration – and (global) exploitation – of locality. We have also suggested, the universal and the indigenous should not be seen as necessarily in opposition: rather, even in the most global of sport sponsorship campaigns, corporations may (sometimes simultaneously) seek to transcend, engage, or even capitalize on cultural, and, in particular, national, difference. The (often deliberately) ambiguous, malleable identities of adidas's global sporting celebrities thus suggest a new landscape of sport sponsorship in which the corporate engagement of celebrity is complex, varied and specific. For corporations and their attendant cultural intermediaries this of course raises a range of questions regarding the strategic development and utilization of new forms of global sport sponsorship and celebrity – many of which may potentially be addressed through the typologies we have proposed herein.

Perhaps more significant questions, however, are those pertaining to how global advertising images are reconstituting our notions of (localized) identity and place, and the potential consequences of commercially constituted conceptions of both ethnicity and nationality. As Robertson (1995, p. 26) has argued, we need to recognize that "much of the promotion of difference is in fact done from above or outside. Much of what is often declared to be local is in fact the local expressed in terms of generalized recipes of locality." What dangers are therefore posed by the reduction of ethnicity to yet another global, market-inspired, commodity-sign? Is the political, or indeed cultural, efficacy of ethnic difference undermined by stripping it from its historical context and deploying it as yet another means to distinguish brand identity in a cluttered global market? There is therefore not only a need to recognize the ways in which global capital engages ever more differentiated spatial markets (national/regional/local) in a manner that capitalizes on cultural difference, but further – especially given the differential relations of power and privilege inherent in global capitalism – a demand for further analysis of how corporate practices such as global sport sponsorship may be affecting traditional, locally specific, bases of identification.

References

adidas-Salomon AG (2001) "British football is different – Premiership stars show why." *adidas-Salomon News Archive 2001*, August, http://www.adidas-salomon.com/en/news/archive/2001/default.asp (accessed April 10, 2004).

adidas-Salomon AG (2002) "Adidas appoints 180/TBWA as global agency network." *adidas-Salomon News Archive 2002*, January 9, http://www.adidas-salomon.com/en/news/archive/2002/default.asp (accessed April 10, 2004).

Andrews, David L. and Steven J. Jackson (2001) "Introduction: Sport celebrities, public culture, and private experience," in David L. Andrews and Steven J. Jackson (eds), *Sport Stars: the Cultural Politics of Sport Celebrity*. London: Routledge, pp. 1–19.

Bourdieu, Pierre (1984) *Distinction: a Social Critique of the Judgement of Taste*. Cambridge, MA: Harvard University Press.

Brownell, Ginanne (2003) "Brand it like Beckham." *Newsweek*, June 30, p. 88.

Carlin, John (2003) "Too sexy for his shirt." *The Observer*, June 15, p. 17.

Carrington, Ben (2001/2002) "Fear of a Black Athlete: Masculinity, politics and the body." *new formations* 45 (Winter): 91–110.

Cashmore, Ellis (2000) "The marketing Midas with the golden boot." *The Times Higher Education Supplement*, May 16, p. 22.

Cashmore, Ellis and Andrew Parker (2003) "One David Beckham?: Celebrity, masculinity, and the soccerati." *Sociology of Sport Journal* 20: 214–231.

Cole, C. L. and Samantha King (1998) "Representing black masculinity and urban possibilities: Racism, realism, and *Hoop Dreams*," in Geneviève Rail (ed.), *Sport and Postmodern Times*. Albany, NY: State University of New York Press, pp. 49–86.

Conrad, Peter (2003) "Blend it like Beckham." *The Observer*, May 25, p. 1.

Deford, Frank (2003) "Extraordinary appeal." *SportsIllustrated.com*, July 30, http://sportsillustrated.cnn.com/inside_game/frank_deford/news/2003/07/30/viewpoint/index.html (accessed October 7, 2003),

Dibb, Sally, Lyndon Simkin and Rex Yuen (1994) "Pan-European advertising: Think Europe – Act Local." *International Journal of Advertising* 13: 125–136.

Dirlik, Arif (1996) "The global in the local," in Rob Wilson and Wimal Dissanayake (eds), *Global-Local: Cultural Production and the Transnational Imaginary*. Durham, NC: Duke University Press, pp. 21–45.

Elliott, Michael (2003) "Brand it like Beckham." *Time*, June 30, p. 40.

Farred, Grant (2002) "Long distance love: Growing up a Liverpool Football Club fan." *Journal of Sport and Social Issues* 26: 6–24.

Gardner, Rachel (2003) "Adidas reveals Rugby World Cup poster ads." *Campaign*, September 26, p. 8.

Giardina, Michael D (2001) "Global Hingis: Flexible citizenship and the transnational celebrity," in David L. Andrews and Steven J. Jackson (eds), *Sport Stars: the Cultural Politics of Sporting Celebrity*. London: Routledge, pp. 201–230.

Goldman, Robert and Stephen Papson (1996) *Sign Wars: the Cluttered Landscape of Advertising*. Boulder, CO: Westview Press.

Hall, Stuart (1997) "The spectacle of the 'other'," in Stuart Hall (ed.), *Representation: Cultural Representations and Signifying Practices*. Milton Keynes, UK: The Open University, pp. 223–290.

Herzog, Boaz (2003) "Nike, adidas toe to toe in Europe." *The Sunday Oregonian*, November 23, p. E1.

Hunter, Sandy (2000) "Border-bending creative." *Boards Magazine*, March 1, p. 15.

Jackson, Steven J. and Brendan Hokowhitu (2002) "Sport, tribes, and technology: The New Zealand All Blacks Haka and the politics of identity." *Journal of Sport and Social Issues* 26: 125–139.

Jeffery, Nicole (2002) "Thorpedo suit gives every Aussie new choice of cossie." *The Australian*, December 5, p. 4.

Kayes, Jim (2002) "A wing and a prayer." *The Dominion Post*, November 23, p. 15.

Kellner, Douglas (1995) *Media Culture: Cultural Studies, Identity and Politics Between the Modern and the Postmodern*. London: Routledge.

Klein, Naomi (1999) *No Logo: Taking Aim at Brand Bullies*. New York: Picador.

Levitt, Theodore (1983) "The globalization of markets." *Harvard Business Review*, 61: 99–102.

McGuire, Michael (2003) "Thorpe wins out of pool." *The Australian*, July 16, p. 3.

McGuire, Michael (2004) "Thorpey's Asian appeal proves a So Natural drawcard." *The Australian*, February 20, p. 23.

McMullen, Paul (2003) "Fates, feats joined in pool." *The Baltimore Sun*, December 23, p. E1.

Milmo, Cahal (2003) "Is there life after David Beckham?: The Beckham industry." *The Independent*, April 26, p. 3.

Mirams, Chris (2004) "Wake up NZRU, Jonah deserves better than this." *The Sunday Star-Times*, February 22, p. 6.

Mitchell, Neil (2004) "Fix this farce – now." *Herald Sun*, March 30, p. 19.

Mitchell, Peter (2003) "US teen sensation targets Thorpedo." *Sun Herald*, September 7, p. 98.

O'Connor, Ashling (2003) "Lomu is true icon, on or off pitch." *The Times*, November 17, p. 36.

Quelch, John (2003) "The return of the global brand." *Harvard Business Review*, 81 (8): 22–23.

Robertson, Roland (1995) "Glocalization: time-space and homogeneity-heterogeneity," in Mike Featherstone, Scott Lash and Roland Robertson (eds), *Global Modernities*. London: Sage, pp. 25–44.

Roche, Maurice (2000) *Mega-Events and Modernity: Olympics, and Expos in the Growth of Global Culture*. London: Routledge.

Saltau, Chloe (2003a) "Thorpe aiming to brush off Phelps and focus on the big picture." *Sydney Morning Herald*, July 19, p. 66.

Saltau, Chloe (2003b) "The rocket man." *The Age*, July 28, p. 4.

Silk, Michael L. and David L. Andrews (2001) "Beyond a boundary?: Sport, transnational advertising, and the reimagining of national culture." *Journal of Sport and Social Issues* 25: 180–201.

Smith, Linda Tuhiwai (1999) *Decolonising Methodologies: Research and Indigenous Peoples*. Dunedin, New Zealand: London Books.

Street, John (1997) "'Across the universe': The limits of global popular culture," in Alan Scott (ed.), *The Limits of Globalization: Cases and Arguments*. London: Routledge, pp. 75–89.

Talbot, Simon and Matt Scott (2004) "Real ready to realise the value of Beckham." *The Guardian*, May 1, p. 4.

Thomson, James (2002) "Ian Thorpe: Mr. Marketable." *Business Review Weekly*, November 28, p. 54.

Weaver, Paul (2002) "Time to worship at feet of Thorpedo." *The Guardian*, July 19, p. 32.

Whannel, Garry (2001) "Punishment, redemption, and celebration in the popular press: The case of David Beckham," in David L. Andrews and Steven J. Jackson (eds), *Sport Stars: the Cultural Politics of Sporting Celebrity*. London: Routledge, pp. 138–150.

Whannel, Garry (2002) *Media Sports Stars: Masculinities and Moralities*. London: Routledge.

Williams, John (1994) "The local and the global in English soccer and the rise of satellite television." *Sociology of Sport Journal* 11: 376–397.

Yeaman, Simon (2002) "The deep end." *Hobart Mercury*, May 18, p. 35.

5

Sports Sponsorship and Tourism Flows

Mike Weed

The interrelationship between sport and tourism has attracted growing interest from academics in a range of disciplines in recent years. Over twenty years ago, Glyptis (1982) examined the links between sport and tourism in five European countries and made comparisons with the UK. Following, and perhaps stimulated by this, there were a number of embryonic studies of sports tourism during the 1980s (e.g. Agne-Traub, 1989; Boon, 1984; Bratton, 1988). Further work by Glyptis (1991) and subsequently the report commissioned by the Sports Council in the UK on the interrelationship between sport and tourism (Jackson & Glyptis, 1992) were also some of the earliest substantive works in the area. Other valuable reviews of the field have been carried out by De Knop (1990), Standeven and Tomlinson (1994), Gibson (1998), Weed (1999a) and Jackson and Weed (2003). Different facets of the interrelationship between sport and tourism have also been researched (e.g. Redmond, 1991; Jackson & Reeves, 1998; Collins & Jackson, 1999; Weed, 1999b; Vrondou, 1999; Reeves, 2000). In addition, commercial analysts have reviewed the volume and value of this emerging sector of the leisure industry (Leisure Consultants, 1992; Mintel, 1999). More recently, a number of complete texts focusing on sports tourism have been published. The first of these was the 1999 offering from Standeven and De Knop which provides a relatively introductory overview, focusing to a large extent on the impacts of sports tourism. The text by Turco, Riley and Swart (2002) approaches the subject from a management perspective, providing an introduction to sports tourism operations and marketing. In contrast, the text by Hinch and Higham (2004) gives a more advanced overview of development aspects of sports tourism, while Weed and Bull (2004) focus on sports tourism as a phenomenon, examining the motivations and behaviors of participants, policy-makers and providers.

This chapter draws on much of this growing body of literature on sports tourism, alongside the broader literature on tourism flows, to understand the relationship between sports sponsorship and tourism. Of course, it is sport's position as an increasingly global product that has led to the growth of sports sponsorship on a global scale. In fact, the same globalizing forces that have led to the expansion of the international tourism trade have also driven the increasingly global reach of sports sponsorship. As such, this book provides a timely opportunity to speculate (because there has been no previous research or investigation in this area) on the relationship between sports sponsorship and tourism. With the exception of tourism that is enabled by sponsorship – largely the travel of elite athletes – the sponsorship-tourism nexus is a relatively straightforward two-way relationship. On one hand sponsorship may generate tourism with, for example, the stimulus for sports spectators to travel being provided by a sponsored event. Conversely, tourism may generate sponsorship as real or potential tourism flows between regions make sponsorship attractive. However, in addition to this two-way relationship, there is also a broader contextual influence arising from what Boyle and Haines (2000, p. 47) refer to as a "triangular relationship" between television, sport and sponsorship. This relationship has led to, for example, world championship boxing matches in the UK being staged in the middle of the night to allow US sponsors to reach their prime-time target markets on the American east coast. Similarly, domestic soccer in England and Scotland, which has traditionally been played on a Saturday afternoon, and thus facilitated traveling support on what is for many a non-work day, can now, due to the influence of television and sponsors, be played on any day of the week at any time, thus making it much more difficult for supporters to travel to watch their team. Such traveling football supporters, like many others whose travel is significant in respect of the sponsorship-tourism relationship, can be labeled as sports tourists. Consequently, a range of sports tourist types will be examined later in the chapter as the "micro" elements of the sponsorship-tourism relationship are examined. However, before this and the "macro" elements of the relationship are considered, some introductory comments relating to tourism definitions and the examination of tourism flows are useful.

Tourism Definitions and the Study of Tourism Flows

There have been many attempts to define tourism. They all emphasize travel away from home and most also stipulate that travel is for leisure purposes, although some still include business trips. While the travel element is a necessary descriptor, the extent to which other characteristics and constraints are included is, in part, linked to different emphases (even motives) behind the varying definitions. For example, some would view tourism as an economic activity or industry and according to Ryan (1991, p. 5) this might suggest tourism being defined as: "a study of the demand for and supply of accommodation and supportive services for those staying away from home, and the resultant patterns of expenditure, income creation and employment." Similarly, Hay (1989) defines tourism as: "...a process concerned with the redistribution of economic resources, from a home community to a host community which involves a trip for leisure purposes." Others highlight the psychological benefits and define tourism in terms of motivations (see Smith, 1989) while tourist organizations often suggest technical definitions which lay down minimum and maximum lengths of stay and strict "purpose of visit categories" in an attempt to isolate tourism from other forms of travel for statistical purposes (Cooper, Fletcher, Wanhill, Gilbert & Shepherd, 1998).

The major distinction between most definitions is whether or not day trips are included. Whereas most earlier definitions of tourism included the requirement of one or more nights away from home (e.g. World Tourism Organisation, 1963, 1991), more recently there has been a willingness to extend the definition to include day trips as well. The problem with including day trips, of course, is that it introduces further definitional issues of what constitutes such a trip. Does it require a minimum length of time and minimum distance travelled away from home? Some definitions have attempted to include precise prescriptions in this respect. The Scottish Tourist Board, for example, sees a leisure day trip as one involving more than three hours and focusing upon a specific activity (quoted in Standeven & Tomlinson, 1994). But essentially such prescriptions are arbitrary. Nevertheless, despite such problems, a number of authorities have suggested a wider more inclusive approach. The British Tourist Authority (1981, p. 3), for example, has defined tourism in rather broader terms as: "the temporary short-term movement of people to destinations outside the places where they normally live and work, and their activities during the stay at these destinations; it includes movement for all purposes as well as day visits and excursions." This is similar to the working definition adopted by Standeven and Tomlinson (1994) who see tourism as ranging from day trips within ones own locality to long-haul package holidays to the other side of the world – but, most importantly, always involving a sense of movement or visit. The key element here is that tourism involves movement away from the usual environment. However, such movement need not necessarily involve a significant distance or an overnight stay, rather the emphasis is on movements that are perceived, by those undertaking them, as being distinct from and outside of their "usual environments." Consequently, such perceptual definitions are inclusive rather than exclusive, and encompass all activities and trips that the tourist considers to be tourism. Such definitions are of little use to those compiling tourism statistics, as they do not provide the parameters by which tourists can be easily identified. However, perceptual definitions are perhaps the most useful in conceptualising the nature of tourism and the behaviours of the tourist and, as such, it is this understanding of tourism and the tourist that will be used in the discussions in this chapter.

Having established the nature of tourism and the tourist, it is possible to introduce the concept of travel propensity. Whilst there are a wide range of individual motivations to travel, travel propensity is a macro concept relating to the propensity of a population to travel (Boniface & Cooper, 2001, p. 13). Travel propensity is usually understood to refer to national populations, but the concept can be applied to any population that exhibits similar characteristics, or that is subject to similar influences. Consequently, a local area's travel propensity might be examined, or the travel propensity of particular subcultures or groups considered.

Travel propensity is a function of contextual, personal and supply factors (Boniface & Cooper, 2001, p. 14). Contextual influences relate to levels of economic development and affluence, population characteristics and, political and/ or power relations. More personal influences are related to variations in lifestyle, life cycle, and personality. Finally, supply factors relate to the availability and perceived availability of tourism opportunities and include such influences as technology, price, frequency and speed of transport, as well as the characteristics of accommodation, facilities and travel organizers.

The travel propensity of a particular population will clearly have an effect on the tourism flows between the regions in which such populations live. As such, travel propensity, and the factors which influence it, are a key consideration in modeling the tourism system (see Leiper, 1979), which illustrates the 'flow' of tourists between regions (see Figure 5.1).

The model of the tourism system shown in Figure 5.1 illustrates not only the 'flows' of tourists between regions, but also the factors that influence such flows. For example, the travel propensity of the tourist generating region is influenced by local contextual and personal factors, by contextual, personal and supply factors local to the tourist destination region, and by global contextual influences. Such global influences also play a part in shaping local influences in both the tourist generating and destination regions. The tourism flows that are a result of these influences are a form of macro spatial interaction between

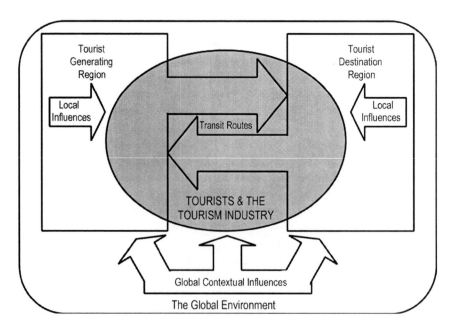

Figure 5.1 *The tourism system (adapted from Leiper, 1979).*

regions (Boniface & Cooper, 2001, p. 5). Such flows are highly complex and, as the model outlined here has begun to indicate, are influenced by a wide variety of interrelated variables.

The purpose of this chapter is to examine both the place of sports sponsorship as one among a number of variables that might influence tourism flows, and the influence that specific actual or potential tourism flows might have on levels of sports sponsorship. At the macro-level this involves a consideration of globalization processes and their effects on tourism flows, alongside the various factors that might influence tourism flows and how sports sponsorship might both contribute to and result from such flows. At a micro-level the emphasis shifts to individual tourism motivations and behaviours, and an examination of the interrelationship between the travel patterns of different types of sports tourists and sports sponsorship. In each case, the discussions are by necessity speculative as the relationship between sports sponsorship and tourism do not appear to have been previously considered or researched.

Sports Sponsorship and Tourism Flows – A Macro Analysis

The starting point for a macro-analysis of the relationship between sports sponsorship and tourism flows is a consideration of globalization processes (see Houlihan, 2003) and the role of the media (see Stead, 2003). Globalization and the existence of global media impacts upon both tourists perceptions and sponsors decisions. Tourists exposed to global media will perceive that there are more places in the world that are accessible to them, whilst sponsors will be interested in the "reach" of products in a global marketplace. However, before proceeding to a more detailed examination of the impact of globalization, some consideration of the use of the term is useful.

Scholte (2000) identifies five types of globalization processes that are in common use. Firstly, globalization as a process of *internationalization* is considered. Internationalization refers to the increase in cross-border exchanges, particularly trade exchanges, but also exchanges of people and ideas (Stewart, 1997). In terms of tourism this will result in an increase in tourism flows as more people travel and people travel more regularly, whilst sports sponsors will increasingly be looking to sponsor products that can have an international impact. The second process of globalization identified by Scholte (2000) is that of *liberalization*, which refers to the removal of restrictions on cross-border business, and is largely a result of the efforts of the World Trade Organization and regional organizations such as the European Union and the North American Free Trade Agreement (Jones, Kavanagh, Moian & Norton, 2001). This results in an increase in global media ownership, and the ability of both sponsors and tourism providers to reach populations that might previously have been beyond them.

The *universalization* of culture is the third globalization process that Scholte (2000) identifies. This simply refers to the convergence and synthesis of existing cultures and the move towards a global culture that produces an increasingly homogenous cultural experience throughout the world (Held, McGrew, Goldblatt & Periaton, 1999). Whilst on the one hand this will mean that many tourists will feel safer when they travel as their experiences will be familiar and therefore unthreatening, it will also mean that more intrepid tourists will have to search more extensively for unusual tourism experiences. For sports sponsors, access to mainstream markets will be easier, but they will have to work harder to reach an increasing number of niche markets. Fourthly, Scholte (2000) discusses globalization as a process of *Westernization* or *Americanization*, where the social structures of inter alia capitalism, modernity, industrialism and representative democracy are spread throughout the world (Axford, 2002). This will result in populations in net tourism destination regions, which are often semi-periphery or periphery countries (Shaw & Williams, 2002), adopting both the methods and the symbols of Western capitalism. Periphery countries are those less-developed nations that have previously been referred to as the 'third world'. However, of importance to both the expansion of tourism and the reach of sports sponsorship are those semi-periphery countries that are developing rapidly and so are not really part of the less developed periphery, but that have not reached the levels of economic development of the more developed areas that Shaw and Williams (2002) characterize as "core" countries. The desire to adopt the methods and symbols of Western capitalism in semi-periphery countries makes them more open to the messages of sports sponsors, and more interested in the activities of international tourists. This could lead to an increase in crime, as Western possessions are coveted, and/or to a more welcoming attitude to such tourists as local populations seek to learn about the cultural (often sporting) icons to which they have been exposed through a global media. The final globalization process described by Scholte (2000) is that of *deterritorialization*, whereby the spatial organisation of social relations is altered as a result in changes in perceptions of space, location and distance (Houlihan, 2003). This will mean that flows from tourism-generating regions increase as tourists perceive that previously inaccessible destinations are within their reach. It also means that aspirations to, and support for, Western sports teams, individuals and products spread far beyond their traditional boundaries, offering many more opportunities for sports sponsors.

In summary, then, globalization processes result in increases in the size and spatial extent of tourism flows, in increases in the global reach of sponsorship messages, in easier access to mainstream markets alongside an increase in the number of niche markets that may be less accessible, and in greater interaction and cultural exchanges, both legal and illegal, between tourists and local residents as cultures converge. The effects of such globalization processes provide the context for a macro analysis of how different forms of sponsorship influence travel propensities, and thus tourism flows, between particular populations, alongside a discussion of the extent to which such travel propensities may influence sports sponsorship.

Robinson (2003) identifies six broad areas of sports sponsorship – event sponsorship, sponsorship of individuals, team sponsorship, competition sponsorship, sponsorship of venues, and sponsorship of sports development schemes. Here, by way of illustration, the macro-relationship between sports sponsorship and tourism flows will be considered in relation to the first three, and perhaps the most widespread of these, event, individual and team sponsorship.

Sponsorship of events can occur at a number of different levels, indeed both Gratton, Dobson and Shibli (2000) and Roche (2001) have proposed typologies of events that illustrate such levels. However, in relation to sponsorship opportunities it is perhaps useful to consider a range of events that begins with global, one-off multi-sport events like the Olympics, moving through regular events like the Wimbledon Tennis Championships and bi-polar exchanges such as golf's Ryder Cup, to smaller national or local level festivals or events.

At the global level, events such as the Olympics are becoming increasingly pervasive and reaching into the lives of a rapidly expanding proportion of the world's population (Maguire, 1999). As global culture becomes more universal and Western/American values increasingly dominate such culture, the impact of sponsorships of such events expand into hitherto unreachable areas (Sport Business, 2003). The promotion of Western/American values and the symbols of Western capitalism increase the desire to travel in semi-periphery countries that are net tourism destination regions (Holloway, 2003). This increased travel propensity in destination regions increases flows to those Western countries that have historically been net generating regions and contributes towards a reduction of tourism balance of payments in such regions. The reach of sponsors to semi-periphery countries is entirely dependent on the development of a global media, as it is through such media that products such as Nike and Coca-Cola become associated with global sport and an increasingly Westernized/Americanized world culture (Rowe, 1999). These influences are contextual and exist at the global level, although levels of economic development in semi-periphery countries that enable travel and the purchase of Western goods are also required for such processes to take place.

Sponsors of events such as the Olympic Games largely target mediated spectators, and such mediated spectators can also be the target of sponsors of events such as the Ryder Cup. However, the experience of those traveling to watch the event is also targeted, with sponsors often trying to create an association not only with the event, but also with the experience of the trip. Here travel propensity factors such as personal lifestyle influences are important as tourists seek to develop an association with particular sports and particular types of travel. This association can be communicated to others through particular products that are seen as part of such a lifestyle (Nixon & Frey, 1996) and in creating such an association sponsors both benefit from, and to a certain extent, generate tourism flows. A good example of the association of products with trip experience is the presence of Robinsons Barley Water at the Wimbledon Tennis Championships. Here the product is associated with the quintessential Englishness of a visit to the

All-England Tennis Club's Open Championships at Wimbledon. The benefits of this association for the sponsor are clearly linked to the trip experience, and the part their product plays in the memories generated by the trip.

For smaller events, travel flows within national boundaries are important (Gibson, Willming & Holdnack, 2003; Higham & Hinch, 2002) and consequently it is local contextual, personal and supply characteristics that are significant. Flows between regions within countries can be submitted to the same sort of analysis as international tourism flows, with some areas being net destination regions, and others being net receiving regions. In the UK in recent years, areas that would traditionally have been tourism-generating regions have attempted to use sports events to reduce their tourism deficit. Sheffield is one such example (Shibli & Gratton, 2001; SCCSDEU, 1995) of a city that has staged a number of events, from large-scale international championships (e.g. World Student Games) to more modest national junior championships in swimming and athletics. The tourism flows generated by these latter smaller events can be attractive to sponsors as junior championships not only attract junior competitors, but also their families, and often members of their extended family and friends (Weed & Bull, 2004). Such a broad captive audience has meant that junior sports events have attracted a wide range of sponsors in recent years, but have also (in the UK at least) been subjected to relatively strict rules in terms of the types of sponsorship allowed for fear of corrupting children with messages aimed at an adult market (sponsorship agreements involving alcoholic products, for example, are not permitted in junior sport).

The second broad area of sponsorship identified by Robinson (2003) is that of sponsorship of individuals (see Grainger et al., this volume, for a more detailed analysis of global sport sponsorship campaigns centred on celebrities). Given increasing internationalization and universalization of culture, sponsors increasingly feel they can reach their mainstream markets through the sponsorship of a key number of individuals who they would see as global properties. Nike's sponsorship of basketball's Michael Jordan and adidas's sponsorship of the English soccer star David Beckham are examples of sponsorships that are seen to have a global reach. However, despite the increasing popularity of American sports such as baseball and basketball in Europe and repeated attempts to interest mainstream American markets in soccer, there are few sports that are both big enough (in terms of fan and player bases) *and* geographically spread throughout the globe to be regarded as having a truly global reach (Lentell, 1997). Athletics is perhaps the biggest sport that can be said to have a truly global geographical spread. However, its spectator and participant base can in no way rival that of soccer, basketball or baseball (Ebersol, 2003). The result is competition among traditional North American sports and traditional European sports for supremacy in the global marketplace, and particularly in the relatively untapped markets in semi-periphery and periphery countries. This is where globalizing forces associated with Americanization have not been as pervasive as in other areas. Furthermore, in addition to European and American sports, there are other sports that are largely associated with the former British Empire (now the Commonwealth), such as rugby union and cricket.

It is in this tension between the cultures and global spreads of different sports that one of the most interesting elements of the relationship between sports sponsorship and tourism manifests itself in the example of the Caribbean. Sporting culture, and indeed much of mainstream culture, in the Caribbean has long been centered on cricket (Burton, 1991). However, the iconic status of American sports stars such as Michael Jordan, largely created through the worldwide marketing of his name and image by his major international sponsors, has meant that for a new generation of young people from the Caribbean, personal lifestyle preferences are moving towards such American sporting cultures rather than the traditional Caribbean sporting culture largely centered on cricket. As a consequence, tourism propensities become shaped by such sporting preferences and, rather than being centered on Commonwealth countries, such travel propensities focus on North America and the culture that many young people associate with it. That such propensities are shaped by international sporting icons, marketed and promoted worldwide largely through their sponsors, serves to highlight the disparate range of areas in which the relationship between sports sponsorship and tourism can be important.

Sponsors of sports teams, the third area of sponsorship identified by Robinson (2003), are similarly interested in "products" that have a global reach. Notwithstanding some of the comments relating to the global nature of different sports above, Manchester United, Chelsea and Arsenal are three examples of teams in the English Premiership (soccer) that can provide exposure into a wide range of markets around the globe. Furthermore, in many semi-periphery countries, that are seen as untapped markets by many potential and actual sports sponsors, football is one of the most popular sports (Darby, 2001). Increasing global de-territorialization, which reduces perceptions of distances and access around the world, coupled with both contextual and tourism supply factors, such as increasing affluence and perceived travel opportunities in semi-periphery countries, sees a broadening travel aspiration from countries that have traditionally been net receiving areas. In many areas sports sponsors seek to tap into this increasingly pervasive Western lifestyle. Both Manchester United and Arsenal are sponsored by mobile phone companies, perhaps one of the strongest symbols of Western capitalism and affluence, and a clear aspirational product associated with Western lifestyles by many people in semi-periphery countries. Such associations serve only to increase the travel propensities of populations, particularly the younger generations, in such countries.

Having discussed three of the most widespread areas of sports sponsorship identified by Robinson (2003) and their macro-level influence on the relationship with tourism, the discussion will now turn to a micro-analysis of this relationship. Here the emphasis is on the travel preferences of a range of types of sports tourists that might either attract or be stimulated by the involvement of sponsors.

Sports Sponsorship and Tourism Flows – A Micro-Analysis

In examining the micro-element of the sports sponsorship-tourism nexus it is useful to refer to Weed and Bull's (2004) Sports Tourism Participation Model. This model identifies a range of sports tourist types and examines how identity can be important in motivating and constructing sports tourism trips. It allows an examination of individual sports tourism profiles as well as facilitating a consideration of the behaviours of a range of sports tourist types. The model incorporates ideas developed through a range of studies at Loughborough University (Jackson & Reeves, 1996; Reeves, 2000; Jackson & Weed, 2003) that proposed the concept of a sports tourism demand continuum. The sports tourism demand continuum takes its basic concept from the English Sports Council's "Sports Development Continuum" (Sport England, 1997) that plots the movement of sports participants from the introductory Foundation level, through Participation and Performance, to the elite Excellence level. The sports tourism demand continuum, similarly, begins with Incidental sports participation on general holidays and moves through various levels of commitment – Sporadic, Occasional, Regular and Committed – ending with the Driven sports tourist involved in year-round travel for elite competition and training. This continuum is incorporated within the Sports Tourism Participation Model, which includes and emphasizes a consideration of the importance of identity (see Figure 5.2)

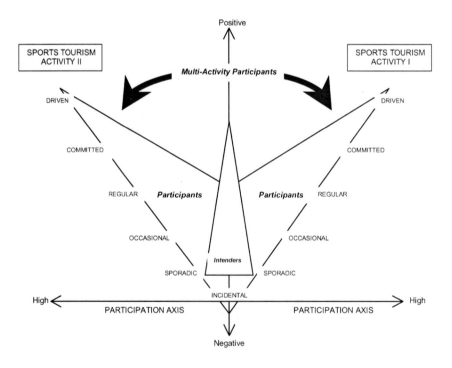

Figure 5.2 *Sports tourism participation model (Weed & Bull, 2004).*

The model plots participation against the importance placed by sports tourists on their sports tourism participation. It also shows that sports tourism participants are likely to take part in multiple activities (Standeven & DeKnop, 1999), and although Figure 5.2 only illustrates two activities (one on the right and one on the left of the central importance axis), the model can be envisaged as three dimensional with a potentially infinite number of activities "growing out" around the center axis to create a "bowl" shape. Including this multi-activity dimension allows for the different characteristics of individual sports tourists to be plotted in relation to their full-participation profile.

A key assumption of the Sports Tourism Participation Model is that for some participants at the Incidental end of the continuum, sports tourism trips may be of significant importance to individual's perceived self-identity (Weed, 2002). Furthermore, for those falling into the two adjacent categories to Incidental participants (Sporadic and Occasional participants), the relatively rare sports tourism trip – or sports opportunity on a general tourism trip – may be of great importance in shaping self-identity and perception on return from such a trip. Consequently, although actual levels of participation may be low, the experience is defined as much by the retelling of participation as by participation itself. MacCannell (1996, p. 4) describes this tourism phenomenon, explaining that "returning home is an essential part of being a tourist – one goes only to return." For MacCannell tourists are people who leave home in the expectation that they will have some kind of experience of "otherness" that will set them apart from their peers on their return. This experience of otherness (i.e. sports tourism) that can be told and retold to peers, often based on only sporadic or incidental participation, is what can make sports tourism important to individuals for whom actual levels of participation are low. For other participants at the incidental end of the continuum, sports tourism can actually be of negative importance – that is, although participation takes place, there is actually an antipathy towards it. This has been evidenced by Reeves (2000), who describes participation that takes place as a "duty" to others such as children or partners.

At the Driven end of the scale, both participation and importance will be high as sport clearly plays a central role in shaping self-identity (Weed & Bull, 2004). Whilst many Driven sports tourists are elite athletes, this is not a defining characteristic of this category. Participants at this extreme may be taking part in non-competitive activities such as potholing, in which case the concept of an elite athlete is difficult to apply, or may simply have very high levels of commitment to the sports tourism, rather than the sports experience. While the English Sports Council's Sports Development Continuum assumes an increase in ability with a move along the continuum, this is not the case with the Sports Tourism Participation Model, as this would call into question the applicability of this model to sports spectators. It is difficult to reconcile the implication that levels of ability increase with a movement along the scale through the categories with the concept of sports spectating, as it is difficult to imagine how one's ability as a sports spectator could be defined. Consequently, the implication that levels of ability increase with a movement along the model is discarded, and the focus, again, is on participation and importance. For sports spectators this might usefully be illustrated by reference to football fans. At the Incidental end of the scale will be a vast number of people for whom identity as a football fan is of great importance, but for whom participation in live football spectating as a sports tourism experience is minimal. Similarly, there will be those who have spectated at football, but for whom it is not an important part of their identity. In fact, it is likely that, for some, it has a negative importance as participation has been out of a sense of duty to others. At the Driven end of the scale, there are those for whom participation as a football spectator is high, and for whom it is a defining part of their lives. Some of the material on football hooliganism is illustrative of this (see, for example, Weed, 2001).

The final aspect of the model is the inclusion of the 'Intenders' group. This group was drawn from work on arts audiences by Hill, O'Sullivan and O'Sullivan (1995, p. 43) and was described as "those who think the arts are a 'good thing' and like the idea of attending, but never seem to get around to it." Such a concept is also useful in relation to sports tourism, and perhaps sports spectators provide the most useful illustration. The growth in televised coverage of sport has created a vast number of sports spectators who are highly committed, and for whom watching sport is important, but who rarely travel to a live event. Many such spectators often express a desire to go to a live event, but like Hill et al.'s (1995) arts intenders, "never seem to get around to it." Of course, some intenders will attend the odd match, and so the boundary with incidental participation is fluid. However, this group is largely made up of those for whom watching sport is important, but for whom attending a live event never becomes more than a whimsical intention.

The Intenders categorization is, of course, equally significant in relation to active sports tourism. In the same research in which he identified holiday sports participation that takes place as a duty to others, Reeves (2000) also describes those who go on holiday with the intention of taking up some of the sports opportunities available, but never actually get round to it. The promotion of the range of sports opportunities available in hotel and resort brochures can create the intention to participate in sport on holiday, but in many cases such intention is not converted into actual participation. Even where such incidental sports opportunities may play a part in resort or hotel choice, and the intention may be described to peers pre-trip as a way of boosting perceived identity, there is no guarantee that such intention will be converted into actual participation. Thus, while importance may be high, participation is very low or non-existent, and such people rarely become actual participants.

Having identified the nature and features of a range of sports tourist types illustrated in Weed and Bull's (2004) model, it is now possible to examine the relationship between the travel patterns of such sports tourists and sports sponsorship. An example from the Driven end of the model is that of the elite athlete, a fairly atypical group in sports tourism terms, but a group that represents some of the most prolific travellers for sports purposes. Earlier in this chapter it was mentioned that elite athletes' travel is often enabled by sports sponsorship, and both Jackson and Reeves (1998) and Jackson and Weed (2003) identify this as a defining feature of this group. It is perhaps interesting to illustrate the extent of the travel flows enabled by sponsorship in this area. Studies of elite British track athletes (Jackson & Reeves, 1998; Reeves, 2000) have shown that the number of days traveled per year can be significant, and ranges from 69 days a year for a junior international to 146 days for an established senior athlete (see Table 5.1)

Table 5.1 *Travel patterns of elite British track athletes*

Two illustrative examples of annual travel volumes for training and competition:

Andrew Young (20) GB & Scotland Junior International, 800m		Mark Richardson (23) GB & England Senior International, 400m	
Days per year traveled for…		*Days per year traveled for…*	
Training in the UK	16	Training in the UK	40
Competition in the UK	29	Competition in the UK	20
Training Overseas	14	Training Overseas	38
Competition Overseas	10	Competition Overseas	48
TOTAL	69 days	TOTAL	146 days

Illustrative comments on training and competition overseas:

"This year I went to Lanzarote for a week at the end of February. I then went to Jamaica for a week in March. I have also been to Portugal, America and Spain to train." (Mark Richardson, 23, GB & England Senior International, 400m)

"I went to Portugal for one week, I have been to Gainsville, Florida for two weeks, I was also in France earlier this year for four or five days, to catch up on a bit of pre-season warm weather training." (Lesley Owusu, 17, GB & England Junior International, 200m)

"I have been to Portugal for two weeks, I have been to New Zealand for a month, I have been to America for a week and I have been to Spain for a week on numerous occasions." (Paul Hibbert, 30, England Senior International, 400m hurdles)

"I've been to Uruguay, Holland, California, Tenerife, Spain, South Africa and most other European countries." (Jackie Agyepong, 26, GB & England Senior International, 100m hurdles)

Sources: Reeves (2000); Jackson and Reeves (1998), presented in Weed and Bull (2004)

Clearly these volumes of travel represent considerable tourism flows, and if they are multiplied across all sports in all countries, then the sponsorship of elite sport is responsible for considerable travel around the world. It should perhaps be noted that if sports sponsorship did not exist, then the travel of elite athletes would not cease, but it would be severely curtailed, and as such in this area alone, the relationship between sports sponsorship and tourism is a significant one.

Moving back along the participation triangle to the committed sports tourist, it is possible to examine the involvement of sponsors in "extreme" and "alternative" sports. An interesting example here is the "X-Games" owned and organized in the USA by ESPN. Conceived by ESPN's Director of Programming in 1993, and first staged in 1995, the "extreme Olympics" provide an example of a sponsor actually owning and organizing a competition. In this case, without ESPN's involvement the X-Games would not exist, and the travel flows generated among the extreme sports subculture would not take place. A key feature of "extreme sport" sports tourists is the centrality of the sports to their identity and their lifestyle, and as such there is a significant amount of importance placed on such trips. Furthermore, the nature of such sports is that while they are undoubtedly competitive, they are also participatory, with the delineation between elite and recreational participants being much weaker than for many mainstream sports (Donnelly, 1993; Lentell, 1997). As such, the X-Games, and a growing number of similar events, stimulate travel among the broader extreme sports subculture, with many people travelling to simply be in the same place as other sports tourists with similar interests to "celebrate the subculture" (Green & Chalip, 1998). Clearly the role of ESPN as event sponsor and organiser is central to the generation of these tourism flows.

Participants in many road running, triathlon and other such mass participation events can be numbered among the "regular" and "occasional" type of sports tourist. For many such participants, sport is often a significant part of their lifestyle (Smith, 1998), and thus important to their sense of identity, but the sports tourism experience is perhaps not so important, hence their characterization as "regular"/"occasional" rather than "committed" sports tourists. However, the participation in a range of events "outside their usual environments" by such people, means that they can be located within the Sports Tourism Participation Model. Furthermore, such events generate considerable travel flows, with many participants traveling with family groups, who are often in attendance as spectators supporting their partners, parents, or in some cases children (Weed & Bull, 2004). Whilst such travel is often day-trip or one-night-stay tourism, the volumes generated can be significant – in fact, the London Marathon accepted 45,500 entrants in 2002 (London Marathon Ltd, 2003). This represents a captive audience of participants with a significant interest in sport and in sports products, along with families and friends of such people who may also have similar interests. While the big city marathons usually generate media interest, sponsors of both these events, and smaller events without media coverage, are attracted to the event by the captive audience generated by the tourism flows to such events.

A prime example of a non-media event that generates significant travel flows and thus interests sponsors is the World Masters Swimming Championships, a participatory competition for swimmers over the age of 25 and up to 90 years plus. A study of the 1996 event in Sheffield (Dobson & Gratton, 1997) found that the event attracted almost 7,000 participants (competitors, coaches, officials, etc.), with the average length of stay being 5.4 nights. When friends and family are added to these numbers, it is likely that the total number attracted would be close to 10,000. For a non-media event, this is a significant captive audience to interest sponsors, and most of the participants are relatively well off (largely social classes ABC1), as evidenced by an average spend per person per day of almost £100. Consequently, the ability of the event to put around 10,000 like-minded people with above average disposable income in one place for a concentrated period of time represents a considerable sponsorship opportunity.

Towards the Incidental end of the Sports Tourism Participation Model, the link between sports tourists and sports sponsorship is weaker, as the travel patterns related to sport of the "incidental" and "sporadic" groups are more erratic and often difficult to predict. There are some examples of sports participation/development programmes, often aimed at children, being sponsored in holiday destinations and holiday "camps" (e.g. Butlins in the UK – see Reeves, 2000). However, generally the relationship at this end of the model is less significant.

It is perhaps worth noting the importance of mediated sponsorship and the "Intenders" group. As described earlier, intenders are positively disposed to the idea of sports related travel, but "never quite get round it." Such positive attitudes towards the idea of sports tourism often means that intenders consume a great deal of mediated sport, and thus are an important target audience for sponsors. The key difference between intenders and ordinary watchers of televised sports is that intenders often make an "imagined journey" (Gammon, 2002) to the destination, and often feel as though they are participating interactively with the event (Weed, 2003). This may result in this group being more open to sponsors' messages than the passive consumer of televised sports events, and is the reason for the scheduling of some sports events to please mediated rather than live spectators as noted in the introduction. The relationship here may be between "virtual" sports tourism and sponsorship, although this is an area about which very little is known.

Summary and Observations

It has been the aim of this chapter to explore some of the areas in which there may be a significant relationship between sports sponsorship and tourism flows. The chapter has sought to be illustrative rather than comprehensive, and as such there are likely to be a range of further areas not discussed in this chapter in which the sports sponsorship-tourism relationship is important. The area has been conceptualized through the employment of Leiper's (1979) model of the tourism system and Weed and Bull's (2004) Sports Tourism Participation Model. At the macro-level, some of the discussions have been necessarily abstract, as there has been no previous research that examines the relationships explored. However, in illustrating the micro-aspects of the relationship it has been possible to identify some clear examples of the issues highlighted.

As a contribution to a text on global sports sponsorship, this chapter is intended to stimulate thinking about the reciprocal relationship between sponsorship decisions and tourism flows. It provides no answers as it is not the result of empirical research, nor has it been possible to draw on relevant empirical material as the area does not appear to have been explored before. Some research has taken place on the ways in which sports tourism facilities and events may secure sponsorship (Delpy, Giabijas & Stefunsitch, 1998), but such a "how-to" approach would not have been appropriate in this chapter, and would make little contribution to the development of a broader understanding of global sports sponsorship that is the aim of this book. Furthermore, the broader focus on tourism flows has illustrated that both sports sponsorship and tourism are global phenomena, and subject to the same globalizing forces. Consequently, as this chapter is read alongside other contributions to this text, the importance of a global perspective on both sponsorship and tourism, and the range of macro-forces that drive the growth of each in a range of cultures and economies around the world is brought into sharper focus. While many would cite economic forces as the most important influence in a global society, the macro-analysis of the sports sponsorship-tourism nexus in this chapter has highlighted the importance of cultural influences in the global spread of both tourism and sport. Furthermore, the importance of an appreciation of subcultures, lifestyles and identities at the micro-level serves to further reinforce the importance of a cultural perspective. While, undoubtedly, it is economic forces that drive the global growth of sports sponsorship, the cultural elements and influences operating in both tourism and sport are likely to have some effect on the extent to which sports sponsorship will be able to reach new and emerging markets in a wide range of disparate populations around the globe.

References

Agne-Traub, L. (1989) "Volkssporting and tourism: something for the working class." *Leisure Information Quarterly*, 15(4): 6–8.

Axford, B. (2002) "The processes of globalisation," in Axford, B., Browning, G. K., Huggins, R., Rosamond, B. and Turner, J. (eds), *Politics: An Introduction*, 2nd edition, London: Routledge, pp. 524–562.

Boniface, B. G. and Cooper, C. (2001) *Worldwide Destinations: The Geography of Travel and Tourism*. Oxford: Butterworth Heinemann.

Boon, M. A. (1984) "Understanding Skiing Behaviour." *Society and Leisure*, 7(2): 397–406.

Boyle, R. and Haines, R. (2000) *Power Play: Sport, the Media and Popular Culture*. Harlow: Longman.

Bratton, R. D. (1988) "Amateur Sport and the Tourism Industry in Calgary: A progress report." *Post Olympic Sociology Colloquium*, Calgary.

British Tourist Authority (1981) *Tourism, the UK – The Broad Perspective*, London: BTA.

Burton, R. D. E. (1991) "Cricket, Carnival and street culture in the Caribbean," in Jarvie, G. (ed.), *Sport, Racism and Ethnicity*. London: Falmer Press, pp. 7–29.

Collins, M. F. and Jackson, G. A. M. (1999) "The Economic Impact of Sport and Tourism," in Standeven, J. and De Knop, P. (eds), *Sport Tourism*. London: Human Kinetics, pp. 169–202.

Cooper, C. P., Fletcher, J., Wanhill, S., Gilbert, D. and Shepherd, R. (1998) *Tourism: Principles and Practice*, 2nd edn. Harlow: Pitman.

Darby, P. (2001) *Africa and Football's Global Order*. London: Frank Cass.

Delpy, L., Grabijas, M. and Stefanovich, A. (1998) "Sport tourism and corporate sponsorship: A winning combination." *Journal of Vacation Marketing*, 4(1): 91–101.

De Knop, P. (1990) "Sport for All and Active Tourism." *Journal of the World Leisure and Recreation Association*, Fall, pp. 30–36.

Dobson, N. and Gratton, C. (1997) *The Economic Impact of Sports Events: Euro '96 and VI Fina World Masters Swimming Championship in Sheffield*. Sheffield: Leisure Industries Research Centre.

Donnelly, P. (1993) "Subcultures in Sport: Resilience and Transformation," in Ingham, A. G. and Loy, J. W. (eds), *Sport in Social Development: Traditions, Transitions and Transformations*. Illinois: Human Kinetics Publishers, pp. 119–146.

Ebersol, D. (2003) "Big 4 Rivals Set for Collapse." *Sport Business International*, October.

Gammon, S. (2002) "Fantasy, Nostalgia and the Pursuit of What Never Was," in Gammon, S. and Kurtzman, J. (eds), *Sport Tourism: Principles and Practice*. Eastbourne: LSA, pp. 61–71.

Gibson, H. J. (1998) "Sport Tourism: A Critical Analysis of Research." *Sport Management Review*, 1(1): 45–76.

Gibson, H. J., Willming, C. and Holdnack, A. (2003) "Small-scale event sport tourism: Fans as tourists." *Tourism Management*, 24.

Glyptis, S. A. (1982) *Sport and Tourism in Western Europe*. London: British Travel Education Trust.

Glyptis, S. A. (1991) "Sport and Tourism," in Cooper, C. P. (ed.) *Progress in Tourism, Recreation and Hospitality Management*, Vol. 3. London: Belhaven Press.

Gratton, C., Dobson, N. and Shibli, S. (2000) "The Economic Impacts of Major Sports Events: A Case-Study of Six Events." *Managing Leisure*, 5(1): 17–28.

Green, B. C. and Chalip, L. (1998) "Sport Tourism as the Celebration of Subculture," *Annals of Tourism Research*, 25(2): 275–291.

Hay, B (1989) "Leisure Day Trips: The New Tourism," in Botterill, D. (ed.) *Tourism and Leisure (Part Two): Markets, Users and Sites*. Eastbourne: Leisure Studies Association.

Held, D., McGrew, A., Goldblatt, D. and Perraton, J. (1999) *Global Transformations: Politics, Economics and Culture*. Cambridge: Polity Press.

Higham, J. and Hinch, T. (2002) "Tourism, sport and seasons: The challenges and potential of overcoming seasonality in the sport and tourism sectors." *Tourism Management*, 23: 175–185.

Hill, E., O'Sullivan, T. and O'Sullivan, C. (1995) *Creative Arts Marketing*. Oxford: Butterworth Heinemann.

Hinch, T. D. and Higham, J. E. S. (2004) *Sport Tourism Development*. Clevedon: Channel View Publications, forthcoming.

Holloway, J. C. (2004) *The Business of Tourism*, 6th edn. Harlow: Financial Times Prentice Hall

Houlihan, B. (2003) "Sport and Globalisation," in Houlihan, B. (ed.) *Sport in Society*. London: Sage, pp. 345–363.

Jackson, G. A. M. and Glyptis, S. A. (1992) *Sport and Tourism: A Review of the Literature*. Report to the Sports Council, Recreation Management Group, Loughborough University. Loughborough: Unpublished.

Jackson, G. A. M. and Reeves, M. R. (1996) "Conceptualising the Sport-Tourism Interrelationship: A Case Study Approach." *Paper to the LSA/VVA Conference*, Wageningen, September.

Jackson, G. A. M. and Reeves, M. R. (1998) "Evidencing the Sport-Tourism Interrelationship: A Case Study of Elite British Athletes," in Collins, M. F. and Cooper, I. (eds), *Leisure Management: Issues and Applications*. London: CABI, pp. 263–275.

Jackson, G. A. M. and Weed, M. E. (2003) "The Sport-Tourism Interrelationship," in Houlihan, B. (ed.), *Sport and Society*. London: Sage, pp. 235–251.

Jones, B., Kavanagh, D., Moran, M. and Norton, P. (2001) *Politics UK*, 4th edn. Harlow: Longman.

Leiper, N. (1979) "The framework of tourism." *Annals of Tourism Research*, 6(4): 390–407.

Leisure Consultants (1992) *Activity Holidays: A Growth Market in Tourism*. Sudbury: Leisure Consultants.

Lentell, R. (1997) "Sport: Origins, Transformation and the Growth of Knowledge," in Scarrot, M. (ed.) *Sport and Recreation Information Sources: Proceedings of a Seminar Organised by the Sport and Recreation Information Group*. Sheffield: SPRIG, pp. 4–21.

London Marathon Ltd (2003) "Marathon Info." www.london-marathon.co.uk/marathoninfo/racehistory.shtml (accessed Mar 13, 2003).

MacCannell, D. (1996) *Tourist or Traveller?* London: BBC Education.

Maguire, J. (1999) *Global Sport: Identities, Societies, Civilisations*. Cambridge: Polity Press.

Mintel (1999) *Leisure Intelligence: Activity Holidays*. London: Mintel.

Nixon, H. and Frey, J. (1996) *A Sociology of Sport*. Belmont: Wadsworth Publishing Co.

Redmond, G. (1991) "Changing Styles of Sports Tourism: Industry/consumer interactions in Canada, the USA and Europe," in Sinclair, M. T. and Stabler, M. J. (eds), *The Tourist Industry: An International Analysis*. Wallingford: CAB International, pp. 107–120.

Reeves, M. R. (2000) *Evidencing the Sport-Tourism Interrelationship*. Loughborough University: Unpublished PhD Thesis.

Robinson, L. A. (2003) "The Business of Sport," in Houlihan, B. (ed.) *Sport in Society*. London: Sage, pp. 165–183.

Roche, M. (2001) "Mega-Events, Olympic Games and the World Student Games 1991 – Understanding the Impacts and Information Needs of major Sports Events," Paper Presented at the SPRIG Conference, UMIST Manchester, May 1.

Rowe, D. (1999) *Sport, Culture and the Media*. Buckingham: Open University Press.

Ryan, C. (1991) *Recreational Tourism: A Social Science Perspective*. London: Routledge.

Scholte, J. A. (2000) *Globalisation: A Critical Introduction*. Basingstoke: Palgrave.

Shaw, G. and Williams, A. (2002) *Critical Issues in Tourism: A Geographical Perspective*, 2nd edn. Oxford: Blackwell

Sheffield City Council Sports Development and Event Unit (SCCSDEU) (1995) *Major Sports Events Strategy*. Sheffield: SCCSDEU.

Shibli, S. and Gratton, C. (2001) "The Economic Impact of Two Major Sports Events in Two of the UK's National Cities of Sport," in Gratton, C. and Henry, I. P. (eds), *Sport in the City: The Role of Sport in Economic and Social Regeneration*. London: Routledge, pp. 78–89.

Smith, S. (1989) *Tourism Analysis: A Handbook*. Harlow: Longman.

Smith, S. L. (1998) "Athletes, Runners and Joggers: Participant-Group Dynamics in a sport of 'Individuals.'" *Sociology of Sport Journal*, 15: 174–192.

Sport Business (2003) *Maximising the Value of Sponsorship*. London: Sport Business International.

Sport England (1997) *England: The Sporting Nation*. London: Sport England

Standeven, J. and De Knop, P. (1999) *Sport Tourism*. Champaign: Human Kinetics.

Standeven, J. and Tomlinson, A. (1994) *Sport and Tourism in South East England: A Preliminary Assessment*. London: SECSR.

Stead, D. (2003) "Sport and the Media," in Houlihan, B. (ed.), *Sport in Society*. London: Sage, pp. 184–200.

Stewart, R. (1997) *Ideas that Shaped our World*. San Diego: Thunder Bay Press.

Turco, D. M., Riley, R. S. and Swart, K. (2002) *Sport Tourism*. Morgantown: Fitness Information Technology.

Vrondou, O. (1999) *Sports Related Tourism and the Product Repositioning of Traditional Mass Tourism Destinations: A Case Study of Greece*. Loughborough University: Unpublished PhD Thesis.

Weed, M. E. (1999a) "More Than Sports Holidays: An Introduction to the Sport-Tourism Link," in Scarrot, M. (ed.), Proceedings of the Sport and Recreation Information Group Seminar, *Exploring Sports Tourism*. Sheffield: SPRIG, pp. 6–28.

Weed, M. E. (1999b) *Consensual Policies for Sport and Tourism in the UK: An Analysis of Organisational Behaviour and Problems* (PhD Thesis), Canterbury, University of Kent at Canterbury/Canterbury Christ Church College.

Weed, M. E. (2001) "Ing-ger-land at Euro 2000: How 'Handbags at 20 Paces' was portrayed as a full-scale riot." *International Review for the Sociology of Sport*, 36(4), 407–424.

Weed, M. E. (2002) "Sports Tourism and Identity: Developing a Sports Tourism Participation Model," in Laaksonen, K., Lopponen, P. Nykanen, E. and Puronaho, K. (eds), *Proceedings of the 10th European Congress on Sport Management*. Jyvaskyla: EASM, pp. 164–165.

Weed, M. E. (2003) "Mediated and Inebriated: The Pub as a Sports Spectator Venue." Paper to the Leisure Studies Association Conference, *Leisure and Visual Culture*, Roehampton, UK, July.

Weed, M. E. and Bull, C. J. (2004) *Sports Tourism: Participants, Policy and Providers*. Oxford: Elsevier.

World Tourism Organization (1963) *United Nations Conference on International Travel and Tourism*. Madrid: WTO.

World Tourism Organization (1991) *Tourism to the Year 2000: Qualitative Aspects Affecting Global Growth*. Madrid: WTO.

6

The [E-]Business of Sport Sponsorship

Detlev Zwick and Oliver Dieterle

Over the last two decades sport sponsorships have matured to play a dominant role in many organizations' promotional mix. Conversely, many sport organizations, sport event managers, leagues and even individual athletes see lavish corporate spending as the most viable, if not the only, path to profitability (cf. Pitts & Stotlar, 1996). The unique role sport sponsorship plays for sport marketers is also evidenced by the fact that many text books and monographs in the field of sport marketing devote entire chapters to the topic (see, e.g., Milne & McDonald, 1999; Pitts & Stotlar, 1996; Shank, 1999). However, while from the perspective of the recipient, sponsorship acquisition is a strategic tool with immediate implications for the organization's (or event's, league's, etc.) bottom line, from the perspective of the sponsor, sponsorships have mostly been considered as one tactical component among others in the company's larger integrated marketing communications strategy (Quester & Thompson, 2001; Weilbacher, 2001).[1] In addition, corporations have become increasingly sophisticated consumers of sport sponsorships, demanding more complete sponsorship packages from their partners. Based on the sponsor's designation of the target market, event sponsorships, for example, may incorporate traditional communication vehicles such as mass advertising, promotions, point-of-purchase merchandising, cross-selling opportunities, and public relations as well as non-traditional Internet-based techniques, including online games and event-specific communities. Hence, unless marketers of sport sponsorships continuously add value to their product, they will see their share in the corporate communication budget dwindle in the future.

As the content of sponsorship packages changes, so does the need for measuring effectiveness (see also Meenaghan, this volume). Yet, in comparison to modern data-driven direct, one-on-one, and relationship marketing techniques, sponsorship represents a crude marketing tool because return on investment is notoriously difficult to measure. Even a seemingly simple task such as comparing brand awareness between sport fans and non-fans poses myriad problems. Linking sport sponsorship dollars to product sales is infinitely more complicated. But as companies feel the pressure to justify large sponsorship investments to employees, investors, clients, and trade partners, proof that brand equity and financial objectives are being achieved is needed. Clients increasingly demand evidence that links fungible deliverables like sales volume and stock price more or less directly to their investment in the sponsorship (Shimp, 1997). Accountability is key and recipients must therefore do whatever they can to support clients in their effort to justify the sponsorship.

The challenge for sport marketers to sell their assets in an increasingly competitive global marketplace is tremendous. Two relatively new forces add additional layers of complexity to the business of sport sponsorship: the Internet[2] and what has been called the globalization of markets (Adam, Awerbuch, Glonin, Wegner & Tesha, 1997; Cairncross, 1997; Quelch & Klein, 1996; Stauss, 1997). To succeed in this brave new world of global e-business, sport marketers must understand what threats the Internet poses to sport *(e-)sponsoring*[3] and what opportunities may be opened up by this new medium. Hence, before integrating the Internet into a sport sponsorship package for a global market, marketers need to be able to judge whether the personality of the sponsor's brand aligns well with the Internet and if the Internet fits with the target audience (see also Madrigal, Bee and LaBarge, this volume). In addition, marketers need to understand how to coordinate an online strategy with an offline strategy and whether the objective of using the Internet for sponsorship purposes is the creation of brand awareness, exploration, or commitment (Rayport & Jaworski, 2001). Beyond such conventional questions about the medium, marketers of global sport sponsorship packages must be sensitized to its unique characteristics, in particular its ability to aggregate global consumers and to create the conditions for intimate consumer relationships (see e.g., Zwick & Dholakia, 2004).

Our goal here is not to provide a step-by-step prescription of how to implement a successful electronic sport sponsorship initiative, although we do have something to say about the "how-to" aspect as well. For the most part, however, we prefer a different route. We suggest that what is needed first and foremost in this rapidly emerging, but still scattered and nebulous e-business landscape is a conceptual understanding of the implications of the Internet for marketing strategy in general. Developing sound business knowledge of the Internet is not a purely theoretical exercise. Rather, this discussion will provide the foundation for proper analyses and strategic implementation. To paraphrase Manuel Castells, 2001, p. 4) our purpose here is analytical because we believe that knowledge should precede action. Special attention will be paid to the transformative power of the Internet on two key concepts in marketing: customer relationships and brands. Armed with an understanding of the new realities of e-business, we will then consider how these general transformations affect the nature and role of global sport sponsorship. In particular, we will sketch out the limitations and promises sponsorships hold for sponsors in the global digital marketplace and what sport marketers trying to attract sponsorships have to do to continuously add value to their clients. Finally, we spend some time pondering the need for global sport sponsoring to exploit the capabilities of e-business if it is to actualize its full potential in a global economy. We suggest that the addition of the "e" to sport sponsorship will make it the promotional tool par excellence for the fragmented, "glocalized" marketplace of the twenty-first century.

Understanding the Internet Revolution: Of Relationships and Brands

Today, not even a decade after its inception as a popular medium, the Internet is everywhere. A wholly pervasive, transformative, threatening and liberating medium, the Internet's cultural, economic and social logic is still largely a mystery.[4] The past several years have been characterized by a frenzy of new ideas, opinions, forecasts, and speculations about the impact of the Internet on business in general and on marketing in particular (e.g. Kelly, 1998; Levine, 2000; Peppers, 2001). As Manuel Castells (2001, p. 3) points out, "[T]he speed of transformation has made it difficult for scholarly research to follow the pace of change with an adequate supply of empirical studies on the why and wherefores of the Internet-based economy and society."

Indeed, the speed with which knowledge is produced and disseminated mirrors the fierce race of companies to innovate and seize new opportunities. On the business-to-consumer (B2C) side, which is the focus of our paper, the attention has been mostly on developing tactics and so-called killer applications (customerization, community, content, personalization, etc.) for the "new economy" (e.g. Godin, 1999; Hagel & Armstrong, 1997; Wind, Mahajan & Gunther, 2002). Experiments with banner ads, e-mail promotions, opt-in/opt-out scenarios, pop-up ads, personalized webpages and many more have been undertaken, modified, adopted and abandoned. As the dust settles a little, it is time to take a more conceptual perspective on the effects of the Internet on marketing management. From our perspective, two key areas of marketing strategy that have been strongly affected by the Internet revolution need to be discussed in more detail because these transformations entail important ramifications for the practice of sport marketing as well. First, the trend of the 1990s towards customer-centric business organizations has received a dramatic push in the age of interactive computer-mediated communication (Hoffman & Novak, 1997). It is no accident that Customer Relationship Management (CRM) has become the buzzword of our times, gradually eclipsing (at least in the trade press and academic writings, if not in strategic importance) previous management paradigms such as Enterprise Resource Planning (ERP), Supply Chain Management (SCM), and Total Quality Management (TQM). The Internet has played a critical role in this shift because it has the potential to bring companies ever closer to the customer, thus ushering in what has been variously called customerization, personalization, or the one-to-one future (Fink, Konnermann, Noller & Schuab, 2002; Peppers, 2001).

Second, as the Internet matures from a sales channel to a multimedia experience, discussion has ensued about the effectiveness and viability of the medium for brand-building initiatives. The success of companies like Yahoo, Amazon and eBay has shown that formidable online brands can be developed and sustained.

But for existing offline consumer brands, things might not be so clear. Should they consider e-business a threat or an opportunity for their brand? Most marketers tend to focus on the potentially brand-strengthening features of the new medium (e.g. innovative content, increased reach, improved targeting, etc.), overlooking that the same medium spawns new forms of customer involvement and consumer behavior that might have *brand-diluting* effects (see Dussart, 2001).

E-business Transformations [1]: Customer Relationship Management

Customer Relationship Management[5] is increasingly taking center-stage in organizations' corporate strategies (Greenberg, 2002; Swift, 2001). Closely related to notions of relationship and database marketing, CRM aims at creating, developing, and enhancing personal and valuable relationships with customers by providing personalized and customized products and services (McKim, 2002; Rigby, Reichfeld & Schefter, 2002). For it to work, a CRM system relies on its ability to swiftly accumulate accurate individual customer records at every organizational touch point.[6] Customer profiles are stored in a central database, making them available to every part of the organization at any time. If well executed, the company gains a 360° vision of each customer, allowing it to very accurately determine for each customer his or her costs to serve, profitability, and customer lifetime value (Ryals & Knox, 2001).

The Internet has increased the level of buyer-seller interactivity (Achrol & Kotler, 1999). In the world of relationship-based electronic commerce, personal information is acquiring enormous financial value and some companies have noticed that their consumers tell them more online than offline (Dussart, 2001). Because a minority of customers account for the bulk of revenue and profits for many companies (Donath, 1999; Libai, Narayandas & Humby, 2002), competitive strategies now emphasize customer retention over customer acquisition in efforts to maximize customer equity (Blattberg & Deighton, 1996). To implement this strategic shift, successful firms increasingly depend on vast amounts of customer data (Baig, Stepanek & Guess, 1999; Shapiro & Varian, 1999). The assumption is that details about customers' real needs and requirements can be extracted from this data to help businesses better satisfy them and build loyalty.

CRM can thus be seen as a company's tactic to gain an "informational edge" (Berthon, Holbrook & Hulbert, 2000) over competitors. In other words, whoever owns the most information about a customer owns the relationship with him or her (Seybold, 2001). Therefore, in the age of e-business all customer-facing organizational touch points should be reconceptualized to capture customer information. The key to success lies in the interactivity and data-capturing capabilities of the Internet. Every interaction between the customer and the company that takes place through this channel is automatically recorded and can be used for targeted promotional and sales efforts.

At the same time, these capabilities however change the expectations regarding marketing and promotional efforts. Traditional mass-media based advertising, for example, while by no means obsolete, has several disadvantages vis-à-vis highly targeted interactive direct marketing techniques such as indeterminable return on investment and one-way communication flows[7] (i.e. no identifiable, collectable, and advertising-related data stream coming back from the customer) (Hoffman & Novak, 1996). Advertising formats that make use of the Internet's interactive capabilities deliver on these dimensions and therefore increasingly end up on management's radar screens. Hence, with growing expectations, metrics for measuring marketing and communication effectiveness change. Accurate ROI evaluations and the amount and quality of customer data gathered – operationalizing "soft" measures like value of relationship or customer lifetime value (Wind et al., 2002) – will increasingly be used to assess the value of marketing efforts.

Traditional vehicles of a company's integrated marketing communication strategy such as sponsorship programs will need to find ways to deliver on the promises of the interactive communication paradigm. In other words, only if the sponsorship activity becomes an interactive customer touch point that generates incoming flows of customer data will it be able to position itself as a valuable promotional tool for the sponsor. We will return to this important aspect later.

E-business Transformations [2]: Branding

The importance of branding in today's overcrowded and hyper-competitive marketplaces can hardly be overstated. Strong brands reduce customer acquisition costs, increase loyalty and customer retention, and protect against competitors undermining the price premium consumers are willing to pay (Aaker, 1996; Aaker & Joachimsthaler, 2000). From a strategic marketing perspective, a strong brand is a key asset in the successful implementation of the relationship paradigm (Fournier, 1998). Creating a strong brand has never been easy but with the advent of the Internet, it has become a whole lot more difficult. Before the Internet became the "channel of universal communication" (Castells, 1998), effectively decentralizing communication flows, companies could exert a tremendous amount of control over the source, form and content of the marketing message. In effect, companies could rely on the structural security of the mass communication model with its one-way communication flow. Consequently, a company could make product claims without being too concerned about direct and immediate customer opposition to these assertions. Consumers hardly ever talked back and therefore brand managers equated control over means of communication with control over the brand.[8]

The Web, however, has changed all of this by opening up a dialogue between consumers and companies (including manufacturers, designers, marketers, etc.) *and,* infinitely more important, between consumers. "Brands are now an open book for all to look into" (Travis, 2001, p. 16). False statements about the performance or quality of a product can be exposed quickly by consumer activists armed with a laptop computer and Internet access. Consumers now talk back to the brand manager and what is more, they talk to each other, effectively *co-creating the brand on a global basis* (Kozinets, 1999). Therefore, the Internet "will drive the last nail into the coffin of controlled branding, selective distribution and set price lists. The power of negotiation that has mostly passed into the hands of mass distributors may end up entirely in those of customers" (Dussart, 2000, p. 390).

The end of brand management may also bring about the end of developing a coherent corporate identity, leaving the business with little more to sell than an aggregation of product and service characteristics. In other words, with brand equity under severe attack, marketers will lose the benefit of distinguishing between representation and reality that hitherto has governed the modern consumer gaze (cf. Harvey, 1996). The manipulation of the product and service on the *symbolic level* for the purpose of perceptual differentiation (Lien, 2000) becomes infinitely more difficult and consumer behavior differentiated by loyalty and price insensitivity becomes less likely.

In short, the Internet, which is here to stay, is not necessarily good news for companies (Porter, 2001). Marketing guru Regis McKenna points to the threat of e-business to commoditize all and everything because the only variable customers are looking for on the Net is price (Kuchinskas, 2000). Furthermore, models like "name your own price," "group buying," "reverse auctions" and "shopbot buying" create markets that ignore the symbolic properties of vendor and product (i.e. the brand) and thus lead to *brand dilution*.

Conceptually, as e-business develops we observe increasing difficulty in creating brand proximity and intimacy. These concepts denote the degree to which a customer perceives a certain brand to address his or her symbolic and material needs (see Figure 6.1).

The important question then for marketers will be to figure out ways to turn some of the obvious negative effects of the Internet – brand dilution due to commoditization and distancing – into positive ones for their brands. In other words, can the Internet be used to resuscitate brands that have been weakened by e-business commoditization? For this to happen, the Internet must be used in ways that help decrease the distance between consumer and brand and to create more proximity and intimacy (see Figure 6.2). We argue below that for a number of reasons, sport e-sponsorship is a very promising proposition for businesses that want to recreate their brands.

Sport Sponsorship in the Age of E-Business

So far, we have discussed two major transformations of marketing strategy in the age of e-business: the radical move towards information-intensive customer relationship management and the dilution of brands characterized by the

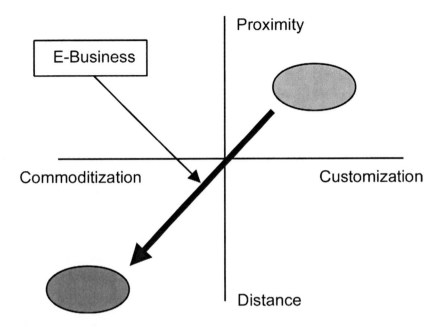

Figure 6.1 *Effect of internet on brand (adapted from Dussart, 2001).*

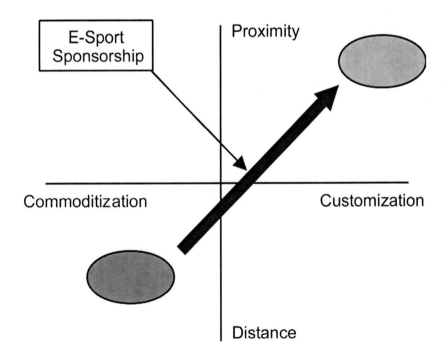

Figure 6.2 *Potential effect of e-sport sponsorship on brand (adapted from Dussart, 2001, p. 634).*

double threat of brand distancing and commoditization. Two imperatives with tremendous implications for sport sponsorship initiatives emerge from these observations: (1) for a good relationship there is a permanent need for up-to-date and detailed *customer information* (Berthon et al., 2000); and (2) there is a need for creating *brand involvement* that brings the customer closer to the brand and defers brand aging (Fournier, 1998). Promotional marketing tactics that can deliver on these needs have a great chance of successfully supporting the entire marketing mix.

The question we need to investigate, then, is whether a sport e-sponsorship can be used to address the two marketing imperatives of information and involvement. In the following we discuss what a sport e-sponsorship that adds value to the sponsor's promotional mix should look like. In a second step, we take a cursory look at some examples to illustrate the still undeveloped use of the medium's interactive capabilities for sponsorship. Finally, we shed light on the opportunities that emerge for sport e-sponsorship within the global marketplace.

The Information and the Involvement Imperative

In the age of information-intensive marketing, the organization must rethink every touch point with the customer as a source of customer knowledge. Previously, advertising was a non-interactive flow of data, streaming one-way as it were, from the organization to the audience. Now, advertising can be created as an interactive experience in which the consumer engages with the ad in active and creative ways. Advertising and promotions are thus no longer passive vehicles for a company's message but rather *co-created brand environments* (cf. Berthon et al., 2000). In these spaces, much more than in their off-line equivalent, customers are willing to tell marketers about themselves. In addition to the increased quantity of customer data, information provided by the customers in these co-created advertising spaces like Amazon's recommendation boards, the discussion forums of the National Basketball Association, or Nike sponsored RunLondon website (http://www.runlondon.com) is much more accurate and hence useful for actual marketing purposes.

The key to a real and shared sense of relationship between the marketer and the customer, indeed the brand and the customer, is whether the message can get the customer involved. Involvement leads to a lasting brand relationship and a greater willingness to share information, which is critical for both electronic customer relationship management and brand equity.

Paradigmatic of involvement-generating use of the Internet is the innovative community site Neopets.com, the most popular youth site on the Web. It counts about 70 million registered users worldwide and records seven billion hits per month. In this community, users begin by designing a virtual pet for which they have to care. The pet demands to be fed and entertained, checked by the doctor, and taken shopping, among other things. To do all of these activities, the pet owner needs NeoPoints which can be collected by playing the games offered in various parts of the site. Users quickly find themselves deeply immersed in a world of games and playful interaction with other pet owners, where the transition from playing the new Spy Kids 3-D game to watching the latest movie trailer in the "Disney Theatre" is seamless. In the Thinkway store, easily accessible with a few clicks, users receive NeoPoints for watching ads for Thinkway's new line of Neopets toys.[9] Not unlike product placement in movies, this type of immersion advertising transforms the brand into a "natural" part of the virtual landscape. Immersion encourages lengthy, intimate, and active interaction with the brand. In fact, the Internet provides the infrastructure for global interactive brand environments that are no longer recognized as channels for corporate marketing communication. Conceptually, Internet-enabled immersion advertising transforms the brand from a selling proposition to a reliable partner who is essential in accomplishing the required task of raising and caring for one's virtual pet. In this way, marketer and pet owner become complicit in creating, maintaining, and advancing the brand.

E-sport sponsorships are uniquely positioned to involve customers with the brand by making them *co-creators of the sponsorship*. In addition to the interactive element of the Internet, which allows for a conversational relationship between brand, customers and marketers (see Zwick & Dholakia, 2004) and the immersive experience described above, the medium attracts a youthful market segment. As the average age is much lower for online sports fans and buyers than for traditional ones, the Internet delivers a powerful strategic vehicle to prevent brand ageing. Finally, given the youthful image of sports in general, Internet-enabled sponsorships align more naturally with the characteristics of the target market than any other marketing communication channel.

As the Nike Runlondon website example shows, with the extension of the sponsorship of the "London 10k" run into virtual space, Nike does more than merely deliver a passive message to its audience. The site allows for some basic form of immersion by inviting runners to interact with its capabilities and to make it "work" for them in several ways, including watching oneself crossing the finish line, connecting with other runners, getting friends involved that are not yet runners, and shopping. In effect, Nike is creating a platform for runners to extend the experience of the run, all the while keeping the runner (inter)actively involved with the brand. By doing so, Nike vanishes as a corporate brand message and re-emerges as a relationship partner in the project of experience creation. Nike is the beneficiary of the information exchange as well as the ongoing economic and symbolic exchange that characterizes brand equity.

Thus to the degree that the sponsorship can be upgraded by the use of electronic media, including effective tie-ins with traditional promotional vehicles, it is more likely to get the desired results. A website is but one of the possibilities for electronic mass interactivity with customers: handheld devices, for example, will play an increasingly important role in companies' promotional strategies and sponsoring will be included there. But the Web is still the most promising vehicle given the multimedia content that can be delivered via high-speed

Internet. However, creating an engaging, involving, and interactive site is not a simple affair. Customers today expect a website to perform like software, full of capabilities, responsiveness and functionality. Disconfirming these expectations of the cyber consumer would lead to a negative attitude toward the site and the sponsoring brand (cf. Brown & Stayman, 1992). The "realness" of the action and interaction allowed by the site can be positively linked to attitude-behavior consistency through the notions of direct versus indirect experiences with an attitude object (Coyle & Thorson, 2001). Specifically, attitudes developed through direct experiences are held more confidently, are more enduring and more resistant to attack than those developed through indirect experience. It has further been argued that more direct experiences with an attitude object lead to more consistency between attitudes and behavior than do indirect experiences (Fazio & Zanna, 1978). Therefore, the capability of the medium to produce a sense of direct and real involvement with the brand, what we call immersion, is crucial for the effectiveness of the sponsor's communication efforts. Hence, the attitude toward the brand as mediated toward the ongoing involvement with the site is continuously shaped even after the main event has ended. The Nike site marks a simple, yet effective execution of e-sponsorship because it addresses better than any other medium both the need for customer information and lasting involvement with the site.

Nike's "London 10k" site is also an example of a global player leveraging the Internet's "placelessness" for developing a highly localized form of sponsorship. Placelessness here refers to the freedom from large transmission sites and printing presses needed for traditional media production. Setting up a website of this kind is very inexpensive – especially when compared to traditional forms of marketing communications like television and newspaper – and its message is highly relevant to a well-segmented and narrowcast audience. This independence from the broadcasting model of traditional media allows the Internet to become the ultimate form of localized communication within a global network of information flows (Wellman, 2001). As we will discuss in more detail below, marketers of sport sponsorships can use the Internet to both localize the package (e.g. tie-ins with local retail promotions, use of local stars for chat events, etc.) and globalize it at the same time. Online communities, for example, are able to draw a highly involved and globally dispersed audience together and align it for the branding efforts of the sponsor.

Companies continue to struggle to leverage the interactive nature of the Internet for sponsorship purposes. Siemens Mobile's (www.siemens-mobile.com) sport sponsorship involvement, for example, is substantial and yet its use of the Internet to support their sport marketing communication efforts is rather basic. The company also follows a philosophy of localized representation; but on a large scale nevertheless. In May 2000 Siemens's mobile branch embarked on a massive soccer sponsorship campaign across Europe combining twenty-four clubs in its portfolio as well as the English FA Premier League. Since 2002, Siemens Mobile has been a sponsor of Real Madrid, arguably the world's most glamorous and prestigious soccer club. In addition, top national soccer clubs Lazio Rome, Girondins de Bordeaux, Olympiakos Piraeus and Aalborg BK count Siemens Mobile as their main sponsor. Siemens Mobile also has a large stake in Formula One racing as the provider of communication equipment. Siemens Mobile customers can sign up for special services such as up-to-date race results or drivers' positions during an F1 race, notifications of breaking news and "trading rumors," and logo downloads to display on the phone's screen. These are early examples of how mobile commerce can be leveraged by generating sales that are directly linked to the sponsored event. Yet, Siemens Mobile's German website, at least on the soccer side of things, is not as good at making use of the company's sponsorship involvement. It is limited to a few general remarks on the game of soccer and a chat archive with two German soccer players. The games available for cellular phones bear no relation to the nature of the sponsorships and there are no opportunities for unique downloads that would leverage the company's involvement such as images from athletes or their cars (as in the case of Formula One), top athletes' personal greetings in lieu of a ring tone, among other things.

Siemens Mobile does a better job using the Internet to leverage its significant presence in Formula One as a technology partner (www.my-siemens.com/f1). The F1-specific website offers a number of interactive activities such as a video game, quizzes, chats with Formula One drivers, e-cards, etc. In order to participate in these activities the user must first register by creating a profile complete with login name and password. Thus, the Siemens Mobile F1-website, thus, offers the usual mix of entertainment, interactive games and information that makes a site sticky. By inviting the visitor to spend time on the F1 site Siemens Mobile hopes to establish an emotional link between the brand and the consumer. In addition, asking the visitor to fill out a brief personal profile questionnaire can be regarded as a valid form of customer information gathering, notwithstanding some problems inherent in this method. When combined with cookies and site tracking tools, a relatively detailed picture of a visitor emerges (Berry & Linoff, 2000; Hoffman, Novate & Penalta, 1999). Tracking software is now able to monitor every minute detail of online consumer behavior (Locke, 2000). Computers record where consumers go and how long they linger at a site. What is more, software can capture whether a consumer who is exposed to company X's banner advertising when visiting website Y, actually visits company X's website, even if she does so three days later (Allard, Graves, Gluck, May & McAteer, 1999). With such information at hand, stored in customer databases, and if needed accessed and analyzed with lightning speed, the sponsor gains invaluable data that can be mined for hidden customer preferences and unexpected correlations (Fayyad, 2001; Fayyad & Uthurusamy, 1996). Whether Siemens Mobile uses these techniques for marketing purposes is another question.

It is significant, however, that on the poorly developed and surprisingly un-professional-looking home page of the Federation Internationale De L'Automobile (www.FIA.com), the governing body of Formula One, no reference is made to Siemens Mobile's involvement and no link can be found to any sponsors' sites. Ignoring these most basic capabilities of the medium is now rare but is by no means unique to the FIA site. Smaller sporting events, in particular, struggle to take advantage of the website's communicatory potential in favor of the sponsor and thereby forgo a legitimate value-added service. The official site for the Kroger St Jude ATP tennis tournament (http://www.atptennis.com/memphis/), for example, exhibits "non-clickable" logos of its sponsors including Conair and Pepsi. Also, the official home page of the 2003 Ford Curling World Championships in Winnipeg, Canada (http://www.wcc2003.ca/index2.php) did not offer any clickable logos of its many sponsors, including what they refer to as the event's Gold Sponsors. Completely absent are any attempts to create an immersive online brand environment (e.g. virtual golf or tennis games) and tie-ins with offline promotions.

Even such a cursory look at a few efforts to incorporate the Internet into the sponsorship package reveals that the website has not yet been discovered as a legitimate aspect of the sponsorship package. It appears that marketers on both sides of the sponsorship dyad still lack a basic understanding of how the Internet can add value to the promotional mix in general and the sponsorship package in particular. Simply transferring the broadcasting model to the Internet does not do justice to the possibilities of the medium. Well-executed e-sponsorships open up ongoing and involving conversations with consumers (Levine, 2000), the foundation of relationship marketing and brand equity in a world of scarce consumer attention and crowded marketplaces.

Globalizing E-Sponsorship

Late capitalist global expansion of markets has forced especially multinational corporations to adapt their promotional strategies to the local contexts in which they seek to place their products (Silk & Andrews, 2001) (see also Silk & Andrews, and Grainger, Newman & Andrews, this volume). Sport sponsorships have proven to be a valuable strategy for addressing consumers and trade on a local level (Gordon, 1994). To be sure, global umbrella campaigns remain indispensable in the battle for market share and mind share but the crisis of the Fordist regime of standardized mass production and consumption in the 1970s and the subsequent transition to flexible production, labor relations, and "postmodern consumption" (Firat & Dholakia, 1998; Lury, 1996) require an accompanying system of signification that allows for the manipulation of the commodity sign on a local scale (Andrews, Carrington, Jackson & Mazur, 1996; Harvey, 1989). In fact, under the post-Fordist mode of production we have also seen a certain promiscuity in the production of locally relevant brand images. Nonetheless, this has not led to true heterogeneity of meaning because companies maintain the "cultural power" to limit the range of possible interpretations of the brand image in the place of reception (cf. Wilson & Sparks, 2001). The strategic "brandscape" envisioned by multinationals is thus characterized by what Wilk

(1995) calls the "structure of common difference" where Appadurai's (1996) "global localities" are being developed according to a Western corporate script.

Here is where the Internet comes in because it delivers to multinational businesses the ability to continuously write and rewrite the dominant script, thus maintaining relative control over their brand image the world over while at the same time diversifying it. In fact, the Internet has emerged as the "globalization tool" par excellence, where companies from Microsoft to Nike author, as it were, their vision of global localities and create the structure of common difference that prove strategically most gainful to them.

The key to the Internet's success as a global-local promotional tool is on the one hand its modular character, which permits rapid production and distribution of slight variations of the overall branding theme, and on the other its global connectivity. Unlike television commercials, flyers, and print ads, which, once produced, are finished products enclosed in themselves, Internet-based messages, services, and environments can quickly become versions of themselves (Rayport & Sviokla, 1995). A website allows for immediate and detailed changes of its content which appeals to the local consumer while at the same time emphasizing the company's global corporate image. The power of versioning of the sponsor's Internet presence according to specific needs of national or regional subsidiaries is amplified by the seamless and effortless distribution of these versions to their appropriate local target markets.

A good example of modular, surface-level adaptations is Nike's corporate website (www.nike.com), where each visitor is encouraged to go to a world region of his or her choice. Based on the region clicked, a unique yet distinctly "Nikean" adaptation of the "original" site appears, catering to the local sporting taste (e.g. soccer in Europe, gymnastics in Hong Kong), average connection speed (basic graphics for Latin America, sound and animation in Korea) and language preferences. If nothing else, the Nike website becomes a metaphor for global localities in which the company realizes its vision of common differences believed to be exhibited by the markets around the world.

From the sponsee's perspective, the website could become a strategic asset that adds significant value to the sponsorship. In the case of events like the World Cup, a global sponsor such as MasterCard (www.mastercard.com) is technically and theoretically able to network its own site to locally relevant content (news, reports and video feeds from individual national teams, online chats with national players, sweepstakes, virtual games, country-specific promotions, etc.) as well as content of global appeal like game schedules and results, global chats with the event's superstars, or a global sweepstake campaign. The ability to deliver a rich and engaging media experience in the context of what is a very emotional issue for many people around the globe fulfills all the prerequisites for an immersive brand experience. As an important by-product, marketers collect exclusive customer data, which supports strategic efforts to improve customer relationships and decrease brand distance for specific target groups. Hence, the strategic significance of the Internet for sport sponsorship marketing is not just its ability to deliver locally relevant versions of the sponsor's message cost-effectively nor just the medium's global reach but the combination of both.

Given the strategic opportunities for "glocalization" of the brand via the Internet, the fact that MasterCard has done almost nothing to exploit this communication vehicle in their massive sponsorship efforts during the soccer World Cups of 1998 and 2002 comes as a surprise. The company's online presence for its sponsorship of the UEFA Champions League competition is even more disappointing. As one of only four official sponsors, enjoying category exclusivity, MasterCard makes very little of this opportunity on its own website, be it the English or the German or any other of the company's nationally specific home pages. Apart from links to the official UEFA site where the visitor is exposed to some banner ads sporting the MasterCard logo and some outdated information about the league's schedule of games, nothing indicates that any effort was made to localize the sponsorship and to use the medium's interactivity for purposes of data collection, customer relationship management and brand management.

Clearly, strategic opportunities to extend a sponsorship into the virtual space abound. Yet, as the case of MasterCard and the other examples discussed above show, sponsors are a significant way from really understanding and actualizing the vast potential of e-sponsorships. This is a challenge and an opportunity for the sport marketer. If he or she can successfully demonstrate the medium's potential for improving customer relationship management and brand proximity as well as its superior structural facility for thinking global and acting local (Macrae & Uncles, 1997), the sponsorship's value will increase exponentially, enhancing the chance for sponsor satisfaction and loyalty and finally, event profitability.

Conclusion

The age of e-business transforms marketing in many ways, from channel, to price, to product strategies. Affected perhaps most of all by this transformation is the promotional ecology because the Internet ushers in enormous opportunities and imposing threats at the same time. As an information-collecting tool, the Internet provides businesses with the unprecedented power to really know their customers and give them what they want. Yet, according to economic theorists (see Brynjolfsson & Kahin, 2000; Nikell, 2000; Varian, 2000), e-business leads to a more transparent and cutthroat marketplace in which products and services become commoditized and sellers are forced to compete on price. As a result, the value per dollars spent on the symbolic power of the brand may decline, brand equity is threatened, and marketers may see consumers becoming less involved with, and more distanced from, the brand.

We argue that in this paradoxical state of affairs electronic sport sponsoring could become a particularly promising tactical tool for marketers because if well managed it can deliver on what we identified as the two imperatives of an information-driven business environment: (1) intimate customer relationships based on rich data profiles; and (2) brand involvement through immersive environments and versioned communication. When we look at CRM and e-branding in this way they emerge as two sides of the same coin. Sport sponsorships should be conceptualized as a relationship-building tool rather than as an advertising or sales vehicle. In the age of instant information flows and global communication networks, the currency of marketing is customers' behavioral information. Especially in a marketplace of global localities that is characterized by structures of common differences (Wilk, 1995), customer information is critical for the creation of a more involving and relevant brand experience. For sport sponsorships to grow on a global scale, they must be turned into interactive, information-driven and immersive customer experiences. Only then will they be regarded as a cornerstone of the overall marketing objectives of building one-to-one customer relationships, providing cross and up-selling opportunities, customizing direct marketing communication, retention and increasing customer equity. What we see so far, however, is a more or less wholesale transfer to the Internet of the unidirectional broadcasting model, ignoring the medium's potential for imagining entirely new types of customer-brand interactions.

To conclude, electronic sport sponsorship represents a powerful proposition in the global marketplace. By combining worldwide reach and low production costs for targeted sponsorship versions with the ability to capture a geographically dispersed but homogeneous customer segment, sport marketers' capacity to add value to a client's integrated marketing communication increases, especially in the age of globalization. The Internet is the post-Fordist accomplice to flexible production and global marketing. It turns trepidation into opportunity by virtue of modular communication formats. Sport marketers who harness the power of decentralized electronic communication networks like the Internet for their clients are likely to succeed *in mobilizing the local consumer as part of the global market* (cf. Miller, 2000; Probyn, 1998). If that happens, sport sponsorships will emerge even more prominently as prime movers of corporate globalization.

Notes

1. Of course, sponsorships can be considered strategic assets, as in the case of MasterCard and its category ownership of the FIFA World Cup. Also, in some instances sport sponsorship takes on strategic importance in brand development as was the case with Mountain Dew's early sponsorship of extreme sports in the early 1990s. Because Mountain Dew's commitment preceded the sport's mass commercialization, the company was able to position itself as a genuine supporter of a cultural movement rather than a corporate parasite (Holt, 2003).

2. We use the Internet here as a short-cut to represent the more general rise of new information, communication, and database technologies (Poster, 1995; Robins & Webster, 1999; Varian, 2000), as well as its much more specific incarnation as e-commerce (see e.g., Dholakia, 1998; Hoffman & Novak, 1997; Siebel & House, 1999).

3. We refer to a sponsorship that has a large digital, interactive and virtual component as electronic, or e-sponsorship.

4. As opposed to the Internet's technological workings, which are quite well understood.

5. With information technology (IT) becoming a critical CRM enabler (Goodhue, Wixom & Watson, 2002), we believe CRM and electronic CRM (eCRM) will converge, if they have not already done so. Thus, we will use these terms interchangeably.

6. Herein lies one of the differences between CRM and database marketing. For database marketing to be successful a company "does not need every customer record populated with data" (McKim, 2002).

7. Other disadvantages are quality of impressions, absolute media cost (although probably not cost per thousand) and segmentation accuracy.

8. Of course, we mean *relative* control. Companies have never had complete control either over communication or the brand. But they certainly used to have a lot *more* of both before information systems and communication processes became decentralized by telecommunicated networks of personal computers (cf. Castells, 1998).

9. Recently, McDonald's in the US launched the Neopets Happy Meal, which comes with one of 109 different toys. We recognize the important ethical, moral, and potential legal questions raised by immersion advertising. We do not endorse NeoPets' business model. We merely wish to draw attention to the company's innovative use of the Internet as a branding tool.

References

Aaker, D. A. (1996) *Building Strong Brands*. New York: Free Press.

Aaker, D. A. and E. Joachimsthaler (2000) *Brand Leadership*. New York: Free Press.

Achrol, R. S. and P. Kotler (1999) "Marketing in the Network Economy," *Journal of Marketing*, 63: 146–163.

Adam, N., B. Awerbuch, J. Slonim, P. Wegner, and Y. Yesha (1997) "Globalizing Business, Education, Culture Through the Internet," *Communications of the ACM*, 40 (2): 115–121.

Allard, K., L. Graves, M. Gluck, M. May, and S. McAteer (1999) "Proactive Personalization," ericaclark.com.

Andrews, D. L., B. Carrington, S. Jackson, and Z. Mazur (1996) "Jordanscapes: A preliminary analysis of the global popular," *Sociology of Sport Journal*, 13 (4): 428–457.

Appadurai, A. (1996) *Modernity at Large: Cultural Dimensions of Globalization*. Minneapolis, MN: University of Minnesota Press.

Baig, E. C., M. Stepanek, and N. Gross (1999) "The Internet Wants Your Personal Info. What's In It For You?" in *Business Week*, April 5, 1984.

Berry, M. J. A. and G. Linoff (2000) *Mastering Data Mining: The Art and Science of Customer Relationship Management*. New York: Wiley.

Berthon, P., M. B. Holbrook, and J. M. Hulbert (2000) "Beyond Market Orientation: A Conceptualization of Market Evolution," *Journal of Interactive Marketing*, 14 (3): 50–66.

Blattberg, R. C. and J. Deighton (1996) "Manage marketing by the customer equity test," *Harvard Business Review*, 74 (4): 136–144.

Brown, S. P. and D. M. Stayman (1992) "Antecedents and consequences of attitudes towards the ad: A Meta-Analysis," *Journal of Consumer Research*, 19 (June): 34–51.

Brynjolfsson, E. and B. E. Kahin (2000) *Understanding the Digital Economy: Data, Tools and Research*. Cambridge, MA: MIT Press.

Cairncross, F. (1997) "A connected world," *The Economist*, September 13: 4–34.

Castells, M. (1998) "Information Technology, Globalization and Social Development," Paper prepared for the UNRISD Conference on Information Technologies and Social Development. Palais des Nations, Geneva.

Castells, M. (2001) *The Internet Galaxy: Reflections on the Internet, Business, and Society*. Oxford and New York: Oxford University Press.

Coyle, J. R. and E. Thorson (2001) "The effects of progressive levels of interactivity and vividness in Web marketing sites," *Journal of Advertising*, 30 (3): 65–77.

Dholakia, R. R. (1998) "Introduction: Special Issue on Conducting Business in the New Electronic Environment: Prospects and Problems," *Journal of Business Research*, 41 (3): 175–177.

Donath, B. (1999) "Fire your Big Customers? Maybe you should," *Marketing News*, 33 (13): 9.

Dussart, C. (2000) "Internet: The One-Plus-Eight 'Re-volutions'," *European Management Journal*, 18 (4): 386–397.

Dussart, C. (2001) "Transformative Power of E-Business over Consumer Brands," *European Management Journal*, 19 (6): 629–637.

Fayyad, U. (2001) "The Digital Physics of Data Mining," *Communications of the ACM*, 44 (3): 62–65.

Fayyad, U. and R. Uthurusamy (1996) "Data Mining and Knowledge Discovery in Databases," *Communications of the ACM*, 39 (11): 24–26.

Fazio, R. H. and M. P. Zanna (1978) "Direct Experience and Attitude-Behavior Consistency," in L. Berkowitz (ed.), *Advances in Experimental Social Psychology*, Vol. 14. New York: Academic Press, pp. 161–202.

Fink, J., J. Koenemann, S. Noller, and I. Schwab (2002) "Putting personalization into practice," *Communications of the ACM*, 45 (5): 41–42.

Firat, A. and N. Dholakia (1998) *Consuming People: From Political Economy to Theatres of Consumption*. London: Routledge.

Fournier, S. (1998) "Consumers and their brands: Developing relationship theory in consumer research," *Journal of Consumer Research*, 24 (4): 343–373.

Godin, S. (1999) *Permission Marketing: Turning Strangers Into Friends, and Friends Into Customers*. New York: Simon and Schuster.

Goodhue, D. L., B. H. Wixom, and H. J. Watson (2002) "Realizing Business Benefits Through CRM: Hitting the right target in the right way," *MIS Quarterly Executive*, 1 (2): 79–94.

Gordon, A. (1994) "Corporate kick," *Sporting Goods Business*, Vol. 27.

Greenberg, P. (2002) *CRM at the Speed of Light: Capturing and Keeping Customers in Internet Real Time*, 2nd edn. Berkeley and London: McGraw-Hill.

Hagel, J. and A. G. Armstrong (1997) *Net Gain*. Boston, MA: Harvard Business School Press.

Harvey, D. (1989) *The Condition of Postmodernity*. Cambridge, MA: Blackwell.

Harvey, P. (1996) *Hybrids of Modernity: Anthropology, the Nation State and the Universal Exhibition*. London and New York: Routledge.

Hoffman, D. L. and T. P. Novak (1996) "Marketing in Hypermedia Computer-Mediated Environments: Conceptual Foundations," *Journal of Marketing*, 80 (1): 50–68.

Hoffman, D. L. and T. P. Novak (1997) "A New Marketing Paradigm for Electronic Commerce," *The Information Society*, 13 (1): 43–54.

Hoffman, D. L., T. P. Novak, and M. A. Peralta (1999) "Information Privacy in the Marketspace: Implications for the Commercial Uses of Anonymity on the Web," *The Information Society*, 15 (2): 129–139.

Holt, D. B. (2003) "What becomes an icon most?," *Harvard Business Review*, 81 (3): 43–49.

Kelly, K. (1998) *New Rules for the New Economy: 10 Radical Strategies for a Connected World*. New York: Viking.

Kozinets, R. V. (1999) "E-Tribalized Marketing?: The Strategic Implications of Virtual Communities of Consumption," *European Management Journal*, 17 (3): 252–264.

Kuchinskas, S. (2000) "The End of Marketing," *in Business 2.0*, October 30.

Levine, R. (2000) *The Cluetrain Manifesto: The End of Business as Usual*. Cambridge, MA: Perseus Books.

Libai, B., D. Narayandas, and C. Humby (2002) "Toward and Individual Customer Profitability Model: A segment-based approach," *Journal of Service Research*, 5 (1): 69–76.

Lien, M. (2000) "Imagined Cuisines: 'Nation' and 'Market' as Organizing Structures in Norwegian Food Marketing," in P. Jackson, M. Lowe, D. Miller and F. Mort (eds), *Commercial Cultures: Economies, Practices, Spaces*. Oxford: Berg, pp. 153–173.

Locke, C. (2000) "Personalization and Privacy: The Race Is On," Vol. 2000: personalization. com.

Lury, C. (1996) "The Stylization of Consumption," in *Consumer Culture*. Oxford: Blackwell Publishers Ltd, pp. 52–78.

Macrae, C. and M. D. Uncles (1997) "Rethinking brand management: the role of 'brand chartering'," *Journal of Product and Brand Management*, 6 (1): 64–87.

McKim, B. (2002) "CRM: Beyond the hoopla," *Target Marketing*, 25 (7): 38 ff.

Miller, D. (2000) *The Internet: An Ethnographic Approach*. Oxford: Berg.

Milne, G. R. and M. A. McDonald (1999) *Sport Marketing: Managing the Exchange Process*. Sudbury, MA: Jones and Bartlett.

Nickell, J. A. (2000) "Hey Big Spender." Retrieved October 12, 2002. http://www. business2.com/articles/mag/0,1640,14192,00.html.

Peppers, D. (2001) *The One to One Future: Building Relationships One Customer at a Time*, New York: Random House.

Pitts, B. G. and D. K. Stotlar (1996) *Fundamentals of Sport Marketing*. Morgantown, WV: Fitness Information Technology.

Porter, M. E. (2001) "Strategy and the Internet," *Harvard Business Review* (March), 62–78.

Poster, M. (1995) *The Second Media Age*. Cambridge: Polity Press.

Probyn, E. (1998) "Mc-Identities: Food and the Family Citizen," *Theory, Culture and Society*, 15 (2): 155–73.

Quelch, J. A. and L. R. Klein (1996) "The Internet and International Marketing," *Sloan Management Review*, 37 (3): 60–75.

Quester, P. G. and B. Thompson (2001) "Advertising and promotion leverage on arts sponsorship effectiveness," *Journal of Advertising Research*, 41 (1): 33–47.

Rayport, J. F. and B. J. Jaworski (2001) *E-commerce*. Boston: McGraw-Hill/Irwin MarketspaceU.

Rayport, J. F. and J. J. Sviokla (1995) "Exploiting the Virtual Value Chain," *Harvard Business Review*, 73 (6): 75–99.

Rigby, D. K., F. F. Reichheld, and P. Schefter (2002) "Avoid the four perils of CRM," *Harvard Business Review*, 80 (2): 101–109.

Robins, K. and F. Webster (1999) *Times of the Technoculture*. London and New York: Routledge.

Ryals, L. and S. Knox (2001) "Cross-functional Issues in the Implementation of Relationship Marketing through Customer Relationship Management," *European Management Journal*, 19 (5): 534–542.

Seybold, P. B. (2001) *The Customer Revolution*. New York: Crown Business.

Shank, M. D. (1999) *Sports Marketing: A Strategic Perspective*. Upper Saddle River, NJ: Prentice Hall.

Shapiro, C. and H. R. Varian (1999) *Information Rules: A Strategic Guide to the Network Economy*. Boston, Mass.: Harvard Business School Press.

Shimp, T. A. (1997) *Advertising, Promotion, and Supplemental Aspects of Integrated Marketing Communications*, 4th edition. Fort Worth and London: Dryden Press.

Siebel, T. M. and P. House (1999) *Cyber Rules*. New York: Currency/Doubleday.

Silk, M. L. and D. L. Andrews (2001) "Understanding globalisation: Transnational marketing and sponsorship," *International Journal of Sport Marketing and Sponsorship*, 2 (3): 129–133.

Stauss, B. (1997) "Global Word of Mouth," *Marketing Management*, 6 (3): 28.

Swift, R. S. (2001) *Accelerating Customer Relationships: Using CRM and Relationship Technologies*. Upper Saddle River, NJ: Prentice Hall.

Travis, D. (2001) "Branding in the Digital Age," *Journal of Business Strategy* (May/June), 14–18.

Varian, H. R. (2000) "Market Structure in the Network Age," in Erik Brynjolfsson and Brian Kahin (eds), *Understanding the Digital Economy: Data, Tools and Research*, Cambridge MA: MIT Press, pp. 137–150.

Weilbacher, W. M. (2001) "Point of view: Does advertising cause a 'hierarchy of effects'?," *Journal of Advertising Research*, 41 (6): 19–26.

Wellman, B. (2001) "Little boxes, glocalization, and networked individualism," in T. Ishida (ed.), *Digital Cities 2*, Berlin: Springer-Verlag, pp. 3–15.

Wilk, R. (1995) "Learning to be Local in Belize," in D Miller (ed.), *Worlds Apart: Modernity through the Prism of the Local*, London: Routledge, pp. 110–133.

Wilson, B. and R. Sparks (2001) "Michael Jordan, Sneaker Commercials, and Canadian Youth Culture," in David L. Andrews (ed.), *Michael Jordan, Inc.: Corporate Sport, Media Culture, and Late Modern America*, Albany: State University of New York Press, pp. 217–255.

Wind, Y., V. Mahajan, and R. E. Gunther (2002) *Convergence Marketing: Strategies for Reaching the New Hybrid Consumer*. Harlow: Financial Times Prentice Hall.

Zwick, D. and N. Dholakia (2004) "Consumer subjectivity in the Age of Internet: The radical concept of marketing control through Customer Relationship Management," *Information and Organization*, 14 (3): 211–236.

7

Global Sport Sponsorship
Towards a strategic understanding

Don Roy

Strategic planning is essential for an organization to survive and prosper long-term. If well-defined goals and objectives are not in place, then it will be very difficult for a business effectively to devise tactics because its destination is unclear. The strategic planning process begins at the organizational level with a situation analysis that identifies relevant internal and external factors facing an organization. Once there is understanding of where the organization is now (i.e. a situation analysis), the organization must articulate what the organization is about (i.e. mission) and where it desires to go (i.e. objectives). Then, mission and organization objectives are shared with all organizational units so that they become the foundation of their strategic plans, too. A strategic approach to planning of the marketing function focuses on establishing desired outcomes that will advance the organization (i.e. objectives) before devising strategies and tactics that should be undertaken in pursuit of objectives.

Strategic planning for firms operating in global markets entails additional issues beyond those faced by domestic firms. For example, the organizational structure of a global firm influences the level of standardization or adaptation in its marketing strategy (van Gelder, 2004). If the organizational structure of a firm is centralized, standardization of strategy across markets is feasible. A "one brand, one voice" approach can be developed in an effort to create economies of scale. On the other hand, a firm with a decentralized organization structure may engage in strategic planning on a market-by-market basis. This approach enables a firm to develop strategies based on the needs and preferences of its customers locally (see Silk & Andrews, this volume).

Sport sponsorship has increasingly figured into marketing strategies of firms that seek to reach their target markets via an association with a sports property that has relevance with customers. While sponsorships can be undertaken by local, regional or national firms, the role of sport sponsorship throughout an organization takes on greater significance for firms operating in a global environment. When companies seek to extend their geographic reach into countries beyond their home markets, they often face cultural and language obstacles that can hinder meaningful communication with customers in those markets.

The use of sport properties as a medium to reach a target audience can be potentially powerful for a firm in at least two ways. First, sport contains a great deal of meaning for many people throughout the world. Whether the sport be football (American football, Australian football or the football played globally known as soccer), ice hockey in Canada, cricket in India, baseball in the United States, or any other sport with which one can associate, sport provides an escape from everyday life and can become a part of one's self-identity. This emotional relationship with sport makes sport sponsorship an attractive vehicle for communicating with customers in a way that overcomes cultural and language differences faced by traditional communication media. Second, certain sport properties such as the Olympics, FIFA World Cup (see Madrigal et al., this volume), and the National Basketball Association have global appeal. Global sport properties provide a common platform for a firm operating in multiple countries to communicate with customers.

In this chapter, the role of sport sponsorship in global strategic planning is discussed. Sponsorships tend to be viewed rather narrowly as a tactic to use in support of marketing communication objectives. The framework for sponsorship planning presented here is based on the idea that responsibility for sponsorship management should not be restricted to those involved with marketing communication. Instead, sponsorship management should permeate an entire organization.

Strategic planning at the organization, marketing, and brand levels should include consideration of how sponsorships can be employed to achieve objectives. First, sponsorship management should begin with corporate level planning to develop sponsorship capabilities and cultivate these capabilities so that they can become sources of competitive advantage. Second, sponsorship resources should be leveraged to play a role in the creation and pursuit of growth strategies that can be undertaken in pursuit of marketing objectives. Third, sponsorship planning at the brand level should focus on how sponsorship resources can be utilized to communicate a brand's position to a target market. The remainder of the chapter addresses these three areas of strategic planning and their relationship to sponsorship management as well as influences on the sponsorship planning process pertinent to global firms.

Organization Level Sponsorship Planning

A great deal of scholarly research has been undertaken in the past two decades that examines influences on firm performance. Industrial organization research, particularly the work of Michael Porter (1980, 1985, 1989), has been particularly prominent in this respect. The foundation of this body of research is that organization-level strategy decisions and external factors (e.g. number of competitors) influence a firm's performance. Another body of research examined the strategy-performance relationship at the marketing management level. The Profit Impact Marketing Strategy (PIMS) project identified marketing-level variables such as spending levels for advertising and promotions, product quality, and product line breadth that influenced firm performance (Buzell & Gale, 1987).

The strategy-performance paradigm was of keen interest to academics and practitioners during the 1980s and into the early 1990s. However, alternative explanations for firm performance have been developed given that empirical assessment of the influence of organization-level strategy on performance suggests that a relatively small amount of variance in performance among firms can be attributed to strategy variables (Amis, Slack & Berrett, 1999). Researchers turned their attention away from strategic moves and market factors and instead focused on the resources firms employ to compete and attempt to differentiate themselves from competition. One view in this area was that firms should develop strategy around its resources rather than its products. The role of an organization's resources should be to create barriers to competition and to serve as a catalyst for growth (Wernerfelt, 1984).

The view that a firm's resources influence performance shifts the emphasis of strategy development to an examination of how a firm utilizes what it owns or can access. A firm's resources can be classified as tangible or intangible. Tangible resources are somewhat difficult to leverage as sources of sustainable competitive advantage because of the potential that other firms can observe and acquire similar resources. On the other hand, intangible resources are much more difficult to emulate. For example, a firm that succeeds in establishing a high level of brand equity for one or more of its brands usually has invested years of time and substantial financial resources into integrated marketing campaigns and strategic brand management. Competing firms may find it difficult to compete unless they, too, make similar investments in branding.

Sponsorship has been touted for its potential to be developed into a resource that can be used to create a distinctive competence for a firm (Amis, Slack & Berrett, 1999). Specifically, sponsorship can be developed into an intangible resource (Amis, Pant & Slack, 1997). Realization of global sport sponsorship opportunities as an organizational resource will likely occur only if a sponsor views sponsorship as it does other resources it possesses; it must view it as an investment that requires cultivation rather than an expense that should be controlled. Many sponsorships end in disappointment for sponsors because they do not perceive the benefits received from a sponsorship justify costs of rights fees to be associated with an event. In some cases, this perception may be accurate; particularly as rights fees for some top-tier properties have spiraled sharply upward in recent years. For example, IBM discontinued its Olympic sponsorship following the 2000 Summer Olympics, ending a forty-year association with the Olympics (Elkin, 2002). The company decided to move sponsorship dollars into other types of events amid rising rights fees and uncertainty surrounding the sponsorship's return on investment.

In other cases, sponsors underestimate the investments of money and time necessary to activate a sponsorship and transform it into a resource. Investment in collateral marketing communication (e.g. advertising, sales promotion and public relations) is considered a necessity in order to reach a target audience and establish a brand's involvement with an event in the audience's mind (Crimmins & Horn, 1996). This becomes particularly important for global events (see Madrigal et al., this volume) that have multiple sponsors and thus may preclude easy association of individual sponsors. Also, sponsors may become impatient as they look for results from sponsorship participation such as increases in sales or market share. If sponsorship objectives are not being reached, participation may be discontinued out of concerns that sponsorship expenditures are not providing an adequate return on investment. This decision may be shortsighted because the brand-building benefits of sponsorship appear to be greater when an association with an event property has a long-term orientation (Cornwell, Roy & Steinard, 2001).

Sponsorship as a Source of Competitive Advantage

Resources that are distinct or unique to an organization give it an advantage over competing firms and potentially allow the firm to exploit those resources for its benefit. Hunt and Morgan (1995) provide an explanation of the role a firm's resources play in its marketing strategies through their comparative advantage theory of competition. Hunt and Morgan's theory posits that a firm's resources extend beyond physical assets and human resources to include such intangible resources as information and relationships. Sponsorships are a type of relational resource a firm can develop to create a comparative advantage. One characteristic of sponsorships that make them potentially valuable resources is that sponsorships are rather immobile. That is, sponsorships cannot be sold or transferred to competing firms as easily as other assets (e.g. equipment and land).

Another characteristic of sponsorships as a resource is that they can be difficult to copy or emulate. Property owners can assist potential sponsors in this area by offering product category exclusivity so that only one firm for a given product category has the rights to be associated with a particular event. While somewhat problematic for properties that reach into multiple national markets, such a practice would make it difficult for competitors to develop similar resources, although the practice of ambush marketing is often undertaken for that purpose. Ambush marketing is a strategy in which a firm attempts to indirectly associate itself with an event to project the appearance of being an official event sponsor (Sandler & Shani, 1989; see also Hoek, this volume). Common ambush marketing practices include buying media advertising time during televised events for which a brand is not an event sponsor (but creates the perception that it is) and establishing a presence at or near events for which a brand is not an official sponsor. Sport properties can add value to their sponsors when they actively manage the size and industry composition of their sponsor rosters as well as police would-be ambush marketers.

Effective management of sponsorships as an organizational resource can transform them into sources of competitive advantage. A firm possesses a competitive advantage when it can serve customers' needs better than its competitors. Sources of competitive advantage often arise from functions such as research and development, manufacturing, or human resources. However, sources of competitive advantage can arise from a firm's marketing activities, too (Ferrell, Hartline & Lucas, 2002). A competitive advantage that is recognized and exploited by a firm can be used to develop a position in a marketplace that is difficult for competitors to copy. A competitive advantage can be particularly difficult to copy when costs required to acquire and cultivate resources needed to create the advantage are high (Hunt & Morgan, 1996). In the case of global sport properties, substantial rights fees and other required investments for marquee events make it unlikely other firms could enjoy similar benefits. For example, Anheuser-Busch brand Budweiser is the official beer of the FA Premier League and the FIFA World Cup, two prestigious global football properties (FA Premier League, 2004). The financial commitment required to associate with such prestigious properties, coupled with exclusive rights afforded Budweiser (e.g. pouring rights at venues and official online partner of the FA Premier League), make it almost impossible for any other beer brand to have the same position with the properties.

One classification of sources of competitive advantage holds that a firm can create a competitive advantage in one of three areas: operational excellence, product leadership, or customer intimacy (Treacy & Wiersema, 1995). Sport sponsorships can be used to create a competitive advantage of customer intimacy. Firms that develop a competitive advantage in terms of customer intimacy usually are recognized as being superior in terms of understanding and meeting customers' needs. For example, IBM (information technology) and Nordstrom (department store) are cited as firms that excel in learning their customers' needs and providing solutions to meet those needs. However, customer intimacy has been described in rather narrow terms of providing exceptional customer service. While such service can indeed by a source of competitive advantage, there are other ways to become intimate, or close to customers.

Sponsorships should be viewed as an extension of the customer intimacy advantage that a firm can create. When a sponsor partners with a sport property, it stands to gain positive benefits such as image transfer from event to brand (Gwinner, 1997, and this volume) and the potential to connect with its target market on an emotional level. For example, fans that have a high level of identification with a particular team may perceive sponsors as a partner or extension of the team (Gwinner & Swanson, 2003). Such perceptions may lead to the creation of favorable attitudes toward a sponsor in potentially disparate overseas markets. If a sponsor can achieve this level of response from the target audience it has succeeded in creating customer intimacy by being associated with something (e.g. a sporting event or team) that is highly relevant to them, and it will be difficult for competitors to occupy similar positions with the same audience.

The resource development implications of sponsorship should be of great interest to firms operating in global markets. As firms extend operations beyond their home countries, resource requirements can increase in terms of investments in manufacturing and human resources as well as marketing investments in product development, market research and marketing communication. Management of sport sponsorship as an organizational resource that can be applied across geographic markets, however, can provide an opportunity to establish efficiencies. If a single sponsorship with a global sport property (e.g. the FIFA World Cup) can be leveraged in several different countries, the benefit is a consistent presentation of the brand across markets. Similarly, if a firm chooses to adapt marketing strategies to local markets, sponsorships of properties relevant to individual markets can be undertaken to build a collection of sponsorship resources.

Marketing Level Sponsorship Planning

Sponsorship objectives, strategies and tactics are often established within the framework of a firm's marketing communication program. That is, sponsorship is viewed as a tool for achieving marketing communication objectives. However, the role of sponsorship in a firm's strategy should be defined early in the strategic marketing planning process. If sponsorships are managed as a resource as discussed in the preceding section, they should figure prominently in a firm's overall marketing strategy and not merely a communication tool employed as part of the marketing mix. One of the first planning tasks required in strategic marketing planning is assessment of a firm's current internal and external environment. Firms that possess sponsorship resources should identify them as an organizational strength just as other resources are treated (e.g. high brand equity or a reputation for quality products). Identification of strengths, coupled with recognition of opportunities that exist in the external environment, can become the foundation of a firm's marketing strategy (Ferrell et al., 2002).

Growth Strategies and Sponsorship Management

After a situation analysis is conducted, it is then possible for managers to establish objectives that a firm desires to achieve through its global marketing strategies. It is at this stage of the strategic planning process that decisions should be made about how to exploit sponsorship resources a firm may possess. A key component of the strategic marketing planning process is identification of growth strategies that a firm will pursue in order to maximize returns in different markets. A widely used growth strategy typology is to identify growth opportunities in terms of a firm's product mix and its customer markets served (Kerin, Mahajan & Varadarajan, 1990). This approach to determining growth opportunities identifies whether growth efforts will focus on development of new products or existing products and whether these products will target existing customer markets or new markets. The role that sponsorship resources can have in pursuing two of these strategies, market penetration and market development, is discussed in the following paragraphs.

Market Penetration   A market penetration strategy seeks to achieve growth by attempting to increase consumption of existing products among existing customer markets. This strategy can take one of two routes: Increasing usage rate among existing customers or persuading competitors' customers to switch brands (Lehmann & Winer, 2002). A market penetration strategy is often employed when products are in the maturity stage of the product life cycle, experiencing low growth rates in terms of dollar sales and number of customers. Many brands in the maturity stage have been in the marketplace for several years, sometimes decades, and enjoy high levels of brand awareness among consumers. In this case, sponsorship can impact brand awareness by serving to remind consumers about the brand and influence a brand's presence in consumers' evoked sets as well as seek to impact top-of-mind brand awareness.

Integration of sponsorship with other marketing communication tools can facilitate implementation of a market penetration strategy. For example, Snickers uses its sponsorship of the National Football League in the United States to create excitement for the brand and stimulate product sales. Snickers supports its NFL sponsorship through advertising on "Monday Night Football" and in *Sports Illustrated*. Also, it developed a "Hungriest Player of the Game" sales promotion, which requires fans to have a code from a product wrapper to participate in an online sweepstakes following a "Monday Night Football' broadcast (Lefton, 2003). In this case, Snickers is seeking to leverage its association with the NFL to positively impact sales and reinforce the Snickers brand name in the minds of football fans. Investments in the NFL sponsorship and supporting marketing communication activities will potentially enable Snickers to strengthen its connection with the NFL and transform the sponsorship into a resource for its parent company, Masterfoods.

An alternative market penetration strategy is to target competitors' customers as a means of growth. This approach contains greater risk for a firm than targeting customers that already purchase its products. The choice of a market penetration strategy that targets competitors' customers places a premium on understanding the customer, including knowing characteristics such as common demographics and benefits sought from product use. In addition to learning these fundamental characteristics, a more intimate knowledge of customers can be utilized to connect with them meaningfully. Insights into such psychographics as customers' lifestyles, interests and values can be utilized to relate to customers on a more personal, emotional level. Firms that succeed in developing such insights have the potential to create a competitive advantage of customer intimacy as discussed in an earlier section.

Sponsorship can play a role in a market penetration strategy that focuses on competitors' customers if it is viewed as a resource. A firm must be willing to invest in a sponsorship beyond the monies paid in rights fees that give it the opportunity to associate itself with an event. Also, the efficacy of sponsorship in targeting competitors' customers is enhanced when a firm can create a distinct position in consumers' minds that its brand should be the only brand from its product category associated with an event. Category exclusivity offered by many properties assists in allowing sponsors to create distinct associations in consumers' minds. A sponsorship that has the potential to attract competitors' customers is the Olympics sponsorship by South Korean electronics firm Samsung. The company competes in several product categories, but it chose to become the official wireless communications sponsor for the Olympics. Samsung claims to be the number one or number two firm in many industries in which it operates, but the wireless communication products category is an exception (International Olympic Committee, 2003).

Sponsorship of a global event such as the Olympics allows Samsung to showcase its products for participants and spectators without facing competition from any other manufacturer. This scenario is preferable to one in which competitors vie for the same consumers through the same type of property. When two competing firms extend their rivalry to similar sponsorships, it is rather difficult for either firm to establish an advantage. An example of such a situation exists in the NASCAR Nextel Cup Series in the United States. The two major firms in the home improvement retail store category, Home Depot and Lowe's, both sponsor racing teams. While their sponsorships of successful drivers (Tony Stewart and Jimmie Johnson, respectively) create a great deal of exposure for their companies, their sponsorships may do more to create competitive parity than to create a unique position in consumers' minds.

Market Development Another basis for a firm's growth strategy is to focus on developing new customer markets. These markets can be defined in terms of customer characteristics (e.g. demographics or psychographics) or geographic areas (e.g. entry into foreign markets). When market development is based on customer characteristics, the goal is to appeal to market segments not presently targeted to expand a firm's potential customer base. An example of a firm that has sought to reach new customer markets is Anheuser-Busch. Although it is the world's largest beer marketer, Anheuser-Busch's objective is to grow revenues both in the United States and in global markets.

Sponsorship has played a key role in Anheuser-Busch's strategy to target specific customer markets. Anheuser-Busch became associated with FIFA World Cup Soccer, sponsoring both the men's and women's World Cup events. The company effectively used these global events to target certain audiences. Anheuser-Busch's Budweiser brand is a sponsor of the men's event, while its Bud Light brand is a sponsor of the women's event. This strategy enables Anheuser-Busch to connect with audiences via a property that has a desirable level of reach yet provides the company an opportunity to customize its communications with male and female audiences.

A firm can also expand its customer base by entering new geographic markets. This strategy has been utilized more frequently as many companies saturate their home country markets and must look to other countries to sustain growth rates to which they have grown accustomed. For example, Anheuser-Busch holds a commanding 49.8% market share in the United States, thus capture of incremental market share is difficult. Domestic sales volume increased by only 0.8% in 2003. The company has an objective of 5% annual volume growth in markets outside the United States (Anheuser-Busch, 2003).

Market development growth strategies can be supported by sponsorships regardless of whether the geographic growth focus is global or specific countries. Anheuser-Busch views China as an attractive growth opportunity and has entered into two sponsorships with global reach designed to create an impact in the country. First, Budweiser became a sponsor of the BMW Williams Formula One racing team. Budweiser's association with Formula One is timely given that the first ever Formula One race in China was held in Shanghai in 2004. Second, Anheuser-Busch has entered into Olympics' sponsorships that will directly impact the company's presence in China. Budweiser was the official beer sponsor of the 2004 China Olympic team. Also, Budweiser will be associated with the 2008 Summer Olympics in Beijing as the exclusive international beer sponsor. Budweiser can use the logo of the Beijing Olympics in its marketing activities, and the cost of the sponsorship through the Beijing Organizing Committee was a fraction that it would have paid for sponsorship of the same event through the International Olympic Committee (Thomaselli, 2004).

Decisions about the types of properties to sponsor and the desired geographic reach of a property are influenced by a firm's approach to marketing in multiple countries. A global marketer's decision about where it will operate along the standardization–localization continuum will guide selection of properties for sponsorship. Some properties support standardization of marketing strategies across countries by virtue of their extensive reach. Other properties may offer reach in a single region or country, which provide a firm with a vehicle for supporting a localization strategy.

Vodafone, a wireless communications marketer based in the United Kingdom, has created a sponsorship portfolio of properties that are relevant to consumers in its home market yet have international reach. Major Vodafone sponsorships include its sponsorship of Manchester United, Ferrari Formula One racing team, and the English Cricket Team (Vodafone Group, 2004). Selection of these properties supports the firm's strategy to move away from local sponsorships and instead sponsor global properties that can be leveraged across multiple countries (Gillis, 2004). However, Vodafone has the flexibility to customize marketing communications (e.g. advertising or sales promotions) tied to these properties to increase effectiveness in individual markets (i.e. support a localization strategy).

Brand Level Sponsorship Planning

Once marketing objectives have been established, the next phase of the strategic marketing planning process is formulation of a marketing mix that outlines the strategies that will be employed at the brand level in pursuit of a firm's market-ing objectives. Often, it is at this stage of the strategic planning process that sponsorships first come under consideration. Sponsorship draws the interest of many managers as they evaluate the promotion element of the marketing mix. Expenditures for sponsorships in the past decade have grown at rates faster than expenditures for mass media advertising and sales promotion (International Events Group, 2002). A primary reason for this trend is that sponsorships avoid media clutter and offer an environment in which a brand can communicate with its target market and distinguish itself from competitors. A key brand-building benefit offered by sponsorship that can be leveraged within the framework of a firm or brand's marketing strategy is articulation of brand position.

Brand Positioning

Intense competition in many industries has created an unprecedented need to differentiate a firm's brand from alternatives in the marketplace. A key branding strategy designed to create this differentiation is known as brand positioning. It is an attempt to create for the brand a unique place in consumers' minds (Davis, 2002). When a brand is effectively positioned, it provides direction for a firm's marketing strategies, meaning that marketing mix decisions should be made with the goal of reinforcing the desired brand position. A marketing manager can position a brand with one of two objectives in mind: Competition-based positioning or goal-based positioning (Tybout & Sternthal, 2001). Competition-based positioning is a necessary first step for a brand, particularly if it is perceived to have few points of difference compared to other brands.

Sponsorship can be used to implement a competition-based positioning strategy. Effective positioning of a brand via sponsorship can influence consumers' beliefs about a brand and its superiority to competitors. One view of sponsorship's influence with consumers is a behaviorist perspective that contends a consumer could be influenced through sponsorship by vicarious learning (Hoek, Gendall, Jeffcoat & Orsman, 1997). Vicarious learning can take place when a consumer observes a player or team using certain products at the event. A consumer might observe, "If Shell fuel is good enough to help Michael Schumacher win seven Formula One driver championships, certainly it is good enough to put in my passenger vehicle." In this case, associating Shell with a championship racecar driver can support a brand position of high quality, and other petroleum fuel brands would have difficulty creating a similar position using a Formula One sponsorship.

A global brand that has used sport sponsorship to achieve competition-based positioning is Avaya, an information technology and communications firm. Avaya is the official "convergence communication provider" of the FIFA World Cup men and women's soccer tournaments (Avaya, 2003). Avaya's products and services are utilized in the staging of the World Cup as well as opportunities to receive global brand exposure during televised matches. The benefit of impacting awareness is substantial, but the brand associations created by Avaya's association with FIFA are instrumental in consumers' understanding of the brand and create points of difference between Avaya and its competitors. Sport properties can add value to sponsorships by offering category exclusivity to sponsors, which effectively allows a brand to receive exposure without concerns about the presence of direct competitors.

A goal-based positioning approach requires that consumers develop a deeper understanding of a brand in order to understand how it can meet their needs or goals. A key to successful goal-based positioning via sponsorship is that a sponsored event must be relevant to a brand's target market (Davis, 2002). Relevance of an event to a brand's target market can influence how consumers perceive a sponsorship. A brand that has excelled at articulating a goal-based position via sponsorship is Mountain Dew. The brand leveraged a product attribute, caffeine, to position itself as a carbonated beverage for young, active people. Sponsorship of action sports has been used to reinforce this position. Mountain Dew has capitalized on the increased interest in action sports in the United States. Among the brand's sponsorships are the Summer X Games, an annual action sports competition, as well as sponsorship of several top individual athletes in BMX biking, skateboarding, inline skating, freestyle motor cross and snowboarding (Mountain Dew, 2003). Competing beverage brands would face a very difficult challenge if they attempted to adopt a similar brand position. Not only has Mountain Dew secured the position of being the carbonated beverage of choice for young people with active lifestyles, it has effectively blocked competitors from using action sports to communicate brand position. Further discussion of action sports as a marketing vehicle is presented in this book in the chapter authored by Gladden and McDonald.

The premise of brand positioning is to articulate an element of a brand's identity and communicate it to target audiences. However, the idea of "one voice positioning" may not be the most effective strategy for global marketers. A firm that operates in multiple countries must be cognizant of how cultural and language differences could impact an audience's response to a brand-event linkage created via sponsorship. An obvious tactic to employ to minimize this risk is to create a sponsorship portfolio of properties with a national, regional or local geographic scope. Such a tactic would be appropriate for a global firm that utilizes a localization approach to operating in international markets.

Firms seeking to create economies of scale in their sponsorship portfolio may rely more on sponsorship of global properties, with customization of brand messages by geographic market. For example, Samsung co-sponsored the first around-the-world Olympic Torch relay prior to the 2004 Summer Olympics. The tour went through more than twenty countries, and Samsung developed a marketing initiative that was localized to each country. Customization of the message included considerations of translation of brand information into local languages and selection of music at the event that was appropriate for each country (Bond, 2004). Samsung's localization efforts created meaningful experiences across many countries without compromising the brand's integrity.

Conclusion

The growth in sponsorship expenditures worldwide in the last decade suggests that many firms recognize sponsorship's capabilities as a communication vehicle. Sponsorship has been widely cited as a creative communication tool that enables a brand to cut through message clutter that plagues mass media. Also, sponsorship is an ideal platform for development of an integrated marketing communication program because of the opportunities available to communicate a sponsorship using promotion mix tools (i.e. advertising, sales promotion, public relations and personal selling).

Perhaps the greatest benefit offered by sponsorship is its ability to allow a brand to communicate with its target market in a *relevant* way. The deep feelings attached to sport are sometimes very obvious; normal activity in an entire nation may cease for a few hours when its national team is involved in an important contest in events such as the Olympics or the FIFA World Cup. Emotional attachments to a sport property run the gamut of global, national, regional, and local properties. When a brand is able to resonate with its target market through sponsorship, the potential payoffs are substantial in terms of effectively articulating brand position and creating customer-based brand equity.

Consideration of the role of sponsorship in a firm's business strategy should appear throughout the strategic planning process. Strategic planning at the organization level should incorporate an understanding that sponsorship planning begins with managing sponsorships as a resource. The result of adopting such an approach is that sponsorships become viewed as investments that should be proactively managed and not expenditures that can easily be reduced or eliminated at the first sign of economic difficulty. When sponsorships are managed as a resource, it is possible to begin exploring opportunities for transforming sponsorships into a source of competitive advantage. Connecting with customers via a relevant, involving medium with which they may be emotionally attached such as a sport property can enable a sponsor to engender feelings of intimacy between customers and the brand.

In turn, establishment of marketing objectives should be undertaken with consideration of how sponsorship resources can be employed. Marketing plan objectives, whether they are based on growth in existing customer markets or development of new markets, can be formulated with the knowledge that sponsorship can be employed in pursuit of such objectives. Brand level marketing tactics will include sponsorship activities, but by this point in the strategic planning process sponsorship issues have received a great deal of consideration. An understanding is already in place of sponsorship's role as a resource and as a catalyst for the establishment and pursuit of marketing objectives.

The strategic planning implications of sport sponsorship discussed in this chapter pertain to firms of all sizes and geographic scopes, but firms operating in global markets should be particularly attuned to issues surrounding development of a global sport sponsorship strategy. Global sport sponsorships can be a resource that is shared across multiple geographic markets, creating efficiencies in marketing communication that project a consistent brand identity that crosses cultures and languages.

A commitment to cultivating sponsorship resources should be made at the highest levels of the organization. An example of a company whose sponsorship vision begins at the top of the organization is US-based financial services firm John Hancock. The company's chief executive, David D'Alessandro, has been at the forefront of efforts to build a visible brand using prestigious properties such as the Olympics, Major League Baseball and the Boston Marathon. Demonstration of commitment to sponsorships by top management can extend to marketing level and brand level planning.

Marketing and brand level sponsorship decisions for global marketers will be influenced by whether a standardization or localization strategy is pursued. When sponsorship resources are built primarily on global properties, a standardization strategy would seem to be appropriate. Consideration of leveraging global sport properties should be concerned with the availability of mediums to send messages to target audiences. A few properties (e.g. the Olympics) have a long-standing global broadcast distribution that enables the event to reach a large audience. Other properties with broad appeal may be lacking a medium that would enable them to reach more people. In recent years, the geographic reach of sport properties has been enhanced significantly by two media innovations: the Internet and satellite television. For example, Formula One racing had little impact in the United States for sponsors because it lacked a broadcast partner for its races. That problem has been eliminated as US F1 fans can now follow the circuit on News Corporation's Speed Channel, available via satellite and cable to more than 66 million households in North America (Speed Channel, 2004).

The ability to standardize the articulation of a global sponsorship is important, but it does not preclude localizing messages delivered via the sponsorship. Articulation of global properties can be tailored to specific audiences in individual markets. For example, a sponsor can use its language or country-specific websites as a vehicle for customizing message content about its sponsorships. Likewise, a sponsor can offer customized content using opt-in e-mail programs, communicating only with those persons who have given the sponsor permission to send information to them.

The decision whether to standardize or localize communication delivered via sport sponsorship may be a moot point in the future. An executive with one of the world's largest global brands signaled a possible end to standardization strategy, as it is known. Larry Light, McDonald's global chief marketing officer, said "Identifying one brand positioning, communicating it in a repetitive manner, is old fashioned, out-of-date, out-of-touch brand communication" (cf. Cardona, 2004, p. 1). The idea that brands hold different meanings for different people means that a single brand position is inadequate. The variation in brand meanings is magnified when the brand operates in approximately 120 countries, as does McDonald's.

The challenge facing global firms in creation of a sponsorship strategy is how to develop resources that can be extended efficiently throughout a firm's geographic markets while creating meaningful communication in each market. In the future, a firm's ability to create maximum audience reach yet tailor communications to specific groups may be a more important determinant of sponsorship effectiveness than its mix of global versus local properties in its sponsorship portfolio. Audience reach must be sufficient to generate a desired return on sponsorship investment that is increasingly being sought by a firm's owners. At the same time, a sponsor must strive to achieve more than mere brand exposure and resonate with audiences on an emotional level, a challenge that is made greater by cultural and language differences.

References

Amis, J., Slack, T. and Berrett, T. (1999) "Sport Sponsorship as a Distinctive Competence," *European Journal of Marketing*, 33 (3–4): 250–272.

Amis, J., Pant, N. and Slack, T. (1997) "Achieving a Sustainable Competitive Advantage: A Resource-based View of Sport Sponsorship," *Journal of Sport Management*, 11 (1): 80–96.

Anheuser-Busch (2003) http://www.anheuser-busch.com/annual/default.htm, accessed December 4.

Avaya (2003) http://worldcup.avaya.com/, accessed September 18.

Bond, C. (2004) "World Drives Go Back to Basics," *Event*, September, 15.

Buzell, R. D. and Gale, B. T. (1987) *The PIMS Principles: Linking Strategy to Performance*, New York: The Free Press.

Cardona, M. M. (2004) "Mass Marketing Meets Its Maker," *Advertising Age*, 75 (25): 1, 25.

Cornwell, T. B., Roy, D. P., and Steinard, E. A. II (2001) "Exploring Managers' Perceptions of the Impact of Sponsorship on Brand Equity," *Journal of Advertising*, 30 (2): 41–51.

Crimmins, J. and Horn, M. (1996) "Sponsorship: From Management Ego Trip Marketing Success," *Journal of Advertising Research*, 36 (July/August): 11–20.

Davis, S. M. (2002) *Brand Asset Management*, San Francisco, CA: Jossey-Bass.

Elkin, T. (2002) "IBM Re-Examines Sponsorships," *Advertising Age*, 73 (8): 3–4.

FA Premier League (2004) http://www.premierleague.com/fapl.rac?command=forwardOnly&nextPage=enPartners&categoryCode=Partners, accessed October 11.

Ferrell, O. C., Hartline, M. D. and Lucas, G. H. (2002) *Marketing Strategy*, 2nd edn. Fort Worth, TX: Harcourt.

Gillis, R. (2004) "Global Deal, Local Glory," *Marketing*, August 11, 36–37.

Gwinner, K. (1997) "A Model of Image Creation and Image Transfer in Event Sponsorship," *International Marketing Review*, 14 (3): 145–158.

Gwinner, K. and Swanson, S. R. (2003) "A Model of Fan Identification: Antecedents and Sponsorship Outcomes," *Journal of Services Marketing*, 17 (3): 275–294.

Hoek, J., Gendall, P., Jeffcoat, M. and Orsman, D. (1997) "Sponsorship and Advertising: A Comparison of Their Effects," *Journal of Marketing Communications*, 3: 21–32.

Hunt, S. D. and Morgan, R. M. (1995) "The Comparative Advantage Theory of Competition," *Journal of Marketing*, 59 (1): 1–15.

Hunt, S.D. and Morgan, R.M. (1996) "The Resource-Advantage Theory of Competition: Dynamics, Path Dependencies, and Evolutionary Dimensions," *Journal of Marketing*, 60 (4): 107–114.

International Events Group (2003) http://www.sponsorship.com/learn/northamericaspending.asp, accessed August 21.

International Events Group (2002) http://www.sponsorship.com/learn/index.asp, accessed January 22.

International Olympic Committee (2003) http://www.olympic.org/uk/organisation/facts/programme/profiles_uk.asp, accessed August 28.

Kerin, R. A., Mahajan, V. and Varadarajan, R. (1990) *Strategic Market Planning*, Boston, MA: Allyn and Bacon.

Lefton, T. (2003) "Snickers Bulks Up NFL Efforts with 'MNF' Tie," *Street & Smith's Sports Business Journal*, 6 (12): 1, 5.

Lehmann, D. R. and Winer, R. S. (2002) *Product Management,* 3rd edition, Burr Ridge, IL: McGraw-Hill Irwin

Mountain Dew (2003) http://mountaindew.com/sports/athletes/, accessed September 12.

Porter, M. (1980) *Competitive Strategy*, New York: The Free Press.

Porter, M. (1985) *Competitive Advantage: Creating and Sustaining Superior Performance*, New York: The Free Press.

Porter (1989) *The Competitive Advantage of Nations and Their Firms*, New York: The Free Press.

Sandler, D. M. and Shani, D. (1989) "Olympic Sponsorship vs. 'Ambush' Marketing: Who Gets the Gold?" *Journal of Advertising Research*, 29 (August/September): 9–14.

Speed Channel (2004) http://www.speedtv.com/speed/press.php, accessed December 5.

Thomaselli, R. (2004) "Bud Skirts IOC for Beijing Gold," *Advertising Age*, 75 (40): 1–2.

Treacy, M. and Wiersema, F. (1995) *The Discipline of Market Leaders*, Reading, MA: Perseus Books.

Tybout, A. M. and Sternthal, B. (2001) "Brand Positioning" in D. Iacobucci (ed.), *Kellogg on Marketing*, New York: John Wiley and Sons, pp. 31–57.

van Gelder, S. (2004) "Global Brand Strategy," *Brand Management*, 12 (1): 39–48.

Vodafone Group (2004) http://www.vodafone.co.uk/cgi-bin/COUK/portal/ep/browse.do?channelPath=%2FVodafone+Portal%2FAbout+Vodafone%2FSponsorship&BV_SessionID=@@@@0315674005.1102171794@@@@&BV_EngineID=cccfadddfefmlhgcflgcegjdgnfdffn.0, accessed November 8.

Wernerfelt, B. (1984) "A Resource-Based View of the Firm," *Strategic Management Journal*, 5: 171–180.

8

Image Transfer in Global Sport Sponsorship

Theoretical support and boundary conditions

Kevin Gwinner

Tostitos corn chips sponsors the Fiesta Bowl, Mountain Dew sponsors the X Games Global Championship, Flybe (a European regional airline) sponsors Birmingham City FC of the English Premier League, Malaysian car manufacturer Proton is the shirt sponsor of Norwich City FC, and Manchester United is paid nearly US$13 million to wear Vodafone patches on its team uniforms. These are only a few of the thousands of sponsorship arrangements being made at all levels of sport all around the world. Further, these are not insignificant arrangements as they can involve huge sums of money being paid by the brands (US Cellular has just signed a 23-year, US$68 million stadium-naming sponsorship deal with the Chicago White Sox) for the privilege of sponsoring the event, the stadium, the team, or even a small and seemingly minor aspect associated with the sport (e.g. Tim Hortons is the official "coffee and baked goods" restaurant of the Canadian Football League).

Why would a firm spend millions of dollars to get their company name on a stadium or brand logo on a uniform? What form of return do companies hope to receive for these global investments (Meenaghan's chapter in this volume on evaluating sponsorship effects may be useful in understanding the different types of objectives in sport sponsorship)? One benefit of sponsorship is the ability of the corporation to use the event as a venue for client cultivation. Skyboxes, VIP passes and other luxuries can be used in efforts to entertain and solicit business from new clients and retain the business of existing customers. At sporting events, a high level of interpersonal interaction is possible, which facilitates deals being made, relationships being strengthened and information being shared. Another important objective for many companies is to use sport sponsorship as an opportunity to build consumer awareness for the brand among key market segments (Turley & Shannon, 2000; Walliser, 2003). With the increase in television and radio coverage of different sport types (and especially in non-traditional sports including snowboarding, rodeo, women's basketball, skateboarding, motocross, women's boxing and lacrosse), the ability of a brand to achieve gains in awareness are increasing. Further, the international popularity and media coverage of many sporting events greatly increases the number of spectators far beyond the boundaries of the particular country in which the sport is played. However, for many "household-name" brands the appeal of added awareness is limited. In a recent article in the *Sydney Morning Herald* discussing the Australian sport sponsorship industry, an industry expert commented that "awareness doesn't mean anything to the likes of Qantas and Telstra any more," adding. "They are looking at connections [with the audience]" (Lee, 2004).

Another goal of sponsorship, and the topic of this chapter, involves the brand leveraging the image of the event (Meenaghan, 2001). That is, it is thought that by connecting the brand with an event, some of the positive associations cosumers have toward the event will be linked to the sponsoring brand.[1] This process is referred to as image transfer. As will be discussed in this chapter, the global nature of many sport sponsorships creates both opportunities (e.g. greater exposure) and challenges (e.g. different markets all exposed to the same image transfer information, even though positioning goals may differ between regions) for managers interested in managing brand image perceptions among target markets.

In the remainder of this chapter, I first discuss the theoretical underpinnings of image transfer and review recent empirical findings of image transfer in a sponsorship context. Second, factors that moderate (alter the strength) of the transfer process are discussed with a particular focus on issues related to sponsoring events in a global environment. Finally, the chapter poses a variety of notable issues related to image transfer that remain largely understudied in the area of global sport sponsorship. Figure 8.1 provides a graphical representation of the concepts and their inter-relationships discussed in this chapter.

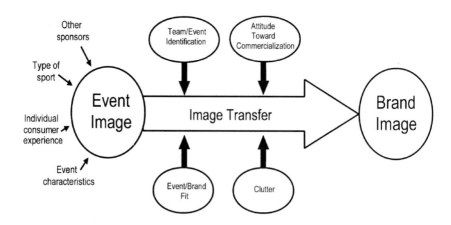

Figure 8.1 *Image transfer in global sport sponsorship.*

Image Transfer

A consumer's knowledge about a brand reflects all of the different types of information that a consumer associates with the brand that is held in their memory (Keller, 2003). These brand associations can take many forms including attributes, benefits, experiences, and attitudes (Keller, 1993, 2003). In his early work on brand equity, Keller (1993) suggested that these "associations" are developed from a variety of sources including brand and product category experiences, product attributes, price information, positioning in promotional communications, packaging, user imagery (e.g. typical brand users), and usage occasion. In addition, brand associations can be influenced through celebrity endorsement and sponsorship activities (Keller, 1993). In the case of event sponsorship, "when the brand becomes linked with the event, some of the associations with the event may become indirectly associated with the brand" (Keller, 1993, p. 11). This linking of event "associations" to the brand is what is meant by the term "image transfer." That is, the image of the event is being transferred to the image of the sponsoring brand when an individual connects information about the event's attributes, event's benefits, or attitudes about the event with the brand in his/her memory.

Keller's views are consistent with the theory of meaning transfer that McCracken (1989) uses to explain the celebrity endorsement process. This theory suggests that consumers assign "meaning" to celebrities based upon an individual's interpretation of the celebrity's public image as demonstrated in "television, movies, military, athletics, and other careers" (McCracken, 1989, p. 315). Meaning moves *from* the celebrity endorser *to* the product when the two are paired in an endorsement capacity (McCracken, 1989). Consumption of the endorsed product then transfers this meaning to the consumer, which, presumably, is a motivating force in the individual's decision to select and purchase the endorsed product.

One can logically extend this concept to a global sponsorship context where the meanings (or "associations" in Keller's terminology) held with respect to an event are transferred to a sponsoring brand, thus providing those consumers who are favorably disposed toward those meanings a reason to purchase the sponsoring brand. While consumers attribute meaning to celebrities based upon their public activities (e.g. sport participation, movie roles, etc.), sporting events develop meaning or associations from their unique characteristics. For example, it has been suggested that part of the meaning consumers attribute to sporting events will be based upon the type of sport (e.g. football versus ice skating), the event's characteristics (e.g. professional status, venue, global exposure, etc.), and individual consumer factors such as one's past experiences with the event (Gwinner, 1997; Meenaghan, 2001; Parker, 1991). In a sports context, and consistent with Keller and McCraken's reasoning, Ferrand and Pages (1996) proposed a model of image transfer based on the concept of social representation. Under this framework, a less recognized brand would be anchored within the context of a more recognized event.

Gwinner and Eaton (1999) demonstrated the image transfer process empirically in a sports sponsorship context. Using an experiment, they found that the image of a specific event and brand were reported to be more congruent by those that had been exposed to the sponsorship, than by those who were not exposed to the sponsorship treatment. Their image transfer measure focused on event and brand "personality" as one aspect of image. Brand personality can be regarded as "the set of human characteristics associated with a brand" (Aaker, 1997, p. 347). Brand personality has been described as an important aspect of brand image that is impacted by one's expectations of the type of person who would use a particular product – user imagery – and in which situations a product might be used – usage imagery (Aaker, 1997; Keller, 1993; Plummer, 1985). Both user and usage imagery can be communicated in an event sponsorship context. The brand personality concept is useful because it serves as a mechanism upon which producers can differentiate their goods and services from competitors. This becomes especially critical when other potentially differentiating features are perceived by consumers as equal across competing brands (Plummer, 1985).

In summary, image transfer occurs in a sponsorship context when the meanings consumers associate with an event become associated with the sponsoring brand. Theoretically, following the associative memory paradigm, the pairing of the event and brand through sponsorship activities (e.g. perimeter signage, media exposure, etc.) provides a link in the consumer's mind between the knowledge they have of the event and their knowledge of the brand.

Boundary Conditions

An important consideration for companies interested in the image transfer aspects of sponsorship is how to leverage the sponsorship to derive the maximum amount of transfer. As such, it is critical to identify factors that may increase or decrease the transfer of image from the event to the brand. As noted earlier, today's global media environment produces both opportunities and challenges for companies engaged in sponsorship arrangements that span across international boundaries. These global sponsorship issues are highlighted within the context of the following four factors that have been discussed in the marketing and sponsorship literature: team identification, attitude toward commercialization, event-brand fit and sponsorship clutter.

Team Identification

Sociologically, sport teams are groups to which individuals relate. Turner (1987, p. 2) describes a group as "one that is psychologically significant for the members to which they relate themselves subjectively for social comparison and the acquisition of norms and values ... which influences their attitudes and behaviors." A spectator is said to be highly identified with a team when they perceive a "connectedness" to the team and feel that the team's successes and failures are also his or her own successes and failures (Ashforth & Mael, 1989;

Gwinner & Swanson, 2003; Hirt, Zillmann, Erickson & Kennedy, 1992; Wann & Branscombe, 1992; Wann, Dolan, McGeorge & Allison, 1994). As such, team identification is a more specific instance of organizational identification (Mael & Ashforth, 1992). Naturally, there are large variations in the extent to which individuals identify with teams ranging from low identified fans to fans that identify highly with the team. Spectators falling on different points of the identification spectrum also act differently toward the team. Low identified fans are likely attracted to the team for the entertainment value and opportunity for social interaction. These fans have little emotional or financial commitment to the team (Sutton, McDonald, Milne & Cimberman, 1997). In contrast, highly identified fans display long-term loyalty to the team and support the team through both their time and financial commitments (Sutton et al., 1997).

Identification with a particular group can serve to increase one's self-esteem (Hogg & Turner, 1985; Tajfel, 1978). In order to accomplish this self-esteem enhancement, the individual must be able to accurately identify group members (in-group) from non-group members (out-group). "To the extent that the in-group is perceived as both different and better than the out-group, thereby achieving positive distinctiveness, one's social identity is enhanced" (Abrams & Hogg, 1990, p. 3). Indeed, the distinctiveness of an organization, how clearly one group is distinguished from other groups, has been shown to be a significant predictor of organizational identification (Mael & Ashforth, 1992). Self-esteem is enhanced by individuals associating themselves with groups they perceive in a favorable way (Cialdini, Boiden, Thorne, Walker, Freeman & Sloan, 1976). More specifically, self-esteem enhancement is accomplished by focusing on the positive elements of the in-group and downplaying their negative aspects (Wann & Branscombe, 1995a, 1995b). Further, emphasizing negative information, and downplaying the positive, among out-groups can similarly contribute to one's self-esteem by elevating the status of the in-group relative to the out-group (Branscombe & Wann, 1994). In general, one's sense of self is enhanced by membership in the group with positive elements and by rejecting membership in the group with negatively perceived elements (Wann & Branscombe, 1990). As such, self-esteem maintenance serves as a motivation for highly identified individuals to actively discriminate between in- and out-group members.

In a sporting context, in-group membership can extend beyond the actual athletes on a team to also include a team's coaches, administrators, and even fans; whereas out-group membership may be assigned to fans and employees (players, coaches, etc.) of rival teams. It is logical to conclude that in a sport sponsorship context, highly identified fans will also extend in-group membership status to brands that sponsor an event or team, because the sponsor is perceived as aiding the team/event in accomplishing its goals (Madrigal, 2000; 2001). Individuals in a sporting context are likely to be especially aware of in-group and out-group membership because intergroup competition (as in sports) has been shown to heighten one's sensitivity to group membership information (Brown & Ross, 1982). Highly identified individuals are more concerned and active (than low identification individuals) in differentiating between in-group and out-group members (Abrams & Hogg, 1990; Wann & Branscombe, 1995a). Thus, those highly identified spectators attending the Asian Windsurfing Tour, a five-event tour in five Asian countries, are more likely to view Lava Eyewear, a sponsor of the tour, as an in-group member.

Potentially, characteristics of a country's national culture may impact the degree to which sponsors are viewed as in-group members. One of Hofstede's (1984) cultural dimensions that is widely discussed is the individualism-collectivism continuum. Those country cultures that are individualistic tend to be characterized by loose ties between people, while collectivist cultures have stronger ties between people. For example, the United States and Canada are individualistic cultures, while Japan and China are collectivist. "Collectivists make heightened distinctions between in-groups and out-groups with reference to the goals and welfare of the in-groups to which they belong" (Hui, Au & Fock, 2004, p. 110). As such, we might expect to see individuals in collectivist cultures to be more sensitive to the manner in which sponsors act as in-group members for the benefit of the group. This added scrutiny places additional responsibilities on sponsors of events that are viewed in collectivist cultures.

The heightened sensitivity exhibited by highly identified fans to in-group and out-group membership will make them more likely to (1) hold a strong image of the event in their mind; and (2) recognize sponsors of the event. This should aid in the image transfer process in two ways. First, a stronger image of the event will better enable the image to be transferred than a weaker image (Keller, 1993). That is, there must *be* an image of the event in the consumer's mind before it can be associated with a sponsor. Highly identified fans have been shown to possess greater objective knowledge about sports and particular teams than low identification fans (Wann & Branscombe, 1995b) and thus are likely to have made stronger connections regarding the event's image in their memory. Second, image transfer requires not only an image of the source of the transfer (event), but also a target (sponsoring brand) to which it can be transferred to. As such, an accurate recall of whom the sponsors are (and are not) will increase the success of the image transfer process. On this second point, sponsor recognition has been shown to be higher among highly identified fans (Lascu, Giese, Toolan, Guetring & Mercer, 1995) and Ashforth and Mael suggest that "awareness of out-groups reinforces awareness of one's in-group" (1989, p. 25). As such, sponsors' in-group status should also aid highly identified fans in correctly recognizing event sponsors, which will have a positive influence on the image transfer process.

To summarize, it is the greater sensitivity to in-group and out-group membership that allows greater image transfer for the highly identified spectator. The potential for self-esteem enhancement motivates the active searching for in-group members and the accurate recognition of sponsors and the enhanced knowledge of the event facilitate the image transfer. Further, national culture difference may influence the manner in which the in-group member is scrutinized.

Attitude Toward Commercialization

It has been suggested that the proliferation of sponsorship in sporting events may lead to negative attitudes toward the events and their sponsors because some consumer segments feel sporting events have become too commercialized, thus detracting from the event itself (Gwinner, 1997; Lee, Sandler & Shani, 1997). Conversely, it has been argued that sponsorship may create feelings of goodwill toward the sponsoring brand/firm if it is perceived as a benefactor who is making the event possible (McDonald, 1991). Indeed, there are many positive consumer benefits provided by commercial sponsorship that are similar to the benefits provided by advertising. For example, the influx of corporate money can reduce event ticket prices and allow games to be shown on network or cable television. An interesting question that has not received attention in the sports marketing literature is how commercialization attitudes may differ by type of sport or even region of the world. That is, there may be particular sports or global regions where sponsorship is well accepted and viewed as a natural component of the event and other sports or regions where sponsorship is viewed more negatively. Thus, in a global media environment, where the same event is viewed across the world, it is possible that the same sponsorship arrangement is viewed positively in one market but negatively in another as a result of consumer's attitudes toward commercialization.

Lee, Sandler and Shani (1997) define attitude toward commercialization as a consumer's reaction to sponsor-initiated commercial activity surrounding an event. Thus, this construct parallels attitude toward advertising in that it represents a favorable or unfavorable attitude toward sponsorship activities in general, rather than an attitude toward any specific commercially oriented sponsorship activity (MacKenzie & Lutz, 1989). Bauer and Greyser (1968) and Andrews (1989) submit that beliefs toward advertising are best described by economic and social dimensions. Specifically, while the general public may understand the economic benefits of corporate commercialization of an event, social attitudes may suggest that corporate sponsorship can be excessive.

Other research in advertising supports this notion. Sandage and Leckenby (1980) and Muehling (1987) have both confirmed that generally individuals have a more positive attitude toward the "institution of advertising" (translated into a sponsorship context as, "the need for events to be sponsored") than the "instruments of advertising" (operationalized in sponsorship as arena signage, changing from traditional stadium names to corporate stadium names, etc.). However, there is a positive correlation between attitude toward the institution of advertising and the instruments of advertising, suggesting that the more favorable one is toward the institution of advertising, the more favorable one will be toward the instruments of advertising, albeit at a reduced rate. Extending these findings into a sponsorship context, if one is favorable toward the institution of sponsorship (e.g. the commercialization of sport), then one typically will be favorable to the vehicles of corporate sponsorship. Further, those individuals with a more positive attitude toward commercialization are more likely to understand the link between the event and sponsorship. In a sporting context, Speed and Thompson (2000) find that perceived sincerity of the sponsor (e.g. sponsorship based on philanthropical concerns) had a significantly positive influence on spectator's attitude toward and intention to use a sponsoring brand. A high level of perceived sponsor sincerity is likely to be inversely related to a negative attitude toward commercialization.

A rather elaborate research stream has provided evidence that one's attitude toward advertising will significantly influence one's attitude toward the ad, which in turn will influence one's attitude toward the brand (e.g. MacKenzie & Lutz, 1989; MacKenzie, Lutz & Belch, 1986; Mitchell, 1986; Mitchell & Olson, 1981; Mittal, 1990). Accordingly, we can expect that one's attitude toward commercialization will impact one's attitude toward both the brand and the event. Specifically, those who have a negative attitude toward commercialization will have an increased negative attitude toward the brand or the event. For example, those who feel that sporting events associated with higher education should focus on their "amateur status" and should not be commercialized, may hold negative attitudes toward those college football postseason bowl games in the United States named after corporate sponsorships (e.g. the Sugar Bowl is currently called the Nokia Sugar Bowl).

While not impacting the strength of the image transfer (weaker or stronger) a negative attitude toward commercialization is likely to taint the type of image transferred. As discussed above, for individuals with a negative attitude toward commercialization, which may be greater in some countries than in others, the meanings associated with the event and brand become linked to negative attitudes due to the perceived inappropriateness of the sponsorship activity.

Event/Brand Fit

Fit, or congruence between objects, is an often-studied phenomenon in the marketing literature. Past research has examined fit in such contexts as a brand and a proposed brand extension, celebrity endorsers and the endorsed goods, and even a brand's name and its country of production (e.g. Häubl & Elrod, 1999; Kahle & Homer, 1985; Kamins, 1990; Lynch & Schuler, 1994; Mirsa & Beatty, 1990; Park, Milberg & Lawson, 1991; Till & Busler, 2000). The interest in this topic is justifiable because the similarity between two stimuli impacts the degree to which knowledge and affect are transferred between the objects (Martin & Stewart, 2001). Given that image transfer is often a goal in sponsorship decisions, a more complete understanding of how event–sponsoring brand fit may impact the image transfer process is needed.

There has been much speculation and empirical assessment in examining brand-event fit in sporting contexts. Meenaghan (2001) reports that focus group participants were able to discern congruence between some event–sponsor pairings, this assessment is based on there being a "logical connection between both parties to the relationship (i.e. sponsor and sponsored activity)" (p. 105). In a recent study examining fit in a sponsorship context it was found that image transfer between event and sponsoring brand was enhanced when respondents perceived either a functional (brand is used in the event) or image based (abstract perceptions) similarity to exist between the event and brand (Gwinner & Eaton, 1999). Using a more generalized measure of event–sponsor fit and a student sample, Speed and Thompson (2000) found a positive relationship between degree of fit and respondent's interest in the sponsor, attitude toward the sponsor, and intention to use the sponsored product. Other research has found fit between brand and sport to be positively associated with the perceived personality match between the two (Musante, Milne & McDonald, 1999). Foster's Beer, the largest selling Australian beer brand in the world, appears to recognize the importance of linking their brand to an event which matches well with their image. In recent communications they have described the pairing as a "partnership between two of the world's most desirable and high profile global properties" where "both Foster's Lager and Formula One are international, fun, aspirational, youthful and glamorous" (Foster's Group, 2004). Of course fit depends upon the perceived image of both the event and the sponsor. Sponsors of events viewed globally have to be particularly careful as the company may be positioning the brand in different ways in different countries. This has the potential to cause a sponsoring brand's image to fit with the event in one country, but not fit in another where the brand's image is different due to different positioning. A similar fit mismatch situation could occur if the brand positioning is consistent across countries, but the image of the event changes. Thus, the fit issue is an important consideration that needs to be taken into account when companies evaluate sponsorship arrangements that span international boundaries.

The theory of associative memory provides the rationale for why event–brand fit will positively moderate event to brand image transfer. Under this framework, one's memory is represented as a series of concepts or nodes that are linked together with ties of varying strength (Anderson, 1983). As discussed earlier, Keller (1993) uses this framework to suggest that the concepts associated with an event can become linked in memory with a brand through sponsorship activities. However, the ease to which an individual processes, encodes and links these concepts is higher when there is a perceived similarity between the concepts (Meyers-Levy & Tybout, 1989). This perspective is consistent with the schema theory based argument for endorser–brand fit advanced by Misra and Beatty (1990). To explain the better recall of respondents in their "congruent" condition, they propose that inconsistent information is filtered out and not brought into memory as well as consistent information (Misra & Beatty, 1990). If the same process holds true for image transfer, then we would expect that when the event and sponsoring brand are more congruent, the task of encoding and linking their respective meanings will be easier for the individual to accomplish. The result is an increasing level of image transfer between the event and sponsoring brand.

Sponsorship Clutter

Another factor influencing the image transfer process deals with the degree to which the brand is recognized as a sponsor of the event. That is, an event's image must have a target in order to be transferred and a variety of factors may come into play that would diminish a spectator's identification of the brand (target) as a sponsor. We will refer to these factors as sponsorship clutter. From a consumer awareness standpoint (one of the other objectives of sponsorship) sponsorship has had its share of criticism. For example, Crimmins and Horn (1996) comment on the difficult task of consumers accurately identifying the sponsors that they are exposed to in a stadium.

Perhaps the most obvious factor contributing to clutter is the sheer number of sponsorships. As more and more sponsors are added, it becomes more likely that any one brand will not be noticed by spectators. One only need look at stadium perimeter signage, signs on scoreboards, and the side of a Formula One racecar to understand how prolific sponsorships have become. Indeed, worldwide sponsorship spending in 2003 was estimated to be US$26.2 billion dollars, a 7.4% increase over 2002 spending (Sport Business, 2004). As a result, identifying and remembering specific sponsors is more challenging for consumers. While increasing numbers of sponsors is generally a positive outcome for teams and events because of the increased sponsorship revenue, it has added a new challenge for brands who are now trying to be recognized in a sea of other sponsors. In response some companies are making conscious decisions to sponsor events where their brand is more likely to stand out. T-Mobile's recent decision to sponsor the Tour of Britain cycling event was based partly on the ability to cut through the clutter of other sponsorships. According to one of the corporate sponsorship managers at T-Mobile, "we sponsor football and cycling but whereas everybody else also sponsors football, not everybody sponsors cycling so in the UK it's a chance for ownership" (Bikebiz, 2004). As such, there is an opportunity for companies to search across countries for lesser known or under-sponsored events where their sponsorship will bring greater recognition to their brand due to the lack of clutter. Additionally, a cluttered sponsorship venue might still be attractive to a potential sponsoring brand if language differences can be exploited. That is, if the event has a strong following in a country where the predominant language is different from the language used by the majority of sponsors, then a sponsoring brand using language familiar to that market would be able to stand out from the other sponsors, which will be less understood by the market.

Another factor that impacts the potential of a sponsor to be accurately recalled is the level of sponsorship. Often sponsorship packages are sold at various levels with higher prices being associated with more visibility for the sponsoring brand (e.g. title sponsorship). Low level sponsorships are likely to be lost in the clutter, and therefore do not add as much value to the brand in terms of image transfer.

The frequency of the event will also impact the recognition of a brand as a sponsor (Gwinner, 1997). According to Turley and Shannon (2000), accurate recall of sponsors increases as the number of times a spectator attends a sporting event increases (i.e. high exposure frequency). Naturally, the more opportunities there are for attendance, the higher the probability that an individual will attend multiple times and have multiple exposures to the sponsor. Repeated exposures to the event-brand linkage will more firmly establish the association of their respective meanings in the consumers mind.

In summary, image transfer will be enhanced the more prominent the sponsor, the more selective the event (i.e. fewer sponsors), and the more often individuals are exposed to the event–sponsor association.

Issues to Consider in Image Transfer

This section concludes the image transfer chapter by posing several questions that brand managers, event managers, academics, and students may want to consider in thinking further about image transfer in event sponsorship in a global environment.

How is Image Transfer Managed in a Global Sport Environment?

That is, as sport broadcasts are increasing global in terms of market coverage does this add new concerns for brands interested in image transfer? Primary among a list of issues would be the concern that the event's image will be interpreted differently in different countries or by different cultures. Thus, the event image transferred in Germany for a given sponsorship might be different when that sport is broadcast in Brazil. Further, even if the image transferred is the same, the image a brand is trying to cultivate may be different in different markets of the world. Hofstede (1991) uses the term "national culture" to describe a multidimensional system of values and norms that are shared by members of a society. This suggests that different national cultures have distinct ways of viewing the world and companies tend to alter their brand's positioning strategy based upon what is most effective in a given culture. One potential problem with global sport sponsorship is that the image transferred cannot be controlled on a national level. That is, as a result of worldwide television coverage, all parts of the globe often view the same event-sponsor pairing (e.g. the Olympics and Kodak Film), however that pairing (and the associations that are transferred to the brand) may not be consistent with the brand's positioning goals in all market segments.

Which Direction Does the Transfer Go?

So far in this chapter we have been making the assumption that image is transferred from the event to the sponsoring brand. However, might there be instances where the opposite is true? That is, the image of the brand is transferred to the sponsored event? Another possibility is that there is a comparatively equal level of reciprocal image transfer, event-to-brand and brand-to-event. If the image is only going in the direction of brand to event, then image transfer effects would obviously not be applicable for the brand's sponsorship selection decision. Assuming image transfer is part of the rationale for entering into the sponsorship arrangement, understanding when these brand-to-event transfers occur is important because brand-to-event directionality implies that no image transfer benefit will accrue to the sponsoring brand.

We might speculate that this situation is more likely to happen if the brand has a strong image and the event has a weak image among a given customer segment. For example, new events, by nature of their short history, may not have strong image associations linked to them yet. Alternatively, events in the process of change (e.g. moving up in terms of level of competition) may be casting off old images and acquiring new ones in the consumer's mind. In this situation, the image of the event may be confusing to relevant customer segments during the transition and thus the brand's image may appear stronger in comparison. Further complicating the situation is that in a global media environment, the strength of an event's image may vary in different regions of the world.

In all likelihood, there is reciprocal transfer going on between events and brands in sponsorship arrangements. As a result, this implies that not only must brands be mindful of the events they elect to sponsor, but also events must be cognizant of the image that a sponsoring brand is bringing to the partnership.

What is the Impact on Image Transfer from Multiple Sponsorships?

When multiple events are sponsored by a single brand, the brand must be aware of how a given market segment might perceive the various event associations that are transferred. This is not a concern when there is consistency of image among the events for the segment, but it becomes problematic when the events have conflicting images associated with them. It is also not an issue if a particular market segment has no (or limited) exposure to the conflicting sponsorship. However, as mentioned above, the frequency of televised events in an increasingly global media environment is making sponsorships visible to more and more consumers.

What is the Impact of Other Sponsors on Image Transfer?

Assuming a reciprocal image transfer influence between events and brands, then an event's image is at least partially determined by *all* of the brands that serve as sponsors. Depending on the nature of the other sponsors, this could serve to enhance or detract from the image transferred to any one brand. For example, a brand hoping to associate with a prestigious event in order to leverage some of the event's prestige image would be disappointed by the event accepting a low prestige brand as a sponsor because it may alter consumer's perception of the event (and thus the image transferred).

Conclusion

This chapter has presented a theoretically based rationale for image transfer in the context of the unique challenges and opportunities associated with global sport sponsorship arrangements. Brand managers should be cognizant of the image transfer effect when making sponsorship selection decisions. In addition, a variety of boundary conditions were identified that can alter the strength or nature of the image that is transferred. Again, from a brand sponsorship selection perspective, firms should consider spectators' level of team identification and their attitudes toward commercialization, as well as the degree of fit between the event and sponsor and the probability that spectators will be able to accurately recall the brand as a sponsor (clutter issues). Further, the challenges and opportunities faced by sponsors in a global media environment where segmenting the market to receive targeted product messages is difficult must be considered. Like much of the sports marketing literature, this is a relatively young field of investigation and many questions remain. This chapter has presented some additional issues that those involved in the business of purchasing, selling and studying global sponsorship arrangements should consider.

Note

1. For simplicity, the term "event" is used throughout this chapter to refer to the *source* of meaning that is transferred to the sponsoring brand. However, this source could also take the form of a facility (e.g. Lincoln Financial Field) or a team (e.g. The Philadelphia Eagles).

References

Aaker, J. L. (1997) "Dimensions of Brand Personality," *Journal of Marketing Research*, 34 (3): 347–356.

Abrams, D. and M. A. Hogg (1990) "An Introduction to the Social Identity Approach," in Abrams, D. and Hogg, M.A (eds), *Social Identity: Constructive and Critical Advances*, Germany: Springer-Verlag, pp. 1–9.

Anderson, J. R. (1983) *The Architecture of Cognition*. Cambridge, MA: Harvard University Press.

Andrews, J. C. (1989) "The Dimensionality of Beliefs Toward Advertising in General," *Journal of Advertising*, 18 (1): 26–35.

Ashforth, B. E. and F. Mael. (1989) "Social Identity Theory and the Organization." *Academy of Management Review* 14 (1): 20–30.

Bauer, R. A. and S. A. Greyser (1968) *Advertising in America: The Consumer View*, Cambridge, MA: Harvard University Press.

BikeBiz (2004) "T-Mobile's Sponsorship Makes Me Proud to Work Here," http://www.bikebiz.co.uk/daily-news/article.php?id=4586, accessed October 1.

Branscombe, N. R. and D. L. Wann (1994) "Collective self-esteem consequences of outgroup derogation when a valued social identity is on trial," *European Journal of Social Psychology*, 24: 641–57.

Brown R. J. and G. F. Ross (1982) "The Battle for Acceptance: An Investigation into the Dynamics of Intergroup Behavior," in H. Tajfel (ed.), *Social Identity and Intergroup Relations*, Cambridge: Cambridge University Press, pp. 155–178.

Cialdini, R. B., R. J. Borden, A. Thorne, M. R. Walker, S. Freeman and L. R. Sloan (1976) "Basking in Reflected Glory: Three (football) Field Studies," *Journal of Personality and Social Psychology*, 34: 366–375.

Crimmins, J. and M. Horn (1996) "Sponsorship: from Management Ego Trip to Marketing Success," *Journal of Advertising Research*, 36 (4): 11–21.

Ferrand A. and M. Pages (1996) "Image Sponsoring: A Methodology to Match Event and Sponsor," *Journal of Sport Management* 10: 278–291.

Foster's Group (2004) "Fosters Personality," http://www.fosters.com.au/corporate/brands/fosters/personality.asp, accessed October 1.

Gwinner, K. P. (1997) "A Model of Image Creation and Image Transfer in Event Sponsorship," *International Marketing Review*, 14 (3): 145–158.

Gwinner, K. P. and J. Eaton (1999) "Building Brand Image Through Event Sponsorship: The Role of Image Transfer." *Journal of Advertising*, 28 (Winter): 47–57.

Gwinner, Kevin P. and Scott Swanson, (2003) "A Model of Fan Identification: Antecedents and Sponsorship Outcomes," *Journal of Services Marketing*, 17 (3): 275–292.

Häubl, G. and T. Elrod (1999) "The Impact of Congruity between Brand Name and Country of Production on Consumers' Product Quality Judgments," *International Journal of Research in Marketing*, 16: 199–215.

Hirt, E. R., D. Zillmann, G. A. Erickson and C. Kennedy (1992) "Costs and Benefits of Allegiance: Changes in Fans' Self-Ascribed Competencies After Team Victory Versus Defeat," *Journal of Personality and Social Psychology*, 63: 724–38.

Hofstede, G. (1984) *Culture's Consequences: International Differences in Work-related Values,* California: Sage Publications.

Hofstede, G. (1991) *Cultures and Organisations: Software of the Mind*, London: McGraw-Hill.

Hogg, M. A. and J. C. Turner (1985) "Interpersonal Attraction, Social Identification and Psychological Group Formation," *European Journal of Social Psychology*, 15: 51–66.

Hui, M. K., K. Au and H. Fock (2004) "Reactions of Service Employees to Organization–Customer Conflict: A Cross-cultural Comparison," *International Journal of Research in Marketing*, 21: 107–121.

Kahle, L. R. and P. M. Homer (1985) "Physical Attractiveness of the Celebrity Endorser: A Social Adaptation Perspective," *Journal of Consumer Research*, 11 (4): 954–961.

Kamins, M. A. (1990) "An Investigation into the 'Match-up' Hypothesis in Celebrity Advertising: When Beauty May be Only Skin Deep," *Journal of Advertising*, 19 (1): 4–13.

Keller, K. L. (1993) "Conceptualizing, Measuring, and Managing Customer-Based Brand Equity," *Journal of Marketing*, 57 (1): 1–22.

Keller, K. L. (2003) "Brand Synthesis: The Multidimensionality of Brand Knowledge," *Journal of Consumer Research*, 29 (4): 595–600.

Lascu, D. N., T. D. Giese, C. Toolan, B. Guehring and J. Mercer (1995) "Sport Involvement: A Relevant Individual Difference Factor in Spectator Sports," *Sport Marketing Quarterly*, 4 (4): 41–6.

Lee, M. S., D. M. Sandler and D. Shani (1997) "Attitudinal Constructs Toward Sponsorship: Scale Development Using Three Global Sporting Events," *International Marketing Review*, 14 (3): 159–169.

Lee, J. (2004) "Branded Sports Heroes Getting Lost in the Sponsorship Clutter," http://www.smh.com.au/articles/2004/06/09/1086749778738.html?from=storyrhs&oneclick=true, accessed October 1.

Lynch, J. and D. Schuler (1994) "The Matchup Effect of Spokesperson and Product Congruency: A Schema Theory Interpretation," *Psychology and Marketing*, 11 (5): 417–445.

Mackenzie, S. B. and R. J. Lutz (1989) "An Empirical Examination of the Structural Antecedents of Attitude Toward the Ad in an Advertising Pretesting Context," *Journal of Marketing*, 53 (April): 48–65.

Mackenzie, S. B., R. J. Lutz, and G. E. Belch (1986) "The Role of Attitude Toward the Ad as a Mediator of Advertising Effectiveness: A Test of Competing Explanations," *Journal of Marketing Research*, 23 (May): 130–143.

Madrigal, R. (2000) "The Influence of Social Alliances with Sports Teams on Intentions to Purchase Corporate Sponsors' Products," *Journal of Advertising*, 24 (4): 13–24.

Madrigal, R. (2001) "Social Identity Effects in a Belief-Attitude-Intentions Hierarchy Implications for Corporate Sponsorship," *Psychology and Marketing*, 18 (2): 145–165.

Mael, F. and B. E. Ashforth (1992) "Alumni and Their Alma Matter: A Partial Test of the Reformulated Model of Organizational Identification," *Journal of Organizational Behavior*, 13 (2): 103–123.

Martin, I. M. and D. W. Stewart (2001) "The Differential Impact of Goal Congruency on Attitudes, Intentions, and the Transfer of Brand Equity," *Journal of Marketing Research*, 38 (November): 471–484.

McCracken, G. (1989) "Who is the Celebrity Endorser? Cultural Foundations of the Endorsement Process," *Journal of Consumer Research*, 16 (3): 310–321.

McDonald, C. (1991) "Sponsorship and the Image of the Sponsor," *European Journal of Marketing*, 25 (11): 31–38.

Meenaghan, T. (2001) "Understanding Sponsorship Effects," *Psychology and Marketing*, 18 (2): 95–122.

Meyers-Levy, J. and A. M. Tybout (1989) "Schema Congruity as a Basis for Product Evaluation," *Journal of Consumer Research*, 16 (June): 39–54.

Misra, S. and S. E. Beatty (1990) "Celebrity Spokesperson and Brand Congruence: An Assessment of Recall and Affect," *Journal of Business Research*, 21 (2): 159–173.

Mitchell, A. A. (1986) "The Effect of Verbal and Visual Components of Advertisements on Brand Attitudes and Attitude Toward the Advertisement," *Journal of Consumer Research*, 13 (June): 12–24.

Mitchell, A. A. and J. C. Olson (1981) "Are Product Attribute Beliefs the Only Mediators of Advertising Effects on Brand Attitudes?," *Journal of Marketing Research*, 18 (August): 318–322.

Mittal, B. (1990) "The Relative Roles of Brand Beliefs and Attitude Toward the Ad as Mediators of Brand Attitude: A Second Look," *Journal of Marketing Research*, 27 (May): 209–219.

Muehling, D. D. (1987) "An Investigation of Factors Underlying Attitude-Toward-Advertising-In-General," *Journal of Advertising*, 16 (1): 32–40.

Musante, M., G. R. Milne and M. A. McDonald (1999) "Sport Sponsorship: Evaluating the Sport and Brand Image Match," *International Journal of Sports Marketing and Sponsorship*, 1 (1): 32–47.

Park, C. W., S. Milberg and R. Lawson (1991) "Evaluation of Brand Extensions: The Role of Product Level Similarity and Brand Concept Consistency," *Journal of Consumer Research*, 18 (September): 185–193.

Parker, K. (1991) "Sponsorship: the Research Contribution," *European Journal of Marketing*, 25 (11): 22–30.

Plummer, J. T. (1985) "How Personality Makes a Difference," *Journal of Advertising Research*, 24 (6): 27–31.

Sandage, C. H. and J. D. Leckenby (1980) "Student Attitudes Toward Advertising: Institution vs. Instrument," *Journal of Advertising*, 9 (2): 29–44.

Speed, R. and Thompson, P. (2000) "Determinants of Sports Sponsorship Response," *Journal of the Academy of Marketing Science*, 28 (2): 226–238.

Sport Business (2004) Maximising the Value of Sponsorship, http://www.sportbusiness.com/static/reports_text/sri, accessed October 1.

Sutton, W. A., M. A. McDonald, G. R. Milne and J. Cimperman (1997) "Creating and Fostering Fan Identification in Professional Sports," *Sport Marketing Quarterly*, 6 (1): 15–22.

Tajfel, H. (1978) "The Achievement of Group Differentiation," in H. Tajfel (ed.), *Differentiation Between Social Groups: Studies in the Social Psychology of Intergroup Relations*, London: Academic Press, pp. 77–98.

Till, B. D. and M. Busler (2000) "The Match-Up Hypothesis: Physical Attractiveness, Expertise, and the Role of Fit on Brand Attitude, Purchase Intent and Brand Beliefs," *Journal of Advertising*, 29 (3): 1–13.

Turley, L. W. and J. R. Shannon (2000) "The Impact and Effectiveness of Advertisements in a Sports Arena," *Journal of Services Marketing*, 14 (4): 323–336.

Turner, J. C. (1987) "Social Identity and Group Cohesiveness," in *Rediscovering the Social Group: A Self-Categorization Theory*. New York: Basil Blackwell, Inc.

Walliser, B. (2003) "An International Review of Sponsorship Research: Extension and Update," *International Journal of Advertising*, 22: 5–40.

Wann, D. L. and N. R. Branscombe (1990) "Die-Hard and Fair-Weather Fans: Effects of Identification on BIRGing and CORFing Tendencies," *Journal of Sport and Social Issues*, 14 (2): 103–117.

Wann, D. L. and N. R. Branscombe (1992) "Emotional Responses to the Sports Page," *Journal of Sport and Social Issues*, 16 (1): 49–64.

Wann, D. L. and N. R. Branscombe (1995a) "Influence of Identification with a Sports Team on Objective Knowledge and Subjective Beliefs," *International Journal of Sports Psychology*, 26: 551–567.

Wann, D. L. and N. R. Branscombe (1995b) "Influence of Level of Identification with a Group and Physiological Arousal on Perceived Intergroup Complexity," *British Journal of Social Psychology*, 34: 223–235.

Wann, D. L., T. J. Dolan, K. K. McGeorge, and J. A. Allison. (1994) "Relationships Between Spectator Identification and Spectators' Perceptions of Influence, Spectators' Emotions, and Competition Outcomes," *Journal of Sport and Exercise Psychology*, 16: 347–364.

9

Using the Olympics and FIFA World Cup to Enhance Global Brand Equity

A case study of two companies in the payment services category

Robert Madrigal, Colleen Bee and Monica LaBarge

A brand may be defined as a name, symbol, design, logo or some combination of them that is intended to identify a seller's (or group of sellers') goods or services, and to differentiate those goods or services from those of competitors (Kotler & Armstrong, 1996). Branding is especially important when consumers are faced with making a choice among competing brands in a given product category. Interestingly, brands extend beyond just products and services. People and organizations may also be viewed as brands. One such example is Michael Jordan whose "brand" influence on ticket purchases, product merchandising, television revenues, Nike products, and value as a product endorser was estimated to exceed US$10 billion in 1998 (Johnson & Harrington, 1998). Similarly, organizations such as the New York Yankees and Manchester United can also represent valued brands to sports consumers.

Sponsored events are yet another unique type of branded product. The current chapter focuses on two such events: the Olympics and World Cup soccer. Although both are global events, they are governed by very different organizing bodies. Whereas the Olympics operate under the auspices of the International Olympic Committee, World Cup soccer is governed by the Fédération Internationale de Football Association (FIFA). Both events have rich and long traditions. By looking at each event from the point of view of a major sponsor in the payment services category, we are able to identify and discuss key differences and similarities in their respective approaches to sponsorship. Specifically, we consider MasterCard's sponsorship of the FIFA World Cup and Visa's sponsorship of the Olympics. Each company is the official payment service provider and provides the exclusive payment card for its respective event.

The chapter begins with an outline of what constitutes a brand and how branding functions in a global context. The focus then turns to the unique nature of sponsorship as a brand-building platform. The following section of the chapter describes the FIFA World Cup and Olympic brands. The MasterCard and Visa brands are subsequently discussed, and then specific examples of how each company activates its respective sponsorship on a global stage are provided. The chapter concludes with a general discussion of implications for global sponsorship strategy and practice.

Understanding Brands

Brands are perceptual entities or mental structures that ultimately reside in the minds of consumers. All the bits of information (e.g. facts, beliefs, perceptions) held in memory that are linked to a specific brand are referred to as brand associations. Brand associations include product-related attributes (e.g. physical composition of the product or service requirements) and non-product-related attributes (e.g. price, user imagery); experiential, symbolic or functional benefits associated with using the product or service; and attitudes related to the overall evaluation of the brand (Keller, 1993). The sum total of brand associations held in memory constitutes the brand's image.

Marketers seek to create strong, favorable and unique brand associations in the minds of consumers in order to distinguish their brands from competitors and, by so doing, enhance brand equity (Keller, 1993). Brand equity refers to the "assets and liabilities linked to a brand, its name and symbol that add to or subtract from the value provided by a product or service to a firm and/or to that firm's customers" (Aaker, 1991, p. 15). Viewed more narrowly from the perspective of the consumer, brand equity reflects "the differential effect of brand knowledge on consumer response to the marketing of the brand" (Keller, 1993, p. 2).

Consumers come to understand what brands represent in one of three ways: direct experience with the product or service; information about the brand provided through company-directed marketing communications efforts, other commercial sources, or word-of-mouth; and belief associations created on the basis of inferences from existing brand associations (Keller, 1993). Regarding the latter, one way that inferences about a brand may arise is because of other generally held associations in memory. For example, consumers may infer greater quality from a higher priced brand. Another type of inferred association occurs when the brand is linked to other associations held in memory that are not directly related to the product or service. Linking the brand to one of these other entities may lead consumers to infer that the two share associations. In effect, the equity associated with the other entity is transferred to the brand. These indirect connections have been termed secondary associations. Secondary associations may arise from a variety of sources, including consumers' primary associations with country of origin, celebrity endorsers and events. When the motivation or ability to process brand information is low, consumers may be more likely to base their purchasing decisions on secondary considerations such as what they think or feel about the other entity.

With respect to global branding, it is important to recognize that cultural differences in consumer behavior are likely to exist that will impact a marketer's communications activities. In particular, Keller (2003) has noted that leveraging secondary brand associations may be especially problematic because the different entities linked to a brand may take on different meanings across countries. That is, the strength, favorability and uniqueness of these secondary associations may vary and, as a result, impact global brand building. Accordingly, marketers must take great care to create secondary associations to entities that are in fact internationally recognized and admired. It is for this reason that sponsorship of major sports properties has become such a useful tool for global brands.

Understanding Sponsorship

To a large extent, brand equity relies on the knowledge structures created in consumers' memories by the marketer's communications efforts. A variety of communications options exist, including advertising (e.g. television, print, online); consumer and trade promotions; publicity and public relations; and event marketing and sponsorship. Our focus is on how the secondary associations arising from the sponsorship of sporting events can be leveraged so as to enhance global brand equity. Sponsorship refers to "a cash and/or in-kind fee paid to a property (typically in sports, arts, entertainment or causes) in return for access to the exploitable commercial potential associated with that property" (Ukman, 1996, p. 1). Sponsorship allows the company to tap into consumers' passion for the property and provides an opportunity for them to interact with the brand in the context of that passion.

Maximizing brand equity through sponsorship requires an integrated approach that maintains or strengthens favorable and unique brand associations in the minds of consumers. Accordingly, we do not view sponsorship as a stand-alone tactic. Rather, sponsorship is conceived here as a marketing platform in which a company's decision to associate a brand with the property is supported by brand advertising, promotions, public relations, and consumer and employee relations (Crimmins & Horn, 1996). As such, a company has the opportunity to activate its sponsorship of a property in a variety of ways.

Sponsorships should begin with objectives and end with objectives. That is, sponsorship is a marketing investment driven by corporate objectives. Companies should clearly identify their corporate objectives prior to purchasing a sponsorship and then evaluate the success of the alignment based on the extent to which objectives have been met or exceeded. In the case of the payment services category, corporate objectives are likely to include new cardholder acquisition, increased card usage, business building for merchants, and member bank involvement. Typically, companies in this category enter into sponsorships in order to gain benefits that can then be passed on to their customers (cardholders, merchants, card issuers). Especially important in this category is transaction volume. Thus, companies seek exclusive use of their cards in and around the event in order to provide incremental revenue.

Overview of the Olympic Games and FIFA World Cup

We turn our attention now to the FIFA World Cup and the Olympics. This section begins with an overview of each of these properties. Next, the psychological basis for fans' cognitive associations to each event is discussed. We then focus on the importance and structure of sponsorship for each of the properties.

Overview

According to IOC President Jacques Rogge, approximately 3.9 billion people tuned in to watch parts of the 2004 Athens Olympics, with the cumulative television audience estimated to be 40 billion (CBS, 2004). The 2002 FIFA World Cup games played in South Korea and Japan also generated a massive television audience. According to the official Television Report for the 2002 FIFA World Cup, over 41,100 hours of dedicated programming in 213 countries generated a cumulative audience of 28.8 billion viewers. The twenty most viewed matches achieved an average television share of 84.8% (percentage of in-use television sets tuned in to a particular show). The FIFA World Cup tournament occurs in a different location every four years, but qualifying matches take place at various locations around the world in the two years preceding the championship rounds. The 2002 FIFA World Cup featured twenty-five match days over this two-year window. The Olympics, on the other hand, take place in a different location every two years (alternating Winter and Summer Games) and each Games lasts sixteen days. More countries are represented in the Summer Olympics (over 200) than in the FIFA World Cup (32 qualifying teams in the final rounds of competition), although the numbers for the World Cup are almost identical as those for the Olympics when one takes into account the qualifying competition.

Basis for Fans' Cognitive Associations with Each Event

Although both are considered marquis global sporting events, the types of associations likely to be held by consumers toward each are quite different. The core values or equities underlying the Olympics brand include (1) hope for a better world through involvement with sport; (2) the inspiration to achieve personal dreams through the lessons of athletes' sacrifice, striving and determination; (3) friendship and fair play; and (4) joy in the effort of doing one's best. Based on research conducted in eleven countries, the attributes perceived to be the most important and most associated with the Olympic Games were friendship, multiculturalism, globality, participation and fair competition (International Olympic Committee, 2004). These primary associations tend to create a positive "halo" effect for companies that associate with the Games (Stipp & Schiavone, 1996). For the most part, the nature of this effect is an affect transfer in which the positive feelings that consumers have toward the values underlying the Olympics rub off on the sponsor (Crimmins & Horn, 1996; see Pracejus, 2004 for a review).

In contrast to the Olympics where most fans lack an enduring involvement with any of the individual sports comprising the event, the basis for most fans' cognitive associations with the FIFA World Cup tends to be their affiliation with the game itself and their respective national teams. There can be little doubt that nationalism also plays a role in the Olympics as evidenced by fans' interest in their own country's medal counts. However, it pales in comparison to the passion that FIFA World Cup fans demonstrate towards their national teams. Thus, rather than a general positive feeling arising from the values associated with the Olympics, the process underlying the type of secondary associations held by fans of the FIFA World Cup is likely to be social identification (see Madrigal, 2004 for a review). Social identity theory maintains that we define ourselves in part by our memberships and affiliations to various social groups (Hogg & Abrams, 1988; Tajfel & Turner, 1979). In a discussion of the solidarity and self-definition existing among British soccer fans, Hogg and Abrams (1988) noted that "support for the home team is more than an act; it is part of identification with that team and/or what it represents" (p. 128). For individuals who are most highly identified, a favored team's successes and failures are viewed as personal successes and failures (Hirt, Zillmann, Erickson & Kennedy, 1992). Moreover, highly identified fans are likely to engage in supportive behaviors that enhance their connectedness to the team (Madrigal, 2000; 2001).

Sponsorship Overview

Approximately 32% of the marketing revenue for the 2001–2004 Olympic period was generated from sponsorship (International Olympic Committee, 2004). Established in 1985, The Olympic Partner (TOP) program operates on a quadrennial basis in which collective global marketing rights are granted for an Olympic Winter Games and an Olympic Summer Games. Eleven of the most prominent brands in the world were TOP sponsors for the Athens 2004 Olympics, including Coca-Cola, Kodak, McDonald's and Samsung, each paying approximately US$65 million. Sponsorship benefits include the use of all Olympic imagery, direct advertising and promotional opportunities, on-site concessions and product showcase opportunities, hospitality, tickets, access to National Olympic Committees, and ambush protection (International Olympic Committee, 2000).

The cost of a FIFA World Cup global sponsorship is approximately US$40 million for a quadrennial term. As in the case of the Olympics, sponsorship is an important income source for FIFA World Cup with over 31% of the all marketing revenue being generated by the Official Partners program (FIFA, 2002b). Fifteen global brands have committed themselves as Official Partners of the 2006 FIFA World Cup, including adidas, Budweiser, Coca-Cola, Fujifilm and McDonald's. Evidence of partner satisfaction with the event can be seen in the decision by twelve current Official Partners to renew their 2002 sponsorship through 2006. Although the benefits received by FIFA World Cup Official Partners are similar to those granted TOP sponsors, a key point of differentiation is the inclusion of on-field signage at the venues where World Cup matches are played – a benefit not available to TOP sponsors. Another advantage of soccer is participation in the game: there are currently over 484 million registered soccer players worldwide (FIFA, 2002a). Unlike the Olympics, most FIFA World Cup fans have actually played the game competitively at one level or another.

An interesting problem for both properties is that sponsorship rights can be bought at an international or national level (Meenaghan, 1996). In the case of the Olympics, a rights hierarchy exists in which a sponsor can, for example, buy an association with (1) the International Olympic Committee as official partners (the TOP program), (2) an Olympic Games Organizing Committee (OGOC, such as Atlanta or Sydney), (3) National Olympic Committees (NOCs), and/or (4) National Governing Bodies (NGBs). Similarly, sponsors wishing to associate with FIFA World Cup can affiliate with national soccer associations and bypass an official global sponsorship. It is also possible for companies to align themselves directly with athletes and bypass official sponsorships altogether. Although TOP sponsors are also granted rights at the NOC and NGB level, it is still possible for competitors to purchase sponsorships at a lower level or hire star athletes as endorsers. Such arrangements are legal and difficult to defend against. Moreover, this sort of activity tends to add clutter and frequently confuses consumers about which companies are the official sponsors (see Dalakas, Madrigal & Burton, 2004 for a review). Accordingly, it becomes critically important for global sponsors to effectively leverage their sponsorships in order to achieve enhanced brand equity.

Overview of MasterCard International and Visa International

Visa International is the world's leading payment brand with more than US$2.7 trillion in annual volume in 2003 and is accepted in more than 150 countries. MasterCard holds the second position in the category with a sales volume of US$1.27 trillion in 2003. The Visa card is accepted at over 29 million locations worldwide compared to 22 million locations for MasterCard. Both companies are membership associations that offer a full range of payment programs and services to their member financial institutions (25,000 MasterCard members, 21,000 Visa members). Neither company, however, offers services directly to end-user consumers. Each company ultimately relies on gross sales volumes to generate profits.

Marketing communications programs are conducted on a region-by-region basis using global brand architecture provided by the company. For example, MasterCard's award-winning Priceless advertising campaign is seen in 96 countries and 47 languages. In the case of sponsorship, each company makes the initial investment at the corporate level and then depends on the promotional commitments by member banks across each global region to involve merchants and cardholders. Member institutions are motivated to participate in sponsorship programs because returns on the investment accrue locally in the form of higher spending volume, greater brand awareness and increased acquisition rates.

Toward this end, both MasterCard and Visa provide turnkey toolkits to aid member banks and their creative agencies in activating the sponsorship locally. The toolkits include sponsorship manuals that outline the rights granted to the member financial institutions, as well as the appropriate approval processes and standards for using the official marks. In addition, conceptual templates for print and television advertising (e.g. pre-approved artwork, layout formula, etc.), and promotional programs are also provided.

Sponsorship evaluation for each of the properties is based on a number of factors. Clearly, the reach and diversity of the television audience for each of the properties is an important indicator of overall consumer interest. Viewership is especially important for MasterCard because one of the metrics used by the company to evaluate the sponsorship is brand exposure time of in-game perimeter signage. Given that both companies offer the same basic services and have similar objectives for sponsorship, a number of common metrics are used by each to evaluate sponsorship success. Of particular interest to both companies is member bank involvement and, by extension, regional participation. In addition to conducting member surveys concerning sponsorship satisfaction, program effectiveness is also evaluated by comparing areas where promotions were executed to control areas on certain key indicators such as brand enhancement for merchants, sponsorship awareness among cardholders, card acquisition, and card usage. Strength in business-to-business channels as a result of hospitality and relationship building activities is also evaluated.

Specific Examples of Global Integration[1]

MasterCard and FIFA World Cup

MasterCard first became involved with the FIFA World Cup as the Official Card and Official Product Licensee of the 1990 FIFA World Cup in Italy. The company stepped up to Official Partner status for the 1994 FIFA World Cup. MasterCard recently renewed its global sponsorship through the 2006 FIFA World Cup in Germany. MasterCard has also renewed its sponsorships of the 2004 UEFA European Football Championship in Portugal, the UEFA Champions League (through 2006), CONMEBOL Copa America (2004), and has a commitment to Copa Toyota Libertadores. By so doing, MasterCard has renewed its commitment to international soccer's five most prestigious events and has significantly reduced the possibility of being ambushed by a competitor. In addition to the properties mentioned above, MasterCard has had a long-term relationship with soccer great Pelé who has served as the "face" of the company's commitment to soccer. Pelé has made over 150 appearances worldwide on behalf of the company, and member banks have used his likeness on affinity cards, cardholder inserts mailings and other promotional collateral materials.

MasterCard activated their global sponsorship of the 2002 FIFA World Cup played in South Korea and Japan using a variety of programs that were executed at the local level. Over half of MasterCard's member financial institutions, representing the majority of credit card gross dollar volume, participated in promotions built around the 2002 FIFA World Cup. Nearly 80% of the tickets received by MasterCard as an Official Partner were directed toward promotions aimed at consumers rather than business-to-business channels. The length of the promotional window for 2002 FIFA World Cup was approximately two years. Promotions began in the year preceding the event and were designed to arouse member interest and participation. Specific brand-building initiatives included the following:

- MasterCard conducted a customer-acquisition program in Korea that entered applicants for a FIFA World Cup-edition card into a sweepstakes for a trip for twenty to a match. In order to qualify, all twenty potential travelers needed to have applied for the card.
- In Europe, MasterCard ran a sweepstakes for trips to watch the finals on television in Sardinia.
- In the United States, where soccer is not as popular, MasterCard activated the sponsorship through its Hispanic marketing group. The group conducted a card-usage promotion with a trip for two to the FIFA World Cup in Japan as the grand prize.
- Sixty-three fans participating in a contest conducted in Malaysia that drew 6000 entries were awarded 2002 FIFA World Cup memorabilia. Participants were asked to answer two simple questions and complete the slogan: "MasterCard brings the game to the people and the people to the game because..." in ten words or less.
- Internet-based promotions conducted at the company's website included "Score a Goal for Your Country" and a "Guess the Moment" trivia contest along with a sweepstakes to win tickets to FIFA World Cup games.
- MasterCard executed a 30-second integrated vignette television spot entitled "Swap" using the Priceless campaign imagery with a soccer theme. It was shown in fifty countries throughout the world, in over twenty languages. The ad extends the tradition of opposing soccer players "swapping" their jerseys following a match – a sign of mutual respect and sportsmanship – to opponents outside the pitch. To provide each region with the option of using the ad in the markets they considered most relevant, thirty different "swaps" were created with actors representing varying nationalities. "Swap" ads shown in Prague featured two commuters swapping T-shirts on a tram ("shirts: 2000 Kr"). In Paris, two waiters from two opposing restaurants swapped aprons outside the street ("aprons: 30 euros"). At a beauty pageant, Miss Venezuela swapped sashes with Miss Puerto Rico ("sashes: 85 dollars"). The subsequent scene in each "swap" ad cuts to two soccer players exchanging jerseys after a match ("football fever: priceless") that integrates the Priceless tag line: "There are some things money can't buy, for everything else there's MasterCard."

Visa and the Olympics

Visa has been a TOP sponsor of the Olympic Games since 1986 and has recently renewed the association through 2012. Visa's goal is to provide meaningful, profit-building, value-added promotional programs for their member institutions and merchants that can be leveraged simply, effectively and economically. The majority of Visa's most prominent financial member institutions participated in the sponsorship platform. As with MasterCard, the majority of tickets received as part of the sponsorship were dedicated to consumer promotions. Activation initiatives included sweepstakes, promotional programs, sports clinics, financial support and other marketing programs.

An especially innovative program has been Visa's support of host cities. Since 2000, Visa has executed a destination marketing campaign linked to the host city and market area. This has involved creating partnerships with state and local tourism associations to increase travel and business to the host cities. Special marketing programs have been created to promote the host city as a travel destination. In Sydney, more than 550 Visa member institutions participated in promotions designed to build tourism and business for Australia's merchants. Over the four years leading up to the 2000 Games, these efforts generated more than US$40 million in incremental marketing value for Australia, along with a 7% increase in tourism and more than US$1.55 billion in additional Visa member revenues. Working in conjunction with the Salt Lake Convention and Visitor's Bureau at the Salt Lake City Winter Olympics, Visa increased its card volume in the host city area by 30% during the Games over the same period in 2001.

For the Athens 2004 Olympic Games, Visa worked closely with the Greek merchant community and partnered with Alpha Bank, the Grand National Sponsor in the banking category, to increase Visa transactions in Greece by 55% in August of 2004 compared to August 2003. The 2008 Beijing Olympic Games presents a unique opportunity for Visa – China has six banks that issue Visa credit cards and just 100,000 businesses that accept payment with a Visa card compared to the US where 5 million businesses accept Visa. Visa is currently working with hotels, restaurants, and retailers to increase acceptance of the cards. Visa is also working with China's national tourism board to create package tour offers for Visa cardholders.

Another unique program designed by the company is the "Visa Olympics of the Imagination" international youth art competition. Launched at the Lillehammer 1994 Winter Olympics, the program challenges school-aged children between the ages of 9 and 13 to use their imaginations to create an original piece of art that represents their thoughts on "How the Olympic Games Can Help Create a Better Future." Since 1994, 175 children from 35 countries have attended the Olympics as guests of Visa. The program is promoted through multitiered marketing and public relations efforts conducted worldwide, integrating extensive in-school outreach with cross promotions involving news media and Visa financial institution members and their merchants. The Athens 2004 competition ran from October 2003 to May 2004 and resulted in almost 1 million entries from around the world. The 29 winners from 17 countries attended the Athens 2004 Olympic Games as guests of Visa International.

Conclusion

In an effort to develop strong, favorable and unique brand associations in the minds of consumers, marketers often align their brands with sporting events. The primary associations held in consumers' memories about these events are often transferred to the brand. The transfer can occur at various levels. For example, brand enhancement might occur as a result of consumer liking of the event or because certain brand attributes are reminiscent of event attributes. At higher levels of cognitive processing, those most highly identified with the event may even be motivated to reciprocate the brand's investment by buying the company's products (Madrigal, 2004; Pracejus, 2004). The extent to which transference will take place depends on the company's willingness to invest in an integrated marketing communications strategy. More specifically, the company must be willing to engage in themed advertising and promotional activities that support the sponsorship platform in order for secondary associations to actually enhance brand equity.

Rather than focusing on developing global brands, Aaker and Joachimsthaler (1999) suggested that companies should instead use global brand leadership to create strong brands in all markets. Global brand leadership suggests that the company uses "organizational structures, processes, and cultures to allocate brand-building resources globally, to create global synergies, and to develop a global brand strategy that coordinates and leverages country brand strategies" (p. 138). The global sponsorships discussed in this chapter illustrate just such an approach to global branding. For both Visa and MasterCard, sponsorship investment occurs at the corporate level. Each company then provides a global execution architecture that allows key partners located in different regions throughout the world with a compelling marketing tool that helps them to achieve their own regional business objectives.

Sporting events are a particularly attractive option for global brand sponsorship. Sports can transcend international boundaries and languages. They represent an alignment for a company that requires little or no translation. In effect, the imagery associated with sports is an international language understood by all. Sporting events allow companies to tap into a broad and diverse audience, of which many members care passionately about the sponsored property. Events such as FIFA World Cup and the Olympics provide promotional platforms that are interesting and exciting to consumers, thus enhancing the likelihood of consumer participation in brand promotions. In regard to the payment services category, major sports properties also provide a multitude of card usage opportunities (e.g. ticket sales, purchasing and merchandising, travel and accommodations) which ultimately lead to increased gross sales volumes – a key objective for companies in this category.

Through innovative marketing programs, it is possible to extend the promotional window for a global sponsorship beyond the actual dates of the event itself. For a property such as the FIFA World Cup, the sponsorship includes activation opportunities in the various locations where qualifying rounds are played during the two years preceding the finals. In contrast, the Olympics do not offer the same sort of opportunity. Nevertheless, Visa's innovative destination marketing initiative provides a creative means for extending the promotional window and for differentiating their brand from other TOP sponsors. Not only does this strategy benefit Visa's partners, it also creates a positive image that enhances the brand equity of the host city and country.

The integrated global communications approach toward sponsorship provides Visa and MasterCard an opportunity to offer their partners a marketing platform that drives business and enhances brand equity. Our chapter provides examples of how global sponsorships can be used to achieve key business objectives at the local level. We also offer a theoretical rationale for explaining how the specific sponsorships of the FIFA World Cup and the Olympics affect consumers' brand perceptions. Sponsorship offers global brands a creative means for aligning themselves with properties that matter deeply to consumers. Successfully leveraging these alignments requires a considerable investment by the company. Execution strategies must be designed so as to generate consumer awareness and interest. Only through successful execution and investment will brand salience, brand perceptions, and brand choice be positively impacted by sponsorship.

Note

1. Sources for much of the information presented in this section include press releases, news articles, and personal interviews with company executives directly responsible for executing the sponsorships.

References

Aaker, D. A. (1991) *Managing Brand Equity: Capitalizing on the Value of a Brand Name*. New York: Free Press.

Aaker, D. A. and Joachimsthaler, E. (1999) "The Lure of Global Branding," *Harvard Business Review*, 77: 137–144.

CBS (2004) http://cbs.sportsline.com/olympics/story/7787174/1, accessed October 15, 2004.

Crimmins, J. and Horn, M. (1996) "Sponsorship: From Management Ego to Marketing Success," *Journal of Advertising Research*, 36: 11–21.

Dalakas, V., Madrigal, R. and Burton, R. (2004) "Understanding Ambush Marketing: Implications of Information Processing," in Kahle, L.R. and Riley, C. (eds), *Sports Marketing and the Psychology of Marketing Communication*. Mahwah, NJ: Lawrence Erlbaum, pp. 293–304.

FIFA (2002a) *Activities Report April 2000 – March 2002*, http://images.fifa.com/events/congress/2002/Activity_Report_2002_EN.pdf, accessed March 29, 2004.

FIFA (2002b) *FIFA Financial Report 2002*, http://images.fifa.com/events/congress/2003/FIFA_Financial_Report_E_2002.pdf, accessed March 29, 2004.

Hirt, E. R., Zillmann, D., Erickson, G. A. and Kennedy, C. (1992) "Costs and Benefits of Allegiance: Changes in Fans' Self-ascribed Competencies after Team Victory versus Defeat," *Journal of Personality and Social Psychology*, 63: 724–738.

Hogg, M. A. and Abrams, D. (1988) *Social Identifications: A Social Psychology of Intergroup Relations and Group Processes*. London: Routledge.

International Olympic Committee (2000) "Marketing Fact File," International Olympic Committee.

International Olympic Committee (2004) "Marketing Revenue," http://www.olympic.org/uk/organisation/facts/revenue/index_uk.asp, accessed October 15.

Johnson, R. S. and Harrington, A. (1998) "The Jordan Effect," *Fortune*, June 22: 124–126, 130–132, 134, 138.

Keller, K. L. (1993) "Conceptualizing, Measuring, and Managing Customer-based Brand Equity," *Journal of Marketing*, 57: 1–22.

Keller, K. L. (2003) *Strategic Brand Management: Building, Measuring, and Managing Brand Equity*. 2nd edn. Upper Saddle River, NJ: Prentice Hall.

Kotler, P. and Armstrong, G. (1996), *Principles of Marketing*. 7th edn. Upper Saddle River, NJ: Prentice Hall.

Madrigal, R. (2000) "The Influence of Sponsee Identification and Group Norms on Intentions to Purchase a Corporate Sponsor's Products," *Journal of Advertising*, 29 (4): 13–24.

Madrigal, R. (2001) "Social Identity Effects in a Beliefs – Attitude – Intentions Hierarchy: Implications for Corporate Sponsorship," *Psychology and Marketing*, 18 (2): 145–165.

Madrigal, R. (2004) "A Review of Team Identification and its Influence on Consumers' Responses Toward Corporate Sponsors," in Kahle, L. and Riley, C. (eds), *Sports Marketing and the Psychology of Marketing Communication*. Mahwah, NJ: Lawrence Erlbaum, pp. 241–255.

Meenaghan, T. (1996) "Ambush Marketing – A Threat to Corporate Sponsorship," *Sloan Management Review*, 38 (3): 103–113.

Pracejus, J. W. (2004) "Seven Psychological Mechanisms through which Sponsorship can Influence Consumers," in Kahle, L. and Riley, C. (eds), *Sports Marketing and the Psychology of Marketing Communication*. Mahwah, NJ: Lawrence Erlbaum, pp. 175–189.

Stipp, H. and Schiavone, N. P. (1996) "Modeling the Impact of Olympic Sponsorship on Corporate Image," *Journal of Advertising Research*, 36: 22–28.

Tajfel, H. and Turner, J. C. (1979) "An Integrative Theory of Intergroup Conflict," in Austin, W. G. and Worchel, S. (eds), *The Social Psychology of Intergroup Relations*. Monterey, CA: Brooks Cole, pp. 33–47.

Ukman, L. (1996) *IEG's Complete Guide to Sponsorship: Everything you Need to Know About Sports, Arts, Event, Entertainment and Cause Marketing*. Chicago, IL: IEG, Inc.

10

Alternative Global Avenues
Action sports and events

James Gladden and Mark McDonald

While interest has been waning for professional sports in recent years, one area experiencing rapid growth is action sports. Action sports are fueled by a passion for risk taking and include, but are not limited to, skateboarding, snowboarding, rock climbing, mountain and BMX/freestyle bike riding, and adventure racing. With name brand events such as ESPN X Games, Gravity Games and the Vans Triple Crown Tour, this category provides an opportunity for corporations to address hard-to-reach Y generation consumers. According to Tim Moufarrige, President, Worldwide, Property representation and sales, Octagon: "As to where future business will come from we have to look at action sports. The young generation is interested in sports but they are taking things to a new level. Advertisers are just screaming for action sports, people are absolutely fascinated by that medium" (*SportBusiness International*, June 2002, p. 31).

While major action sports events have thus far been mostly limited to the United States, there is evidence suggesting that their popularity is global. For one, viewership of action sport events is about the same across the world. Second, action sports-influenced apparel and hard goods sales are comparable in the USA, Europe and Asia. According to Bill Carter, Principal of Fuse Integrated International, a sponsorship consultant to the action sports industry, approximately one-third of Burton's snowboard sales are in the USA, while one-third are in Europe and one-third are in Asia (Bill Carter, personal interview, June 12, 2003). Third, as of 2001, Extreme Sports Channel, based in the United Kingdom, had 7.9 million subscribers in twenty European markets (Koranteng, 2001). The global appeal of action sports has attracted sponsorship involvement from large multinational corporations (e.g. Sony, Motorola, McDonalds, GM).

This chapter will explore the realm of global action sports sponsorships, addressing a series of related questions. What accounts for the growth in action sports? Who are the consumers participating and watching these sports? What is the scope of action sports coverage? Why do sponsors choose to be involved with action sports? Are the methods used to activate action sports sponsorships different than those used to activate mainstream sport sponsorships? What does the future hold for sponsors of action sports?

To answer these questions, we draw on all available research, both academic and sport industry-related. In addition, because the action sports industry is still very young (first ESPN X Games in 1995), there is a limited base of information available regarding the sponsorship of action sports. As such, we also undertook personal interviews with two industry experts to further our understanding of the current state of action sports sponsorship.

Growth in Action Sports

With the launch of the ESPN Summer X Games in 1995, interest in action sports has spread throughout the world. Globally, an estimated 150 million people participate in action sports (Salmon, 2004). In the USA alone, 40.6 million people participate in either aggressive in-line skating or skateboarding, and 7.2 million are involved in snowboarding (*Street & Smith's SportsBusiness Journal*, 2002). Besides participation, other indicators of the prominence of action sports are increased events/major tours, endorsements and corporate sponsorships (Bennett, Henson & Zhang, 2003); all fueled by fan and spectator interest. According to ESPN Sports Poll, 71.3% of Americans between the ages of 18 and 34 consider themselves either fans or avid fans of action sports (*Street & Smith's SportsBusiness Journal*, 2002). Also according to ESPN research, 80% of US males between 8 and 18 have a strong interest in action sports (Gillis, 2002). While these last two statistics are provided by a company (ESPN) that has a vested interest in promoting the action sports movement (i.e. it owns the X Games), data from other and more independent sources are consistent with the above statistics. For example, among American children aged 6–17, the only event with more appeal than the X Games is the Olympic Games (Ruibal, 2000).

Growing involvement with these high-octane sports may have come at the expense of mainstream sports. Raymond (2002) notes "These high-intensity, individualistic sports, which involve everything from the ultra-hip snowboarding to Moto-X (a strange, scary contest that has motorcyclists attempt ski jumps) have encroached upon traditional sports – especially group sports – in popularity" (p. 28). In 2002, for example, more Americans rode skateboards than played the national pastime, baseball (Sporting Goods Manufacturers Association, 2003). Not surprisingly, extreme activities particularly appeal to males. In 2003, action sports-related purchases accounted for approximately one-third of all sporting goods purchases (Liberman, 2004a). In 2001 the winner of the Favorite Male Sports Star category at the Nickelodeon (children-oriented cable television station) Kids' Choice Awards was not a mainstream athlete but the skateboarder Tony Hawk (Wendel, 2001). Increased interest in these sports is not limited to the USA. The world's largest extreme sports theme park is currently under construction in Shanghai, China. This 27,000-square-meter park will provide the venue for the Chinese to host national and international events and also spur the development of action sport participation (*China Daily*, 2004, April 27). While China has not yet produced an international action sport icon,

X Games event manager Bill Cooper predicts an explosion in this market when the breakthrough occurs (Ng, 2003).

Impact of Generation Y

Much of the growth in action sports has been driven by the consumption habits of Generation Y, comprised of people born between 1977 and 1996. Approximately 25% of the world's population is between the ages of 10 and 24, with more than 560 million teens from 15 to 19 (Kamenick, 2000). Referred to variously as Gen Y, Millennials or Echo Boomers, this cohort has significant buying power, estimated at more than US$250 billion for just the American youth between the ages of 10 and 24. This is a primary reason why corporations such as Motorola, AT&T Broadband, PepsiCo, Ford, Morningstar Foods and even the US Marines spend heavily to reach Gen X and Gen Y males (Kleinfeld, 2002).

Understanding the differing values of Generation X (people typically born between 1961 and 1977) and Generation Y is crucial. While Generation X is viewed as "slackers," Generation Y is more positive and self-confident, valuing diversity and education (Koranteng, 2001). Additionally, they understand technology and utilize the Internet extensively, are goal-oriented, and value honesty and integrity. Research indicates that Gen Y is spontaneous, realistic, action-oriented and highly intelligent (Fanning, 2004).

Unfortunately, for marketers, this group of influential kids has a fragmented brand consciousness and can't be reached with classic shotgun marketing messages. Brands must bring their message to where Gen Y gather, which could be the Internet, cable TV or a snowboarding event (Neuborne & Kerwin, 1999). However, Gen Y can also react negatively to both big brands and the over-commercialization that can occur through various marketing platforms. Therefore, it is sometimes better to use subtle messages at the grassroots level to reach Gen Y. According to *Promo* magazine: "The trick in reaching Gen Y is to infiltrate their lifestyles without letting them know you're infiltrating their lifestyles" (Making the Grade, 2001, p.19). Keith Deutsch (1999), summarizing proprietary research by retailers and advertisers on reaching Generation Y concludes: "So retailers better learn to stay loose (phat?), keep their eyes on the music, and fragment their advertising campaigns with lots of offbeat small brands based on the concepts of the hot retailers that are selling – until a brand hits it big – then extend that brand identity for all its worth in every marketing medium technology offers" (p. 1). The good news for sport marketers is that the subculture of action sports combines sport, music and fashion into a lifestyle receptive to interactive branding.

Action Sport Events/Media

While part of this phenomenon represents pull from Generation Y consumers, there is also the aggressive push from practitioners marketing not just action sport, but also a lifestyle with associated music and fashion. The 2004 Vans

Warped Tour, for example, makes fifty stops across the USA, combining action sports with six to ten stages of live music (Liberman, 2004b). In 2004, the Vans Warped Tour drew 650,000 fans (paying US$25 per ticket) (Liberman, 2004b). This movement has spurred a growing number of major events globally, all with extensive corporate involvement. In the USA, these include the ESPN Winter and Summer X Games, NBC Gravity Games, Gorge Games, Great Outdoor Games, Vans Warped Tour and Boom Boom HuckJam Tour. The ESPN X Games are still the clear standard-bearer. The eighth Summer X Games (August 2002), held in Philadelphia (USA), drew 221,352 fans over just five days (admission was free though) earning a reported US$12 million profit (Ostrowski, 2002a).

Outside of the USA, events such as the Winter & Summer Planet X Games, Planet X Jam & Slam Tour (Australia), as well as X Games qualifiers throughout the world have been created to satisfy the needs of these consumers. Since the first Asian Games were held on Thailand's Phuket Island in 1998, interest in action sports has spread to China and throughout Southeast Asia. Recently, the Asian X Games held in Kuala Lumpur Malaysia attracted 200 athletes from fourteen countries. According to ESPN's Mark Reilly, "Asia is leading the way in action sports as this is the fifth time the regional X Games is being held. Latin America is going into their second year while Europe is now into their third year" (Ng, 2003). However, to date, the USA has been the host for the majority of the major action sports events. Wade Martin, General Manager of the Dew Action Sports Tour, suggests that this is largely due to the fact that significant corporate support (sponsorships and advertising buys) are needed and thus far such support has been harder to find in other parts of the world (Wade Martin, personal interview, June 17, 2003).

Furthermore, there is no end in sight, with broadcasters and agencies continuing to launch new events and brand extensions. Originally a strategic partnership between NBC, Octagon (a sport marketing agency) and Primedia (a content and marketing solutions company), the Gravity Games was purchased by the Outdoor Life Network in 2004 and is now pursuing a growth strategy (Liberman, 2004c). In addition to resurrecting the Winter Gravity Games (which had not occurred since 2000), OLN created the Gravity Games H2O, action sports on water, held in Australia in 2004 (Bernstein, 2004a). Other action sports brand extensions could include camps, skate parks, licensing opportunities and grass-roots tours (Gillis, 2002). In 2003, ESPN created an event called the X Games Global Championships. A unique twist on the X Games concept, this event involves six teams representing countries or regions from around the world competing in eleven events, earning both individual and team points. At the conclusion, one team was crowned the world X Games champion. This event, launched in 2003 simultaneously in both warm weather and alpine venues, filled the gap between the Winter and Summer X Games, providing a major action sports property to advertisers during the second quarter (Bernstein, 2002a). The newest action sport property, the Dew Action Sports Tour, will be launched in June 2005. Owned by NBC and Clear Channel, this property will include five events with a cumulating points system, essentially creating an entire season of action sport competition in skateboarding, BMX and freestyle motocross (Lefton, 2004a).

In addition to providing live entertainment, pre-existing and newly developed networks have aired these events globally. ESPN, launched in the USA in 1979, airs around 900 hours of action sports annually (Cleland, 2001). Europe-based Extreme Sports Channel, available worldwide via satellite, is 100% dedicated to airing action sports. Similarly, Fuel is an action sports channel with over 10 million cable television subscribers in the USA (Bernstein, 2004b). With the exception of ESPN's X Games, NBC's Gravity Games and the Planet X Games in Australia, however, the quality of television coverage of action sports has been questionable. Television coverage is almost always taped and not live. Additionally, the coverage in some cases has not been of the highest quality. According to Damien Bray of Planet X, Australia's premier extreme event, "To date there have been volumes of low budget, low production quality product on the market for these sports that essentially provide wallpaper-type fill, primarily for pay-per-view sports distribution channels" (Gillis, 2002, p. 39).

Beyond networks, other suppliers to the industry have incentives to produce action sports content. Quiksilver, a boardwear company, for example, plans on creating a division focusing on developing and promoting TV programming, music and movies. By utilizing connections with athletes such as Tony Hawk and Kelly Slater in entertainment projects, Quiksilver aims to increase demand for the company's action sports gear (Ostrowski, 2002b). T-Mobile, a wireless communication provider, is staging, and sharing title sponsorship with Nokia of "Ramps and Amps," a free eleven-city action sports tour. This provides an opportunity for T-Mobile to showcase five top athletes recently signed to one-year deals to wear the company's logo while competing in events (Lefton, 2003).

Another testament to the strength of the action sports industry is the presence of marketing agencies specifically dedicated to action sports athletes and events. For example, The Familie is an agency that specializes in representing action sports athletes, while On-Board Entertainment is focused on developing action sports properties (Bill Carter, personal interview, June 12, 2003). Then there is Fuse Integrated Marketing, a Burlington, Vermont agency that specializes in helping corporations maximize their involvement with action sports (Carter, personal interview). Beyond these "niche" agencies, larger sport marketing agencies such as Octagon, IMG (with the US Open of Surfing), The Marketing Arm and Millsport all have personnel or a division focused on action sports (Carter, personal interview). The fact that agencies and divisions within agencies are viable is further support for the notion that action sports will be a prevalent force in the sport industry for the near future.

Sponsorship of Action Sports: Scope, Objectives, and Activation

The growth in action sports, both participation and spectatorship, has fueled significant interest from corporate sponsors. In this section, we will first provide a brief overview of the scope of sponsor involvement with action sports. Next, we discuss the variety of objectives possessed by action sports sponsors. Finally, the unique aspects of activating action sports sponsorships are discussed. Throughout, we attempt to provide links between practice and existing research on sponsorship.

Scope of Sponsorship Involvement

Significant sponsorship dollars are being invested in both action sports athletes and action sports events. As it relates to athlete endorsements, the most prominent example is skateboarder Tony Hawk. Given his name recognition to mainstream sport consumers, it is not surprising that Tony Hawk has amassed a business empire worth an estimated US$250 million annually, with sales of his video game over US$500 million (*SportsBusiness Daily*, 2003, February 20). His two most recent endorsement deals with Frito-Lay's Go Snacks and Morningstar Foods' Hershey's Milk and Milkshakes both involve estimated US$15 million national media buys (*SportsBusiness Daily*, 2003, February 20).

Other athletes, while not synonymous with their sports like Tony Hawk and skateboarding, are also flushed with endorsements. Snowboarder Ross Powers may become the first pro snowboarder to earn a million dollars a year, having recently re-signed a five-year deal with Burton Snowboards worth more than US$3 million (*SportsBusiness Daily*, 2002, October 22). IMG's X Sports Division signed snowboarder and skateboarder Shaun White to represent him in management, marketing, sponsorships, appearances and other areas. White has deals with Burton, Oakley, Target, Volcom, Birdhouse and Sony PlayStation (*SportsBusiness Daily*, 2003, January 28). The market for action sports athletes is currently so hot that companies, just like in basketball, are prospecting for the next superstar. A six-year-old skateboarding prodigy, Mitchie Brusco, currently has nine endorsement deals, largely for free merchandise. SMGA President Mike May notes: "The beauty of so-called extreme sports is that there are no rules in marketing. A youngster can make a living at an earlier age than in any other sport. There are no parameters as to what's right or wrong" (*SportsBusiness Daily*, 2003, March 13). While the marketing to and recruiting of young children may seem like an opportunity for some corporations, there are host of ethical issues that arise. As Shaw's chapter on sport sponsorship and ethical decision-making illustrates, sponsorship very often raises significant ethical concerns (for more on the ethical issues associated with global sports sponsorship, see Shaw, this volume).

As with any athlete endorsement, there are inherent risks. Two athletes, Jeremy Stenberg (motocross) and Jen O'Brien have appeared in *High Times*, a magazine for marijuana users. While O'Brien's agent Steve Astephan reacted strongly when confronted about this information, it is noteworthy that Stenberg said "some of his sponsors even called to congratulate him... A lot of people in the motocross industry smoke. Even the guys in the three-piece suits" (*SportsBusiness Daily*, 2003, May 5).

While endorsement income has begun to flow for well-known action sport athletes, networks and events depend heavily on sponsors to help fund made-for-TV events. ESPN continues to experience sponsorship success with the inaugural ESPN X Games Global Championship, airing a combined twelve hours on ABC, ESPN and ESPN2. McDonald's, GM and 1–800–CALL-ATT all signed on as Gold sponsors of this new event (*SportsBusiness Daily*, March 4, 2003). Through offering three levels of sponsorship, The Vans Warped Tour has also brought major corporations on board: title sponsor (Vans); national sponsor (Amp, Motorola, Sony Computer Entertainment America, The Truth, Transworld Media, Yoo-hoo); and endemic sponsor (*SportsBusiness Daily*, 2002, August 2). The newly created Dew Action Sports Tour will receive US$3.6 million from Mountain Dew to be the tour's title sponsor (Lefton, 2004b). The Dew Action Sports Tour will also receive US$1.75 to US$2 million each from Toyota, Vans, Panasonic, Sony PlayStation and Gillette to be the sponsors of the individual tour stops (Lefton, 2004a)

Sponsorship Objectives

What are corporations tying to achieve when they sponsor action sports? In many cases, the objectives of action sports sponsors are quite similar to those of mainstream sport sponsors as documented by a variety of researchers (e.g. Meenaghan, 1991; Irwin & Assimakopoulas, 1992; Cornwell, 1995). For example, creating awareness, generating sales and enhancing brand image are all objectives of action sports sponsors. Also similar to nearly every other sponsorship endeavor, action sports are seeking to reach a specific market segment. According to Wade Martin: "The common thread is that [action sports sponsors] are trying to reach the youth market. The 12 to 24 and even sometimes the 10 to 18 market" (personal interview, June 17, 2003). Similarly, Brad Adgate, senior vice president and corporate research director at Horizon suggests: "This is a demographic sweet spot. The games are an incredible success story in combining sports with entertainment, while targeting a specific market" (Kleinfeld, 2002). Today's youth are quite adept at doing multiple tasks at once (i.e. "multi-tasking"). Therefore, the manner in which action sports include facets beyond sports provides a very effective means to communicate with these consumers. According to Martin, "[sponsors] see that action sports, and the byproduct of action sports – music, lifestyle, and fashion – is how you reach this group most effectively."

Action sports sponsors appear to seek more than awareness with their sponsorships. As Matthew Kinsman of *Promo* magazine contends, "...getting in-park signage, brand placement on scoreboards, or even 30-second Super Bowl spots aren't carrying the weight they used to" (Kinsman, 2002). Rather, sponsors are seeking to make a direct connection to consumers (Kinsman, 2002). Action sports events provide a platform for this to happen. Given their format and layout, action sports events afford corporations a variety of opportunities to have one-on-one interactions with customers. For example, at the 2000 X Games, there were more than forty corporate sponsor booths that were well visited by attendees (King & Kang, 2000). Sponsor messages can also be integrated into action sports extensions such as compilation videos and video games.

In a number of cases, action sports sponsors are seeking to position or reposition their brands through an action sports sponsorship. As Gladden and Wolfe (2001) suggest, "...the goal of sponsorship could be to create a link whereby image attributes are transferred or shared between the corporation and the sponsored entity" (p. 46). Prior research suggests that the degree to which consumers perceive a match or "fit" between the image of the sponsor and the image of the event is important to the overall success of the sponsorship (e.g. Aaker & Joachimsthaler, 2000; Musante, Milne & McDonald, 1999; Kinney & McDaniel, 1996). Beyond this, Javalgi, Traylor, Gross and Lampman (1994) suggest that the image of a corporation can be positively or negatively impacted by sponsorship. In their interpretation of prior research, Cornwell, Pruitt and Van Ness (2001) suggest that where a strong link does not occur, the marketer can still build such a link through advertising. It is this latter tactic that seems to be occurring in the action sports industry. Rather than seeking events that project a similar image to the corporation, some action sports sponsors appear to be seeking an image modification or enhancement.

The classic image-transfer sponsor case study is the soft drink Mountain Dew. Launched in 1960, until 1992 Mountain Dew was perceived as a drink of people that lived in rural areas. This changed when the "Do the Dew" marketing campaign swung into gear, showing people involved in extreme sports. Mountain Dew was the fastest-growing soft drink in the 90s. Furthermore, there was a 10% increase from 1998 to 2001 of teens saying "Mountain Dew is a brand for someone like me" (Kleinfeld, 2002). At least partially using action sports imagery, Mountain Dew created an image that included attributes such as cool, attitude, momentum, excitement and edge (Prince, 1998). In support of this repositioning, it is estimated that Mountain Dew has spent US$6 million annually on action sports sponsorship (not including their recent commitment to the Dew Action Sports Tour!) (Lefton, 2004b).

LG Electronics, the South Korean manufacturer of consumer electronics with annual revenue of about US$30 billion, hopes to increase brand awareness and modify its image though involvement with action sports. Even though LG is the world's largest producer of goods such as computer screens, liquid-crystal displays and DVD players, it wasn't listed among the top 100 global brands in the 2004 Interbrand survey. By sponsoring the World Action Sports championships in Pomona, California, LG is trying to change this perception. According to Les Edwards, vice president in Seoul of ad agency Lee DDB: "LG's image is practical, mainstream and homey. What they need to do is really leverage this property and transfer its edginess across all their communications disciplines" (Salmon, 2004). To reach beyond the USA with action sports, LG plans on African, Middle Eastern and European tours (Salmon, 2004).

Beyond the above mentioned brand attributes, Layden (2002) suggested action sports are also associated with genuine energy and passion for sport, an element that is often perceived to be missing from mainstream team sport today. In summarizing the difference between action sports and mainstream sports after watching Tony Hawk practice for a crowd, Layden captured the essence of the difference: "Translation: Never mind the medals podium, let's elevate the sport. Entertain the crowd. Hawk landed the trick, the first time any skater has done it. The arena went nuts and Hawk's fellow skaters mobbed him. It was pure joy. I'm sure baseball was that way once, a long time ago" (Layden, 2002). From an image-matching perspective, energy, passion and achievement could be very desirable brand attributes for a corporation to seek through an image transfer.

In addition to reaching a segmented market and realizing an image transfer, action sport sponsors are also trying to increase sales. For example, Bagel Bites signed on as a sponsor of the 2000 X Games and realized a 26% increase in consumption in the eight weeks after the event (Cleland, 2001). Experts argue that one of the reasons that action sports sponsors might see an increase in sales is that action sports consumers are extremely loyal to the brands that support action sports. According to Wade Martin:

> There is a tremendous brand loyalty (not unlike a NASCAR) to sponsors of action sports if they are perceived as being authentic to the sports. That stems from an actual recognition that sponsorship drives these events that drives these sports … a recognition that I don't think you can find in other sports. A sponsor may change, but they won't take the NFL away … there is a true connection between sponsors supporting these lifestyles and brand loyalty. (Personal interview, June 17, 2003)

Martin is arguing that action sports consumers see the sponsors as essential to the existence of the events and participation of the athletes and thus feel strongly toward those brands that support action sports. This is consistent with prior research by Madrigal (2000), who found that high levels of identification with a particular team can lead to positive purchase intentions towards sponsor products. If this thinking is extended into action sports, it would be identification with action sports athletes and/or the action sports movement that could engender positive feelings towards those companies that support these entities.

However, capitalizing on this brand loyalty is not as easily achieved as placing a sign at an action sports event. As previously noted, Generation Y tends to be sensitive to the domination of mega brands. For example, some of the best snowboarders do not compete at the Olympic Games because they see "…the Olympic machine squeezing the soul out of competition" (Ruibal, 2000, p. 1C). For many action sports athletes and supporters, the Olympics are over-commercialized (Roberts, 2002). Related to this, Wade Martin of the Dew Action Sports Tour contends that the loyalty to action sports only transfers to sponsors if the action sports sponsor is perceived to be genuinely interested in action sports and not just trying to capitalize on it for commercial gain (personal interview, June 17, 2003). According to Martin, "there is more importance placed on the authenticity of how you are sponsoring these things. In other sports, you could just get away with being a 'broadcast advertiser.' I think it is really important to have a well-rounded campaign that shows you are just not buying your way into these sports…" Bill Carter, President of Fuse Integrated Marketing, sees it a little bit differently, suggesting that in addition to incorporating all of the traditional elements of sponsorship (signage, television ads, on-site sampling, etc.), sponsors must be perceived as giving something back to the sport: "We are saying 'listen we know the deal here'. We know we are using the imagery of your sport for mass advertising. But, we are going to give something back to you so that you do not turn your back on our brand" (Carter, personal interview, June 12, 2003). How sponsors achieve such a perception in the minds of action sports consumers is discussed in the next section.

The Activation of Action Sports Sponsorships

"Activation" refers to the tactics sponsors use in an attempt to reap benefits from their sponsorship with a particular sports property. In many cases, the activation methods used by corporations associated with action sports are the same as the activation methods used by those associated with mainstream sports. For example, signage, broadcast advertising, retail promotion and on-site sampling are all tactics used by action sports sponsors. However, there is a significant difference in a sponsor's understanding as to how to activate action sports sponsorships. Bill Carter best summarizes this challenge:

> There is a disconnect between the consumer, the end user, the teen and the systems that the sponsorships are often bought to support. If you and I work in an agency and we work on behalf of Pepsi, we might want to buy a Major League Baseball sponsorship and then we hand it over to our system, which is the Pepsi bottling system and it gets activated in every MLB city across the country. The system, the bottlers, who are generally white men in their 50's know baseball and they get exactly what we are giving them. If you do the same thing with action sports … they have no idea what you are talking about. (Personal interview, June 12, 2003)

Carter is suggesting that even if a company sees the merits of sponsoring action sports, sponsors have to spend an inordinate amount of time (compared to mainstream sports sponsorships) educating their different internal constituents as to how to maximize their involvement with action sports. For example, Mountain Dew initially had to educate their bottlers as to why action sports are important and why they are relevant to teens (Carter, personal interview).

A lack of understanding can lead action sports enthusiasts to perceive a sponsor's involvement as inauthentic. In a number of cases, corporations have not fully understood the tastes of 12–24 year olds and have used imagery, graphics or language that is off-target or perceived as not genuine (Wade Martin, personal interview, June 17, 2003). Research conducted by the sponsorship research agency Performance Research found that 46% of X Games attendees felt that sponsors of the event were "only trying to sell me something" (Extreme Games, Commercialism…, 1996).

A major challenge to achieving an authentic perception in the eyes of action sport consumers is what Bill Carter refers to as the different "layers" of action sports consumers. Carter argues that for a corporation to achieve business objectives through action sports, it must sponsor the major events such as the X Games because of the visibility it affords a sponsor. However, according to Carter:

> There is a whole other portion of teens that we want to reach that don't particularly care about the X Games and may even be turned off by the X Games because they are the big corporate monster that gets too much attention while some more core grass roots properties don't get any attention but get all the respect from those that are the most hard-core participants in the sport. (Bill Carter, personal interview, June 12, 2003)

While this "second layer" is small in comparison to the masses that follow the X Games, they are very influential with their peers. Finally, there is a third layer of "ultra hard-core participants," which is very small in size, but again terribly influential with their peers. Carter argues that the influencers in this second and third group must be convinced that sponsors are "there to do good and not evil" (Bill Carter, personal interview, June 12, 2003).

To create a perception that a sponsor is an "authentic" supporter of action sports, corporations must fully integrate their sponsorships and even sponsor events that might not provide significant return on investment. For example, Mountain Dew created an 18–stop amateur skateboarding tour entitled the "Mountain Dew Free Flow Tour." The goals of this tour are more focused on building goodwill among the second and third layers of action sports enthusiasts (i.e. the influencers) as opposed to increasing sales (Bill Carter, personal interview, June 12, 2003).

Beyond making a significant monetary commitment to action sports such that a fully integrated marketing program is put in place, action sports also offer some unique opportunities for sponsors to achieve their objectives. For example, most action sports events have a significant musical element. The Gravity Games has a main stage where music performances are concurrent with the action sports event. One way sponsors can better integrate their sponsorships at the Gravity Games is to purchase the title sponsorship to the music stage (Wade Martin, personal interview, June 17, 2003).

Given Gen Y's propensity to multi-task and seek experiences, technology-based extensions of the action sports culture afford sponsors another opportunity to integrate their marketing communications around action sports. For example, highlight videos associated with action sports events present another unique sponsorship opportunity. Action sports enthusiasts enjoy reliving great action sports performances through compilation videos that are often sold at specialty stores (Carter, personal interview, June 12, 2003). According to Wade Martin, these videos are a great marketing tool for action sports sponsors: "[The music] has some great activation applications like a DVD sampler that can be distributed through street teams. So, it is something that can live on beyond the event" (Martin, personal interview, June 17, 2003). Action sports video games are also quite popular and afford sponsors another unique activation opportunity. For example, the Tony Hawk Pro Skater Series video games present a number of in-game branding opportunities. Such marketing opportunities provide another way that corporations can demonstrate their support for action sports events and athletes, and as a result move toward being perceived as being authentic by action sports enthusiasts.

The Future of Action Sports Sponsorship

Action sports are still on the fast paced growth portion of the product life cycle. Gravity Media Owner George Krieger notes,

> It is a category that continues to attract advertisers and marketers, and some of them are leading a demand for new programming. The smart advertisers have grasped on to a way to get young adults who drink soda, play video games, buy packaged goods and watch movies as well as other activities. I think in addition to just action footage on TV, you'll start to see more programming that goes to the lifestyle of these kids. (*SportsBusiness Daily*, 2003, April 16)

But, as action sports have become more mainstream, marketers walk a fine line between maintaining an image of nonconformity to appeal to the young male demographic and making these sports and athletes palatable to the mass market. The popular X Games, for example, draws a family audience more in tune with SUVs than dirt bikes. According to Ron Semiao, ESPN's vice president, programming and managing director of the X Games, "What puts us on the edge is the athletes. They're so legitimate, they bring the character. But from an event staging standpoint, we have to be more on the family side" (Bernstein, 2002b). As noted in the activation section of this chapter, appealing to the masses while still maintaining a relationship with the core action sports participants, who have tremendous influence over their peers, is a difficult challenge facing action sports sponsors.

In addition, some industry experts suggest action sports will have to evolve if they are going to be successful. For example, action sports argue that the competitive aspect of action sports needs far outshine the music and video elements (Liberman, 2004a). Will the Dew Action Sports Tour help in this respect? It is yet to be determined. Additionally, experts suggest action sports events must also be on live (not taped) television if they are going to be sustainable (Liberman, 2004a). While the 2005 X Games and the 2005 Dew Action Sports Tour will both be televised live, it is yet to be determined whether or not ratings will support this effort. As it specifically relates to the sponsorship of action sports, experts such as Martin argue that sponsors and properties need to become more sophisticated in their action sports involvement (Liberman, 2004a).

Conclusion: What Merits Our Attention?

Considering the fact that action sports events have only been on the global sports landscape for slightly more than a decade, action sports sponsorship may also be in its infancy. From a global perspective, large events are starting to become more prevalent in Europe, Asia and Australia. Multinational companies such as LG, Sony and Panasonic are investing sponsorship dollars in action sports. Perhaps because action sports are in an early growth phase, an in-depth understanding of the impact of these sponsorships is difficult to provide. Beyond some basic anecdotal information on increased sales and improved brand image, a number of intriguing questions warrant further examination.

Beyond Bennett et al. (2003), there has been scant examination of the action sports sponsorship realm. Clearly, the unique differences and nuances associated with this highly targeted vehicle warrant close examination, particularly as it relates to the theoretical issues raised herein. For example, to what degree does an action sports enthusiast's identification translate into loyalty toward the action sports sponsor's products? Similarly, how successful are action sports sponsors in repositioning themselves as having brand attributes typically associated with action sports? While we have anecdotal evidence that such an image transfer has occurred in one case (i.e. Mountain Dew), has such an image transfer occurred for other action sports sponsors? Related to this, what happens when mainstream, dominant brands attempt to sponsor action sports? Are they unilaterally perceived as inauthentic or is it possible for a market leader to also successfully garner loyalty from action sports enthusiasts? Answers to these questions may very well go a long way to determining the long-term viability and size of the action sports industry.

References

Aaker, D. A. and Joachimsthaler, E. (2000) *Brand Leadership*, New York: The Free Press.

Bennett, G., Henson, R. and Zhang, J. (2003) "Generation Y's Perceptions of the Action Sports Industry Segment," *Journal of Sport Management*, 17: 95–115.

Bernstein, A. (2002a) "National Teams to Battle in X Games Addition," *Street & Smith's SportsBusiness Journal*, May 27–June 2: 3.

Bernstein, A. (2002b) "Walking Line Between Cool, Conventional: Fans, Sponsors Give X Games Stroll a Mainstream Feel," *Street & Smith's SportsBusiness Journal*, August 26–September 1: 33.

Bernstein, A. (2004a) "Winter Gravitys will return on OLN," *Street & Smith's SportsBusiness Journal*, October 11: 7.

Bernstein, A. (2004b) "Fox's Fuel nears a deal to add Adelphia homes," *Street & Smith's SportsBusiness Journal*, May 10: 5.

China Daily (2004, April 27) "Sports Venues Going to Extreme," accessed through Lexis-Nexis Academic.

Cleland, K. (2001) "Action Sports Form Fabric of Generation: Marines to Mountain Dew Quick to Join Games in Search of Teens," *Advertising Age*, 72, April 16: 22–24.

Cornwell, T. B. (1995) "Sponsorship-Linked Marketing Development," *Sport Marketing Quarterly*, 4(4): 13–23.

Cornwell, T. B., Pruitt, S. W. and Van Ness, R. (2001) "The Value of Winning in Motorsports: Sponsorship-Linked Marketing," *Journal of Advertising Research*, 41(1): 17–31.

Deutsch, K. (1999, June) "Why Generation Y? Here's Why!" www.specialtyrealestate. net/issues/june99/why.htm, accessed December 6, 2003.

Extreme Games, Commercialism Taken Too Far? (1996) Performance Research. Retrieved June 27, 2003 from http://www.researchsponsorship.com/espn_xgames.htm.

Fanning, C. (2004) "The Class of 2004," *Northeast Pennsylvania Business Journal*, 19(7), June 1: 1.

Gillis, R. (2002) "Action Stations," *SportBusiness International*, March, 38–42.

Gladden, J. M. and Wolfe, R. (2001) "Sponsorship of Intercollegiate Athletics: The Importance of Image Matching," *International Journal of Sports Marketing & Sponsorship*, 3(1): 41–65.

Irwin, R. L. and Assimakopoulas, M. (1992) "An Approach to the Evaluation and Selection of Sport Sponsorship Proposals," *Sport Marketing Quarterly*, 1(2): 43–51.

Javalgi, R. G., Traylor, M. B., Gross, A. C. and Lampman, E. (1994) "Awareness of Sponsorship and Corporate Image," *Journal of Advertising*, 23(4): 4–58.

Kamenick, A. (2000) "Firms Reach Out for Generation Y: Billions in Buying Power," *The Business Journal (Minneapolis/St. Paul)*, July 3, www.twincities.bizjournals.com/ twincities/stories/2000/07/03/story4.html

King, B. and Kang, P. (2000) 'X Markets the Spot', *Wired News*, August 17. Retrieved June 27, 2003 from http://www.wired.com/news/culture/0,1294,38275,00.html.

Kinney, L. and McDaniel, S. (1996) "Strategic Implications of Attitude-Toward-the-Ad in Leveraging Sport Sponsorships," *Journal of Sport Management*, 10(3): 250–261.

Kinsman, M. (2002) "Pick-Up Promotions," *Promo*, December 1. Retrieved June 27, 2003 from www.promomagazine.com.

Kleinfeld, M. (2002) "Going to extremes," *American Demographics*, June: 28–30.

Koranteng, J. (2001) "Extreme Ambitions," *AdAgeGlobal*, 1(7), March: 14.

Layden, T. (2002, August 23) "Sport Like it Oughta Be: X Games Athletes put Competition and Fans First," Retrieved June 27, 2003 from http://sportsillustrated.cnn.com/ inside_game/tim_layden/news/2002/08/23/layden_veiwpoint/

Lefton, T. (2003) "T-Mobile Gets More From Action Sports with Tour and Athletes," *SportsBusiness Daily*, May 14, www.sportsbusinessdaily.com/

Lefton, T. (2004a) "5 Sponsors Choose to do the Dew," *Street & Smith's SportsBusiness Journal*, October 4, 1, 35.

Lefton, T. (2004b) "Mountain Dew will title Clear Channel-NBC tour," *Street & Smith's SportsBusiness Journal*, July 12, 1, 39.

Liberman, N. (2004a) "New heights or a crash landing?" *Street & Smith's SportsBusiness Journal*, July 12, 25–27.

Liberman, N. (2004b) "Vans thins events but not spending," *Street & Smith's SportsBusiness Journal*, September 20, 8.

Liberman, N. (2004c) "Sources: Outdoor Life buying Gravity Games," *Street & Smith's SportsBusiness Journal*, January 12, 4.

Madrigal, R. (2000) "The influence of social alliances with sports teams on intentions to purchase corporate sponsors' products," *Journal of Advertising,* 29(4): 13–24.

Meenaghan, T. (1991) "The Role of Sponsorship in the Marketing Communications Mix," *International Journal of Advertising*, 10: 35–47.

Musante, M, Milne, G. R. and McDonald, M. A. (1999) "Sport Sponsorship: Evaluating the Sport and Brand Image Match," *International Journal of Sports Marketing and Sponsorship*, 1(1): 32–47.

Neuborne, E. and Kerwin, K. (1999) "Today's Teens – the Biggest Bulge Since the Boomers – May Force Marketers to Toss Their Old Tricks," *Businessweek online*, February 15 (www.businessweek.com)

Ng, E. (2003) "Extreme Sports Make Strong Inroads into Asia," *Agence France Presse*, January 28, accessed through Lexis-Nexis Academic.

Ostrowski, J. (2002a) "Sources: ESPN Considers an X Tour," *Street & Smith's SportsBusiness Journal*, August 26–September 1, 33.

Ostrowski, J. (2002b) "Alt-sports' Quiksilver Gives showbiz a Go," *Street & Smith's SportsBusiness Journal*, July 1–7, 7.

Prince, G. W. (1998) "Give Them Their Dew: Credit Pepsi for Marketing a Mountain of a Brand," *Beverage World*, January, 54.

Promo Magazine (2001, August) "Making the grade," 19.

Raymond, J. (2002) "Going to Extremes," *American Demographics*, June, 28–30.

Roberts, S. (2002) "Olympics: Some Winter Stars Prefer Green to Gold," *New York Times*, February 7, 1.

Ruibal, S. (2000) "Aging X Games Seek Sharper Edge: Staying Cool is a Hot Issue," *USA Today*, August 17, 20C.

Salmon, A. (2004) "On Advertising: LG Defines its Image with Sports," *International Herald Tribune: The IHT Online*, September 27.

SportBusiness International (2002, June) "Thinking Allowed: Kevin Roberts Talks to Mark McCormick, Michael Payne and Tim Moufarrige about the Future of Sports Marketing."

Sporting Goods Manufacturers Association (2003) *Superstudy of Sports Participation*, North Palm Beach, FL.

SportsBusiness Daily (2002, August 2) "Spons-o-Meter: Seven Partners Align with Vans Warped Tour."

SportsBusiness Daily (2002, October 22) "Burton Snowboards, Malibu Boats Acknowledge Powers That Be."

SportsBusiness Daily (2003, January 28) "Names and Games: IMG X Sports Unit Inks First Athlete."

SportsBusiness Daily (2003, February 20) "Tony Hawk: Pro Endorser? Thought it Was Pro Skater."

SportsBusiness Daily (2003, March 4) "Deals and Dollars: Global X Games Inks Three Gold-Level Deals."

SportsBusiness Daily (2003, March 13) "Names and Faces: Endorsements Entering Realm of Child's Play."

SportsBusiness Daily (2003, April 16) "NBC Looks to Rekindle '02 Olympic Magic with Adrenaline X."

SportsBusiness Daily (2003, May 5) "Is There Concern Marijuana is Infiltrating Action Sports?"

Street & Smith's SportsBusiness Journal (2002) *By the numbers: the authoritative annual research guide and fact book.*

Wendel, T. (2001, August 19) "Going to X-Tremes," *USA Weekend.com*, Retrieved June 27, 2003 from http://www.usaweekend.com/01_issues/010819/010819xtreme.html.

11

Ambush Marketing
Research and management implications

Janet Hoek

Several researchers have discussed sponsorship's extraordinary growth over the last two decades and its increasingly commercial and global orientation (Crimmins & Horn, 1996; Meenaghan, 1998a; Tripodi & Sutherland, 2000). However, although managers' escalating use of sponsorship is well known, few researchers have discussed the growth of what has become colloquially described as "ambush marketing" and even fewer have considered how managers might avoid this problem. As sponsorships extend beyond national boundaries, managers' need to protect their brands from ambushers has become more urgent and more complex. Global sponsorships, such as the Olympics and the FIFA World Cup, involve multiple sponsors from many nations, thus increasing the potential for conflicts to arise between legitimate sponsors. Event owners operating in this global environment face the dual challenge of ensuring consistency within their sponsor profile, while sponsors themselves must guard their rights across multiple jurisdictions.

According to Meenaghan (1994), ambush marketing occurs when "another company, often a competitor, intrudes upon public attention surrounding [an] event, thereby deflecting attention toward themselves and away from the sponsor" (p. 79). This "intrusion" may create or contribute to consumer confusion over the real sponsor and can reduce the benefits the actual sponsor might otherwise have realized. Critics of ambushing argue that it transfers the benefits of sponsorship to non-sponsors, who become the real beneficiaries of the event (Sandler & Shani 1989; Bean 1995; Meenaghan, 1996; 1998a).

Ambush marketing thus amounts to a form of passing off, where non-sponsors imply or create an impression that they have an association with an event when this is not the case. Meenaghan (1994) stimulated debate over ambush marketing by asking whether it was an "immoral or illegal" practice. However, although he outlined two clear perspectives, marketers have focused less on their legal position than on the ethics of ambushing.

Predictably, event owners and official sponsors have regarded attempts to deflect attention away from the official sponsor as immoral, because it threatens their ability to sell events or recoup investments made in these. For example, Payne described ambush marketers as "... thieves knowingly stealing something that does not belong to them" (Payne, 1991, p. 24) and later argued that "ambush marketing breaches one of the fundamental tenets of business activity, namely truth in advertising and business communications" (Payne, 1998, p. 323; see also Townley, Harrington & Couchman, 1998).

However, Welsh, a former marketing executive at American Express, criticized the "weak-minded view that competitors have a moral obligation to step back and allow an official sponsor to reap all the benefits from a special event" (Meenaghan, 1996, p. 108). He further stated that competitors had "not only a right, but an obligation to shareholders to take advantage of such events" and that "all this talk about unethical ambushing is ... intellectual rubbish and posturing by people who are sloppy marketers" (Meenaghan, 1996, p. 108).

Given these very different views of ambush marketing, sponsors wishing to protect their investment cannot necessarily assume competitors will share their ethical perspective and so need to consider the legal remedies open to them (Hoek & Gendall, 2002a). As the courts determine these remedies, Meenaghan's question is more aptly rephrased as whether, and in what circumstances, ambush marketing is illegal.

This chapter begins by discussing the development of ambush marketing before analysing specific practices said to constitute ambushing, the global context within which these occur, and their legal status. The chapter suggests how sponsors could reduce the risk that competitors will detract from their sponsorship investment and concludes that marketers need to place more emphasis on the legal status of their competitors' behavior. That is, although sponsors may feel aggrieved by competitors' behavior, unless a breach of trademark or some form of passing off has occurred, their ability to pursue the matter will be limited.

Evolution of Ambush Marketing

Researchers have documented many reasons for sponsorship's rapid growth, including its novelty relative to traditional mass media advertising and the stronger cut-through it arguably achieves. Sponsorship offers and delivers truly global audiences, creating opportunities for brand exposure that are virtually unrivalled. For event owners, sponsorship's revenue generating potential has led to an increase in the variety of sponsorship packages now available (Altobelli, 1997; Meenaghan, 1998a). Graham, Goldblat and Delpy (1995) noted that the promise of exclusivity within sponsorship levels enabled the IOC to make a profit of over US$200 million from the 1984 Olympic Games.

However, whereas companies once secured sponsorship contracts relatively easily, exclusivity clauses reduced the number of sponsors that could associate themselves with specific events. Furthermore, the cost of obtaining sponsorship rights increased to compensate for the decrease in the number of sponsors and to reflect the wide-ranging audiences delivered. As a result, some companies found themselves excluded from sponsoring an event either because they could no longer afford the cost of procuring these or because a competitor had secured them. However, despite the structural changes that affected access to various sponsorships, companies that had formerly sponsored events still wished to associate themselves with these. The changes to sponsorship contracts thus created conflicts that some companies resolved by engaging in alternative promotions. Where these alternative promotions (including alternative sponsorships) appeared to threaten the publicity associated with the sponsored event, they became known as ambush marketing.

Sandler and Shani (1989) suggest that the first instance of ambush marketing occurred when Kodak failed to secure sponsorship rights for the 1984 Olympic Games to Fuji. Undeterred, Kodak sponsored the ABC's broadcasts of the 1984 Games, became the "official film" of the US track team, and obtained Olympic rights for some Kodak cameras (p. 11).

Although Sandler and Shani indicate that Kodak's behavior was an isolated event in 1984, they argue that, in the following Olympics, "ambush marketing was the name of the game" (p. 11). In 1988, Kodak had reasserted itself as an official Olympic sponsor and Fuji, having learned from its experiences in 1984, ran what Sandler and Shani describe as a very visible promotion that involved sponsorship of the US swimming team (see also Bayless, 1988).

Since then, competitors of a sponsor routinely undertake promotions that coincide with the sponsored event. For official sponsors and event owners, the problem of rival promotions is even greater when the event is international, since competitors may undertake alternative promotions in any one of the countries represented. One example of this problem occurred when Coca-Cola secured official worldwide sponsorship rights to the 1990 Football World Cup, but Pepsi sponsored the high profile Brazilian soccer team (Falconer, 2003). For Coca-Cola, Pepsi's sponsorship threatened their exclusivity and had the potential to confuse soccer fans and the wider public exposed to the Football World Cup, particularly given the high profile of the Brazilian team. However, although irritating to Coca-Cola, Pepsi's behavior was not illegal as the sponsorships it entered into were all legally available to it.

A related conflict occurs for sportspeople, who may belong to teams that have sponsorship contracts, enter into contracts in their own right, and participate in events that have sponsorship links. In early 2003, the Indian cricket team came close to boycotting the ICC Champions Trophy tournament because of differences involving individual and event sponsorships. Several members of the Indian cricket team held lucrative personal endorsement contracts that clashed with the ICC anti-ambush rules and threatened the exclusivity the ICC had promised to official sponsors (Reuters, 2002).

Growth in sponsorship and the opportunities to reach global audiences offered by major sports sponsorships have contributed to an increasingly competitive promotion environment. Social changes, particularly the cult following that major sportspeople such as David Beckham attract, have also added to the competition for sponsorship opportunities. Paradoxically, high profile sportspeople may both increase the premium event owners can charge and the potential for conflict, given their wide range of personal endorsements. However, although few would dispute that these conflicts have increased in number and scope, considerable debate over what constitutes ambush marketing still exists. The following section examines specific instances of alleged ambush marketing in more detail and considers the extent to which these breach fair-trading and trademark statutes.

Ambush Marketing Strategies

Meenaghan (1996, p. 106) identified five commonly employed ambush marketing strategies. These include sponsoring media coverage of an event, a subcategory within the event, or contributing to a "players' pool." Meenaghan also noted that advertising coinciding with a sponsored event or other promotion, or deflecting attention away from the event, could be considered ambushing. Even when considered on a local or national basis, these strategies encompass many activities; when viewed in a global context, it is clear that the potential for conflicts to arise between sponsors is considerable. The remainder of this section examines the strategies Meenaghan outlined and the extent to which these breach relevant statutes or torts.

Sponsoring Media Coverage of an Event

Depending on the relationship between event and media owners, an event owner may offer sponsorship contracts that provide rights to association with an event, but that do not include media rights. Meenaghan (1998b) noted that sponsors should spend up to twice the amount invested in sponsorship rights on promotions and advertising to reinforce their link with the sponsored event. Securing media rights to the event offers an efficient means of promoting the sponsorship association; however, the increasing costs of sponsorship rights can limit the funding available for additional promotions. Where sponsors need to purchase event and media rights independently, rival companies may outbid the event sponsor and thus legitimately obtain alternative sponsorship rights. Ironically, media sponsorship of international sporting events may enable rival sponsors to generate a higher profile than the event sponsor, despite the latter's official status. Lyberger and McCarthy (2001) noted media sponsorship "may result in far greater exposure, as the media audience of major sport events is, typically, significantly larger than the on-site audience" (p. 131). In addition, they suggest the growth of web casting could further increase the opportunities for non-sponsors to develop media associations with major events.

Not surprisingly, event owners view media sponsorship by rivals of the event sponsor with considerable skepticism. Payne, an IOC representative, argued that official sponsors who have purchased exclusive rights to an event have a legitimate right to any publicity the event generates (Payne, 1991, 1998). Purchase of media sponsorship by a rival compromises the event sponsor's access to this publicity and, from Payne's perspective, amounts to corporate theft (see also Townley, Harrington & Couchman, 1998).

However, others have questioned event owners' behavior, calling on them to liaise more effectively with the media to reduce the potential for conflicting sponsorships (Falconer, 2003). Others have queried the proliferation of sponsorship levels and categories, suggesting that event owners' greed has contributed to the increase in sponsorship incompatibilities (Shani & Sandler, 1998).

The Kodak-Fuji sponsorships of the 1984 and 1988 Olympic Games illustrate the problems created when sponsorships are inadequately coordinated. While Payne (1991) criticized the media sponsors for gaining an association with the event and access to its audience, his arguments assume that the Olympic Games have a sacrosanct status that sponsors and non-sponsors alike should respect. This moral claim sits uneasily alongside the commercial reality that competitors of official sponsors face. Major events such as the Olympic Games command a large international audience, thus reducing the reach achieved by other media options and increasing the pressure on non-sponsors to maintain their brands' salience.

From a legal point of view, it is clear that in both 1984 and 1988, the media sponsors' behavior did not breach the contract the official sponsor held with the IOC. Instead, it is arguable that the IOC, in its eagerness to maximize its revenue from both sponsors and broadcasters, failed to protect its sponsors sufficiently. If official sponsors believe they were misled into believing their contract with the IOC included broadcasting rights, their recourse was to sue the IOC for breach of contract. Alternatively, if official sponsors had not assumed broadcasting rights were included in the sponsorship contract, they were either remiss in failing to secure these or naïve in believing that competitors would overlook a legitimate opportunity to associate themselves with the event.

Sponsoring a Subcategory within an Event

Meenaghan (1996) also suggests subcategory sponsorship, which occurs when a rival of an overall event sponsor obtains rights to sponsor a specific activity within that event, could constitute ambushing. Several researchers have noted the rapid growth in sponsorship categories, which Lyberger and McCarthy (2001) describe as creating "a myriad of opportunities for corporations who do not wish to pay the fees associated with being top-category sponsors" (p. 131). These comments also raise interesting questions about the genesis of ambushing and whether it results from predatory competitive behavior, as event owners such as Payne (1998) have alleged, or from excessive exploitation of an event's potential, as Shani and Sandler (1998) suggested.

Kodak's 1988 worldwide category sponsorship of the Olympic Games and Fuji's sub-sponsorship of the US swimming team, which it went on to promote aggressively, illustrates the conflict that can occur when multiple sponsorship levels are available (Fannin, 1988, pp. 64–70; Bayless, 1988, p. B1). Although event owners viewed Fuji's behavior as clear evidence of ambushing, closer analysis suggests a more ambiguous situation. While Fuji had not retained the official sponsorship rights they held in 1984, they remained able to take advantage of other opportunities. Given Kodak's actions during the 1984 Olympic Games, it would be surprising if they had not foreseen this possibility, although they do not appear to have attempted to forestall rivals' access to other sponsorship options. Legally, Fuji's actions did not appear to constitute a breach of any fair-trading or trademark statutes, making it difficult for either Kodak or the IOC to seek redress from Fuji. Even if Kodak's contract with the IOC entitled them to full exclusivity at all sponsorship levels, their case would be against the IOC, rather than Fuji.

Falconer (2003) discussed a similar dispute that occurred between Master-Card and Sprint Communications, both of which held sponsorship associations with the 1994 World Cup. However, whereas MasterCard was an official sponsor, Sprint was an official partner, a lower-level sponsorship category. The dispute between the two sponsors occurred when Sprint featured the World Cup logo in promotions of its pre-paid telephone cards. MasterCard claimed that these promotions infringed their right to the exclusive use of the World Cup logo in relation to "card-based payment and account access devices" and, in the case that followed, the US Federal Court found in favor of MasterCard. The Court concluded that consumers exposed to a Sprint card would "mistakenly assume that Sprint had rights in a category that, in fact, belonged exclusively to MasterCard" (Falconer, 2003).

More recently, Lyberger and McCarthy (2001) suggested that even supply contracts might disrupt sponsorship arrangements. They noted that the Sydney 2000 Olympic Games organizers used TNT to distribute Olympic tickets, even though UPS, a rival courier company, was an official IOC partner. Failure to use the services of official sponsors may reflect nothing more than an administrative oversight, however, the public may interpret it as suggesting a lack of confidence in the sponsor. This type of conflict highlights the growing complexity of international sports sponsorship management, and the need to design management systems capable of identifying these.

In the future, clear coordination of all sponsorship categories, and a reduction of the number of sponsorship opportunities available, could resolve the problem of subcategory sponsorships conflicting with higher-level sponsorship contracts. However, as the UPS example suggests, event organizers need to consider whether supplier contracts will conflict with sponsorship contracts before they address the problems caused by rival sponsors.

Making a Sponsorship-Related Contribution to a Players' Pool and Sponsorship of Players

In some events, such as the Rugby, Football or Cricket World Cup, players do not represent their usual club or team, but play for their country. Lyberger and McCarthy (2001) note that the stipends paid to national team members are typically very small compared to the salary they earn from their club. Companies wishing to support the players can contribute to a players' bonus pool and, in doing so, obtain the right to associate themselves with the team.

Many companies also sponsor individual athletes and teams; for example, sportswear manufacturer adidas sponsors the New Zealand All Blacks and Jonah Lomu, a former All Black. Problems arise when individual sponsorship contracts conflict with the sponsorship arrangements event owners have made. At the Sydney 2000 Olympic Games, adidas's sponsorship of Australian swimmer Ian Thorpe created problems for Nike, which was the official clothing supplier for the Australian Olympic team. Curthoys and Kendall (2001) noted that Thorpe was photographed with his towel draped over Nike's logo at a medal presentation ceremony (para 69), a gesture they suggest was necessary to avoid breaching his personal contract with adidas. McDonald and Davidson (2001) noted a similar dilemma when Nike-sponsored players from the US men's basketball team covered the Reebok logos on their tracksuits when receiving their medals.

Curthoys and Kendall (2001) also commented on the conflict faced by Cathy Freeman, the Australian athlete who opened the Olympic Games. Freeman appeared in advertisements for Telstra, an official Olympics sponsor, and Optus, a rival of Telstra that held no official sponsorship rights but that had a long history of sponsoring Australian athletics. Curthoys and Kendall (2001) raised several important questions about the management of conflicts such as these.

> Should Cathy Freeman have been prohibited from appearing in advertisements for non-official sponsors for a period before the Sydney 2000 Games? While the IOC Charter (binding all athletes) restricts athletes from engaging in marketing activities during the Games period, would it have been fair, even ethical, to limit her activities prior to the Games? Equally, should Optus, the sponsor of athletics in Australia for over 5 years, have been prevented from sponsoring her? (para 73).

These questions highlight the practical difficulties in defining ambush marketing, particularly where two companies may have had ongoing commitments to events or participants within these. Conflicts between individual team members and event owners also raise the question of whose rights should prevail – those of individual athletes or teams, or those of sporting associations and event owners. The Indian cricket team members' dispute with the ICC, outlined above, clearly illustrates the potential for conflict between event sponsors and individual sponsors. Where individuals obtain considerable personal revenue from brand endorsements, they are understandably reluctant to relinquish these, even if they run counter to the event owner's sponsorship commitments.

Disputes between Reebok, which was official apparel supplier to the US team at the 1992 Olympics, and Nike, which contracted the US track and field team to wear Nike clothing when competing, also illustrate this problem. Reebok considered Nike had stolen exposure and publicity they believe they had purchased when they obtained the apparel sponsorship for the entire US team. However, Nike argued they simply exploited a legitimate sponsorship opportunity open to them. Moreover, Nike noted their contracts with some of the athletes, for example Michael Johnson, existed well before the 1992 Olympics.

Conflicts between event owners and stadium owners may also disrupt sponsorship arrangements. Wadell (1995) reported a dispute between the National Football League (NFL) and the owner of the Dallas Cowboys, Jerry Jones, who also owns the Texas Stadium. At the time, the NFL held a sponsorship contract with Coca-Cola that entitled Coca-Cola to use NFL team logos. (Although PepsiCo became official soft drink sponsor of the NFL in 2002, this dispute pre-dates the change in official sponsor.) However, Jones entered into a separate contract with Pepsi, who obtained sole pouring rights in the Texas Stadium. He argued that his team was worth more than the revenue obtained through NFL shares, and that only independent marketing enabled the team's potential to be realized.

Although some of the disputes outlined above involve conflicting contractual terms, subcategory sponsorship is not inherently illegal and individual sponsorships, in particular, exist well before bidding for event sponsorships commences (Curthoys & Kendall, 2001). The existence of earlier sponsorship contracts questions the level of exclusivity that event owners can offer prospective sponsors and suggests a reconsideration of the benefits "exclusive" sponsorship can actually deliver is timely. The fact the event owners do not own media, venues or competitors, means they cannot exert full control over all other contracts that may exist, a point that could be more explicitly stated in sponsorship contracts. Contracts that specified contingences within and outside event owners' control would help clarify sponsors' expectations and make them more alert to their competitors' likely behavior. Clauses such as these seem particularly important in international sponsorships, where event owners may be able to exert less control over local supply arrangements. For sponsors, clearer definition of their entitlements could provide a stronger basis from which to take any legal action, should a rival's actions breach the contract.

Engaging in Advertising that Coincides with a Sponsored Event

Although many examples of "ambushing" involve other sponsorship arrangements, rivals of official sponsors can also purchase normal advertising time and space, which official sponsors have also regarded as ambush marketing. Large international sporting events, such as the Olympic Games or Football or Rugby World Cups attract very large audiences, at least some of whom will see or hear advertising that screens during interval periods. Where non-sponsors promote their brands heavily during event broadcasts, viewers may come to associate non-sponsors' brands with the event.

Official sponsors have expressed even more concern about themed advertising that features competitors from an event. For example, during the 1992 Winter Olympics, McDonald's were the official sponsors of the US team, yet Wendy's featured Kristi Yamaguchi, an Olympic champion figure skater, in its advertising (see Jensen, 1995, p. 3). However, while McDonald's viewed Wendy's behavior as ambushing, Wendy's argued they were within their rights to promote their brand during the Olympic Games, using airtime available to all advertisers.

Falconer (2003) noted the aggressive advertising American Express and Visa engaged in during the 1994 Winter Olympics in Norway. Visa, an official sponsor, developed a television advertising campaign to promote the fact that the Olympic Village would not accept American Express cards. In response, American Express ran a campaign stating that their card was accepted throughout Norway and that tourists did not need a 'visa' to visit Norway. Falconer suggests that American Express's clever use of double entendre may have led viewers to conclude that American Express did have an official association with the Winter Olympics.

During the 1992 Barcelona Olympics, Nike held press conferences for Olympic athletes it sponsored and displayed large murals of members of the US basketball team on buildings in Barcelona, even though they were not the official sponsors. Lyberger and McCarthy (2001) noted: "...the sheer magnitude of [Nike's] presence at the venues effectively deflected attention from official sponsors" (p. 132). Davis (1996) reported that Nike manager Mark Pilkenton rationalized these actions by stating: "...we feel like in any major sporting event, we have the right to come in and give our message as long as we don't interfere with the official proceedings."

Curthoys and Kendall (2001) discussed Qantas's campaign in the period preceding the 2000 Sydney Olympics, which involved a series of advertisements featuring famous Australian athletes and posters with slogans such as "Australia Wide Olympic Sale." Although Ansett sued Qantas, the issue settled, though not before nearly 60% of the public believed Qantas was the official Olympic airline (compared with the 38% who correctly identified Ansett as the official sponsor). While the Australian public appeared confused, it is difficult to attribute their confusion to the advertising campaign alone, which did not appear either to breach any trademarks or imply official associations that did not exist.

Although event owners clearly resent these activities, Welsh challenged their thinking: "The ... notion, that non-sponsors have a moral or ethical obligation to market themselves away from the thematic space of a sponsored property, is nonsense. Smart marketers have long recognized that view as a commercial non-starter and an intellectual affront" (reported in *Marketing UK*, p. 15). Non-sponsors' rights, according to this reasoning, extend to everything not specifically prohibited by law or by a legally enforceable contract.

One of the few cases to reach the courts, NZO&CGA Inc. v Telecom New Zealand Ltd, (1996 7 TCLR 167) assessed an ambushing claim made by the New Zealand Olympic and Commonwealth Games Association. The NZO&CGA alleged that Telecom, the largest New Zealand telecommunications company, had "ambushed" Bell South, a rival company that was New Zealand's official telecommunications sponsor of the 1996 Atlanta Olympic Games. Telecom had developed an advertisement that featured the word "Ring" five times in the Olympic colors to promote their mobile phone system's global capability. More specifically, Telecom claimed that their mobile network would allow consumers to use their mobile phone, should they travel to Atlanta for the Olympic Games. Given the comparatively low levels of cell phone penetration in 1996, Olympic sponsorship represented a key opportunity to reach an international audience likely to be receptive to international communications.

In assessing the NZO&CGA's application, Justice McGechan considered the actual claims made in the advertisement and found no evidence of a deliberate falsehood, as Telecom had not claimed an association with the New Zealand Olympic team. He also considered how a casual reader would interpret the advertisement and found that readers were unlikely to assume that "this play on the Olympic five circles must have been with the authority of the Olympic Association, or through sponsorship of the Olympics. It quite simply and patently is not the use of the five circles as such" (NZO&CGA v Telecom) (Hoek, 1997).

However, although the New Zealand courts did not uphold this alleged instance of passing off, in 2002, an Argentinean Court ordered PepsiCo to cease using an advertisement that implied a relationship between PepsiCo and the FIFA World Cup. PepsiCo's advertising used the phrase "Tokyo 2002" and featured footballers and imagery that the Court ruled could create confusion among viewers. While these two cases were heard in quite different jurisdictions, the Argentinean outcome suggests the courts may be adopting a more sympathetic stance. Whether this is the case will, however, depend on the development of a body of case law that clarifies the distinction between harmless insinuation and passing off.

Development of Other Imaginative Ambush Strategies

Marketers' use of new media such as text messaging, event merchandising and sales promotions has opened up new "ambushing" opportunities. McKelvey (1994) summarizes several of the more innovative promotions that have featured at recent international sporting events. "...non-sponsors handing out coupons and caps to spectators, hanging banners from tall buildings, running 'good luck' and 'congratulations' ads, purchasing billboards around the venue, using World Cup tickets in consumer sweepstakes etc.... ." (p. 20). Rivals to official sponsors have often provided spectators with merchandise to ensure their brand imagery features at the event. McKelvey (2003b) has even noted the use of temporary tattoos, or "body billboards" on athletes as presenting another challenge to event owners in their fight to preserve the exclusivity of official sponsorship rights.

Increasing awareness of the use of merchandise to promote a rival's brand has seen event officials screen spectators and prohibit entry to those who wear apparel that bears a rival's logo, lest these feature in international media coverage of the event. A South African newspaper reported that schoolchildren with Coca-Cola in their lunch boxes had to peel off the can labels and remove Coca-Cola logos from bottle tops and lids before they could enter a World Cup cricket match (*Natal Witness*, 2003).

Attempts by rivals of official sponsors to expose their brands have gone well beyond the distribution of merchandise. At the 1996 Atlanta Olympics, Nike built a large sports centre called Niketown near a key Olympic venue. More recently, Nike and Columbia Sportswear, neither of which were official sponsors of the 2002 Winter Olympics, contracted to outfit teams and media officials (Hegedus, 2002).

The activities outlined above have irritated official sponsors, but have provided few grounds for action. However, a sales promotion that allegedly misled consumers is one of the few activities to have been ruled on by the courts. Bean (1995) discussed a recent Canadian case, where the National Hockey League (NHL) sued Pepsi for what the NHL alleged was an ambush campaign. The NHL represents twenty-one ice hockey teams, and generates considerable revenue by selling licenses to manufacturers; these manufacturers are then entitled to use the NHL logo, or the logos of its member teams.

Coca-Cola entered into a contract with the NHL to become official soft drink supplier. However, Pepsi obtained advertising rights through Molson Breweries, which held broadcast sponsorship rights to the NHL. As well as advertising, Pepsi ran a promotion in which consumers predicted NHL Playoff results using information found on Pepsi bottle caps. Despite this link to the NHL, Pepsi did not refer to the NHL and included disclaimers on its merchandising and advertising material that stated the items were not associated with the NHL. In addition, Pepsi did not use the teams' trademarked names, but referred to them generically, through their city.

From the NHL's point of view, Pepsi's campaign involved several activities they considered had ambushed Coca-Cola's sponsorship contract. Pepsi made use of a similar promotion, scheduled to run simultaneously with the original event, and employed a variety of supporting promotions that paralleled aspects of the original event. The NHL thus alleged that Pepsi's promotion deliberately created confusion over the sponsor of the NHL Playoffs and sued Pepsi for alleged trademark infringement, passing off and interference with the NHL's contractual arrangements. However, Pepsi's care in not using registered trademarks and their disclaimer led the judge to conclude that their conduct fell short of breaching Canadian law (*NHL v Pepsi 92 DHR 4th 349*).

The NHL could not prevent Pepsi from running its competition. However, a more robust contract with Coca-Cola would have included broadcast rights or some provision that prevented the holder of these from on-selling them to Coca-Cola's competitors. A restraining provision such as this would have reduced the exposure Pepsi were able to obtain for their competition. McKelvey (2003a) notes that *NCAA v Coors,* a very similar case to *NHL v Pepsi* but to be heard in the USA, is likely to provide an important precedent in determining the extent to which themed promotions run by non-sponsors constitute behavior that is likely to mislead consumers.

Although irksome to official sponsors, the activities outlined above draw on opportunities legitimately available to advertisers. While considerable debate over the ethics of these promotions continues, this debate offers no new insights into their legal status or the remedies available to official sponsors, particularly those operating in the global arena. Until specifically prevented from utilizing promotion opportunities, competitors will claim the right to promote their brands using media opportunities that sponsors or event owners do not own.

However, the fact that so many media opportunities remain available for rivals to exploit suggests a need for greater coordination between media and event owners. In addition, event owners may need to be more circumspect about the levels of exclusivity they offer sponsors. The following section analyses these and other remedies that may be open to event owners and sponsors.

Possible Remedies and Research Implications

Commercial pragmatism may, over time, promote a more logical discussion of ambush marketing. Meenaghan (1996, p. 108) has already noted that many of the activities previously labeled ambush marketing, such as competitive advertising during and around sponsored events, are now regarded as legitimate activities. This suggests that at least some event owners and sponsors have accepted that the brand competition apparent in other media will also occur in sponsorship and supporting promotions.

Aside from adopting a more realistic perspective, event owners could implement other options. Although unlikely to meet with approval from event owners, one obvious solution to the conflicts outlined above would see a reduction in the number of sponsorship categories sold. As the revenue from sponsorship has increased, the temptation to increase the number of sponsorship levels and classes has also grown. While this practice increases income for the event owner, it heightens the chance that rivals might secure rights to a subcategory of the event, especially if rights packages are sold in several countries. More importantly, proliferation of sponsorship categories has reduced the public's ability to differentiate between sponsorship classes. Indeed, Shani and Sandler (1998) reported that more than two thirds of the people they interviewed were unable to differentiate between different sponsorship levels.

Given the inconsistencies that have emerged between event sponsorship and broadcast sponsorship, event owners need to manage the sale of these rights carefully. As Shani and Sandler (1998) noted, event owners can generate considerable revenue by accepting bids for telecast rights. However, broadcasters must also recoup the expense of securing rights, which may entail selling more advertising space and offering sub-sponsorship rights within event telecasts. Shani and Sandler (1998) reported that over a third of their survey respondents thought only official sponsors could advertise during an event telecast. Sale of advertising space to rivals who may operate in several countries thus appears to create considerable confusion among the public. Where sponsorships deliver global audiences, the need to ensure carefully coordinated subcategory packages is further heightened. To address this problem, Shani and Sandler (1998) suggested event owners should reduce the cost of broadcast rights in return for obtaining more control over whom these are sold to.

Event owners have also moved to develop legal protection of the rights they sell to official sponsors. The organizing committee for the Sydney 2000 Olympic

Games successfully lobbied for new legal protections as part of a comprehensive brand protection strategy (see Roper-Drimie, 2001, pp. 151–153). The Sydney 2000 Games (Indicia and Images) Protection Act 1996 and the Olympic Arrangements Act 2000 formed part of a strategy designed to reduce the incidence of ambushing at the 2000 Olympic Games (though Curthoys and Kendall (2001) question the strength of the former Act's provisions). While the former Act attempted to protect Olympic imagery and control how, where and by whom this could be used, the latter Act prohibited rival companies from using billboards, signs or posters near any of the Olympic venues. In addition, an aircraft exclusion zone operated during the Olympics to prevent balloon advertising, sky-banners and sky-writers from promoting non-sponsors' brands (Simmons, 2000).

Similarly, the introduction of the Merchandise Marks Amendment Act 2002 by the South African government responded to the International Cricket Council's call for support to reduce ambushing at the 2003 ICC World Cup. This legislation even contains provisions to jail directors of companies that engage in ambushing activities.

Before the introduction of specific legislation to address the potential for ambush marketing, event owners and sponsors had to rely on trademark and fair trading statutes and, where breaches occurred in several countries, they needed to seek redress in each of these. However, very few ambushers use the exact logos or insignia of the event owner; instead, ambushers typically create images or devices that allude to or connote the event or team without using a trademark. The New Zealand "Ring Ring" case illustrates the imaginative use of a visual device that, on close reading refers to the Olympic Ring symbol (Hoek, 1997). Similarly, Pepsi's use of NBL teams' hometowns, instead of the team names themselves, avoided breaching trademarked names.

Even general commercial protection may not afford the protection from ambushing desired by sponsors. Event owners must also clearly state the actual rights purchased and ensure these are protected via tighter contractual provisions with all parties. Hoek and Gendall (2002b, p. 88) point to tighter sponsorship contracts that better define event owners' responsibilities and sponsors' rights as providing more grounds for action and a greater range of remedies. Shiu (2002) outlined specific points that ought to be made clear in contracts, including the rights licensed, the terms of the license, prohibited uses, and rights regarding signage, trademarks and hospitality (p. 16). This latter issue is important in preventing what McDonald and Davidson (2001) refer to as "promotional creep," which occurs when sponsors attempt to spread their sponsorship rights beyond the specific activity to which they have rights.

An IOC report on the Salt Lake City 2002 Winter Olympic Games also set out several measures used to reduce the incidence of ambush marketing. These included full registration of trademarks and copyright material at state and federal levels, and internationally. In addition, the IOC undertook close monitoring of the manner in which Olympic marks were used and prohibited unauthorized use of these, including suing companies they considered had breached their trademarks. They also instituted audit programs, together with photo audits of commercial activity within the Olympic venues and mystery shopper programs to detect unauthorized merchandise. In line with this advice, the Sydney Organizing Committee prevented tickets to any Olympic event from being used in other promotional activities (thereby ensuring non-sponsors would not use tickets as prizes in competitions).

Shani and Sandler (1998) recommended the use of an education program to ensure consumers are aware that not all advertisers are official sponsors of an event and the IOC has developed programs to increase knowledge of ambush marketing and to discredit alleged ambushers. Their aggressive advertising campaigns castigate alleged ambushers as cheats that deserve public approbation. These advertisements suggest that ambushers are attempting to dupe the public and freeload on the values of the official Olympic movement by undermining the rights secured by their competitors. However, it is not clear whether this advertising clarifies the status of the official sponsors; ironically, it could actually reinforce awareness of the rival.

As noted earlier, Meenaghan (1998b) argued that sponsors should purchase mass-media time and space to promote their sponsorship and they may need to spend two to three times the cost of the sponsorship rights to promote their association with an event. Strong and obtrusive supporting advertising could diminish the effects any rivals' promotions may have, although this suggests the logical means of combating ambush marketing is to purchase all the media and subcategory sponsorship rights to the event. Shiu (2002) summarizes this view when he suggested controlling ambush marketing involved buying up all "rights to all the teams, or all the broadcast rights, or all the space for 10 miles around ... if you won't or can't do that, then you open the door to [ambushers]" (p. 17). The costs of implementing this advice would be considerable even at a national level; where global events, covering multiple venues, are involved, adopting these suggestions could be prohibitively expensive.

Despite the protection afforded by new legislation or the sponsors' promotions, the onus is still on event owners to prove that a breach occurred or a rival trader's behavior would create confusion among consumers. Thus, although the courts will enforce sponsors' and event owners' rights if a rival breaches trademark or copyright legislation, or when their actions constitute passing off under the law, event owners still need to demonstrate that a breach occurred. Both parties may thus rely increasingly on consumer evidence to support the presence (or absence) of deception. As Hoek and Gendall (2003) have noted, adducing robust and persuasive consumer evidence is more difficult than marketers may recognize.

This situation highlights the need for additional research into the effects of sponsorship passing off on major sponsors and event owners. While there is ample evidence that non-sponsors have sometimes engaged in imaginative and perhaps gray activities, there is little evidence to show how these activities have affected consumers, or whether cultural factors affect consumers' responses to instances of alleged ambushing. Although some researchers have reported consumer confusion over official sponsors, the source of this confusion is not always clear. Even if consumers believe a non-sponsor is an official sponsor, their views could be based on their own usage behavior or even on a perception of the market structure. That is, if unsure of which brands sponsor an event, consumers may suggest either the brands they use, or the brands they know to be successful within a product category. Additional research that examines the role of brand usage and market structure in consumers' perceptions of sponsors is thus urgently required to examine how other factors contribute to consumer confusion. Given that brand profiles and shares are likely to differ across countries, a multinational study may be required to fully understand the role played by usage and brand perceptions.

Researchers need also to turn their attention to the behavioral consequences of sponsorship passing off. If consumer confusion can be reliably attributed to a non-sponsor's promotions, official sponsors need to estimate the effect this confusion has had on their business and the return they might otherwise have expected. At present, there is surprisingly little evidence about how confusion affects consumers' behavior. This question will require greater attention if sponsors plan to sue rivals for damages they believe to have resulted from misleading or deceptive promotions.

Conclusions

The creative use of ambush marketing tactics will probably always irritate event owners and their official sponsors. Ironically, although global sponsors invest heavily in event rights, they could be at greatest risk of ambushing because of the difficulty of monitoring the international activities of their rivals. As Curthoys and Kendall noted: "The law as it now stands seems unable to accommodate the concerns of official corporate sponsors. There is no limit to human ingenuity. As such, ambush marketing at the margins will arguably always occur" (Curthoys & Kendall, 2001, para 78).

However, while regulating against every possible "ambushing" initiative may prove difficult, several measures could clarify and protect sponsors' rights. More specific and better-coordinated contracts could reduce the range of opportunities currently open to rival traders. In addition, the normal protection provided by trademark, copyright and passing off laws needs to be supplemented by tighter contractual provisions between all parties involved in sponsoring an event; these, in turn, need to recognize differences in fair-trading and passing off statutes across participating countries. Greater clarity and more detailed sponsorship contracts could foster more pragmatic expectations about sponsorship's likely benefits. Activities not prohibited by law or the contract would be legitimate marketing tactics; however, their potential effect should be more explicitly recognized during negotiations between event owners and prospective sponsors.

Given that regulation and tighter contracts may not deter non-sponsors wishing to associate themselves with an event, researchers need to address the effects of passing off as it affects sponsorship. If sponsors can separate out the confounding effects of past usage behavior and market perception, they will be able to estimate the effects of a rival's promotions. More critically, research into the behavioral effects of sponsorship passing off will provide sponsors with the means of quantifying the damages they may have suffered from competitors' behavior.

Although Payne and other IOC officials may wish "ambush marketing" would disappear, this appears to be a naïve hope, especially as the cachet of key sportspeople and teams increases and their global profile expands. For sponsors of multinational events, the need to check and coordinate sponsor profiles in participating countries is a challenging task. Funding purchase of global media rights to protect the sponsorship may also represent a considerable financial burden, especially when coupled with the growing costs of sponsorship rights to international events. Ultimately, sponsors' and event owners' best hopes of countering this phenomenon may instead rely on increased collaboration to protect each others' interests and a more realistic assessment of what sponsorship can actually achieve.

References

Altobelli, T. (1997) "Cashing in on the Sydney Olympics," *Law Society Journal*, 35 (4): 44–46.

Bayless, A. (1988) "Ambush Marketing is Becoming a Popular Event at Olympic Games," *The Wall Street Journal*, February 8.

Bean, L. (1995) "Ambush Marketing: Sports Sponsorship Confusion and the Lanham Act," *Boston University Law Review*, 75 (September): 1099–1134.

Crimmins, J. and Horn, M. (1996) "Sponsorship: From Management Ego Trip To Marketing Success," *Journal of Advertising Research*, 36: 11–21.

Curthoys, J. and Kendall, C. (2001) "Ambush Marketing and the Sydney 2000 Games (Indicia and Images) Protection Act: A Retrospective," *Murdoch University Electronic Journal of Law*, 8 (2): http://www.murdoch.edu.au/elaw/issues/v8n2/kendal1182.html, accessed August 6, 2003.

Davis, R. (1996) "Ambushing the Olympic Games," *Sports and Entertainment Law Journal*, 3 (2): http://vls.law.vill.edu/students/orgs/sports/back_issues/volume3/issue2/ambushing.html, accessed August 8, 2003.

Falconer, R. (2003) "Ambush Marketing and How to Avoid it," http://www.geoccities.com/Athens/Acropolis/5232/ambush.html, accessed August 6, 2003.

Fannin, R. (1988) "Gold Rings or Smoke Rings?" *Marketing and Media Decisions* 23 (9).

Graham, S., Goldblat, J. and Delpy, L. (1995) *The Ultimate Guide to Sport Event Management and Marketing*. Chicago: Irwin.

Hegedus, M. (2002) "Ambush marketing hits Salt Lake City," http://www.msnbc.com/NEWS/712031.asp, accessed August 6, 2003.

Hoek, J. (1997) "*Ring Ring:* Visual pun or passing off?" *Asia-Australia Marketing Journal,* 5: 33–44.

Hoek, J. and Gendall, P. (2002a) "When Do Ex-Sponsors Become Ambush Marketers?" *International Journal of Sports Marketing & Sponsorship,* 3 (4): 383–402.

Hoek, J. and Gendall, P. (2002b) "Ambush Marketing: More than Just a Commercial Irritant?" *Entertainment Law,* 1 (2): 72–91.

Hoek, J. and Gendall, P. (2003) "David vs Goliath: An Analysis of Survey Evidence in a Trademark Dispute," *International Journal of Market Research,* 45 (1): 99–121.

Jensen, J. (1995) "Atlanta Games Craft Barriers to Ambushers," *Advertising Age,* March 13, 66 (11): 3.

Lyberger, M. and McCarthy, L. (2001) "An Assessment of Consumer Knowledge of, Interest in, and Perceptions of Ambush Marketing Strategies," *Sport Marketing Quarterly,* 10 (2): 130–137.

McDonald, J. and Davidson, J. (2001) "Avoiding Surprise Results at the Olympic Games," http://www.managingip.com, accessed August 6, 2003.

McKelvey, S. (1994) "Sans Legal Restraint, No Stopping Brash, Creative Ambush Marketing," *Brandweek,* April 18: 20.

McKelvey, S. (2003a) "Unauthorised Use of Event Tickets in Promotion Campaign May Create New Legal Strategies to Combat Ambush Marketing: NCAA v Corrs," *Sport Marketing Quarterly,* 12 (2): 117–118.

McKelvey, S. (2003b) "Commercial 'Branding': The Final Frontier or False Start for Athletes' Use of Temporary Tattoos as Body Billboards," *Journal of Legal Aspects of Sport,* 13 (2): in press.

Marketing UK (2002) "Are Ambush Marketers 'Ethically Correct'?" April 7: 15

MasterCard International Incorporated v Sprint Communications Co v ISL Football AG, 30 USPQ 2d 1963 (SDNY 1994); 23 F3d 397 (2d Cir. 1994),

Meenaghan, T. (1994) "Point Of View: Ambush Marketing – Immoral or Imaginative Practice?" *Journal of Advertising Research.* 34 (3): 77–88.

Meenaghan, T. (1996) "Ambush Marketing – A Threat to Corporate Sponsorship," *Sloan Management Review,* 38: 103–113.

Meenaghan, T. (1998a) "Ambush Marketing: Corporate Strategy and Consumers' Re-actions," *Psychology and Marketing,* 15 (4): 305–322.

Meenaghan, T. (1998b) "Current Developments and Future Directions in Sponsorship," *International Journal of Advertising,* 17 (1), 3–28.

Natal Witness (2003) "Ambush Marketing Fight at World Cup Sinks to New Lows," 19 February. http://www.legalbrief.co.za/view_1.php?artnum=9133, accessed August 7, 2003.

New Zealand Olympic and Commonwealth Games Association Inc v Telecom NZ Ltd 1996 7 TCLR 167.

Payne, M. (1991) "Ambush Marketing: Immoral or Imaginative Practice." Paper presented at Sponsorship Europe '91 Conference, Barcelona, Spain.

Payne, M. (1998) "Ambush Marketing: The Undeserved Advantage," *Psychology and Marketing,* 15 (4): 323–331.

Reuters (2002) "World Cup ambush marketing could mean jail terms – ICC," http://www-usa.cricket.org/link_to_database/ARCHIVE/CRICKET_NEWS/2002/DEC, accessed August 6, 2003.

Roper-Drimie, M. (2001) "Sydney 2000 Olympic Games – 'The Worst Games Ever' for Ambush Marketers?" *Entertainment Law Review,* 5.

Sandler, D. and Shani, D. (1989) "Olympic Sponsorship vs 'Ambush' Marketing: Who Gets the Gold?" *Journal of Advertising Research,* 29: 9–14.

Shani, D. and Sandler, D. (1998) "Ambush Marketing: Is Confusion to Blame for the Flickering of the Flame?" *Psychology and Marketing,* 15 (4): 367–383.

Shiu, F. (2002) "You've Been Ambushed!" *Asian IP,* 1 (5): 12–17.

Simmons, M. (2000) "The Other Side of the Olympic Games." http://www.askmen. com/sports/business/13_sports_business.html, accessed August 6, 2003.

Townley, S., Harrington, D. and Couchman, N. (1998) "The Legal and Practical Prevention of Ambush Marketing in Sports," *Psychology and Marketing,* 15 (4): 333–348.

Tripodi, J. and Sutherland, M. (2000) "Ambush Marketing: An Olympic Event," *The Journal of Brand Management,* 7 (6).

Wadell, R. (1995) "Cowboys Rewriting NFL Revenue Rules?" *Amusement Business,* 107 (38): 1–3.

12

Examining International Alliances through Sponsorship

Francis Farrelly and Pascale Quester

Recent developments in the field of sponsorship suggest that much is to be gained from examining the sponsorship relationship as a strategic alliance. These developments include: the growing use of sponsorship as a vehicle to achieve strategic ends such as corporate and brand positioning objectives; the increasingly substantial budgets invested in sponsorship and the prominence it has assumed in the marketing efforts of many organizations; and the growing incidence of "sponsorship-linked marketing" (Cornwell, 1995), where sponsorship is used as the platform for the development of marketing strategy. Despite casual references to the sponsorship relationship as an alliance (Crompton, 1993) and calls for dyadic research to better understand the mechanics of relationships (Olkkonen, 2001), the relationship between sponsors and their properties remains largely unexplored in terms of its potential as a strategic alliance.

Anecdotal evidence abounds of sponsorship alliances being formed to help sponsors compete in domestic and international markets, and even on the global stage. There is growing recognition that sponsorship of sport has become the communications tool of choice for multinational companies such as Heineken, Visa and Coca-Cola. This is because sport (and the commercial message built around it) has a unique capacity to transcend cultural boundaries with non-verbal and universal messages of hope, pain, competition and victory, and because the same or similar communication message can be used in many markets.

For example, a motivation for Telstra (Australia's largest telecommunications company) to invest in excess of A$100 million dollars as part of its Sydney 2000 Olympic sponsorship campaign was to showcase its technologies to other parts of the world in addition to Australia, particularly Southeast Asia, a rapidly emerging market for such services. Similarly, Qantas's and Foster's decisions to sponsor the Formula One Grand Prix in Australia is not just because of domestic market opportunities (F1 Racing is not such a popular sport in Australia as compared to some other sports) but because the race is broadcast into Europe, particularly the UK, and South America, where it has a large and loyal following, and where both companies compete.

This paper examines sponsorship as a tool for international or global strategic alliance. It begins with an argument in favor of the conceptualization of sponsorship as an alliance and identifies key construct deemed important for its development. The paper then discusses the specific case of MasterCard, an organization that uses sponsorship alliances as a platform for global marketing and to project the global stature of its brand. The paper then reports the findings of a qualitative study involving a series of in-depth interviews conducted with leading Australian sponsors dealing with properties enjoying international reach. The paper concludes with a conceptual framework and reflects on issues pertinent to the management of sponsorship as an international or global alliance.

Our findings suggest that sponsorship is well suited to building strategic alliances, including international ones, and that it can be used to activate effective international marketing strategies. However further research is clearly required to better understand those conditions most appropriate for engaging sponsorship as the basis for an alliance, and the determinants of sponsorship alliance success, including the cause and effect of particular alliance attributes such as strategic compatibility, communication and commitment between focal partners.

Sponsorship as a Strategic Alliance

Strategic alliances are now a familiar feature of the competitive landscape. In particular, alliances with a marketing emphasis – joint product development, joint branding and reciprocal marketing alliances – have become increasingly widespread (Varadarajan & Cunningham, 1995). For example, a study conducted by Simonin and Ruth (1998) examined the "growing and pervasive phenomenon of brand alliances as they affect consumers' brand attitudes" (p. 30). These authors found that brand alliances of various types significantly affect the respective partnering brands but do not necessarily benefit both partners equally.

According to Varadarajan and Cunningham (1995), "strategic alliances, a manifestation of interorganisational cooperative strategies, entails the pooling of skills and resources by the alliance partners, in order to achieve one or more goals linked to the strategic objectives of the cooperating firms" (p. 283). They note that a strategic alliance can be structured as either a distinct corporate entity in which alliance partners hold an equity position, or alternatively, as a distinct inter-organizational entity to which the organizational partners commit resources or skills without sharing equity in the relationship. Sponsorship is typical of the latter: parties to the sponsorship agreement share resources and skills. This may be in the form of alignment of intangible assets such as brand image and/or skills in marketing planning and implementation.

Strategic alliances, however, are distinct from cooperative arrangements (Varadarajan & Cunningham, 1995). While cooperation is clearly an important facet of the strategic alliance, it is not its defining characteristic. A strategic alliance can only be viewed as such where cooperation is established to facilitate defined strategic initiatives to achieve a competitive advantage, and where the focal parties make an equitable contribution towards achieving this advantage.

Clearly, sponsorship can be viewed as a strategic tool used in the pursuit of competitive advantage. Indeed it is often initiated to achieve both corporate and brand image objectives, and on occasions, can even be employed as the platform of corporate and brand positioning strategies and the basis on which marketing activities are conceived and implemented (Cornwell, 1995). In such instances, major strategies are created and activated based on the sponsorship investment, including co-branding initiatives, advertising campaigns, sales and trade promotion and so forth. Sponsorship may also be used as a foundation for international market entry and diffusion strategies (James, 1999).

According to Douma, Bilderbeek, Idenburg and Looise (2000), the success of an alliance is predicated upon "an alignment between the partners involved." Such a fit has long been considered a key element of sponsorship agreement, with "fit" defined either in terms of product category relatedness (Johar & Pham, 1999; Quester, 1997) or in terms of historical development (Quester & Lardinoit, 2001a). Whether such alignment is at strategic or operational level (Niederkofler, 1991), it appears just as vital for sponsorship as for any other alliance. The drivers of "fit" proposed by Douma et al. (2000) are articulated around six core issues, namely:

- shared strategic vision on developments in the alliance environment;
- compatibility;
- strategic importance to both partners;
- complementary balance (mutual dependence);
- added value for clients and partners;
- market acceptance by the partners' market.

It is clear that these drivers are also relevant in determining the fit between the sponsor and property from a relationship perspective. And while the degree to which mutual dependence in different sponsorship dyads will vary, only those sponsorship relationships where some complementary balance is achieved may accurately be considered alliances. The more predatory or exploitative situation, where one party tends to dictate terms, should more appropriately be considered a Principal–Agent type of relationship and, while more common for smaller sponsorship agreements, it is not the focus of this chapter. Instead, we propose to examine, first with a case study and then based on a qualitative survey of international sponsors, the relevance and importance of several key relationship factors to the international sponsorship alliance.

Key Constructs of the International Sponsorship Alliance

Establishing successful sponsorship relationships depends to a large extent on both partners' understanding of those relationship antecedents and attributes which are key to the sponsorship alliance. Hoffman and Schlosser (2001) argue that the decision to cooperate should be based on specific strengths and resource complementarity, a perfect description for the sponsor/property motivation. The process followed by sponsors seeking a partner, therefore, is a search for the ideal alliance partner, with an emphasis on trust-based relationships and collaboration. In the global setting, partners seeking an alliance through sponsorship often do so on the assumption that the association will itself lend international credibility and stature. Hence, just as the Olympic Games selected ten global brands for their TOP program, so too were these ten brands immediately conferred global status as they signed their sponsorship contract with the IOC.

The design of the partnership itself, according to Hoffman and Schlosser (2001), should entail a precise definition of rights and duties (usually embodied in a contract in the case of sponsorship) in order to identify areas of *strategic compatibility*, achieve equitable contribution (which captures sponsorship in Meenaghan's 1983 original definition), seek value creation (Farrelly & Quester, 2003), build *trust* and avoid opportunistic behavior (Farrelly & Quester, 2003; Medlin & Quester, 2002). This is vitally important when considering sponsorship as a platform for an international alliance given the complexity of managing the relationship from multiple offices in different locations, and at various geographic levels (international, domestic and local). Moreover, the management of the alliance should encompass the establishment of good information sharing systems (Hoffman & Schlosser, 2001), and hence *effective communication* processes, as indeed must the sponsorship alliance (Farrelly & Quester, 2003). Communication will be particularly vital in the international context, given the well-known pitfalls created by cultural and national differences. Finally, alliances also require top management support, as has been demonstrated in the case of sponsorship management in the USA and Australia (Farrelly & Quester, 1997).

Furthermore, in the case of sponsorship (as in all other business-to-business relationships) the concept of trust seems inseparable from that of *commitment*. The intangible nature of the exchange, particularly for the sponsor who secures access to the commercial potential of an event, sports or personality against a cash or in-kind investment in the property, requires that trust and commitment go hand in hand. In the relationship marketing literature, both concepts are believed to interact in a mutually reinforcing manner with researchers showing one as the antecedent (Selnes, 1998) or outcome of the other (Farrelly & Quester, 2003), an expected finding given the iterative nature of the relationship over time. Regardless of the specific causality between the two constructs, they are both recognized as key to relationship success (Andaleeb, 1996; Morgan & Hunt, 1994). In the international setting the importance of these two building blocks to the relationship would only be increased, as both sponsorship partners manage a larger, more diverse and complex set of variables in both the micro- and macro-environments, there are higher levels of commercial risk, and each party must often deal with the relationship from a distance.

When considering the outcome of such relationships in the business-to-business context, *satisfaction* has been defined as the overall evaluation of relationship fulfilment by the firm (Dwyer, Schurr & Oh, 1987) or as the positive affective state resulting form the appraisal of all aspects of a firm's working relationship with another (Gaski & John, 1985). In a similar vein, sponsorship satisfaction can be defined as the overall evaluation of the relationship binding the sponsors with the properties they sponsor. Whilst the international scope of a sponsorship alliance will make the process of evaluation more complex, satisfaction will retain its central influence on the longevity of any such relationship and hence should require especially closer analysis in the global setting.

Early work by Dwyer (1980) and Ruekert and Churchill (1984) established satisfaction as critical to the understanding of channel relationships and to their viability. For example, satisfaction has been found to act as an incentive to collaborate (Schul, Little & Pride, 1985), develop integrated management practices (Brown, Lusch & Smith, 1991), or even as a barrier to exit (Hunt & Nevin, 1974). However, some differences have emerged as to the definition of satisfaction: some researchers (e.g. Brown et al., 1991 or more recently Nowak, Boughton & Pereira, 1997) conceptualize it as a primarily economic phenomenon; others (e.g. Anderson & Narus, 1984) define it in non-economic terms, as an emotional, psychosocial response by one partner toward the other.

It may be useful, therefore, to retain two separate types of satisfaction (Geyskens, Steenkamp & Kumar, 1999): *Economic satisfaction* is defined by the positive affective response to economic rewards that flow from the relationship whereas *non-economic satisfaction* is the positive affective response to the psycho-social aspect of the relationship in that interactions with the partner are fulfilling, gratifying and easy (e.g. Mohr, Fisher & Nevin, 1996). Altogether, however, satisfaction is a key evaluative outcome of relationship interaction and, as such, is likely to be an indicator of relationship renewal (Dwyer, 1980).

Empirical results ascertaining the effects of the satisfaction construct itself have been mixed, sometimes because of the variety of variables used to define it, at other times because of the context within which the studies were undertaken. As reported by Geyskens et al. (1999) as a preamble to their meta-analysis of the construct of satisfaction, an additional difficulty has emerged when researchers have substituted trust and commitment to explain channel relationships without attempting to relate these constructs to satisfaction (Anderson & Weitz, 1989; Morgan & Hunt, 1994). This is problematic as the constructs of satisfaction, trust and commitment have been found empirically to be fundamentally different, albeit correlated. Importantly, economic and non-economic satisfactions have also been found to represent two distinct constructs (Geyskens et al. 1999).

There has been, to our knowledge, no previous attempt in the sponsorship literature to identify or define the construct of satisfaction in the context of sponsorship. One reason for this may well be the notoriously difficult task faced by sponsors who try to evaluate sponsorship effects and outcomes (see Meenaghan in this volume for a discussion of mechanisms of, and difficulties with, global sponsorship evaluation). It is likely, however, that both types of satisfaction are pertinent for organizations engaged in sponsorship. In other words, as much as the sponsor values *what* has been done by the property in terms of achieving the objective, it would also assess *how* this was done. That satisfaction is more complex and multifaceted in the business-to-business context than is commonly acknowledged in the literature has motivated some researchers to advocate the adoption of phenomenological approaches rather than the use of more quantitative and reductive methodologies (Tikkanen, Alajoutsijarvi & Tahtinen, 2000), a major motivation for the qualitative approached undertaken in the study that follows the case study below.

International Sponsorship Alliances: The Case of MasterCard

MasterCard is an association made up of over 25,000 member financial institutions spanning the globe. The sheer volume of sponsorship arrangements managed by a major global sponsor like MasterCard suggests that potential efficiencies can be gained through formal structured alliances with their sponsored properties. In addition, the multilayered nature of these relationships, presenting international, national and local leveraging opportunities, also clearly demonstrates the vital importance of a sound strategic rationale underpinning the choice of partner.

Priceless – MasterCard and the World Game

Forming alliances is common practice for credit card companies. MasterCard, for instance, has been involved in numerous alliances with a range of retailers across the globe. This has included highly successful nationwide pricing ventures with American chain stores such as K-mart and Toys-R-Us, and similar strategic alliances with a variety of brand name manufacturers such as Mattel. They have also formed alliances with organizations in a range of other industries, including AT&T (telecommunications), Coca-Cola (soft drinks) and several others, with leveraging activities spanning national and international markets (Magrath, 1991).

Table 12.1 shows some of the sponsorships MasterCard has invested in. These sport sponsorship relationships offer local, national and international reach. MasterCard is clearly one of the largest sport sponsors worldwide and these relationships are key components of an overall, integrated global marketing strategy that has the following objectives (MasterCard Sponsorship Activities Factsheet, 2003):

- generate business-building card usage or issuance and acquisition opportunities for MasterCard members and merchants,
- reinforce brand preference, loyalty, image and awareness,
- create brand differentiation,
- provide exclusive added value to MasterCard cardholder's.

At the heart of MasterCard's global sponsorship effort is the association with the "world game": soccer (see also Madrigal et al., this volume). In a significant integration of its global marketing initiatives, MasterCard International recently

Table 12.1 *MasterCard sponsorship programs*

MasterCard: Sport Sponsorship Across the Globe	
Baseball	US Major League Baseball (since 1997)
	Team sponsorships (US teams such as Pittsburgh Pirates, Atlanta Braves, Cleveland Indians, LA Dodgers, New York Mets, Boston Red Sox)
Formula One	Jordan Grand Prix Formula One Team
Golf	PGA Tour
	MasterCard Championship (Senior PGA Tour)
	The British Open
Hockey	National Hockey League USA (NHL)
	Canadian Hockey League (CHL)
	NHL All-Star Weekend
Soccer	FIFA World Cup (since 1990 through to 2006),
	FIFA Women's World Cup (since 1999)
	FIFA World Youth and U/17 Championship
	UEFA Champions League (since 1994)
	UEFA European Football Championship (since 1992)
	National Teams (France, Finland, Netherlands, Sweden)
	Copa America (South American Soccer Federation)
	Pelé (MasterCard Spokesperson)

renewed its commitment to five of international football's most prestigious events. These included extending its Official Sponsorship status of the FIFA World Cup to include the event in 2006 in Germany, the UEFA Champions League (through 2006), CONMEBOL Copa America (2004), and Copa Toyota Libertadores. MasterCard's association with FIFA can be seen to reflect and reinforce the global stature of the brand, falling neatly into the categories articulated by Douma et al. (2000) under "shared strategy vision," "strategic importance" and "complementary balance." The FIFA alliance is key to MasterCard's ability to assist its member institutions to forge business relationships and to market to their target customers. It also serves as a highly effective means of motivating member institutions and merchants to actively promote the MasterCard brand.

MasterCard describes its relationship with FIFA as a strategic alliance and its approach to the relationship has all the traits of an alliance (or portfolio of alliances) as described in the literature and mentioned in introduction to this paper. Crucial to its decision to expand the FIFA alliance was the opportunity to develop a long-term association with an organization it deemed compatible on a series of vital strategic dimensions (MasterCard, Press Release, 2003).

They included:

- a compatible approach to strategic marketing and market development,
- a partner organization committed to global reach and presence,
- a partner that offered global, domestic and grass roots branding opportunities,
- the potential for target market crossover worldwide,
- synergies on the symbolic attributes of both brands, linkage with the Master-Card brand in an emotional context – in this case a football match denoted by the FIFA/MasterCard "priceless moments" worldwide positioning statement.

MasterCard's research has indicated that more than 2,300 of its members activated the FIFA World Cup in Korea/Japan in 2002, resulting in a 12.5% increase in related member spend compared to the 1998 World Cup in France (Hunter, 2003). The sponsorship alliance with FIFA has been pivotal in MasterCard's efforts to differentiate the brand on a global stage whilst maintaining relevance at the local level. Importantly, the issue of market acceptance is one that favours sponsors as research suggest that even ethnocentric consumers tend to view global sport sponsors favourably (Quester & Lardinoit, 2001b).

Given the anecdotal evidence provided by MasterCard that sponsorship acts as an international strategic alliance, we then proceeded with a qualitative examination of the key constructs identified in earlier sections of this paper.

A Qualitative Study of International Sponsorship Alliances

In order to investigate the nature and articulation of the constructs discussed above and with the view of developing a conceptual framework of sponsorship strategic alliances at the international level, a qualitative study was undertaken of a number of major international sponsors. The study involved interviewing seven of the largest sport sponsors in Australia. Personal interviews were conducted with the marketing manager of companies that operated in a range of industries including brewing, sports apparel, insurance and investment, telecommunications and automotive.

Each of the respondents included in our study had experience managing sponsorship arrangements with international, and on occasion global, marketing objectives, and had one or more current relationships with sports properties enjoying a significant international reach. Sample selection was based on a purposive method (Beverland & Bretherton, 2001). To gain a sense of the complexities of managing major sponsorship relationships across national borders, companies were chosen where practitioners were known to have had experience in the international domain. The interviews lasted between sixty and ninety minutes. Where the respondents elaborated on pre-identified issues, the interviewer avoided prompting other than to ensure that the interview focused on one relationship from beginning to end (in instances where they were involved in more than one relationship). Consistent with the approach pioneered by Belk, Sherry and Wallendorf (1988), interview data were triangulated (for authenticity and validation purposes) via the use of company reports, promotional material, and on occasions, through checks with other staff from the responding organization. Follow-up calls were also made with many of those interviewed to clarify some of the issues discussed.

Following the principles of phenomenological inquiry advocated by Fournier and Mick (1999), the interviews started with the prompt, "Tell me what you believe constitutes a strategic or co-marketing alliance." Informants were thus allowed to select what they thought were the key dimensions of a co-marketing alliance and to state impressions of the sponsorship relationship as a co-marketing alliance. Interviewers then probed for elaboration on the basis of informants' own words (e.g. evaluative expressions describing what was critical if a relationship was to function as an effective alliance).

Analysis took place both during data collection, to enable follow up probing of emergent ideas, and afterward, to group insights in view of the overall output of the interview (and interviews previously conducted). Notes were taken during interviews on a pro-forma that categorised key themes. A memo summarizing the interpretations of each interview was also completed soon after in order to capture a full appreciation of respondent views and experiences. Key findings of this analysis are provided in the following sections.

Strategic Compatibility

Encapsulating several of the aforementioned criteria identified by Douma et al. (2000), Shamdasani and Sheth (1995) define strategic compatibility as "the extent to which an alliance partner has complementary goals and shares similar orientations that facilitate co-ordination of alliance activities and execution of alliance strategies" (p. 49). Strategic compatibility was considered a vital issue for the sponsorship alliance for a host of reasons, not least because it was a catalyst for partners to reach common ground on the underlying motives for the association. For instance, where a global sponsor may seek greater exposure for its brand of soft drinks, a property may seek an increase in grass roots participation. Strategic compatibility is important to determine potential overlap in the objectives sought by both partners. The sponsor's desire for greater exposure could, for example, overlap neatly with the property's aim for greater financial resources, as greater exposure will be typically associated with more valuable broadcast rights. Establishing strategic compatibility should also reveal the level of import each part attributes to the relationship and the level of marketing resources, knowledge and skills they can call on to influence relationship outcomes.

It was clear from the interviews that all respondents considered strategic compatibility with a property partner vital. The importance of a shared vision of market development opportunities was noted, especially in the case of sponsorship led initiatives that spanned several international markets. The response centered on two factors. First, a number of interviewees procured sponsorship rights specifically to tap into emerging markets in Southeast Asia, and/or established ones in Europe where they were attempting to grow market share. Our informants believed that without a common motivation on the part of both parties to grow their respective positions in these new markets, there was limited scope for success.

Second, a shared sense of strategic purpose was deemed essential to overcome the difficulties that inevitably surface when planning and executing sponsorship programs across borders, and in markets where promotion and distribution practices may differ quite considerably. Shared belief in common strategic opportunities was also perceived as a binding force in the relationship, assisting the resolution of conflicts and misunderstandings typically associated with international alliances. Indeed, a unified sense of the "bigger picture" motivated partners to overcome unexpected relational problems unique to alliances, including those that can hinder the achievement of strategic objectives. Moreover, and consistent with the partner criteria identified by MasterCard, a shared strategic philosophy was also seen as instrumental to establishing mutually beneficial goals and to enable partners to react swiftly to changes in the environment.

Partners exhibiting strategic compatibility were better able to grasp and accept the roles and requirements of each party in relation to the leveraging of the investment. In the words of one of the respondents:

> It is vital that both the property and sponsor share a sense of the opportunities and responsibility the relationship brings in various markets. There must be a complete understanding of the markets to be targeted, and a genuine belief that the sponsorship association can be activated to great effect in these markets. This will also mean that parties can reconcile their structural preferences for the relationship.

Finally, strategic compatibility was thought to be essential for the organizations to allocate the complementary resources each had to offer as well as to identify, in some detail, and right from the outset, such resource requirements at a national and international level. Consistent with the motives for entering an alliance noted by Varadarajan and Cunningham (1995), the sponsors interviewed appeared to have developed a clear strategic intent in terms of the level of impact they expected from the relationship across different markets. They were also categorical about their objectives for each market, as well as ready to customize their approach to leveraging the relationship according to the nature of the markets' cultural distinctions or level of maturity. For example, in mature markets like Australia, objectives included "brand authentication," whereas for less developed markets including regions of Southeast Asia, the aim was to generate maximum exposure and awareness.

Alliance Development Factors

Communication   Responses highlighted that communication was vital to bridge what were often quite contrasting organizational cultures between the sponsor and the property. While language was also at times a barrier in the international context, it appeared less of an issue than problems associated with a lack of process or structure for communicating operational intentions and requirements. Respondents noted that formal, structured communication was essential to explore issues and opportunities meaningfully.

Respondents stressed the importance of periodic face-to-face meetings with property staff (or agents) in international markets to establish and maintain rapport, and to ensure bilateral ownership of key leveraging initiatives. Formal, structured (and recorded) dialogue of this nature overshadowed the importance of other aspects of communication, including the frequency of interplay between the focal sponsor partners. The following two quotes from the interviews capture the importance of formal communication:

> Unless formal communication structures are put in place early in the relationship too little time is spent scoping strategic direction and desired outcomes of both parties, and how this translates across the markets in question. A complex matrix of opportunities exists when dealing with international sponsorship arrangements. To realise these partners must come to the table with a detailed sense of where they wish to take their respective brands, how sponsorship fits into the broader picture, and what shape the locus of control will take.

> A series of formal planning sessions are required in the formative stages to plot the strategic course of the sponsorship. Intentions must be explicit, and in our experience one must use these meetings to ensure the property (and sponsor) is fully appraised of the benefits of the relationship above and beyond rights fees. Without full realisation of such opportunities and benefits it can be difficult to convince the property to invest which can be a critical impediment to the growth and longevity of relationship.

In addition to formality, however, one respondent noted that frequency in communication was also required when dealing with property offices in international markets because it was often necessary to coordinate with multiple individuals before resources could be mobilized.

Commitment   Anderson and Weitz (1992), Selnes (1998), Siguaw, Simpson and Baker (1998) and others have demonstrated empirically the importance of commitment in business-to-business relationships. In the interviews conducted for this study a behavioural focus was adopted with attention focused on investment-related actions. It has been demonstrated empirically that companies must "leverage" a sponsorship to achieve any real degree of success (e.g. Quester & Thompson, 2001), and it was believed that leveraging by both sponsorship parties would signal a "desire to develop a stable relationship," and "confidence in the stability of the relationship," issues emphasised by Anderson and Weitz (1992) in their conceptualization of commitment.

Sponsors considered that commitment to the alliance in the form of leveraging expenditures was a basic requirement from both parties. This was due to the magnitude of the sponsorship rights fees typically invested by the sponsor; the subsequent benefits accrued by the property; and the shared opportunities sponsorship afforded both parties in different markets. The sponsors' own level of commitment reflected the properties' direct level of contribution to performance and such reciprocity and bilateral commitment was deemed vital to maximize the opportunities afforded by the alliance. The following two quotes illustrate this sentiment:

> Properties and sponsors must have a genuine desire to grow their reach and impact in the selected markets. If this is not abundantly clear, the likelihood of both parties jointly activating the opportunity is significantly diminished ... if both parties don't invest to activate to a level at least roughly on par with the gains they expect to realise, it is highly unlikely that either, and certainly not the sponsor, will be fully satisfied with the experience or the outcome.

> We are one of the largest multinational organizations in the world, widely regarded as a leading brand marketer. We can assist them (the property) to achieve one of their primary marketing objectives, to increase involvement in the event and in related merchandise internationally, however they too must support that aim with satisfactory resources.

Sponsors also felt that for an alliance to truly succeed it must generate synergies above and beyond brand complementarity, including synergies between the management teams. To this end, they noted that such synergies were predicated on direct investments from both parties into the relationship. Akin to the ideas expressed Kamath and Liker (1994), a party in an inter-firm relationship "earns" more decision-making responsibility by volunteering greater asset specificity.

Trust   Researchers have long examined the different dimensions of trust. In this study, trust in the sponsorship relationship was investigated along its two most commonly researched attributes, namely credibility and benevolence (Ganesan, 1994). Several respondents emphasized the rational (i.e. credibility) component of trust during the interviews, and in particular, stressed the importance of being confident that the property had both the intent and the ability to meet their obligations and fulfill their (promised) contribution to the alliance.

In two instances, some doubts were expressed as to whether the property would ultimately bring significant levels of marketing expertise to the fore. This response was based on previous experience and was consistent with similar caveats expressed elsewhere in the literature. Indeed, it has been suggested that properties have been inclined to remain passive in the sponsorship relationship (e.g. Farrelly, 2002), their marketing expertise with respect to core business activities (i.e. marketing to fans, members, spectators, etc.) often not carrying over to the sponsorship relationship.

On the whole, however, the sponsors included in this exploratory study felt that trust was vital to the relationship. According to a majority of them, trust tends to manifest itself rationally, for example where there was a demonstrated understanding of each partner's position in the relationship, and where each partner possessed a genuine knowledge of the relationship, including the objectives set and their strategic rationale. However, one respondent mentioned the importance of benevolence and the 'soft side' of the relationship, by saying: "There has to be the belief that you are serving each others' best interest if a shared mentality and cooperative chemistry is to permeate the relationship."

Satisfaction   This study followed an emergent theme in the literature by deconstructing the concept of satisfaction into two dimensions, economic and non-economic satisfaction. As noted earlier, Geyskens et al (1999) conclude that the differences between "economic" and "non-economic" satisfaction are significant, and should be addressed in business-to-business research to advance the understanding of the construct.

Sponsors expressed a clear sense of non-economic satisfaction with their current international alliances. For example, achieving multiple objectives with a property partner across multiple markets was a major source of pride in the relationship. Sponsors included in this study spoke of "great rapport" and "strong working relationships" with property counterparts as being a major source of satisfaction. One of our interviewees stated that: "It is important for each party to feel the other is dependable. Where relationship roles and performance expectations were clearly spelled out early on both parties took ownership and could be relied on. This feeling is reassuring and motivating, especially when you may be dealing with partners many thousands of miles away."

Sponsors also generally noted that the relationship had produced economic results that increased the value of their respective brands, and in the majority of cases, they established this value on a market-by-market basis. In three of the interviews, there was also evidence that more was needed to fully exploit the opportunities in the relationship. This included jointly exploring activation opportunities at a deeper level in markets where previous performance had been weak. Sponsors believed that properties should exploit alignment opportunities in all markets designated in the original agreements, rather than specific target markets which for "internal reasons" were a point of focus. In these instances, economic satisfaction was apparent where a sense of the value achieved for both brands existed, and when the level of joint efforts was deemed consistent with the expectations stipulated in the contractual arrangement. For example, in the words of one of our respondents:

The value of the investment will always be considered in terms of its contribution to the brand, and this will also be weighed up against what was set down in the original agreement such as the level of penetration of the markets being targeted.

Being able to build brand loyalty and sales through jointly organized media activity and retail promotions provides a great sense of relationship satisfaction.

A Conceptual Framework of Global Sponsorship Alliances

Sponsorship is an alliance between those who market sport with those who market through sport. It is a business-to-business relationship that, when dealing across national borders, can benefit greatly from a tightly structured collaborative alliance. The findings described in this chapter confirm the value of conceptualizing sponsorship as an alliance, and the need to better understand alliance attributes that determine performance. Yet this study appears to be the first attempt to investigate the sponsorship relationship as an international or global strategic alliance, even though developing a better understanding of sponsorship relationship has, for some time, been flagged as a key goal for future sponsorship research (Cornwell & Maignan, 1998). Introspective examination of this nature is crucial not just from a research perspective, but also because it may prompt new ways of approaching relationship structures and strategy.

The discussion provided in this paper and the qualitative evidence reported therein helps to elucidate some of the issues surrounding sponsorship as a co-marketing alliance and can be used to put forward the conceptual framework shown in Table 12.2. Future research should aim to develop from this framework a more causal model and a set of related and testable hypotheses that could be the object of future empirical work in the area of international and global sponsorship alliances.

Table 12.2 *Conceptual framework of sponsorship global alliances*

Strategic compatibility	Key relational constructs	Key alliance outcomes
• Shared vision • Compatibility • Importance • Complementary balance • Added value • Market acceptance $\Big\} \Rightarrow$	• Communication • Trust • Commitment $\Big\} \Rightarrow$	• Economic satisfaction • Non-Economic satisfaction

Obviously, the qualitative evidence presented here clearly needs to be further strengthened by formal quantitative research examining not only the constructs identified in this paper but other alliance performance indicators such as market share, consumer loyalty or profitability. In particular, future research should examine the returns properties realize as the result of the sponsor actively promoting its association on an international or global scale, as this could prove vital to the collective investment in the relationship and to the achievement of alliance synergies.

Nevertheless, when working at an international level, sponsors and properties must recognize the need to formally examine the extent of their strategic compatibility. This would include identifying dimensions of corporate or brand image complementarity. According to our findings, formal communication may also be critical, especially in the formative stages of the sponsorship relationship, so as to clarify strategic compatibility including responsibilities and leveraging expectations. This may be particularly significant in older sponsorship relationships as the cultures of focal partners are often markedly different (e.g. a football league and a major financial institution) and such differences can only be further magnified when dealing with international alliances. Time and effort must be spent exploring such issues if partners are to be motivated to work together (Bucklin & Sengupta, 1993). Formal communication should also facilitate the development of mutually informed frameworks to guide planning and execution.

Commitment is critical to relational bonding (Mavondo & Rodrigo, 2001) and related investments must be deemed credible if an alliance is to thrive. Ganesan (1994) describes "credible commitments" as relationship-specific inputs of a magnitude befitting the size and nature of relationship. Ring and Van de Ven (1994) note that partners in strategic alliances may "rely more heavily on equity than efficiency in assessing their relationship" (p. 94). In a horizontal partnership such as the sponsorship alliance, commitment will often be evaluated in relative terms and should be a function of each party's perceived investment relative to their respective return from the relationship. This would likely fuel a sponsor's motivation to leverage opportunities and so should be explored fully in future research.

Reciprocity between partners is an important dimension when evaluating the success of a strategic alliance and this will also be the case in the international or global setting. Strategic dependence on the alliance determines the power structure and impact upon the level of reciprocity: an unequal power structure leads to instability. It was not within the scope of this chapter to explore such issues; however, our research suggests that power and dependence are likely to be highly relevant and this may be particularly so on the global scale.

Defining further the nature of the sponsorship alliance may also warrant closer scrutiny by potential partners seeking to develop an international alliance. Two types of alliances identified in the literature may provide some insight in this regard, although how appropriate they are in capturing the sponsorship alliance is not immediately clear. A joint marketing and promotion alliance typically involves partners marketing the same product under the same or different brand names, which does not, strictly speaking, apply to the sponsorship association. Yet the other obvious alternative, a licensing agreement, "by which one firm buys the right to use an asset for a period of time … typically involve a narrow purpose and limited time frame" (Borys & Jemison, 1989, p. 245) is too confined in scope especially given the propensity for commitment inequity as identified here.

Sponsorship relationships as a vehicle to achieve international or global marketing objectives, such as that between MasterCard and FIFA, are likely to grow in the future. Some argue that single country bound sports will find it increasingly difficult to attract sponsors because of the far greater opportunities offered by their multinational property counterparts (Westerbeek & Smith, 2003). Events, teams and leagues with genuine international exposure (e.g. Olympic Games, the NBA, Tennis and Golf Grand Slams, World Cup and European Champions League Soccer and F1 Racing) will continue to attract the lion's share of sponsorship investment, enabling them to expand their reach and penetration further. With this in mind, it is increasingly relevant and important to explore the sport sponsorship agreement as a strategic alliance, especially where its management and marketing span international boundaries.

References

Andaleeb, S. S. (1996) "An Experimental Investigation of Satisfaction and Commitment in Marketing Channels: The Role of Trust and Dependence," *Journal of Retailing*, 72: 71–93.

Anderson, E. and Weitz, B. (1989) "Determinants of Continuity in Conventional Industrial Channel Dyads?" *Marketing Science*, 8 (4): 210–323.

Anderson, E. and Weitz, B. (1992) "The Use of Pledges to Build and Sustain Commitment in Distribution Channels," *Journal of Marketing Research*, 29: 18–34.

Anderson, J. C. and Narus, J. A. (1984) "A Model of the Distributor's Perspective of Distributor-manufacturer working relationships. *Journal of Marketing*, 48: 62–74.

Belk, R., Sherry Jr, J. and Wallendorf, M. (1988) "A Naturalistic Inquiry into Buyer and Seller Behavior at a Swap Meet," *Journal of Consumer Research*, 14 (March): 449–470.

Beverland, M. and Bretherton, P. (2001) "The Uncertain Search for Opportunities: Determinants of Strategic Alliances," *Qualitative Market Research: An International Journal*, 4 (2): 88–99.

Borys, B. and Jemison, D. B. (1989) "Hybrid Arrangements as Atrategic Alliances: Theoretical Issues in Organisational Combinations," *Academy of Management Review*, 14 (2): 234–249.

Brown, S., Lusch, R. and Smith, L. (1991) "Conflict and Satisfaction in an Industrial Channel of Distribution," *International Journal of Physical Distribution and Materials Management*, 21 (6): 15–26.

Bucklin, L. P. and Sengupta, S. (1993) "Organizing Successful Co-marketing Alliances," *Journal of Marketing*, 57 (April): 32–46.

Cornwell, T. B. (1995) "Sponsorship-linked Marketing Development," *Sports Marketing Quarterly*, 4 (4): 13–24.

Cornwell, T. B. and Maignan, I. (1998) "An International Review of Sponsorship Research," *Journal of Advertising*, 27 (1): 1–21.

Crompton, J. L. (1993) "Understanding a Business Organisation's Approach to Entering a Sponsorship Partnership," *Festival Management & Event Tourism*, 1: 98–109.

Douma, M., Bilderbeek, J., Idenburg, P. and Looise, J. (2000) "Strategic Alliances: Managing the Dynamics of Fit," *Long Range Planning*, 33 (4): 579.

Dwyer, F., Schurr, P. and Oh, S. (1987) "Developing Buyer-seller Relationships," *Journal of Marketing*, 51: 11–27.

Dwyer, F. R. (1980) "Channel-member Satisfaction: Laboratory Insights," *Journal of Retailing*, 56 (2): 45–65.

Farrelly, F. (2002) *A Predictive Model of Sport Sponsorship Renewal in Australia*. Unpublished PhD, Monash University, Melbourne.

Farrelly, F. and Quester, P. (1997) "Sports and Arts Sponsors: Investigating the Similarities and Differences in Management Practices," paper presented at the American Marketing Association Conference: New and Evolving Paradigms, Dublin, Ireland.

Farrelly, F. and Quester, P. (2003) "The Effects of Market Orientation on Trust and Commitment: The Case of the Sponsorship Business-to-business Relationship," *European Journal of Marketing*, 37 (3/4): 530–553.

Fournier, S. and Mick, G. (1999) "Rediscovering Satisfaction," *Journal of Marketing*, 63 (4): 5–23.

Ganesan, S. (1994) "Determinants of Long-term Orientation in Buyer-Seller Relationships," *Journal of Marketing*, 58: 1–19.

Gaski, J. F. and John, R. N. (1985) "The Differential Effects of Exercised and Unexercised Power Sources in a Marketing Channel," *Journal of Marketing Research*, 22 (2): 130–142.

Geyskens, I., Steenkamp, J. and Kumar, N. (1999) "A Meta-analysis of Satisfaction in Marketing Channel Relationships," *Journal of Marketing Research*, 36 (2): 223–238.

Hoffmann, W. H. and Schlosser, R. T. (2001) "Success Factors of Strategic Alliances in Small and Medium-sized Enterprises; An Empirical Survey," *Long Range Planning*, 34 (3): 357–381.

Hunt, S. D. and Nevin, J. R. (1974) "Power in a Channel of Distribution: Sources and Consequences," *Journal of Marketing Research*, 11 (May): 186–193.

Hunter, H. (2003) "Global Sponsorships," *Business Picture Magazine,* February 3: 12–15.

James, R. (1999, April) "Sponsorship in International Markets," *Thompson Business*, 3: 12–14.

Johar, V. G. and Pham, M. T. (1999) "Relatedness, Prominence, and Constructive Sponsor Indentification," *Journal of Marketing Research*, 36 (August): 299–312.

Kamath, R. and Liker, J. (1994) "A Second Look at Japanese Product Development," *Harvard Business Review*, 72: 154–170.

Magrath, A. J. (1991) "Collaborative Marketing Comes of Age – Again," *Sales and Marketing Management*: 24–29.

MasterCard (2003) Press Release, http://www.mastercardinternational.com/newsroom/sponsorship_overview.html.

Mavondo, F. T. and Rodrigo, E. M. (2001) "The Effect of Relationship Dimensions on Interpersonal and Interorganizational Commitment in Organizations Conducting Business between Australia and China," *Journal of Business Research*, 52 (2): 111–121.

Medlin C. and Quester P. G. (2002) "Inter-Firm Trust is not a Multi-Dimensional Construct," Proceedings of the 2002 IMP Conference, Perth, December.

Meenaghan, J. (1983) "Commercial Sponsorship," *European Journal of Marketing*, Special Issue: 1–73.

Mohr, J. J., Fisher, R. J. and Nevin, J. R. (1996) "Collaborative Communication in Interfirm Relationships: Moderating Effects of Integration and Control," *Journal of Marketing*, 60 (3): 103–117.

Morgan, R. M. and Hunt, S. D. (1994) "The Commitment-trust Theory of Relationship Marketing," *Journal of Marketing*, 58 (July): 20–38.

Niederkofler, M. (1991) "The Evolution of Strategic Alliances: Opportunities for Managerial Influence," *Journal of Business Venturing*, 6 (4): 237–247.

Nowak, L. I., Boughton, P. D. and Pereira, A. J. A. (1997) "Relationships between Businesses and Marketing Research Firms," *Industrial Marketing Management*, 26 (6): 497–495.

Olkkonen, R. (2001) "Case Study: The Network Approach to International Sport Sponsorship Arrangement," *The Journal of Business & Industrial Marketing*, 16 (4): 309–327.

Quester, P. G. (1997) "Awareness as a Measure of Sponsorship Effectiveness: The Adelaide Formula One Grand Prix and Evidence of Incidental Ambush Effects," *Journal of Marketing Communications*, 3 (2): 24–31.

Quester, P. G. and Lardinoit, T. (2001a) "Attitudinal Effects of Sponsorship on Television Audiences and the Influence of Sponsors: Prominence: Interaction and Main Effects of Two Types of Sponsorship," *Journal of Advertising Research,* 41 (1): 48–58.

Quester, P. G. and Lardinoit, T. (2001b) "Sponsors' Impact on Attitude and Product Involvement: A Longitudinal Study of the 2000 Olympic Games," *Proceedings of the 2001 ANZMAC Conference*, December, Albany, CD ROM.

Quester, P. and Thompson, B. (2001) "Advertising and Promotion Leverage on Arts Sponsorship Effectiveness," *Journal of Advertising Research*, 41 (1): 33–47.

Ring, P. S. and Van de Ven, A. H. (1994) "Developmental Processes of Cooperative Interorganizational Relationships," *Academy of Management Reveiw*, 19 (1): 90–118.

Ruekert, R. W. and Churchill, G., Jr. (1984) "Reliability and Validity of Alternative Measures of Channel Member Satisfaction," *Journal of Marketing Research* 21: 226–233.

Schul, P. L., Little, T. E. and Pride, W. M. (1985) "Channel Climate: Its Impact on Channel Member's Satisfaction," *Journal of Retailing*, 61 (2): 9–31.

Selnes, F. (1998) "Antecedents and Consequences of Trust and Satisfaction in Buyer-seller Relationship," *European Journal of Marketing*, 32 (34): 34–42.

Shamdasani, P. N. and Sheth, J. N. (1995) "An Experimental Approach to Investigating Satisfaction and Continuity in Marketing Alliances," *European Journal of Marketing*, 29 (4): 18–24.

Siguaw, J. A., Simpson, P. M. and Baker, T. L. (1998) "Effects of Supplier Market Orientation on Distributor Market Orientation and the Channel Relationship: The Distributor Perspective," *Journal of Marketing*, 62 (3): 99–111.

Simonin, B. and Ruth, J. (1998) "Is a Company Known by the Company it Keeps? Assessing the Spill Over Effects of Brand Alliances on Consumer Brand Attitudes," *Journal of MarketResearch*, 35 (February): 30–42.

Tikkanen, H., Alajoutsijarvi, K. and Tahtinen, J. (2000) "The Concept of Satisfaction in Industrial Markets: A Contextual Perspective and a Case Study from the Software Industry," *Industrial Marketing Management*, 29: 373–386.

Varadarajan, P. R. and Cunningham, M. H. (1995) "Strategic Alliances: A Synthesis of Conceptual Foundations," *Journal of the Academy of Marketing Science*, 23 (4): 282–296.

Westerbeek, H. and Smith, A. (2003) *Sport business in the global marketplace*, 1st edn. Hampshire: Palgrave Macmillan.

13

Evaluating Sponsorship Effects

Tony Meenaghan

Sponsorship, as a social and business phenomenon, has evolved significantly over its relatively brief history. While many differences can be observed over this period, two interrelated changes are important to the focus of this chapter, namely the increased scale of sponsorship expenditure and the changed corporate perception of sponsorship. Worldwide sponsorship expenditure has increased fourteen-fold in the 19-year period to 2004. This increased scale of expenditure would suggest that sponsorship be regarded in investment terms with attendant corporate expectations in terms of accountability and return on investment. In effect increased expenditure and the related development of an investment orientation demand the proper evaluation of benefits accruing to the sponsor. However despite such expectations many sponsors still seem reluctant to evaluate their sponsorship investments rigorously. This chapter is fundamentally a review of sponsorship evaluation. It initially seeks to examine the nature of sponsorship and its perception as somehow "different" and the implications of such features for sponsorship evaluation. By way of background current industry practices with respect to sponsorship evaluation are examined. Finally, the various methods of sponsorship evaluation currently employed in practice are critically examined, using case examples drawn from a broad range of markets and industries.

Where the sponsorship program is global in nature, the task of sponsorship evaluation is inevitably rendered more complex in strategic and operational terms. Strategic complexities arise where the role assigned to sponsorship varies by market with obvious consequences for sponsorship objectives. As sponsor brands are rarely at the same point on their life cycle or face similar competitive environments in all markets, a sponsorship program may be required to create brand name awareness in a new market while simultaneously driving brand image in a more mature market for the brand. Further complexity is likely to arise where the chosen sponsorship vehicle (whether sports, arts, etc.) varies by market in terms of exposure and popularity (e.g. soccer in the US market compared to England) or indeed where the image values of the chosen sponsorship vehicle varies by market (e.g. rugby in Italy compared to New Zealand). Such strategic issues obviously have implications for the evaluation of sponsorship effects on a global basis.

In operational terms, sponsorship evaluation is likely to be more complex and indeed cumbersome in an international arena. Central to any international sponsorship program is the relationship between corporate head office and the various national sales companies who ultimately are responsible for sponsorship activation and execution at individual market level. Working frameworks must be established which specify levels of local autonomy, including discretion in decision-making on all local market issues, including evaluation. In this regard such frameworks must encompass issues of research budgets, research priorities and objectives, information requirements as well as desired research methodologies and the appropriate choice of research agency.

Sponsorship: Scale and Perception

Commercial sponsorship has for many years been one of the most rapidly growing areas of marketing activity. Largely used by business today as a method of corporate marketing communications, the scale of growth in commercial sponsorship is indicated by the fact that sponsorship expenditure in the USA has grown from US$850 million in 1985 to a projected 2005 expenditure of US$12.09 billion (IEG Sponsorship Report 2004) while sponsorship expenditure worldwide increased from US$2 billion in 1984 to US$28 billion in 2004 (IEG 2004).

A revised corporate view of both the role and nature of sponsorship has coincided with this increased expenditure. A feature of the "early days" of sponsorship was "corporate uncertainty" about exactly "what it was" and "what it could do." Sponsorship seemed to exist in a 'nether land' between philanthropy/patronage and commercial marketing communications. Its versatile nature suggested that it was capable of delivering on a peculiar mixture of objectives ranging from corporate goodwill generation and a variety of marketing benefits to corporate philanthropy and indeed personal motives. It also seemed capable of addressing a broad range of corporate publics, often simultaneously. Furthermore, perhaps because of this versatility, uncertainty also surrounded the most appropriate location of sponsorship decision-making and management in the corporation.

While the inherent versatility of sponsorship continues to benefit sponsors, increased levels of expenditure have resulted in greater precision regarding its role. Today sponsorship is primarily regarded as a marketing activity employed in support of brand communications and relationship management. It is increasingly located within the marketing function and in the case of sophisticated sponsors operates under an integrated marketing communication framework alongside other marketing and communication methods.

Sponsorship is Different?

While the above discussion suggests reduced "uncertainty" regarding aspects of sponsorship, there is still a lingering industry belief that "sponsorship is different," a belief often advanced without necessarily specifying "what it is different from" and "on what dimensions is it different." The suggestion that sponsorship is "different" has in the past been advanced to argue that it is less amenable to conventional management practices, including the evaluation of effects, as is evident in the accompanying quotation:

Marketing has become so organised and pseudo-scientific that it is only relatively uncharted areas like sponsorship that hunch and flair still thrive. It is virtually impossible to evaluate the effectiveness of any single piece of sponsorship... Market research techniques cannot in general help all that much in the evaluation of sponsorship beyond answering the basic questions of awareness, understanding and interest. The whole delicate relationship between sponsorship activity and ultimate product sales remains something of a mystery, which makes marketing much more interesting. And it is probably best to treat sponsorship as an extension of public relations activity... and good PR men quite rightly resist the slide rule of the marketing researcher on the grounds that such activity cannot be scientifically evaluated. Sponsorship should be viewed in much the same light. (Mintel 1980)

While management thinking has moved considerably beyond the views expressed in the above quotation, there is still the residual belief that particular features of sponsorship render it less susceptible to evaluation. All elements of marketing/marketing communications (sales promotion, direct marketing, etc.) possess unique features and capabilities, however sponsorship is most often compared with advertising (Hastings, 1984; McDonald, 1991; Hoek, Gendall, Jeffcoat & Orsman, 1997; Meenaghan, 2001a). In this comparison a range of differences are discernable. These include the following:

1. Mutuality of Benefit   Sponsorship is often defined in terms of benefit to both sponsor and sponsored party. It is seen as bestowing benefit on an activity (sport, team, individual) with whom consumers have relationships as fans and audience (Meenaghan, 2001b). This key distinction has lead to sponsorship being defined as 'advertising plus' (McDonald, 1991). Advertising by contrast is seen as primarily serving a corporate agenda.
2. Consumer Interaction Process   Sponsorship, by its very nature, involves a sponsor in the emotional relationship between the consumer (as fan) and their preferred activity (sport, team). In this regard sponsorship has greater potential for engagement and interaction, both positively and negatively, between brand and consumer. Perceived benefit to the activity by the sponsor can result in higher levels of brand attachment with consequent positive marketing effects. (Meenaghan, 2001b)
3. Communications Process   Advertising is a direct, verbal and visual method of communication capable of product demonstration, feature display, information provision, etc. Sponsorship is an indirect, relatively "mute" mode of communications that operates "by reflection" off the sponsored property to create brand awareness and image transfer. Through delivering benefit to the sponsored property it can also enhance the consumer/brand relationship.
4. Sponsorship – "The Leisure End of Marketing"   The involvement with social, cultural or indeed leisure activities, as well as the corporate hospitality/ entertainment element of sponsorship and the occasional charge of the "chairman's choice" syndrome in selection, have perhaps caused sponsorship

to be seen as a less than wholly commercial business activity. While sponsorship is increasingly seen in commercially legitimate terms, corporate doubts and uncertainties still linger as to its nature, its effects and its capacity for rigorous management, including evaluation.

Quite evidently the foregoing discussion clearly shows that sponsorship is different in many and various ways from other forms of marketing communication, however the real question for this chapter is, do these differences preclude the rigorous evaluation of sponsorship effectiveness? The answer must be in the negative. While the "differences" discussed above may impact on whether and even on how it is evaluated, the key difference between advertising and sponsorship is the sheer scale of the latter's versatility. This feature of sponsorship has immense consequences for its evaluation, in terms of the range of objectives pursued and audiences addressed. However this feature in itself must represent a hurdle rather than an obstacle to the evaluation of sponsorship effects.

Sponsorship – The Versatile Medium

Sponsorship is widely regarded for its versatility on two key dimensions (a) the range of publics capable of being targeted and (b) the range of objectives capable of being pursued. Figure 13.1 below indicates the range of objectives and publics potentially appropriate to sponsorship.

Range of Publics

Sponsorship has the capacity to address a broad range of publics simultaneously, often in the context of a single campaign. This range of internal and external publics is illustrated in Table 13.1.

Range of Objectives

Sponsorship clearly has the ability to undertake a number of roles on behalf of a corporation which will be reflected in a variety of objectives with a broad range of corporate publics. The range of publics, objectives and effects listed in Table 13.1 are possible, however corporations will vary in terms of choice and emphasis. A construction company may seek to use sponsorship to fulfil a corporate hospitality/relationship management function with business associates, politicians and regulators. A brand driven FMCG (fast moving consumer goods) company may seek a branding role for sponsorship with its target market.

Irrespective of the specific role assigned to sponsorship, sponsors must seek to evaluate the effectiveness of their sponsorship investment with the publics targeted and against the objectives specified for that public. Some sponsors may evaluate effects with each specified public, perhaps varying the quality of evaluation according to the importance of that public. Other sponsors may only undertake evaluation with certain publics, deeming other objectives and publics as not justifying the cost of a detailed evaluation of effects.

Table 13.1 *Sponsorship objectives, publics and effects*

Public	Objective	Effects
General public	Corporate citizenship	Enhanced corporate image
	Corporate social responsibility	Goodwill generation
Internal staff	Corporate culture	Enhanced staff pride, morale.
	Corporate image	Image building
Politicians/Regulators	Corporate hospitality Goodwill generation	Entertainment provision, Relationship building, Lobbying aid/platform
Media	Corporate hospitality	Positive corporate portrayal
Shareholders	Omnipresence Visibility	Reassurance
Suppliers (Materials, Finance)	Relationship management	Improved business relationships
Trade buyers (Dealers, Wholesale Retail)	Relationship management	Improved business relationships
Target market	Brand exposure Brand/sponsorship association	Awareness building Drive brand values Attitude change
	Brand relationship	Build brand affinity
	Sales	Drive trial, sales
Self/Peers	'Chairman's choice' Personal enhancement	Status-reinforcement Ego-fulfillment

Each public represents a potential audience for the evaluation of sponsorship effectiveness.

Quite evidently it is not possible within the confines of this chapter to examine the evaluation of sponsorship effects against each objective and with each corporate public listed in Table 13.1. As such this chapter will continue with an examination of sponsorship effects with the main corporate public for sponsorship – i.e. the target market of final consumers. In this regard the chapter will focus on the commonly used quantitative measures rather than the qualitative measures which are increasingly employed.

Sponsorship Evaluation – Basic Principles

Prior to embarking on an analysis of sponsorship metrics, a number of important facts deserve mention: These include:

Need for Objectives

The specification of clear and precise objectives is an absolutely essential ingredient of all successful evaluation programmes. While objectives vary by sponsor and for each targeted public, sponsorship objectives must be detailed in terms of desired outcomes. Based on the role assigned to sponsorship, there is a need to agree the outcomes or effects being sought. Loose statements of aspiration such as 'to improve brand image' are of little real value in this regard. In the case of this example there is a need to specify the brand values on which movement is sought and to clarify the expectations for each year of the sponsorship's anticipated life. (For a review of sponsorship, including objective setting see Pope, 1998; Cornwell & Maignan, 1998; Meenaghan, 2001b and Walliser, 2003.)

Target Market Specification

The precise target audience must be described in measurable terms at the outset. Too often seemingly impressive results are advanced by interested parties as "proof" of significant return on investment, but when considered against the intended target audience, they quickly lose their impact.

Life of the Sponsorship Program

Sponsorship programmes usually involve a minimum three–year commitment and indeed much longer terms are commonplace. Objectives will vary over time, thus expectations must be updated regularly and specified annually over the anticipated life of the sponsorship.

Evaluation – Multi-interventions

In order to evaluate sponsorship effectiveness there is a need for several research interventions as follows:

- At the Outset   Research is necessary at the outset to establish benchmarks for the various metrics being employed as the basis for measurement, e.g. awareness levels, attitudes held, etc.

- Ongoing Tracking   In the event of a long-term sponsorship commitment, it is advisable to undertake measurement on the various metrics on an ongoing basis. The frequency of such measurements will be determined by likely variability in results over time as well as obvious cost factors.
- Final Evaluation   At the end of the sponsorship programme final evaluation can determine the scale of movement on the various metrics achieved over the life of the sponsorship program.

Marketing – Situational, Changing, On-going

The role of sponsorship with regard to the target market will vary between companies. It may fulfill brand awareness objectives for one company while another sponsor may seek the reinforcement of existing brand perceptions from their investment. Similarly the role of sponsorship, even for an individual sponsor will vary over time, being concerned initially with brand awareness building and perhaps moving on to image reinforcement/change later in the life cycle.

Market Segmentation

Even within the context of a defined target market, sponsorship can be called upon to achieve differential effects with different audience segments. Not all segments of the market are similar in terms of the consumer/brand relationship or indeed in terms of their relationship with the sponsored property or activity. It may therefore be important that specified segments be treated differently in terms of sponsorship activation/leveraging and observed differently in terms of sponsorship evaluation.

Having examined the suggestion of sponsorship as "different" and key basic principles of sponsorship evaluation, it is perhaps opportune to examine the practice of sponsorship in the marketplace.

Evaluating Sponsorship Effects – Praxis

Despite the increased scale of sponsorship expenditure, many sponsors still treat their sponsorship investments differently in terms of evaluation. Current research suggests that sponsors exhibit considerable reluctance to measure the effects of their sponsorship investments. A recent IEG/Performance Research study (2003) of US sponsors found that some 32% of respondents spent nothing on research while a further 48% spent less than 1% of the property rights fee on research (see Table 13.2). Research in this instance includes both research prior to selection as well as the evaluation of effectiveness post-implementation (the latter being the subject of this paper). A range of other sponsorship research results confirm sponsor reluctance to undertake adequate levels of evaluation of effects (see reviews of sponsorship, including evaluation by Pope, 1998; Cornwell & Maignan, 1998; Meenaghan, 2001b and Walliser, 2003). Despite the lack of supporting research, sponsors generally express themselves satisfied with the return of their sponsorship investments, which "creates a seeming paradox of

Table 13.2 *Percentage of rights fee spent on research*

Percentage of rights fee spent on research	Percentage of sponsors
Nothing	32%
Less than 1%	48%
1–5%	19%
More than 5%	1%

Source: IEG/Performance Research, *2003 Survey of Sponsorship Decision-Makers*, Chicago, IEG.

satisfaction with sponsorship results without quantitative or qualitative measures of what these results are." (Thjomoe et al, 2002, p. 10)

Where research is undertaken by sponsors to evaluate effectiveness, sponsors tend to rely on relatively basic methodologies. A recent IEG/Performance Research study (2003) of US sponsors is illustrative, as can be seen from Table 13.3.

Table 13.3 *Bases for performance analysis*

Method	Frequency of Use (%)
Internal feedback	53
Sales/promo bounce-back measures	39
TV exposure analysis	26
Print media analysis/clipping	26
Primary consumer research	23
Dealer/trade response	18
Syndicated consumer research	8

Source: IEG/Performance Research, *2003 Survey of Sponsorship Decision-Makers*, Chicago, IEG.

Internal feedback (53%) and media exposure analysis (TV and print – 52%) were the most widely used methods of evaluation, with research undertaken among consumers less likely to be used. Primary consumer research, which enables the measurement of a standard range of sponsorship effects, such as sponsorship awareness, sponsorship image and sales-related effects, still seem a relatively low priority for many sponsors today. Quite evidently, despite the increased scale of expenditure, many sponsors seem to treat sponsorship differently from other methods of marketing communications, at least with regard to the evaluation of effectiveness.

Methods of Sponsorship Evaluation

Having outlined various background issues with regard to sponsorship evaluation, attention will now focus on the various methods of evaluation currently applied in practice. Sponsorship evaluation can take place at several stages on the objectives–effects continuum: exposure → awareness → image → affinity → sales. Each stage is now examined in turn.

Sponsorship Exposure

The use of media coverage analysis to indicate sponsorship effects has generally been reported as the most common form of sponsorship evaluation undertaken by sponsors. Sponsorship exposure measurement can involve several sequential stages;

Collecting the Coverage   This initial stage involves the collection of all media coverage of the event and its sponsorship. The media examined for collection purposes generally involve press, television and increasingly online sponsorship exposure. Other media, including radio, are often not included in such evaluations. In the case of large-scale coverage, a sampling approach is often used, which is then scaled up. As stated, web-presence as a leveraging medium is increasingly important. An example of this form of monitoring is indicated in Table 13.4.

Table 13.4 *Volvooceanrace.org to July 1, 2002 – site performance statistics*

Unique visitors	3.05 million
Pages viewed total	102,379,494
Pages viewed per day	349,418
Visits total	17.5 million
Average daily visits	59,902
Average visit length	9.26 minutes
Highest number of unique visitors	93,169*
Highest hits	23 million**
Total hits	1,669,729,414

* June 9, Finish in Kiel
** May 29, 2002, End of leg to Göteborg

Source: Marketing through the Volvo Ocean Race, 2005–2006, p. 21. Hampshire, UK, Volvo Ocean Race.

Valuing the Coverage   While some sponsors are satisfied with merely collecting and "weighing"/counting the coverage received, for others the next step is the valuation of this coverage. The standard practice is to apply an advertising-media equivalent value to the coverage achieved. Essentially this involves applying the advertising rate card value (cost per thousand, CPT) to the coverage achieved (in terms of space or time). Once this has been completed, practices vary by individual sponsor and in relation to different media. In the case of press coverage, the advertising equivalent value (based on SCI rate card costs) is sometimes factored up. This is based on the argument that media coverage is "editorial" rather than advertising. Some analysts multiply the press coverage valuation by a factor of three, based on the perhaps unprovable PR industry argument/convention that 'editorial' is three times more valuable than "advertising."

In the case of television, there are three inputs to the determination of value, namely scale of sponsor exposure (i.e. in-focus time of logo, brand name, etc.), the audience for the exposure and the relevant CPT rate. Unlike the case of press exposure, television exposure is generally discounted to determine final value. In the case of major events, incredible amounts of coverage can be generated as indicated in the following quotation which discusses the sponsorship property, Ferrari rather than any particular sponsor.

> In winning the 2000 F1 Championship for the first time since 1979, Ferrari achieved even more television presence than in 1998. At that time SRi calculated that Ferrari's annual combined worldwide television presence was worth up to a (gross) equivalent of $3 billion, had that time been purchased at commercial rates. This year that figure rises to $3.9 billion. As usual in comparing sponsorship with advertising the discounting factor is highly specific to the individual sponsoring company, sport and brand. However, even discounting this figure by a theoretical (and extremely high) 95%, a sponsor legible for just one percent of the time Ferrari is present returns almost $2 million. This figure takes into account only live broadcasting, on to which should be added other types of broadcast such as news and recorded highlights. Figures based on a daily analysis of every type of broadcast, including news, general and lifestyle programmes in seven European countries from January to November show that 5% of total F1 broadcasting is contained within news broadcasting. This is impressive given the short durations of coverage.
>
> During all forms of F1 related television broadcasts in the countries monitored, Ferrari and McLaren have together attained 54.9% of the available share of voice or "presence." No other team won a race in 2000, and even more markedly than usual the share of voice falls steeply away from the leading teams. (SRi 2000)

Refining the Value   In the case of press, the value of coverage can be refined using weighting systems which are either established by the sponsor as agreed valuation templates or created by an external media monitoring/valuation agency. An example of the latter approach is shown in Table 13.5. A rating scale can also be applied to the press coverage to reflect its "favorability" to the sponsor.

Sponsorship Exposure – Recent Developments

Sponsorship exposure valuation generally consists of several elements, the determination of coverage/exposure, the size of audience and the relevant advertising CPT rate. In its early days, exposure monitoring was quite basic. In the case of television, exposure analysis was undertaken by an individual (often using a stop-watch) who monitored and logged key aspects of the exposure (e.g. duration of exposure, quality of branding). This basic approach has had huge implications for cost and variability. In the 1990s the introduction of computer automated signal reading, initially on video and later DVD, enabled greater accuracy and lower levels of human input.

Table 13.5 *Analysis of press coverage*

Category	Relative weighting
Heading mention	0.20
Sub-heading	0.15
Body text mention	0.10
Classified	0.15
Colour photograph	0.50
Black and white photo	0.33
Photos sized ½ page or above	2.00

Source: Echo Research – See Kolah, Ardi (2003) *Maximising the Value of Sponsorship*, London, Sports Business Group, p. 109.

In more recent times a range of computer-based monitoring approaches, based on advanced image recognition technology, have been launched (Hollis, 2003). Key advantages of these approaches are consistency of application as well as improved computation of brand exposure (i.e. location, size and quality of exposure on screen). While such improvements inevitably advance the quest for a standardized valuation system, this improvement is confined to television exposure, and does not yet address the huge variation amongst sponsors and agencies (once exposure time has been agreed) in the application of value. The suggestion that this recent development will provide a sponsorship industry equivalent to the 30–second advertising slot as the basic currency for sponsorship transactions would appear to be somewhat optimistic at this time.

Media Exposure – Summary Analysis

The widespread popularity of media exposure analysis as a basis for evaluating sponsorship effectiveness can perhaps be attributed to the following:

- Practicability   In an environment where uncertainty regarding the ability to measure sponsorships effects still exists and where adequate budgets for research are not always available, the popularity of this approach lies in its practicability, i.e. it is something that sponsors can do.
- Comfort Factor   In a world of "uncertainty," such results at least provide a tangible indication of benefit, even if its validity is often suspect.
- Consistency of Evaluation   The ongoing application of the same measure, even if of doubtful validity, does have the benefit of facilitating year-on-year comparisons, which indicate whether the sponsored activity is growing/fading, etc.

While the above factors suggest certain merits in this approach there are a number of important points to bear in mind.

- Publicity is not Effects   The use of media exposure as the basis for evaluating sponsorship effectiveness fails to appreciate that media exposure resulting from sponsorship, is publicity. It is *not* a measure of the effects of such publicity wrought upon the consumer. It is merely equivalent to suggesting that the effectiveness of advertising can be determined by counting the number of advertising slots purchased.
- Sponsorship is more than a Media-buy   Even if one were to accept media exposure as a measure of effectiveness, this approach treats sponsorship merely as a media buy and takes no cognisance of the message element which is inherent in any brand/sponsorship relationship.
- Lack of Standard Approach   Sponsors vary markedly in terms of how they undertake media exposure analysis. Some merely collect, others go on to greater refinement, yet vary in terms of degree of refinement. For example, some sponsors discount in-focus board signage by a factor of twenty while others equate its value with television advertising. Currently there is no real basis for comparing the publicity effects achieved by particular sponsorships in terms of a universally accepted industry model.

This section has sought to examine media exposure monitoring as a proxy indicator of sponsorship effectiveness. Despite considerable reservations, this approach can represent a useful indicator of certain effects, particularly if its capabilities are not exaggerated and its limitations understood.

Awareness Measures

Sponsorship researchers have for many years adopted basic advertising effectiveness measures to indicate the effects of specific sponsorship programmes. Key measures in this regard are recall and recognition measures (aka spontaneous and prompted awareness). Such measures can be applied to both the property and sponsor.

Awareness of the Property   As sponsorship represents an association with a socially intrusive event or activity, it is useful to monitor the extent to which the sponsorship property functions as a medium in terms of its "well-knowingness" or social intrusiveness. Comparisons between events across categories (sports/arts) or within categories (sport) or within particular activities (sailing – America's Cup versus Volvo Ocean Race) are possible.

Sponsorship Awareness   Sponsorship awareness indicates the extent to which a brand is associated with a particular event or activity. It is a useful measure of effectiveness in that it indicates how successful the sponsor has been in creating a linkage in the consumer's mind between the sponsor's brand and the sponsored activity (e.g. Vodafone and Manchester United). This linkage or association is critical to successful sponsorship in that it represents first base without which subsequent sponsorship effects (image transfer, sales, etc.) cannot occur.

Table 13.6 *Unprompted awareness of companies commercially engaged in football (UK market)*

Company	Unprompted awareness score
Vodafone	17
Barclaycard	14
O2	12
Nike	11
Carlsberg	11
Nationwide	11
adidas	10
Carling	9
NTL	8
Worthington	6
Ford	6
Coca-Cola	5

Source: Sports and Market, AG (2003) *European Football Monitor, 2002/2003* – Wave 1, Cologne, Germany. Sports and Market AG.

Sponsorship awareness can be measured on both a prompted and unprompted basis with the former delivering a higher score while the latter probably represents a truer measure. Table 13.6 shows unprompted awareness scores for companies engaged in UK sponsorship (based on a telephone survey of 600 British males (15–69) with an interest in football). Vodafone, sponsors of Manchester United, Barclaycard, sponsors of the English Premiership and O2, sponsors of Arsenal, all achieve significant scores.

Brand Attitude/Imagery

The next stage at which sponsorship can be evaluated is in terms of attitude to the brand/image of the brand. Measures employed at this stage can vary in complexity. Favorability measures such as "I am favorably disposed towards Brand X," indexed over time and attributable to the sponsorship, represents a simple, but limited surrogate measure of attitude to the brand. More complex and indeed costly measures rely on standard brand image type research to indicate sponsorship effects. Such measures indicate the extent of image transfer from the sponsored property to the sponsor's brand.

The extent to which sponsorship brings about brand image change can be measured in survey research using standard semantic differential and Likert scale approaches. Image data from a well-known case study of sponsorship effectiveness evaluation is shown in Figure 13.1. At the time of the launch of the CD player in the mid 1980s, Philips sponsored the rock band Dire Straits to achieve a range of objectives, including image effects. In order to evaluate sponsorship effects they undertook a significant research program in the Austrian market, using both

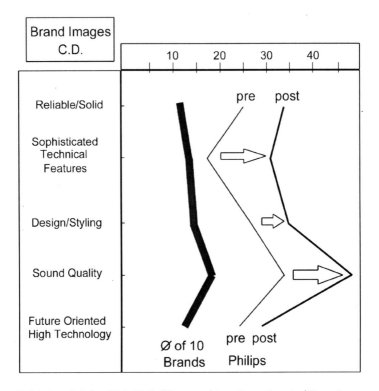

Source: Kohl, F. and Otker, T. (1995), "Sponsorship – Some Practical Experiences in Philips Consumer Electronics," in Meenaghan T. (ed.), *Researching Commercial Sponsorship*, Amsterdam, ESOMAR: 55–74.

Figure 13.1 *Effects of sponsorship on selected brand image dimensions.*

pre- and post-research waves, to indicate movement on selected dimensions. In the case of image, Philips measured the movement of its brand image, both pre and post the sponsorship, on a range of image dimensions such as "sophist-icated technical features," "sound quality," etc. against a battery of ten competing brands. The research results showed significant image benefits to the Philips brand resulting from this sponsorship as can be seen from Figure 13.1.

It is also possible to use Likert scales to indicate sponsorship effects, an example of which is shown in Table 13.7. In this case Texaco sought to measure the effects of its involvement with Formula One on its brand image. The results shows the scale of agreement with specific image-related statements, cross-tabulated against those who were aware/not aware of the sponsorship. The difference in terms of agreement is regarded as the effect of the sponsorship on the brand image. For example 49% of those who were sponsorship-aware agreed with the statement that Texaco 'has a passion for motoring' compared with 24% for those who where not aware. This delineation of sponsorship aware/not aware as the basis for isolating sponsorship effects is examined later.

Table 13.7 Texaco Formula One sponsorship

	Sponsorship awareness	
	Aware	Unaware
Fuel is better for your vehicle	20	11
Has friendly and helpful staff	41	32
An original brand which stands apart from the rest	26	17
A more pleasant place to refuel your vehicle	25	17
A brand that you feel is improving	26	16
Lively and upbeat	29	17
Really understands the needs of motorists	37	27
Has an American Heritage	41	29
Has a passion for motoring	49	24
Fuel will improve your vehicle's performance	19	11

Research Period: Feb. 1997 – June 1998 Strongly agree: % saying 8+/10

Source: Millman, Ivor (2000) "Broadcast Sponsorship Works," Admap, April, p. 15.

Affinity Measures

Marketing, for decades obsessed with the concept of the "sale," has in the last decade focused on customer-relationship management. Against this backdrop and a view of marketing communications as essential to the consumer/brand relationship, the task of evaluating how and the extent to which consumers bond with brands is increasingly important in sponsorship research. The measurement of (brand) affinity is reflected in research statements such as "Brand X is for people like me" or "Brand Y is my type of brand." An example of this type of research is shown in Table 13.8 below which indicates the differential effects of sponsorship on affinity to the Guinness brand. For example, 46% of the total population claim to be "close to the brand as a result of the sponsorship" compared to 54% of 35–55 year olds and 60% of 18–34 year olds. Again the

Table 13.8 *The Guinness All-Ireland Hurling Championship*

Close to the brand as a result of the sponsorship	Nov '00 %	Feb '01 %	Mar '01 %	July '01 %	Aug '01 %	Sept '01 %
Total population	37	38	40	35	46	48
35–55 Target market	n/a	47	51	49	54	54
18–34 Target market	n/a	50	50	48	60	57

Source: Amarach Consulting (2002), *The Guinness All-Ireland Hurling Championship*, Research Report prepared for Guinness Ireland, Dublin, Amarach.

challenge is to link brand affinity movements to sponsorship activity, rather than to other marketing inputs.

Sales Effects

The ability to relate sales outcomes to specific marketing inputs such as advertising has long been recognized as problematic. Sponsorship is no different in this regard, however a range of what might be described as sales-related outcomes can be measured as indicators of sponsorship effectiveness. The extent to which these measures may be used will vary by sponsor and related industry-type, e.g. mobile phone company, brewing company, etc. Sales and sales-related measures can include the following:

- Tastings/Product trials/Lead generation
- Consideration set
- Intention to purchase
- Actual/Claimed purchase
- Repeat purchase/Loyalty

Tastings/Product Trials/Lead Generation   Not all sponsors can use product tastings/trial as an element of their sponsorship programme, however for some sponsors it is an obvious objective for sponsorship involvement and effects evaluation. For example, Guinness sponsored a two-day rock music festival in Ireland called Witness, which provided the sponsor with substantial tasting/sales opportunities with the recruitment sector of the drinks market. On its introduction in the UK, Baileys, the cream liqueur drink, sponsored classical music concerts in English stately homes, which provided a major opportunity for product sampling. Other sponsored events may provide sponsors with sales leads whose ultimate conversion rates can be linked to the sponsorship program.

Intention to Purchase   Intention to purchase represents an important measure of sponsorship effects. An example of this measure used in survey research is provided by the Philips CD/Dire Straits case mentioned earlier. As can be seen from Figure 13.2, buying intention increased significantly between the pre and post research waves as a result of the sponsorship program. In a recent study of the effects of web-sponsorship, Harvey (2001) found that sponsorship delivers a range of improved benefits such as consideration set inclusion, willingness to purchase as well as enhanced brand perceptions.

Actual/Claimed Sales   Relating actual sales outputs to specific marketing inputs has long been recognized as problematic due to the range of marketing and marketing communications elements impacting on sales outcomes, with obvious difficulties in terms of input/output linkage. A similar situation applies in sponsorship, however in certain instances it may be easier to observe the linkage of sales to sponsorship. This may occur where a sponsor has certain sales rights surrounding a sponsorship programme, e.g. food or beverages rights.

Buying Intention

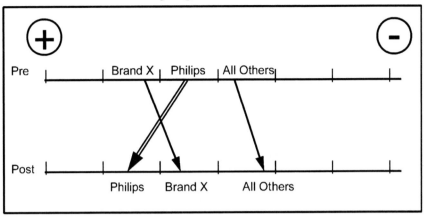

Source: Kohl, F. and Otker, T. (1995), "Sponsorship – Some Practical Experiences in Philips Consumer Electronics," in Meenaghan T. (ed.), *Researching Commercial Sponsorship*, Amsterdam, ESOMAR: 55–74.

Figure 13.2 *Effect of sponsorship on buying intention.*

Kentucky Fried Chicken sponsors gospel and country music festivals while a brewing company such as Guinness sponsors music festivals as well as a program of local festivals. In such instances the sponsor's product has either exclusive or preferential sales rights with obvious linkage potential.

Claimed sales, though less tangible, can be measured through specific survey research programs where such claimed sales can be linked to particular consumer responses (e.g. levels of sponsorship exposure, awareness, image, etc.). In other instances it may be possible to indicate sponsorship effects by proxy. For example, where the sponsorship programme involves particular tasks which are capable of being quantified i.e. the collection of tokens, the redemption of coupons, etc. In the case of some cause-related marketing programs, quantifications may be possible. For example, in the case of a bank it may be possible to link certain outcomes such as the number of new accounts/cards opened or transaction numbers to the sponsorship.

In the case of the Guinness sponsorship of the 1999 Rugby World Cup (RWC), volume sales increases were reported across several world markets. Sales volume increased 37% year on year for the period of the tournament in France and 24% in South Africa. In Australia a "buy 10 pints" sticker collection promotion prompted a 9% increase in sales. Fifty thousand T-shirts were distributed through the promotion (Rines, 2002).

Repeat Purchases/Loyalty Again the linkage between repeat sales and brand loyalty claims and sponsorship can be examined in survey research where such claims are related to specific consumer responses (e.g. levels of sponsorship awareness, image and affinity). In the USA it was found that fans of NASCAR racing and the NFL were twice as likely to have switched brands as a result of sponsorship compared with non-fans. Similarly they were twice as likely to remain brand loyal to the sponsor brand compared to non-fans (SRi, 1995; Hitchen, 1998).

Sponsorship Evaluation – Isolation and Attribution

The foregoing discussion examined a series of research methods commonly used to evaluate sponsorship effects. As is the case with all forms of marketing and marketing communication inputs, the real challenge is to find clean lines of attribution between particular inputs (in this case sponsorship) and specific effects (in this case sponsorship awareness, image, affinity and sales). In this regard two specific points are worth noting. Firstly, it is relatively easy to relate inputs and effects where sponsorship is the only input, however in reality, this situation rarely occurs. Secondly, it is more difficult to isolate out the specific effects of any input, whether advertising or sponsorship, as one proceeds along the continuum of objectives–effects outlined in Table 13.1 earlier. Clear lines of attribution between sponsorship and effects are more difficult to observe in the case of actual sales than for effects sought earlier on the objectives–effects continuum (e.g. awareness, image levels).

In order to examine the specific effects of sponsorship using different sponsorship metrics (sponsorship awareness, image, affinity and sales), a range of approaches can be used. Survey research will generally incorporate standard segmentation or respondent classification data such as socio-economic, user status (user/non-user) as well as lifestyle data, cross-tabulated with the particular metrics (e.g. sponsorship awareness), in order to illustrate any variation in effects by sub-segment. Due to the nature of sponsorship and its engagement with particular activities (e.g. sports, arts, teams, individuals, etc.), it is quite common for survey research results to be cross-tabulated against specific features of the consumer as "fan." This can be as simple as delineating fan/non-fan or to examine degrees of "fandom" based on volume consumption of the sponsored property; for example, games attended, televised matches watched, etc. (Eilander and Koenders, 1991). A further refinement is to measure fan involvement, which is the emotional attachment to the sponsored property (e.g. Manchester United, New York Yankees, etc.). While the importance of "fan involvement" is recognized as critical to sponsorship effectiveness, (Shani, Sandler & Spencer, 2000; Pham, 1992), to date its measurement as a construct in sponsorship evaluation is still in its infancy (Meenaghan, 2001b).

The standard method of isolating sponsorship effects used in survey research is to compare the responses of respondents aware of the sponsorship and those not aware of the sponsorship (e.g. Table 13.7) and attribute the difference between respondent group scores on the specific dimension (sponsorship aware-ness, attitude, image, intention to purchase, claimed purchase, etc.) as the effect of the sponsorship. This approach has come in for some recent criticism, with some critics (Walshe, 2002; Thompson & Vickers, 2002) claiming that the comparison of exposed versus non-exposed responses is a truer measure of sponsorship effects.

Versatile Medium–Multiple Measures of Effects

Versatility as discussed earlier in terms of roles, publics, objectives and effects is identified as a key differentiating feature of sponsorship. This feature has significant implications for the evaluation of sponsorship effects in that the multiple objectives sought and multiple publics targeted will generally require a much more extensive evaluation program using multiple metrics than is likely to be required with other methods of marketing communication, including advertising

In 2001 BT Cellnet, the British Telecom mobile service sponsored the Channel 4 broadcast of the Big Brother series on Channel 4 in the UK, a program that generated huge levels of public interest and involvement. This particular case provides a useful example of the range of evaluation metrics applicable to sponsorship. Having used the sponsorship as a multi-platform, multimedia campaign, evaluation was undertaken using a variety of metrics on the proposed objectives/effects continuum as shown in the selected excerpts below:

Exposure Effects

The series was the highest rating programme on Channel 4 for 16–34-year-old adults in 2001, attracting between four and five million viewers per episode

Against Cellnet's core target of 16–34-year-olds, Channel 4 and E4 activity achieved 4363 TVRs, 83.3% cover at a staggering 52.4 OTS overall. Compared against a typical burst of TV activity, this was a massive achievement, and made the brand very conspicuous for the 16–34-year-old audience

The broadcast sponsorship credits alone delivered BT Cellnet value in excess of £10m at realistic media buying rates, with on–line and Interactive activity taking the sponsorship to greater heights.

PR alone generated 108m OTS across press and radio and the on–line viral marketing campaign generated 230,000 hits in just 5 weeks

Awareness Effects

In fieldwork conducted during the first 2 weeks of the series, 40% of 16–34-year-old mobile users were aware that BT Cellnet was the sponsor. This rose to 66% by the series end, beating the figure for Nescafe's long–running association with Friends

Spontaneous awareness was strong too. 31% of the target knew which company was the Big Brother series sponsor. This was higher amongst BT Cellnet's key targets – 16–24-year-olds (36%), lower social grades, and readers of mid–market and popular newspapers

Image Effects

Brand perceptions among Big Brother 2 viewers increased significantly versus non-viewers in all key image statements including "Straightforward," "Passionate," "Approachable," "Fun," "Open," "Clear" and "Trusted."

Sales Related Effects

Beyond the communications effect of exposure to sponsorship credits, it was clear that huge numbers of consumers got involved with Big Brother via branded BT Cellnet interactions.

- Over 5 million Big Brother gossip text alerts were sent out via BT Cellnet.
- A total of 172,000 people signed up for the basic text alerts service.
- There were 150,000 calls to the audio line for real time live feeds from the house.
- In all, 26,000 vouchers were sold at £4.99 through High St retail outlets for access to the premium Big Brother services, plus an additional 34,000 calls to the voucher registration line, and 3,600 to the voucher download line.
- Altogether, 227,000 people called the Big Brother information line.

In addition to the "brand experience" effect, the scale of this activity generated £880,000 in additional revenue to BT Cellnet. (Griffin & Regan, 2003

The sponsorship also enabled BT Cellnet to promote its recently developed WAP services. Using continuous updates the Big Brother site recorded some 21 million WAP page impressions, equivalent to 286,000 per day. As well as the exposure gained, this also allowed the sponsor to monitor site usage, thereby enhancing company learning as well as providing consumer sampling and interaction with the new technology WAP (Griffin & Regan, 2003).

Conclusion

This paper has sought to examine the evaluation of sponsorship effects. It noted industry perceptions of sponsorship as "something different," perceptions that seem to translate into the less rigorous evaluation of sponsorship effects. In particular this chapter underlined the versatility of sponsorship in terms of publics capable of being addressed and objectives capable of being achieved and the implications of this versatility for sponsorship evaluation. It further proposed an objectives–effects continuum as a useful framework for the analysis of sponsorship effects with final consumers.

While current practice suggests some sponsor reluctance to undertake the proper evaluation of effects, ongoing corporate investment in sponsorship will continue to translate into pressure for greater accountability. Today sponsorship is a major global industry that has drawn the attention of global services providers such as advertising agencies, research companies and management consultants, each competing to deliver improved solutions to sponsor needs. The relatively brief history of sponsorship has witnessed the continuing development of techniques and tools as aids to all aspects of sponsorship management. In terms of sponsorship evaluation, existing approaches are being refined and new approaches developed to accommodate the versatile medium that is sponsorship. Suggestions of "difference" are unlikely to withstand the collective pressure from all parties to the sponsorship industry globally.

References

Amarach Consulting (2002) *The Guinness All-Ireland Hurling Championship*, Research Report prepared for Guinness Ireland, Dublin, Amarach Consulting.

Cornwell, T. Bettina and Isabelle Maignan (1998) "An International Review of Sponsorship Research," *Journal of Advertising*, 27 (1): 1–21.

Eilander, Goos and Henk Koenders (1991) "Communication Research into the Effects of Short and Long-term Sponsorship," paper presented at *Sponsorship 91' Conference*, Barcelona, Spain, October 23–25th, Organised by Expoconsult, Holland, Conference Proceedings, pp. 62–79.

Griffin, Adele and Tony Regan (2003) "BT Cellnet – How Broadcast Sponsorship of Big Brother 2 Series Became a Business Partnership and Consumer Brand Experience," *Advertising Works 12*, London, IPA, pp. 137–152.

Harvey, Bill (2001) "Measuring the Effects of Sponsorships", *Journal of Advertising Research*, 41 (1): 59–65.

Hastings, G. B. (1984) "Sponsorship Works Differently from Advertising," *International Journal of Advertising*, 3: 171–176.

Hitchen, Adrian (1998) "Who Does Sponsorship Persuade Most ?", paper delivered at IEG Sponsorship Conference *"Meta-Sponsorship"*, March, Chicago, IEG.

Hoek Janet, Philip Gendall, Michelle Jeffcoat and David Orsman (1997) "Sponsorship and Advertising: A Comparison of their Effects," *Journal of Marketing Communications*, 3: 21–32.

Hollis Sponsorship Newsletter (2003) "Putting Price on Exposure", UK, Hollis Publishing Ltd, September, pp. 1–2.

IEG Sponsorship Report (2004) "Sponsorship Spending to see Biggest Rise in Five Years," December 27, Vol. 23, No. 24, pp. 1–2.

IEG/Performance Research, *2003 Survey of Sponsorship Decision-Makers,* Chicago, IEG.

Kolah, Ardi (2003) *Maximising the Value of Sponsorship*, London Sportsbusiness Group.

Kohl, Franz and Ton Otker, (1995) "Sponsorship – Some Practical Experiences in Philips Consumer Electronics," in Meenaghan T. (ed.), *Researching Commercial Sponsorship*, Amsterdam, ESOMAR, pp. 55–74.

Marketing through the Volvo Ocean Race, Hampshire, UK, Volvo Ocean Race, 2005–2006, p. 21.

McDonald, Colin, (1991) "Sponsorship and the Image of the Sponsor," *European Journal of Marketing*, 25 (11): 31–38.

Meenaghan, T (2001a) "Sponsorship and Advertising – A Comparison of Consumer Perceptions," *Psychology and Marketing*, 18 (2): 191–215.

Meenaghan, T (2001b) "Understanding Sponsorship Effects," *Psychology and Marketing*, 18 (2): 95–122.

Millman, Ivor (2000) "Broadcast Sponsorship Works," *Admap*, April: 13–15.

Mintel Special Report on Sponsorship, (1980) London, Mintel Publications Ltd.

Pham, M. Tuan (1992) "Effects of Involvement, Arousal and Pleasure on the Recognition of Sponsorship Stimuli," *Advances in Consumer Research*, 19: 85–93.

Pope, Nigel (1998) "Overview of Current Sponsorship Thought," *Cyber-Journal of Sport Marketing*. http://www.ausport.gov.au/fulltext/1998/cjsm/u2n1/pope21.htm

Rines, Simon (2002) "Guinness Rugby World Cup Sponsorship: A Global Platform for meeting business objectives," *International Journal of Sports Marketing and Sponsorship*, 3 (4): 446–465.

Shani, David, Dennis Sandler and Earl Spencer (2000) "Audience Level of Involvement: The Key to Effective Sponsorship," *Marketing in a Global Economy*, Conference Proceedings, Melbourne.

Sponsorship Research International (SRi) (1995) "Effects of Sports Sponsorship on Product Trial/Brand Switching" (Press Release), November, London (SRi).

Sponsorship Research International (SRi) (2000), "Ferrari: The Four Billion Dollar Man," Press Release, 21/12/00, London, SRi.

Sport + Market AG (2003) *European Football Monitor, 2002/2003* – Wave 1, Cologne, Germany, Sport + Market AG.

Thompson, Ian and Sara Vickers (2002) "Sponsorship: The Real Deal," *Admap*, 432 (October): 19–22.

Thjomoe, Hans Malhias, Erik L. Olsen and Peggy Simeic Bronn (2002) "Decision-making Processes Surrounding Sponsorship Activities," *Journal of Advertising Research*, 42 (6): 6–15.

Walliser, Bjorn (2003) "An International Review of Sponsored Research: Extension and Replication," *International Journal of Advertising*, 22: 5–40.

Walshe, Peter (2002) "What Price 'Sponsorship Awareness'?," *Admap*, July: 32–34.

14

While the rich get richer…
Challenging Inequities in Conventional Sport Sponsorship

Sally Shaw

As the introduction to this volume suggests, sport sponsorship has grown exponentially over the past 20–30 years. Testament to global sport sponsorship's value to business is exemplified by the actions of multinational companies such as Coca-Cola and Nike, and local companies such as Speights brewery in New Zealand (sponsors of Otago Rugby and Speights Otago Rebels netball), and their enthusiasm for manipulating this potent element of the marketing mix. Sport sponsorship is also of obvious benefit to an exclusive band of athletes on the global stage, with Venus Williams, Tiger Woods and Manchester United's soccer star Wayne Rooney reportedly earning US$8 million, US$62 million and £30 million respectively, per annum, from endorsements alone (The Celebrity 100, 2003; Wayne Rooney, 2004).

From its prevalence in the global market, sport sponsorship appears to be an appealing process for many firms. Global companies such as Nike develop relationships with sport celebrities who fit with the firm's requirements for an advertising medium. In turn, athletes, such as Tiger Woods, who gain sponsorship agreements may become fantastically wealthy and often earn more through endorsements than they do in their chosen field of play (The Celebrity 100, 2003). Athletes' associations with global companies ensure that they become truly international figures. For many sports, athletes and businesses, this is certainly an ideal situation. For others, notably those sports and athletes who do not "fit" the precise wishes and image of companies that engage in global sponsorship, this exclusive, exclusionary relationship is far from ideal. Even athletes and teams who are successful are often not recognized by global corporations' sponsorship strategies. For example, the New Zealand (NZ) Black Ferns, who won consecutive Rugby World Cups in 1998 and 2001, have struggled unsuccessfully to secure any commercial funding other than that arranged by their national governing body, the New Zealand Rugby Union NZRU, for all national teams (Personal Communication, May 8, 2003).

Given the increasing popularity of rugby on a global scale, this lack of sponsorship for the NZ Black Ferns indicates that there may be inequities within sponsors' decision-making processes. The processes involved in global sport sponsorship are far from straightforward and result in something of a financial inequity for athletes who "have" and those who "have not" access to lucrative sponsorship contracts with global companies such as Coca-Cola or adidas. The purpose of this chapter is to explore how these imbalances are created by global organizations' decisions to sponsor some sports but ignore others, who may have similar abilities but lack the "fit" that is conventionally demanded by sponsors. Further, the possibility of challenging these global practices, without reducing the long-term appeal of sponsorship to interested companies, is considered. In order to achieve these aims the chapter is divided into three parts. First, I outline some of the dominant, globally prevalent power relations that sponsors are influenced by, and create, which result in them entering only into sponsorship agreements that will have a very specific image "fit" (Shaw & Amis, 2001). This fit is often based on powerful, sponsor-led conventions that are dictated by firms' values and beliefs, industry mimetic pressures, and ever-present media pressures. I argue that the development of "fit" is based on a "process of exchange" (Bauman, 1990) in which firms aim to gain as much as possible from their sponsorship agreement without necessarily questioning the philosophies that underpin their behaviour.

In the second part of the chapter, I argue that while the process of exchange is currently dominant, it is possible to challenge it and to develop a potentially more equitable process of sponsorship based on an ethic of "moral sensitivity" (Bauman, 2001). In this alternative practice, "fit" between sponsor and athlete or sport would still be defined through the firm's values and beliefs, mimetic pressures and media coverage. The underlying philosophy of the sponsorship agreement, however, would shift from a process of exchange to an ethic of care (Bauman, 2001). This shift in philosophy may produce a more equitable outcome for athletes and sports. Further examples are outlined to argue these points, many of which come from a local (i.e. national or regional) perspective. These are used to demonstrate how local sponsors may be more aware of the benefits of an "ethic of care," and may offer some alternatives to global sponsors in planning a strategy based on an "ethic of care."

Finally, I argue that the proposed shift in sponsorship ideology represents a sound investment for sponsoring firms. Rather than returning sponsorship to a seemingly prehistoric age of philanthropy, I suggest that firms' decisions to determine their sponsorship spend ethically will appeal to consumers who are increasingly looking to spend their disposable income on the products of ethically minded organizations (Strong, 1996). Thus, the dominant practices of global sport sponsorship may be challenged, and possibly changed, by adopting an ethic of care.

The Pressure to "Fit": Firms' Decisions to Sponsor

With increasing pressures on businesses to show returns on their marketing initiatives, it is unsurprising that most firms which decide to enter into sponsorship on the global stage follow some tried and tested decision-making processes. Three factors that inform the decision whether or not to sponsor are outlined by Shaw and Amis (2001). These are: the necessity of a fit between the values and beliefs of the sponsoring firm and the athlete or sport; mimetic behaviors, which ensure that potential sponsors are likely to follow similar firms into similar sponsorship deals; and the positive media representation of the sport or athlete in question.

Values and Beliefs

The values and beliefs of a firm may be expressed through their decision to sponsor a sport or athlete. Finding a fit between a sport and the firm's values and beliefs may be understood as an external expression of the organization's culture (Martin, 2001). For example, Tag Heuer's President and CEO, Jean-Christophe Babin, suggested that the prestigious watch manufacturer's sponsorship of Tiger Woods was a valuable partnership because; "[Woods'] personality – his obsessive quest for superior achievements and perfection, his ability to withstand pressure, his commitment to live up to expectations and then surpass them and also his passion for discipline – seemed to make this a natural and appropriate partnership" (Ligerakis, 2002, p. 1). The comments from Babin express the desire of Tag Heuer to be associated with, and express, values of hard work, trustworthiness and indefatigable energy. They also underline how clearly sponsoring firms understand that their values and beliefs are expressed on the international stage through their choice of sporting sponsee.

While athletes such as Woods have clearly benefited from such relationships with sponsors, the pursuit of high-value, high-profile agreements by sponsoring firms has also led to the creation of relative "have nots." So what about those sports in which athletes are dedicated, hard working, disciplined and successful (i.e. expressing all the values of Tiger Woods and other sport celebrities) but are unable to secure commercial sport sponsorship? It is possible to suggest that firms exert powerful messages that force athletes to conform not only to the sponsors' values and beliefs but also to express specific behaviors to be granted sponsorship. Those who fit with sponsors' values and beliefs but also express "other" views are unlikely to receive endorsement. Martina Navratilova, for example, has often claimed that she missed out on millions of dollars of sponsorship due to historical discrimination against lesbians in sport (Elliot, 2001). This is despite her dedication to tennis that is exemplified by over 230 victories on the professional Tour, which represents a global stage upon which sponsors could position themselves. Attitudes towards Navratilova have changed recently, enabling her to develop some sponsorship deals later in her athletic career. Yet it is clear from her case that global corporations have strong, historical assertions that they do not wish to be associated with homosexual athletes, however successful they may be. Such influences were also evident when French tennis player Amelie Mauresmo was warned by the WTA to limit displays of affection with her partner Sylvie Bourdon in case it jeopardized the Tour image and firms' willingness to sponsor it (Henderson, 2000). The bold double standard that is set by this pressure is noteworthy as sponsors often encourage heterosexual displays of affection by their sponsees (McDonald, 2000). Other circumstances that appear to be distasteful to sponsors include illness, as Lance Armstrong discovered during his recovery from cancer. During that period, most of his team sponsors lost interest in Armstrong as they did not want to be associated with an athlete that had been "tainted" by potentially terminal illness (Armstrong & Jenkins, 2000).

Firms are therefore very aware of the values and beliefs that their association with certain athletes entails. While hard work and perseverance are rewarded with lucrative deals (e.g. Tiger Woods and Tag Heuer) those rewards can be severely limited or non-existent if those values are "tarnished" by, in the examples above, homosexuality or illness. While these examples only represent a small representation of unacceptable associations for sponsors, they indicate that firms have the power to strongly express which views they do not want to be associated with. This desire *not* to be associated with certain views appears to be driven by strong, conservative, and seemingly globally influential discourses, which overwhelm some athletes' own expressions of values and beliefs.

It is possible to argue that firms' decisions to sponsor and the values and beliefs that they are willing to express through their sponsees are underpinned by a process of exchange (Bauman, 1990). In this process firms operate on the selfish premise of giving away as little as possible to receive as much as possible in return (Bauman, 1990). For sponsors, this means having "their" values and beliefs expressed by "their" sponsees on the global stage, and an unwillingness to entertain any compromise or diversion from that message. The strength and ubiquitous nature of these views ensures that organizational decision-makers are unwilling to challenge them. This would require self-reflection and critique, which are both contrary to the process of exchange (Bauman, 1990).

Mimetic Pressures

The influence of mimetic pressures, in which firms in an industry will mimic their established competitors' sponsorship agreements (DiMaggio & Powell, 1983), is so great partly because of the frailty of sponsorship deals. It only takes a foolish act in front of millions of TV viewers (e.g. David Beckham's kick at an opponent in the 1998 Football World Cup) or the accusation of drug use (e.g. Jennifer Capriati in her rebellious teenage years) to tarnish a sponsor's image and render their sponsorship investment worthless. Sponsoring an athlete who is outside the norm for firms within a specific industry, and thus challenging mimetic pressures, represents a real risk. It is unsurprising, therefore, that firms tend to "follow their leader" and engage in mimetic practices. Such practices, however, ensure that only those athletes who will satisfy the requirements of their sponsors will gain and keep a sponsorship deal with a firm, or with other firms in a specific industry.

Athletes who might choose to use their status to express a political, religious or social message, which is considered by their sponsors to be outside the athlete's jurisdiction as an advertisement for the firm, may very quickly see their sponsorship deals vanish. For example, sponsorship pressure has led to a ban on soccer players in many countries who had traditionally celebrated goals by dramatically removing their playing shirts to reveal political or religious messages on an undershirt (Cronin, 2003; Reuters, 1997). It is not sponsors' wishes to save their image from potentially offensive messages that is of concern here. What is concerning is that sponsors' desire to fit with industry values appears to encourage them to step over into dictating issues that "their" athletes may or may not choose to support. As such, athletes become somewhat dehumanized, pressured into becoming ambulatory billboards, who are discouraged from presenting their own views.

Once again, this practice may be linked to the process of exchange. Sponsors are happy to use the image of successful soccer players to sell their product in the global marketplace but are unwilling to entertain a compromise in which the athlete may be able to support their own social causes. Mimetic pressures, which are underpinned by the process of exchange, contribute to the constant undermining of certain athletes and sports because they do not fit with the powerful, specific requirements of the firms in an industry that follow a certain mold.

Media Representation of Sports

The final pressure that is exerted on firms to sponsor certain athletes and sports over other and perhaps the most influential, is that of the media portrayal of sports (Berrett & Slack, 2001). With their characteristically narrow view of what makes a "newsworthy" sport (Theberge, 1991), the various global media conglomerates largely dictate who will receive sponsorship money and who will not. If an athlete or sport is not receiving consistent positive media attention, then there is little chance that they will be entertained by corporate sponsors (Amis, Pant & Slack, 1997; Berrett & Slack, 2001; Meenaghan, 1991). The sponsorship practices of ANZ bank, which sponsors the ANZ Golf Championship in Australia, provide an example of the pressures that influence international sponsorship agreements. As the Head of Brand and Sponsorship at ANZ bank, Amanda Duggan stated "we look at measures of awareness [of our sponsorship] and do tracking on a weekly basis. Each sign [on the course] that is publicised receives a certain amount of points which are tallied up" (Plaskitt, 2003). This point system has a direct link to justifying the placement of ANZ advertising hoardings around the golf course. Duggan further suggested that accurate measurement of the amount of media time given to the ANZ hoardings was vital in order to "show the Board [of ANZ] the tangibility of the returns obtained" (Plaskitt, 2003).

In short, the pressures that are placed on a sponsored event or team to obtain media time for their sponsor are great if they are to retain their agreement. It is therefore unlikely that the sports which do not fit with the conventions of traditional sponsorship and struggle to offer media presence will break into the sponsorship "scene." Indeed, some minority sports may face a "false dawn" in which they secure some media coverage but lose it after the novelty of their sport or event has worn off (Personal Communication, May 8, 2003). The media themselves are unlikely to take a step into changing which sports are favored. As New Zealand Rugby International suggested

> the media need an angle. Historically, it was "oh look it's women playing a team game and they're not wearing skirts." That novelty angle has gone now [with the development of women's rugby in New Zealand] but the media still feel they have to have an angle [and so don't cover us]. I wish they didn't [feel that they need an angle], that they would just follow us for playing rugby. Like they do with the guys. (Personal communication, May 8, 2003)

It would appear from these comments that the "angle" required by the media is once again an indication of the powerful influences that are exerted by sponsors. If a "minority" athlete or sport cannot provide an "angle" that will last through the false dawn that was experienced by the NZ Black Ferns then corporate sponsors are unlikely to retain an interest in that sport. The requirement to have an "angle" also indicates the nature of the process of exchange with relation to global media pressures. Sponsors, it would appear, are only willing to engage in agreements with sports that can give them an "angle." They are unwilling to promote the "angle" themselves or help the sport develop an angle; nor are they willing to resist the trend of ignoring physical women's sports and encourage global media organizations to work with them to increase women's and their own sponsorship profiles in what would be a risky venture.

With firms' potent combination of a desire to express conventional values and beliefs, a seeming inability to move away from the traditions of their industry peers' choices in sponsorship and a reliance on the narrow view held by dominant media groups about what makes "good TV sport" it is hardly surprising that global sponsorship is framed by the influential, traditional requirements of sponsoring firms. It follows that if a sponsoring organization, which follows the process of exchange, can invest in an athlete who fits its needs immediately and without much nurturing, such a sponsee will be more sought after than one who does not. In current management parlance, a sponsorship agreement that expresses the features of the process of exchange might well be considered to be effective in achieving an organization's outcomes and efficient in doing so with as little extra expenditure as possible. Such a sponsorship may indeed be praised for achieving the marketing aims of the organization in which it was generated (Amis, Slack & Berrett, 1999; Meenaghan, 1991; Shaw & Amis, 2001). Yet this practice of slavishly following the status quo creates a gulf between the "haves" and the "have nots" and does little to encourage and develop those sports with athletes who are hard-working, diligent and often successful, but are underfunded. Is there a solution to the lose/lose situation in which some successful sports do not "fit" within firms' narrow view of worthy sponsees? In the next section I suggest that, with a little imaginative thinking from sponsors and engagement with a moral sensitivity and ethic of care (Bauman, 2001), there is.

Challenging the Rules: Alternative Options for Sponsors

Is there an alternative to the process of exchange within the context of global sport sponsorship? Bauman (2001) suggests that we live in a world that is dominated by rules and structures that benefit those engaging with the exchange process. In the global sport sponsorship industry, it is in the interests of those who benefit from the process of exchange to keep the status quo and express certain values and beliefs, succumb to mimetic pressures and leave the power of the media unchallenged. Yet, as seen above, this creates an unjust situation of "haves" and "have nots." Bauman (2001) suggests that it is possible to challenge this status quo with a change in the philosophies that underpin our decision making processes. It is the responsibility of individuals, including organizational decision-makers, to strive consistently towards the development of a just society that is characterized by moral sensitivity (Bauman, 2001). Interestingly, some local companies already express an element of this in their sponsorship deals and, as the following sections indicate, global corporate sponsors may learn something from their approach. It may therefore be the case that conventional wisdom, which suggests that local sponsors should copy their global "superiors" in decision-making (Amis, Pant & Slack, 1997), may need to be challenged in order to develop more equitable power relations in sport sponsorship.

Moral Sensitivity and Sport Sponsorship

While Bauman does not specifically engage with sport or sponsorship, his ideas on societal change can be applied to this field. In the context of global sport sponsorship a more just distribution of income could be underpinned by sponsorships that still require a fit between sponsor and sponsee, but are based, to a degree, on moral sensitivity rather than the immediate pursuit of revenue through the process of exchange. Bauman (2001) does not present us with an easy definition of what moral sensitivity might entail. Rather, he suggests that the adoption of moral sensitivity in general decision-making processes could develop a "just society." This, according to Bauman (2001) is a "society which thinks it is not just *enough* ... and considers justice always to be a step or more ahead. Above all, it is a society which reacts angrily to any case of *injustice* and promptly sets about correcting it" (p. 61).

Such a flexible definition of what justice is (or is not) may appear to be unhelpful in terms of determining an alternative to conventional forms of global sport sponsorship. However this definition does enable us to seek a just alternative to conventional sponsorship as opposed to accepting the unjust situation that sponsorship currently creates. It also encourages individuals in sponsoring organizations to be self-reflexive in our understanding of justice and does not allow us to "pass the buck" regarding the responsibility for justice. Furthermore, if our vision of justice regarding sponsorships is always a "step or more ahead" (Bauman, 2001, p. 61), then we can acknowledge that working towards a moral society, specifically the just or more equitable distribution of global sponsorship, is a long-term commitment.

It is not enough to engage with moral sensitivity in a superficial sense, as moral sensitivity needs to be excessive to be sufficient (Bauman, 2001). With this long-term view in mind, decision-makers in organizations who see their commitment to moral sensitivity as occasionally passing a few dollars, pounds or euros to "good causes" are not engaging in the development of a morally sensitive sponsorship agreement. Consequently, a move towards global sport sponsorship decisions that are underpinned by moral sensitivity may seem intimidating. Managers are so constrained by the short-term pursuit of profit and dominant characteristics of a good fit, that the courage required to challenge convention may be lacking. Yet it is perhaps only in facing such uncertainty that managers can make meaningful, thoughtful decisions, rather than basing their ideas on the "recipe books" of management. As Bauman (2001) suggests "the sole choice we face is one between loyalty to the humiliated and to beauty. It is like any other choice a moral being confronts: between taking and refusing to take responsibility for one's responsibility" (p. 47). If managers make the choice to be loyal to the humiliated (in sports sponsorship, the have nots) over beauty (the haves) then they are engaging with moral sensitivity, which according to Bauman (2001), is the "preliminary condition of a just society" (p. 68). In the following sections, I address each component part of the fit between sponsor and sponsee and indicate how they may be developed with moral sensitivity as a defining feature of global sport sponsorship.

Values and Beliefs in a Morally Sensitive Sponsorship

As noted above, it is necessary for organizations to enter into sponsorship in which their values and beliefs are reinforced by the athlete or sport (Shaw & Amis, 2001). This remains the case in a sponsorship that is founded on moral sensitivity because a "low fit [of values] reduces the favourability of attitudes towards the sponsorship ... because incongruity is negatively valued ... Low fit makes people less certain of the firm's positioning" (Becker-Olsen & Simmons, 2002, p. 287). The suggestion for a morally sensitive sponsorship, however, is that this fit of values and beliefs is thought of in a broad sense that can include sports and athletes who are traditionally marginalized by conventional conceptualizations. This shift in thinking may encourage firms to think about challenging traditional global sponsorship patterns and developing a more just distribution of sponsorship funds.

Is this view of moral sensitivity altruistic? Laughable in the global corporate age? Perhaps for some it is. For Adecco Recruitment Services, a Swiss-based firm with international offices, and the Australian Women's baseball team, however, this mix has provided a strategic approach to sponsorship. The baseball team has historically been caught in the lose/lose situation in which many sports find themselves. It was a minority sport in a country where cricket, rugby league and Australian rules football reign supreme. Baseball was not entitled to funding from the government until it "better establishe[d] itself" (Rao, 2001), nor was it likely to receive commercial funding until it received media presence. Its chances of commercial sponsorship or government funding were therefore very slim. Yet the Australian branch of Adecco have stepped in as the baseball team's major sponsor with a $A20,000 sponsorship agreement. According to Allison Lee, Director of Impact Communications Australia and a sponsorship consultant to Adecco "[we] are there because the team does not have a high profile. The sponsorship aims to develop women's baseball, which needs to get ahead" (Rao, 2001).

Adecco's involvement was not based on philanthropy, as the company expressed its satisfaction with the fit with the "Adecco Aussie" baseball team. It is suggested on Adecco's website that the "teamwork, commitment, dedication, energy and enjoyment" (Adecco, 2002) that are inherent in sport also fit with the values and beliefs of Adecco as an organization. Adecco's actions also represent an example of a global company that has registered the importance of working locally with a struggling "humiliated" sport, in order to improve the sport's situation, whilst heightening its own profile. This may also be considered a long-term commitment as it has continued for over two years (Adecco, 2002). It is too early in the agreement to measure its commercial success but, as the "Adecco Aussies" have been successful in two World Championships (Australian Baseball, 2002; 2003), it is possible that commercial spin-offs may follow.

It is not only "Down Under" that evidence can be found of sponsorships that are based on moral sensitivity, which enable previously unsponsored teams to gain through sponsorship and in which teams are trusted by sponsoring firms to express their values and beliefs. Rich Thrall, Managing Partner of LandLink Consulting Ltd, which sponsors the Canadian Women's Rugby team, expressed this view. In his statement in March 2002, he announced:

> This [rugby] team embodies the traditional Canadian characteristics of hard work, tenacity and innovation. The LandLink corporate goal of "moving ideas to reality" parallels the National Women's transition of vision... We are confident that the spirit of the LandLink organization will be very well represented by the indomitable spirit of our National Women's Team. (Goff, 2002)

The element of moral sensitivity that underpins this sponsorship agreement lies, once again, in its developmental nature. That is, women's rugby is considered to be a sport that is extremely hard to find commercial sponsors for, as it has minimal media presence (Personal Communication, May 8, 2003). Historically, the Canadian women's team have had to pay player fees to attend the World Cup, despite their ranking as fourth in the world (Goff, 2002). Yet, as Roxanne

Butler, National Women's Team Director for the Canadians suggested, the efforts of the athletes has paid off in terms of the decision by LandLink to make this contribution to their effort. She noted that "[the agreement with LandLink] means that Women's Rugby is finally starting to be noticed in the sport marketplace" (Goff, 2002). It would appear, as the sponsorship with LandLink has been renewed, that women's rugby has also sustained its place in the sport marketplace (Personal Communication, Roxanne Butler, May 16, 2003).

In the Adecco and LandLink sponsorships, both companies acted with a sense of moral sensitivity. Both sponsors were able to work beyond the traditional, global mimetic pressures that limit minority sports' appeal to sponsors and focus on the positive elements of the commitment of the team. The sponsors were able to articulate an element of moral sensitivity and therefore show how it can provide a basis for sponsorship, which may lead to long-term, and potentially profitable, agreements. Global corporate organizations, which have a duty to reflect on their own justifications for sponsorship, would do well to take heed of this approach, and consider it within their negotiations with sports and athletes.

In the opening discussion of values and beliefs, I noted how homosexuality and illness, amongst others, have been seen as a problematic association for sponsors. While the difficulties faced by "out" homosexual athletes are analysed by Lenskyj in the next chapter, it is worth noting that it is possible, with increased sponsorship interest in events such as Gay Games VI in Sydney, that there may be a shift in attitude towards these athletes. There is no clear answer as to whether homosexual athletes will gain sponsorships that equate to their heterosexual colleagues. It is possible, however, that through the development of morally sensitive sponsorship sponsors will focus on the athletes' playing abilities rather than be constrained by prejudices that are based on socially constructed discrimination. Regarding illness, one of Lance Armstrong's sponsors was able to see past his cancer and imagine his ability to ride again (Armstrong & Jenkins, 2000). In a rare act of sensitivity, Nike's ability to act morally and think past his immediate future has been more than amply repaid by Armstrong's successes on the professional cycling tour. While associating Nike with "moral sensitivity" is problematic without a sense of cynicism (Sage, 1999), it is possible to suggest that this global conglomerate may have acted with some sense of morality, which might indicate to other corporate organizations that challenging traditional values and beliefs in sponsorship might pay dividends.

Moral Sensitivity and Mimetic Behavior

A key to sustained sponsorship is the development of mimetic behavior by sponsoring organizations that favors specific sports and athletes (Shaw & Amis, 2001). If mimetic pressures are to be influenced by a long-term framework of moral sensitivity, then it is important that the global sponsoring community perceives this framework to be of benefit to them. Initially, this may seem to be a difficult hurdle to overcome, as businesses may be wary of working with sports or athletes that may be perceived as minority or "also rans." There are, however, some signs within recent sponsorship agreements, which suggest that there may be some move towards more morally sensitive sponsorship. In their study regarding companies' interests in sponsoring charities, Bednall, Walker, Curl and LeRoy (2001) suggest that sponsors such as German car manufacturers BMW are beginning to recognize benefits by associating their products with charities. Bednall et al. (2001) argue that the benefits to the sponsoring company include access to a diverse customer base, the potential for the company to be viewed as a good corporate citizen, and impress staff and customers; "there was also some acceptance that [the firm] had a duty to support community organizations" (p. 177). Finally, and importantly regarding mimetic pressures, companies who were contemplating morally sensitive sponsorships were swayed by mimetic pressures. Bednall et al. (2001) found that "if competitors supported a particular [sponsorship] relationship ... the reporting business was more likely to be doing so" (p. 178). If this is the case, then if a small number of global sponsors are willing to take a risk and engage in moral sensitivity, others may follow, thus impacting the global sponsorship market.

Moral sensitivity is not only a one-way relationship. Sports and athletes who are struggling to find sponsorship may be able to encourage mimetic behaviour, which has positive benefits for them, by approaching a number of sponsors and indicating possible partnership links. For example, the National Collegiate Athletic Association's (NCAA) Big South Conference has developed a sponsorship package linking eight sponsors who previously worked in competition with each other (IEG, 2001). In developing this partnership, the sponsors have developed additional links and agreements that are not related to the initial Big South sponsorship deal. It is possible that some struggling minority sports and athletes may be able to develop this scenario for their own use: why not raise the profile of sponsors and encourage the development of mimetic pressures, which benefit the "have nots," by encouraging such partnership sponsorship arrangements? Similar moves in which athletes manipulate sponsors might also ensure that the power relations in sponsorship deals shift towards sponsees. This would represent another challenge to, and possible change within, the global sponsorship market.

Media

For athletes and sports that are in the minority, the inability to attract media presence is a significant deterrent to gaining sponsorship (Personal Communication, May 8, 2003; Personal Communication, April 30, 2003). Yet, even with this seemingly substantial barrier to sponsors who might otherwise engage in morally sensitive sponsorship, there is some hope that recent changes in global TV coverage may be beneficial. First, it is timely that new TV channels, devoted to covering traditionally underrepresented sports are developing quickly in the digital TV age (Burke, 2003). For those organizations that have the courage to sponsor less well-known athletes and sports, access by these new channels to at least 40 million homes in the USA alone (Burke, 2003) represents the potential exposure of their products and return on sponsorship via the elixir of marketing – media coverage.

Second, while not all countries have the development of TV markets that are noted in the USA, there is the potential to work towards increased media coverage for the "have nots." In smaller markets improved, proactive communication by sports' governing bodies with media organizations may lead to increased TV, newspaper and/or radio coverage for previously marginalized sports. For example, the NZ Black Ferns, who have traditionally lost out on sponsorship because of a low media presence, played two international games as "curtain raisers" for televised men's games in the 2003 season (New Zealand Rugby Union, 2003). This move by NZRU indicated that the door is opening for an opportunity for a commercial sponsor to investigate the possibility of an agreement with players from this successful side. As the Canadian rugby example indicated, there are potential benefits to sponsoring marginalized sports, and with the extra coverage afforded by NZRU, sponsors may gain yet more from sponsoring the world champion Black Ferns.

It is possible to suggest that with the development of TV channels in populous countries like the USA and the UK (Extra BBC Channels, September 30, 2004), and more far-sighted vision from powerful national governing bodies of sport, the media may open up for marginalized sports and athletes, and thus encourage global sponsors to engage in sponsorship. These changes may, however, be considered to be risky and dismissed by some short-termist decision-makers. Yet Bauman (2001) argues that individuals and decision-makers are never truly engaging in morally sensitive behavior unless there is some element of risk. By managing and working through the potential risk of sponsoring a minority sport, then a just end may be achieved through a morally sensitive process. This process includes questioning global sponsoring companies and encouraging them not to hide behind the traditional, commercial and often profit-driven conventions of traditional sponsorship. In the penultimate section I propose some long-term benefits for those companies who do engage in morally sensitive sponsorship.

What about the Long Term? Investment in Ethical Companies

Imagine for a moment that a good number of sponsoring companies decided to take a risk and invest in minority, underfunded, yet successful athletes and sports. While the athletes would undoubtedly be thrilled (Goff, 2002) at having financial worries alleviated, what would it mean for the sponsors' long-term return on their investment? This is, without doubt, a question that needs to be addressed before any but the most courageous potential sponsor would make such an investment. Equally, it is one whose answers are hard to find and can only be alluded to by making educated forecasts based on current methods of evaluation (see Meenaghan in this volume).

So, if a company does take the plunge and decide to invest with moral sensitivity, will they see financial return? There is a varied and wide debate over the returns to "ethical" companies and those who do not focus on ethical investment. Some researchers suggest that, while many consumers would like to consider themselves "ethical," when the choice comes down to fashion (do you buy a sneaker from a multinational who has been accused of sweatshop practices or a much less fashionable, or possibly less comfortable shoe from an ethical provider?) or cost (do you buy coffee beans from an ethical trade organization that may cost more than those from an allegedly unethical producer in your supermarket?) then consumers tend to opt for the less ethically driven company (Carrigan & Attalla, 2001). In the case of moral sensitivity, is it likely that a consumer would change their spending habits just because a company has illustrated its desire to sponsor an unheard-of athlete? For some researchers, possibly not (Carrigan & Attalla, 2001).

Yet others suggest that ethics do matter, particularly to higher income groups (Strong, 1996). If global sponsoring organizations can persuade higher income consumers that their purchase will support an investment based on moral sensitivity then financial reward could be achieved. Indeed, a recent report in New Zealand suggests that 62% of New Zealanders had bought a product or service because of its links with a good cause or charity (AC Nielsen, 2004). More significantly, however, 57% suggested that they would "buy products or services which were more expensive than similar products" if they were linked to a social cause (AC Nielsen, 2004, p. 1). It was also suggested that similar trends and interest in social responsibility were evident internationally, in countries such as the UK and Australia. It is therefore possible to argue consumers are becoming more aware of the power of their spending and the implications for businesses that act with a degree of social responsibility, a trend that global sport sponsors should be aware of and act upon.

Further, many investors and consumers are jittery after the collapse of corporations such as Enron (Harrigan, 2002) and wish to see that their investment and consumer dollars are going towards ethical ends. Companies who sponsor with moral sensitivity can manipulate these market nerves to their own ends in order to encourage "ethical investors" to invest in them. Finally, it has also been argued that not only does the consumer benefit and have greater choice from morally sensitive actions but also employees (Lantos, 2002). It is possible to invest strategically but with an eye to ethical decision-making that may not only have financial reward but also contribute to the 'feel good' factor of a company's employees (Lantos, 2002).

Conclusion

In this chapter, I have outlined how the pursuit of a conventional "fit" between global sponsors and their sponsees has created a vast gulf between the "haves" and the "have nots." I have attempted to challenge some of the traditional thinking regarding a "good fit" and suggested that there are practical ways in which this imbalance can be addressed. The contribution of this chapter to the global sport sponsorship literature is to argue that an alternative to traditional approaches to sponsorship is possible. Specifically, it is possible to use social theorists, such as Bauman (1990, 2001), to frame an alternative to the current global sponsorship status quo. Furthermore, I have highlighted the opportunity for global sponsors to learn from the actions of companies such as Adecco and LandLink and act in a morally sensitive manner.

When such actions seem too risky, it is possible to work with that risk to make change. To engage in moral sensitivity requires an ability not only to challenge comfortable assumptions but also act upon the risks that may be thrown up by those challenges. In an industry that is notoriously conservative, such action may appear daunting. By taking small, experimental steps towards change, rather than trying to make sweeping changes, it may be possible to alter the current status quo within global sport sponsorship. Further, global sponsors may be able to take advantage of changes to media coverage, and consumer tastes towards ethical companies. In the long run, taking advantage of these changes may lead to greater financial gain than a process of exchange alone may offer.

If managers' sense of moral sensitivity is weak, then it is hoped that this chapter may have presented some alternative reasons that global sport sponsors might wish to maintain the momentum that some have started with a morally sensitive intention. If more equitable distribution of global sponsorship dollars is to occur, then it is the duty of sport managers and sponsoring organizations to consider the various alternatives that are presented here, and elsewhere in this book, as they work towards developing such agreements.

References

AC Nielsen (2004) "The Proof is in the Numbers … Groundbreaking Social Responsibility Research," available at www.acnielsen.co.nz/news/asp?newsID=339.

Adecco (2002) "Sporting Values: A Selection of Adecco Sponsorships around the World," available at http://www.adecco.com/channels/adecco/press+office/sponsorships+and+partnerships1.asp.

Amis, J., Pant, N. and Slack, T. (1997) "A Resource Based View of Sponsorship," *Journal of Sport Management*, 11: 80–96.

Amis, J. Slack, T. and Berrett, T. (1999) "Sport Sponsorship as a Distinctive Competence," *European Journal of Marketing*, 33: 250–271.

Armstrong, L. and Jenkins, S. (2000) *It's not About the Bike. My Journey Back to Life*, NSW: Allen and Unwin.

Australian Baseball (January, 2002) "Australian Team Wins Gold in 2002 Women's World Baseball Series," available at http://www.isport.com.au/baseball/wmnsopen/index.cgi?E=htstart&PT=ni&Y=2002&nd=3–01–03&newsID=wmnsopen&newsClub=AA&seq=1.

Australian Baseball (January 2003) "Australia Wins Gold," available at http://www.isport.com.au/baseball/wmnsopen/index.cgi?E=htstart&PT=ni&Y=2002&nd=3–01–03&newsID=wmnsopen&newsClub=AA&seq=1.

Bauman, Z. (1990) *Thinking Sociologically*, Oxford: Basil Blackwell.

Bauman, Z. (2001) *Conversations with Zygmunt Bauman/Zygmunt Bauman and Keith Tester*, Cambridge: Polity Press.

Becker-Olsen, K. and Simmons, C. J. (2002) "When do Social Sponsorships Enhance or Dilute Equity? Fit, Message Source, and the Persistence of Effects," *Advances in Consumer Research*, 29: 287–289.

Bednall, B., Walker, I., Curl, D. and LeRoy, H. (2001) "Business Support Approaches for Charities and Other Nonprofits," *International Journal of Nonprofit and Voluntary Sector Marketing*, 6: 172–187.

Berrett, T. and Slack, T. (2001) "A Framework for the Analysis of Strategic Approaches Employed by Non-profit Sport Organisations in Seeking Corporate Sponsorship," *Sport Management Review*, 4: 21–45.

Burke, M. (March 17, 2003) "For the Love of the Game," *Forbes Magazine*, available at http://www.forbes.com/forbes/2003/0317/058.html.

Carrigan, M. and Attalla, A. (2001) "The Myth of the Ethical Consumer – Do Ethics Matter in Purchase Behaviour?," *Journal of Consumer Marketing*, 18: 560–578.

Cronin, C. (2003) "Colombian Ban on Shirt Celebration," *RTE Sports*, available at http://www.rte.ie/sport/2003/0401/soccer.shirts.html.

DiMaggio, P. and Powell, W. (1983) "The Iron Cage Revisited: Institutional Isomorphism and Collective Rationality in Organizational Fields," *American Sociological Review*, 48: 147–160.

Elliot, S. (2001) "A Natural Marketing Alliance Finally takes some Tentative Steps: Gays and Sports," *The New York Times*, July 9.

Extra BBC Channels (September 30, 2004) available at http://www.bbc.co.uk/digital/.

Goff, A. (2002) "Canada Women Land Sponsor," *Goff on Rugby*, available at http://www.goffonrugby.com/Articles/canwomspons032202.htm.

Harrigan, M. (2002) "Wind of Change," *Guardian Newspaper*, available at http://money.guardian.co.uk/ethicalmoney/story/0,1356,787541,00.html.

Henderson, J. (2000) "Sex and the Singles Women," *Observer Sport Monthly*: 18–23.

IEG (December 24, 2001) "Eight Sponsors are Better than Two, Property Decides," *IEG Sponsorship Report*.

Lantos, G. P. (2002) "The Ethicality of Altruistic Corporate Responsibility," *Journal of Consumer Marketing*, 19: 205–230.

Ligerakis, M. (October, 2002) "Tiger Ticks TAG as Latest Sponsorship Partner," *B&T Marketing and Media*, http://www.bandt.com.au/articles/d7/0c0116d7.asp.

Martin, J. (2001) *Organizational Culture: Mapping the Terrain*, Thousand Oaks, CA: Sage.

McDonald, M. G. (2000) "The Marketing of the Women's National Basketball Association and the Making of Postfeminism," *International Review for the Sociology of Sport*, 35: 35–47.

Meenaghan, T. (1991) "The Role of Sponsorship in the Marketing Communications Mix," *International Journal of Advertising*, 10: 35–47.

New Zealand Rugby Union (May 9, 2003) "Black Ferns' Home Tests Confirmed," *New Zealand Rugby Union*, available at http://www.nzrugby.com/news/stories/may0903_02.asp.

Plaskitt, S. (May 6, 2003) "ANZ Birdies its Golf Sponsorship," *B&T Marketing Media*, available at http://www.bandt.com.au/articles/19/0c013d19.asp.

Rao, S. (July, 2001) "Corporate Sponsorship of Women's Sport. The Hard Sell," *Australian Home Page*, available at http://www.aushomepage.com.au/Article/450/.

Reuters (1997) "Liverpool Footballer Fined for Supporting Dockers," *Labour net*, available at www.labournet.net/docks2/9703/fowler.htm.

Sage, G. H. (1999) "Justice do it! The Nike Transnational Advocacy Network: Organization, Collective Actions, and Outcomes," *Sociology of Sport Journal*, 16: 206–235.

Shaw, S. and Amis, J. (2001) "Image and Investment: Sponsorship of Women's Sports," *Journal of Sport Management*, 15: 221–248.

Strong, C. (1996) "Features Contributing to the Growth of Ethical Consumerism – A Preliminary Investigation," *Marketing Intelligence and Planning*, 14: 5–13.

"The Celebrity 100" (June 19, 2003) *Forbes Magazine*, available at http://www.forbes.com/static_html/celebs/2003/index.shtml.

Theberge, N. (1991) "A Content Analysis of Print Media Coverage of Gender, Women and Physical Activity," *Journal of Applied Sport Psychology*, 3: 36–48.

"Wayne Rooney's Romps could Cost him £30 million in Ad Revenues" (September 28, 2004) available at http://news.newkerala.com/sports-news-india/index.php?action=fullnews&id=9666.

15

Gay Games or Gay Olympics?

Corporate sponsorship issues

Helen Jefferson Lenskyj

The Gay Games (GG), originally called the Gay Olympic Games, were first held in San Francisco in 1982. A sporting and cultural celebration organized by and for gay and lesbian people on the principles of inclusion, participation and community-building, the Gay Games welcome "all people without regard to their sexual orientation, gender, race, religion, nationality, ethnic origin, political belief(s), athletic/artistic ability, age, or health status" (Federation, 2003). Gender parity in committee structures has been an overriding principle from the outset.

The overall purpose of the GG was "to foster and augment the self-respect of lesbians and gay men ... and to engender respect and understanding from the non-gay world" (Federation, 1997a).[1] In the last twenty years, the GG have grown into an international sports spectacle and business enterprise, with more than twenty core sporting events, fierce competition between bid cities, budgets exceeding US$7 million, and more participants than most Olympic Games.

In the early 1980s, liberal gay and lesbian sports activists in the United States and Canada tended to focus on policy and legislative change, with the goal of reforming mainstream sport to make it more welcoming towards gay and lesbian people (Lenskyj, 2003). The stated goal of GG pioneers, however, was potentially more radical: An alternative, inclusive model of sporting competition, with participation and personal bests valued more highly than qualifying trials and international records. But, as the following discussion will reveal, key components of the GG, rather than pioneering radical alternatives, tend to emulate the Olympic industry model – that is, a media spectacle built on multinational sponsorships (see Lenskyj, 2000; 2002).

For their part, corporate sponsors recognized that these games, like other global multi-sport events, could deliver significant numbers of consumers to their advertising campaigns. Although television coverage has until recently been minimal, GG participants and spectators accounted for significant numbers of potential buyers who were accessible to advertisers before, during and after the event. Member groups of the Gay Games Federation, together with local gay and lesbian sport groups affiliated with these national organizations, formed a global network of gay men and lesbians committed to sport. Companies could readily tap this consumer base through advertising in gay and lesbian magazines, sport newsletters and websites, as well as through their highly visible logos at sporting events. Moreover, a sizable percentage of this niche market – white, middle-class gay men living in the United States, Canada, Europe and Australia – had substantial disposable incomes, as well as a demonstrated interest in fitness and personal appearance.

Gay Games: In the Beginning

The first two GG, held in San Francisco in 1982 and 1986, were organized by San Francisco Arts & Athletics, a group founded by Tom Waddell in 1981 and, significantly, a group not identifiable by name as lesbian or gay. By 1989, this organization had become the Federation of Gay Games – a name that still omitted the word *lesbian* – and included board members from countries outside North America.

In the homophobic climate of American sport in the 1980s, the group's use of the word *Olympic* (or more accurately, *Olympic* preceded by *gay*) met with Olympic industry opposition from the outset. GG organizers engaged in a four-year court battle against the United States Olympic Committee (USOC) for the right to call the event the Gay *Olympic* Games – this despite the fact that similar organizations such as the Special Olympics and the Police Olympics were using the "O" word in their names without incident (Booth & Tatz, 1997).

In the course of this struggle, Sara Lewinstein, Waddell's partner, told the press, "The perception has been created that somehow gays hate the Olympics … we love the Olympics. We just don't like the dumb bureaucrats who run the USOC" (Waddell & Schaap, 1996, p. 234). Apart from the problem of sweeping generalizations about gay and lesbian people's alleged "love" of the Olympics, GG history has shown continued ambivalence on this issue: On the one hand, GG organizers' liberal embrace of the Olympic model, and, on the other, their radical call for alternative visions of sporting participation and competition.

The Metropolitan Vancouver Athletic/Arts Association (MVAAA), Canada, was the first group outside the United States to host the event, which attracted over 7,000 athletes to the 1990 GG. Writing in the Toronto lesbian and gay publication *Rites*, Ann Vespry and Shawn Syms were critical of the MVAAA's "assimilationist" approach to advertising. They claimed that its "straight-looking, straight-acting" board members, its "puritan image," and the omission of words like *gay* or *queer* from advertising in the mainstream media rendered lesbian and gay people invisible. The fact that the MVAAA faced virulent right-wing opposition may have accounted for this approach, but it could be argued that the GG principle of inclusion required, at the very least, unequivocal solidarity with openly lesbian and gay members of the community, including the large numbers who rejected the option of "passing" as heterosexual (Syms, 1990; Vespry, 1990). Indeed, the Federation website, gaygames.com, presents this message: "While, individually, participants celebrate personal achievement, collectively, we experience the solidarity of community and celebrate the diversity and scope of the gay, lesbian, bisexual and transgender community" (Federation, 2003).

Statements made by GG founder Tom Waddell, a former Olympic decathlete, demonstrated emerging issues in GG development:

> The message of these games goes beyond validating our culture. They were conceived as a new idea in the meaning of sport based on inclusion rather than exclusion. (Waddell cited in Coe, 1986, p. 7)

> To do one's personal best is the ultimate level of all human achievement. (Waddell cited in Forzley & Hughes, 1990, p. 12)

> This event is becoming an important opportunity for gay men and women all over the world to demonstrate that our character has a wide and varied range... It is an opportunity to expand beyond a falsely tainted image. It is an opportunity to show that gay men and women, like all other responsible citizens of the United States, participate in the same ideal. (Waddell & Schaap, 1996, p. 147)

Waddell's early ideas on lesbian and gay community development appeared in an interview with sport sociologist Mike Messner in a pro-feminist men's magazine (Messner, 1984). It appeared that Waddell directed his citizenship arguments primarily towards prospective financial supporters of the GG, and these ideas were taken up by mainstream commentators like *Sports Illustrated* journalist Dick Schaap, who compiled Waddell's 1996 biography (Waddell & Schaap, 1996). As the GG evolved, it became clear that there was an underlying tension between the liberal goal of good citizenship and sportsmanship and the more radical goal of transforming lesbian and gay communities, and lesbian and gay sports.

While Messner was responsive to Waddell's vision of an exemplary community, journalists like Schaap tended to be more interested in the Games' function of challenging "homosexual stereotypes" (Schaap, 1987; Waddell & Schaap, 1996). In the extensive gay and lesbian media coverage, official GG reports and photojournals, and athletes' first person accounts, there was a clear emphasis on using mainstream (heterosexual) sporting practices to counter homophobic stereotypes and to achieve gay and lesbian visibility and empowerment. Lesbian and gay print journalists, as well as their supportive non-gay counterparts, focused on hetero-normalizing the GG and GG participants. There was consistent emphasis on similarity rather than difference: lesbian and gay athletes can break (heterosexual) records, can produce the biggest and best sporting spectacle in the world, and can organize federation-sanctioned sporting competitions.

In *The Story of Gay Games II*, Roy Coe described them as "an important demonstration of our love for each other and our presence in the world community. Our statement as a minority group was clearly made through the wonderful spirit of camaraderie and friendly competition" (Coe, 1986, p. 7). And, in the 1990 photojournal of Gay Games III, the editors stated that they symbolized "for thousands of gay men and women one more step along the road of self-discovery ... without ever having to apologize for their existence, or even having to suffer the strain of maintaining an appearance alien to their very nature" (Forzley &

Hughes, 1990, p. 110). These liberal notions of individual self-discovery and self-expression overlooked the multiple oppressions suffered by minority members of lesbian and gay communities. Furthermore, simply bringing together diverse groups of gay and lesbian people in sport did not in itself guarantee "love for each other," and it was naive to hope that the spirit of the GG would transcend racism, sexism, classism and other entrenched forms of discrimination that divided sexual minority communities.

In 1994, Gay Games IV brought about 11,000 athletes from 45 countries to New York to a celebration that included the twenty-fifth anniversary of Stonewall, and injected more than US$300 million into the local economy (Federation, 2000). This was the first time that there had been competition among bid cities, with the Federation choosing New York over Sydney, and, for the 1998 GG, there were three bid cities. By 1997, the annual general meeting had to be extended by one day in order to hear presentations from the five cities competing for the 2002 GG. Sydney, making its third attempt, was finally successful in this round. The Federation subsequently decided to limit the number of bidding cities to four because of the time and money involved.

By the end of the decade, the bid process was increasingly resembling the Olympic model. An initial deposit of US$5,000 was required with letters of intent, and the four finalists were each charged US$7,500. Sydney organizers were initially expected to pay the Federation a licensing fee of US$1 million (in contrast to New York's US$55,000 just twelve years earlier) but eventually managed to renegotiate the payment schedule and to reduce the fee to a mere US$695,000 (Boson, 1997b; McQuarrie, 1998). The Federation's explanation for increasing costs included members' on-site visits to bid city finalists, and the expenses incurred in copying and distributing bid books and holding meetings for bid cities' multimedia presentations (Federation, 2000).

The early growth in participation and the economic boost continued for Gay Games V in Amsterdam, the first to be held off North American shores. Since travel costs were prohibitive for many overseas GG participants, the Amsterdam '98 Organizing Committee, supported by the Dutch Government, offered financial assistance to forty-seven developing countries, with priority given to women and to those active in human rights or gay and lesbian emancipation. Sydney 2002 organizing committee included Asia/Pacific, South America and Southern Africa in its outreach program, and steps were taken in Bangkok and Hong Kong to help develop teams for Amsterdam '98 (Wardell, 1997). However, at least one critic (Clark, 1997) claimed that, before Amsterdam, the Federation and its 65% North American membership paid little attention to facilitating the overseas travel of the 20% of participants who had to fly to the United States or Canada to attend the GG.

Mainstreaming the Gay Games?

Developments in AIDS activism and fund-raising in the 1980s and early 1990s, when there were ongoing debates in lesbian and gay communities about the "ownership" of AIDS, are relevant to this discussion. Some lesbians and gay men demanded recognition from non-gay communities for their longstanding record of activism, education and care-giving in the struggle to deal with the epidemic, and were justifiably proud of the success of grassroots safer sex campaigns, and the changing sexual practices of significant numbers of gay men (Myers, 1993). However, given the pressing need for funds for AIDS research, education and medical services, they also recognized that support from governments and non-gay communities was critical. This process of mainstreaming AIDS philanthropy inevitably called for the mainstreaming of the disease (Stratton, 1991). In other words, fundraising in privileged, white, heterosexual circles was more effective when the threat to this population was stressed. But while slogans like "AIDS is an equal opportunity disease" de-emphasized the gay male connection, they also decontextualized and depoliticized the epidemic. In other words, they conveyed the false idea that a gay man's experience living with HIV or AIDS would be the same as that of a heterosexual person in North America.

This is not to suggest that attempts to hetero-normalize gay and lesbian sports are in any way as significant or as serious as AIDS-related fundraising initiatives aimed at enlarging the donor base. Rather, the purpose in drawing parallels is to identify the pitfalls of calling upon some utopian idea of shared humanity when a radical social analysis demands that oppression, discrimination and prejudice be named and challenged.

Despite the philosophical stance underlying their statement of purpose, there is ample evidence that, since their inception, the GG have used the Olympics as a template for their organization and marketing. In addition to the escalating costs involved with bid city selection procedures, discussed earlier, there were parallels in a number of other areas. They operated on a four-year cycle (coinciding with the Winter Olympics), opening and closing ceremonies were held, winners were named, medals were awarded in podium ceremonies, records were kept, increasing numbers of events were sanctioned by mainstream international federations, and corporate sponsors were wooed and rewarded with exclusive marketing rights. Like organizers of other hallmark sporting events, GG committees identified specific categories of corporate sponsors that were needed: running shoes, sportswear, bottled water, energy drinks, information technology, airlines, cellular phones, and so on. In other words, the model "gay consumer" was not very different from his/her counterpart in Olympic industry advertising.

With the advent of the "Gay Olympics," talented athletes whose careers had suffered because of institutionalized homophobia in mainstream sport now had their own "Olympics." Numerous high-profile GG supporters and organizers were mainstream sporting celebrities and/or former Olympic athletes, including Tom Waddell, Betty Baxter, Bruce Hayes, Martina Navratilova and Greg Louganis. Biographies of Federation representatives and bid committee members usually included their *competitive* sporting credentials (except for those organizing the Cultural Festival), and the individualistic liberal notion of gay and lesbian celebrities as "role models" appeared to hold sway with little or no critique of its limitations.

Another aspect of mainstreaming relates to the increased competition between bid cities, and pressure on gay and lesbian media to limit any negative commentary during the bid process. In this respect, members of GG bid committees followed some of the worst practices of the Olympic industry (Booth & Tatz, 1994; Lenskyj, 2002, Chapter 1). Gay and lesbian media were expected, even instructed, to support the bid in terms of editorial content as well as value-in-kind contributions in the form of free advertising space or infomercials.

During and after Sydney's successful bid for the 2002 GG, the city's gay and lesbian newspaper, the *Sydney Star Observer*, published mostly positive articles on the topic, and encountered criticism from Team Sydney when it didn't, or when the timing of a particular article didn't suit organizers' purposes. The *Star's* sport reporter, Mary Boson, continued to write critical pieces that probed some of the bigger political issues behind fundraising, sponsorships, niche marketing and so on (Boson, 1997a, 1997b, 1997c, 1998a, 1998b). Her contributions, I would argue, exemplified the kind of healthy debate that lesbian and gay publications have a responsibility to foster. However, community newspapers also rely on advertisers' dollars for their continued existence, and it is possible that editorial decisions are influenced by this reality.

An unnecessary level of secrecy surrounding bids – a long-standing feature of the Olympics – also began to appear in GG contexts. For example, my attempts to contact Team Sydney representatives to obtain a copy of their bid for research purposes in June 1997 were met with considerable suspicion. I was told that since two Canadian cities were competing and since I was a researcher from Canada, I could not expect to be given any inside information, despite my assurances that I had no formal involvement with Team Toronto or the Federation. Moreover, these conversations took place three months after the deadline for bid submissions, and so it was impossible for any information I received to have any bearing on the outcome of the vote.

Gay Games as Business

Since the early 1980s, two related trends have served to entrench the status of the GG as a global business enterprise: the lesbian and gay "consumer revolution" and the exponential growth of the GG themselves.

The first pattern in mainstream advertising grew out of increasing recognition that white, middle class, gay men constituted a lucrative niche market. Members of this group had considerable disposable income and leisure time, demonstrated brand loyalty, high interest in health and fitness and frequent use of gyms and sports facilities (Booth & Tatz, 1997; Leblanc, 1997; Lukinball, 1995; Pitts, 1988–89, 1998b, 1998c; Pronger, 1990). These factors promoted mainstream as well as gay and lesbian perceptions of the last four Gay Games as positive influences on the local economy and tourism.

There was ample evidence of the view of the GG as good for business in Sydney, where even the liberal daily newspaper, the *Sydney Morning Herald*, greeted the announcement of Sydney's win with the headlines like "We win – and it will be worth millions" and "Pink Olympics could earn US$80m" (Bernoth, 1997; Delvecchio, 1997). The reference to "we" rather than "they" suggests a sense of heterosexual ownership of these Games, at least as a source of tourist dollars, a view that was supported by earlier *Herald* articles on the bid (e.g. Fitzsimons, 1997). The *Herald's* inclusion of a Gay and Lesbian Mardi Gras Festival Supplement for the first time in 1998 provides further evidence of its positive view of lesbian and gay tourism, which since 1991 had been vigorously promoted by the Australian Gay and Lesbian Tourism Association. While Toronto bid representatives reported some positive coverage in local newspapers and radio, mainstream interest in gay and lesbian tourism did not approach the Sydney level.

Some earlier proponents of the "gay and lesbian consumer revolution," as Lukinball (1995) called it, claimed that while niche marketing to gays and lesbians rarely produced backlash from homophobic heterosexual consumers, companies that alienated gay and lesbian customers were likely to become targets of well-organized boycotts. The Colorado tourism industry's US$26 million loss following anti-gay legislation in 1996 provided a graphic example (Baker, Strub & Henning, 1995; Leblanc, 1997). However, these assertions pre-dated more recent examples of successful rightwing backlash, such as the Southern Baptist Convention's boycott of Disneyland after that company introduced same-sex employee benefits, and right-wing advertisers' withdrawal from the television series "Ellen" after the main character/actor came out as lesbian. Clearly, gay-oriented advertising is a two-edged sword from a corporate perspective.

On the issue of niche marketing, some commentators – supportive as well as hostile – have fallen into the trap of viewing "the gay and lesbian market" as a group undifferentiated by gender, socioeconomic status, race/ethnicity or ability. Warnings that mainstream failure to recognize gay and lesbian markets would mean at least a 10% loss (e.g. Booth & Tatz, 1997; Lukinball, 1995) were based on false assumptions that every gay or lesbian consumer has the same purchasing power. A much-quoted 1988 marketing survey of male readers of gay magazines, published in the *Wall Street Journal* to boost gay niche marketing, was put to good use by the right-wing American Family Association. They claimed that this survey supported their argument that "homosexuals are one of the most affluent groups in America" and therefore not deserving of high levels of federal spending on AIDS research and prevention (Homosexuality, 1998). In the same vein, the Community and Family Rights Council of Hobart (Australia), claimed that "homosexuals as a class seem to be economically, socially and politically successful, according to their own publicity, and do not qualify for [anti-discrimination] protection" (quoted in Boson, 1997c).

Surveys of specific subgroups may well have predictive power for white, middle-class, healthy gay men in urban centers (e.g. Lukinball, 1995) but sweeping generalizations about "the gay and lesbian market" fail to take socially disadvantaged subgroups into account. For example, the unspecified "gay and lesbian consumer" touted in various Sydney 2002 publications and on their website was a person who earned more than the "average" Australian, and spent more on alcohol, books, magazines, restaurant meals, entertainment and overseas travel than the average consumer. Apparently failing to see the possible negative consequences, it boasted that this typical gay/lesbian consumer spent over $A42 per week on alcohol, a statistic that could readily be used by rightwing groups to support arguments of affluence and/or decadence. Clearly, this consumer was not a gay man living with HIV/AIDS or other disability, or an unemployed or Indigenous gay man, or a lesbian of any ethnic background, given the well-documented gender differences in earnings.

Furthermore, even if the "double income no kids" description fitted some gay and lesbian couples, the authors of *Cracking the Corporate Closet* correctly pointed out that "many gay people resent the notion that they are somehow more valuable to society because they have a lot of money to spend" (Baker, Strub & Henning, 1995, p. 9). They also noted, perhaps redundantly, that corporate advertising to gay and lesbian consumers was motivated more by the profit than by any concern for equal rights (p. 11).

In view of daily experiences of heterosexist and homophobic harassment and discrimination, it is not surprising to find that some middle-class gays and lesbians are pleased to be considered a legitimate market and to avail themselves of goods and services designed to meet their specific consumer needs. On the topic of brand loyalty and GG sponsorships, Brenda Pitts's research demonstrated that "as an oppressed population slowly gaining recognition and acceptance, lesbian and gay people seems to be much more appreciative of support and will reward it with loyalty" (Pitts, 1998a). However, as contributors to the anthology *HomoEconomics* argued, the social and economic success of some privileged gay and lesbian people serves capitalism remarkably well, but has a deadening effect on the radical political activism that used to characterize American lesbian and gay communities (Gluckman & Reed, 1997). Therefore, a lesbian/gay group operating on the principle of inclusion, such a GG bid or organizing committee, should acknowledge the problem of erasure of culturally and/or economically disadvantaged minorities that stems from the mainstream marketing notion of "*the* gay and lesbian consumer." Similarly, they should pay more than lip service to the goal of outreach to these disadvantaged groups.

The notion of gay and lesbian sport as a new and lucrative marketing vehicle was exemplified in the sales pitch to corporate sponsors developed by the (American) Gay and Lesbian Athletics Foundation prior to its first conference, held at Harvard University in March 2003. Positioning itself unproblematically and uncritically within the mainstream US$213 million sports industry, this organization called for sponsors to seize the opportunity to market their products to "a loyal 'influencer' base." These consumers, it was claimed, are "highly educated with disposable income ... the majority with advanced degrees ... and a pre-disposition to spend on products from companies they feel understand them" (gayconference.org). The pre-registration figures showed 77% male attendance; 30% earned over US$85,000, and 50% made sports purchases at least monthly – hardly a representative sample of gay and lesbian consumers. The inclusion of sports technology and fashion shows on the conference program further attests to the presumed interests of this audience.

There is evidence that many GG organizers are increasingly influenced by the gay and lesbian "consumer revolution" and hence are viewing the Games primarily as business. Sydney 2002, for example, was the first bid team to prepare an economic impact statement, which estimated a flow of $A60–75 million into the New South Wales economy (Sydney 2002, 1997c); its rationale was to persuade the state government to fund both the bid and the Games (Boson, 1997c). The NSW sports minister, cited in a newspaper report, subsequently inflated the economic impact figure to $A100 million (Bernoth, 1997).

The significant growth in GG participation has necessitated increases in paid staff, higher administrative and advertising costs, and more attention to public liability and equipment insurance. I would argue, as some others have – for example, Joe Clark (1994) and Brian Pronger (quoted in Clark, 1994) – that market forces are threatening the underlying philosophy as well as actual sporting practices of the Games. The increased number of events sanctioned (approved for record-keeping purposes) by international federations has been justified on the grounds that the "ready-made pool of officials" and international rules enhanced safety and reduce liability (Clark, 1994). And, while the Federation's 1997 guidelines for Gay Games VI bids gave priority to the Fundamental Principle of Inclusion, they also stated that sports should be sanctioned if the Federation considered it important for safety or liability reasons (Federation Sports Committee, 1997b).

Sydney 2002 representatives agreed that increased knowledge of event management would increase safety and decrease liability, and their plans for volunteer training included a reciprocal arrangement with the organizing committee for Sydney 2000 to enable GG 2002 volunteers to benefit from prior training and experience in the Olympic Games. Although this appeared financially and logistically sound, the Sydney 2000 volunteer training program had come under criticism for its excessive screening of applicants, which included "character tests" and checks on criminal records by state police (Lenskyj, 2002, pp. 117–120). This kind of volunteer training model did not appear compatible with the community empowerment emphasis of the GG movement, particularly since members of sexual minorities were more likely than heterosexuals to have been unfairly targeted by police.

The Bottom Line: Toronto and Sydney

In a community meeting prior to the Federation meeting in November 1997, Team Toronto representatives were unequivocal in framing the Games as "business." They spoke of the Board's primary role in building infrastructure as the business component; community participation would focus on "filling" the infrastructure. Sydney 2002 representatives whom I interviewed similarly viewed the business approach as a means to an end and noted the impracticality of mounting such an event without commercial sponsorship. Both groups viewed "business consciousness" and fiscal responsibility to partners and sponsors as essential, but at the same time they maintained that the Games were "first and foremost" a gay and lesbian community event.

The Sydney budget for the five-year preparation period 1998–2002 included salaries, consultant, accountant and legal fees, office costs, computers, insurance, travel, and conferences, for a total of US$2.312 million in administration, while in the Toronto budget this figure was over US$3 million. Sydney spent approximately US$150,000 on its bid; US$56,000 was contributed by the Special Events Unit, Tourism New South Wales, and the NSW Minister for Transport and Tourism (Australian Labor Party) was present at the launch of the bid in March 1997. At the federal level, the bid was registered with the Australian Sports Foundation, thereby enabling corporate donations to be tax-deductible (*Under New Skies*, 1997).

Toronto's costs for the bid were lower, at approximately US$56,000, with an equal amount of value-in-kind donations. There was no government financial support for Team Toronto's bid, and the rightwing Ontario Premier's office belatedly endorsed it just days before the Federation meeting. The total cost of all five bids for the 2002 GG exceeded the budgets for the first two GG themselves (Boson, 1998b) – an indication of the growing tendency to emulate some of the worst features of the Olympics, most notably the expensive bid competition and the "gigantism" problem.

There were clear differences between Sydney's and Toronto's relative reliance on government, community and corporate funding (see Table 15.1). Team Toronto

Table 15.1 *Fundraising and sponsorships* *

	Toronto	Sydney
Corporate	$2,940,000	$563,000
Business partnerships (in kind)	$342,510	nil
Cultural subsidies	nil	$225,000
Government	nil	$1,125,000
Fundraising events	$441,000	$375,000
Community (private donors & small businesses)	$588,000	$188,000
Total	$4,311,510	$2,476,000

Sources: Sydney 2002 Bid Book, 1997a; Team Toronto Bid Book, 1997

Note: *There were no major differences between Sydney's and Toronto's projected figures in the remaining categories – registration fees, opening ceremonies and athletic events – and therefore these have not been included in the table.

organizers recognized the pressure on the "gay dollar" and hoped to attract three or four major corporate funders. Sydney had the advantage of supportive local and state governments, primed by twenty–year history of gay and lesbian tourism to Mardi Gras, the buildup to the Sydney 2000 Olympics, and the anticipated boost to the local economy (Delvecchio, 1997; Fitzsimons, 1997). The two-week Mardi Gras festival was estimated to provide about $A100 million to the New South Wales economy. A 1998 Mardi Gras economic impact statement found that international visitors spent on average about $A370 a day during a three-week visit. Mardi Gras attracts more than 5000 international and 7000 interstate visitors to Sydney. (Ironically, Mardi Gras itself went into receivership in early 2002 following record financial losses).

There were further significant differences between Sydney and Toronto: Projected income from closing ceremonies (US$1.125 million to US$617,400), cultural events (US$236,000 to US$91,875), and festivals and parties (US$638,000 to nil). These figures indicate that Sydney expected to generate about US$1.3 million more than Toronto from these three categories of non-sporting events, and hence, an extra US$1.3 million from the projected 25,000 interstate and overseas visitors as well as from the local gay and lesbian community (see Delvecchio, 1997). Almost US$3 million was to be generated from ticket sales, and, with Sydney's projections, this would amount to an average expenditure of US$100 per person (both residents and visitors) during the Games. A visitor from North America would already have paid at least US$1,500 for travel, with European tourists paying significantly more. Even for a Sydney participant with no travel costs, registration for one event, plus tickets, would amount to about US$200.

These figures shed a different light on the notion of "community" contributions. If Sydney area gay and lesbian communities were indeed overwhelmingly supportive of the GG, as the Bid Book asserts, the depth of their support would have been demonstrated in their (average) purchase of US$100 worth of tickets during the Games, and in their annual collective contribution of US$75,000 to fundraising events in the five years' leading up to the event. Although the Toronto budget did not rely as much as Sydney on ticket sales for non-sporting events, the projected community contribution to fund-raising was higher, with US$205,800 to be raised annually up to the year 2002. Team Toronto members, however, were aware of the pressure on the "gay dollar" in Toronto, where many gay and lesbian community groups were struggling for survival (Kealy, 1997), whereas Sydney 2002 members felt that the projections of community support were reasonable. However, the fact that the Sydney GG suffered ongoing financial problems, culminating in a financial crisis due to low ticket sales, suggests that gay and lesbian communities both domestically and internationally were not able to keep up the expected levels of support.

Bid committees for GG generally anticipate that local gay and lesbian sport organizations will be a major source of support. Toronto had twenty-five gay and/or lesbian sport and recreation organizations listed in its gay and lesbian newspaper, *Xtra*, in November, 1997, while the *Sydney Star Observer* listed forty, a difference partly attributable to relative populations. In both cases, the bid committees made contact with all relevant gay and non-gay state/provincial sports associations and were successful in gaining support from most of them. Of course, with the 1993 announcement that Sydney was the host of the 2000 Olympics, there was already widespread public interest in international sporting competition, and, more importantly, millions of dollars of taxpayers' money were earmarked for construction of state-of-the-art sporting facilities (Lenskyj, 2002).

In terms of lesbian and gay community support, Team Sydney had the advantage of having prepared two prior bids while this was Toronto's first attempt. Throughout most of the 1990s, Sydney's Mardi Gras celebrations included a major sport festival somewhere in Australia, and the Sydney Bid Book boasted that Team Sydney's hosting of the 24–event, ten-day sport festival in 1996 had attracted over 1,100 athletes. This and other Mardi Gras activities produced a number of community members with extensive experience in large event management. In Sydney, support was also extended by members of Womensport Australia, and Sydney 2002 board member Cathy Verry was invited to write a full-page article for this group's newsletter (Verry, 1998). There was no evidence of a similar level of support for Toronto's bid on the part of the Canadian national women's sport organization. Clearly, the Sydney team generated a high level of interest and support in both gay and non-gay circles.

What Price Politics?

In an insightful piece titled "Are we cheap dates?" *SSO* journalist Mary Boson identified the danger that lesbian and gay organizations such as Team Sydney were abandoning their social justice agendas in the rush to get government and corporate funding and to demonstrate the power of the "pink dollar" to the non-gay world (Boson, 1997c). It was particularly ironic to note that, in the lead-up to the 2000 Olympics, while Sydney-based anti-globalization protesters were targeting Olympic sponsors like Nike (for human rights infringements) and Coca-Cola (for poor environmental practices), Sydney GG organizers, despite their progressive image, were wooing the same kinds of multinationals as potential sponsors (Lenskyj, 2002, Chapter 7).

These were not, of course, new developments. New York's 1994 Gay Games, estimated to have brought over US$400 million into the city's economy, had AT&T (telephone company), Miller Beer and Continental Airlines among its sponsors. In an unprecedented coup, 1998 Amsterdam Gay Games organizers boasted that they had secured Kodak, Avis, Levi Strauss, Miller Beer and about forty other major companies, some national and some multinational, as corporate sponsors. In the case of Sydney 2002 Gay Games, Qantas Airlines, American Airlines, Hertz, Vodaphone (with mobile phone networks in twenty-eight countries over five continents), and Sheraton, Intercontinental and Novotel Hotels were among the major sponsors. Vodaphone's press release pointed out that sponsorship would give the company "significant branding impact with exposure to 4,000 Gay Games volunteers."

In similar developments in the United States, the first Gay Rugby Tournament, held in San Francisco in June 2002, included Nike, Guinness, Calistoga (bottled water) and Red Bull (energy drink) as its "major league sponsors." A Nike spokesperson was quoted as saying that it was not specifically targeting the gay "demographic" through rugby, but rather was focusing on sport-specific media for more efficient outreach to audiences. Other major companies sponsoring gay rugby, softball and hockey in the United States since 2001 included Galiano, Smirnoff, Miller Lite, Coors Light, Powerbar and United Airlines (Wilke, 2002). In 1991, Coors had the distinction of being the first company to use an openly gay athlete, Bruce Hayes (not coincidentally, an Olympic as well as a Gay Games medallist), in its print media campaign (Elliott, 2001).

Nike had also been named, unproblematically, as a potential corporate sponsor in Team Toronto's 2002 bid. A major sponsor of the 2000 Olympic Games in Sydney, Nike employed about 300,000 grossly exploited outworkers throughout Australasia, and labor practices in Nike's Asian sporting goods factories were well documented. By exporting work to Third World countries, Nike profited from cheap labor, a non-unionized workforce (predominantly women and children), minimal safety and environmental standards, repressive political climates, and favorable tax breaks (Klein, 2000; Lenskyj, 2002).

Screening Sponsors: Some Suggestions

The pioneering political efforts of a Toronto-based group, Workers Organizing Rainbow Coalition (WORC), could be used to good effect by GG organizers in their relationships with sponsors. WORC developed a Corporate Code of Conduct in 1998 at a time when the Toronto lesbian and gay communities were grappling with issues of corporate sponsorship of Pride Day events, including the parade, concerts, parties and beer gardens. The code recommended that potential sponsors be screened through a questionnaire about their business practices. They would be asked, for example, about their contributions to non-profit lesbian and gay community groups, their history of putting employment advertisements in the lesbian and gay press, their training of employees regarding the Ontario Human Rights Code, and the unionization of their workers. In an article on these debates in *Xtra* (Noorani, 1998), the Pride committee chair was quoted as saying that a boycott against a company would automatically disqualify it as a potential sponsor. This is a telling statement in view of Team Toronto's plan, just a few months earlier, to solicit the involvement of Nike, arguably the most boycotted sporting goods company in the world.

Conclusion

The GG are no longer a community-based, alternative sporting festival, and the issues discussed here reflect the tensions between their radical roots and their current liberal emphasis on staging an international sporting spectacle dependent on corporate dollars. Rather than conceptualizing the GG as a radical alternative to the Olympics, it is more accurate, given the evidence here, to position the GG on a spectrum of global, multi-sport events that rely on corporate sponsorships for their ongoing operation. The Olympics would occupy the "high end" of the spectrum in terms of corporatization, and the GG, the "low end."

It is possible, too, to conceptualize a spectrum of community-based gay and lesbian sport that offers a genuine alternative – for example, Toronto's lesbian Notso Amazon Softball League, which was financially self-sufficient and autonomous, with no links to corporate sponsors or mainstream sports governing bodies (Lenskyj, 2003, Chapter 6). GG organizers could avoid the worst features of corporatized global sport sponsorship with adequate government support, carefully screened corporate sponsorships, sensitivity to the already depleted "gay dollar," and an uncompromising stance on all the issues of inclusion, participation, accessibility and empowerment.

Notes

1. Although the Games are open to participants who are gay, lesbian, bisexual, transgendered and heterosexual, the terms most often used in reference to the GG community during the timeframe discussed here are "gay and lesbian."

2. In March 1998, I met with Team Toronto co-chair, Jennifer Myers, and Community Outreach Coordinator, Walter Dimini. In April 1998, I conducted telephone interviews with Tom Sneddon, Sydney 2002 Chair, Cathy Verry, Director, Government Support, and met with Mary Boson, *SSO* sports writer. I would like to thank all of them for their time and for the valuable information they gave me. Thanks also to Roger Leblanc, New Zealand delegate to the Federation of GG, for generously providing me with copies of materials from the November 1997 Federation meeting, and Brenda Pitts, for sending me her publications on these issues.

References

Baker, D., Strub, S. and Henning, B. (1995) *Cracking the Corporate Closet.* New York: Harper Business.

Bernoth, A. (1997) "We win … and it will be Worth Millions," *Sydney Morning Herald,* November 15.

Booth, D. and Tatz, C. (1994) "Sydney 2000: The Games People Play," *Current Affairs Bulletin,* 70 (7): 4–11.

Booth, D. and Tatz, C. (1997) "Pink Dollars," *Inside Sport,* June: p. 22.

Boson, M. (1997a) "We Won! Government Goes for Gold," *Sydney Star Observer,* November 20.

Boson, M. (1997b) "Gay Games Licence: Sydney Hit with $1.4 million Fee," *Sydney Star Observer,* December 11.

Boson, M. (1997c) "Are we Cheap Dates?" *Sydney Star Observer,* December 18.

Boson, M. (1998a) "Yanks Stay Home," *Sydney Star Observer*, February 20.

Boson, M. (1998b) "Games Bids 'too Costly,'" *Sydney Star Observer*, May 1.

Clark, J. (1994) "Realness ... or Sellout? Sanctioned Events in the Gay Games", www. interlog.com/~joeclark/sanctioning.html.

Clark, J. (1997) "First Briefing on the Toronto Bid," www.interlog.com/~joeclark/2002_ Toronto1.html.

Coe, R. (1986) *A Sense of Pride: The Story of Gay Games II*. San Francisco: Pride Publications.

Delvecchio, J. (1997) "'Pink Olympics' Could Earn $80m," *Sydney Morning Herald*, August 9.

Elliott, S. (2001) "Gays and Sports in Ad Alliance," *New York Times*, July 9.

Federation of Gay Games (1997a) "The Purpose," Federation Website

Federation of Gay Games (1997b) "Sports Committee: Requirements for GG VI 2002 Contract," Annual General Meeting Materials (November 13).

Federation of Gay Games (2000) "Gay Games VII Deadline Two Months Away" (March 25), Federation website.

Federation of Gay Games (2003) "Games can Change the World!" Federation website.

Fitzsimons, P. (1997) "Sydney Bids for 2002 GG," *Sydney Morning Herald*, March 27.

Forzley, R. and Hughes, D. (eds) (1990) *The Spirit Captured: The official photojournal of Celebration '90. Gay Games III*. Vancouver: For Eyes Press.

Gluckman, A. and Reed, B. (eds) (1997) *HomoEconomics*. New York: Routledge.

"Homosexuality in America: Exposing the Myths" (1998) American Family Association, afa.net/tables.htm.

Kealy, M. (1997) "Is there Enough Cash to go Around?" *Xtra*, December 18: 17.

Klein, N. (2000) *No Logo*. Toronto: Knopf.

Leblanc, R. (1997) "The 'Pink Dollar' in Sport," paper presented to the Gender, Sexualities and Sport Symposium, Victoria University, Australia, June.

Lenskyj, H. (2000) *Inside the Olympic Industry: Power, Politics and Activism*. Albany, NY: SUNY Press.

Lenskyj, H. (2002) *The Best Olympics Ever? Social Impacts of Sydney 2000*. Albany, NY: SUNY Press.

Lenskyj, H. (2003) *Out on the Field: Gender, Sport and Sexualities*. Toronto: Women's Press.

Lukinball, G. (1995) *Untold Millions*. New York: Harper.

McQuarrie, V. (1998) "Money Marathon," *Sydney Star Observer*, December 10.

Messner, M. (1984) "Gay Athletes and the Gay Games: An Interview with Tom Waddell," *M: Gentle Men for Gender Justice*, 13 (Fall): 22–23.

Myers, T. (1993) *The Canadian Survey of Gay and Bisexual Men and HIV Infection: Men's Survey*. Ottawa: Canadian AIDS Society.

Noorani, A. (1998) "Taming the Corporate Beast," *Xtra*, June 18: 43–45.

Pitts, B. (1988–89) "Beyond the Bars: The Development of Leisure Activity Management in the Lesbian and Gay Population in America," *Leisure Information Quarterly*, 15 (3): 4–7.

Pitts, B. (1998a) "An Analysis of Sponsorship Recall during Gay Games IV," *Sport Marketing Quarterly*, 7 (4): 11–15.

Pitts, B. (1998b) "From Leagues of their Own to an Industry of their Own: The Emerging Lesbian Sports Industry," *Women in Sport and Physical Activity Journal*, 6 (2): 109–139.

Pitts, B. (1998c) "Let the Gaymes Begin!" A Case Study of Sports Tourism, Commercialization, and the Gay Games V," paper presented to the "Queer Games? Theories, Politics, Sports" Conference, Amsterdam.

Pronger, B. (1990) *The Arena of Masculinity*. New York: St. Martins.

Schaap, D. (1987) "The Death of an Athlete," *Sports Illustrated*, July 27: 26–32.

Stratton, A. (1991) "Of Largesse and Neglect," *Xtra*, February: XS1.

Sydney 2002 (1997a) *Sydney Gay Games VI: Under New Skies* (Bid Book).

Sydney 2002 (1997b) "Support for the Bid," www.sydney/2002.org.au/support.html (updated October 16).

Sydney 2002 (1997c) "Economic Impact Study," www.sydney/2002.org.au/econ.html (updated July 22).

Syms, S. (1990) "Celebration '90: Physique and Critique," *Rites*, September: 13.

Team Toronto (1997) *Toronto 2002 Gay Games VI* (Bid Book).

Under New Skies Newsletter (1997) Vol. 3 (October).

Unity: A Celebration of Gay Games IV and Stonewall (1994) San Francisco: Labrecque Publishing.

Verry, C. (1998) "Gay Games 2002 – Sydney," *Womensport Australia Newsletter*, March: 14.

Vespry, A. (1990) "Reflections on the Gay Games," *Rites*, September: 11–13.

Waddell, T. and Schaap, D. (1996) *Gay Olympian: The Life and Death of Dr. Tom Waddell*. New York: Knopf.

Wardell, R. (1997) "Spanning the Globe," *Federation Forum*, Fall: 4.

Wilke, M. (2002) "Guinness and Nike Sponsor Gay Rugby Tournament," *Commercial Closet* (June 24).

Websites

Sydney Star Observer, www.sso.rainbow.net/au

Sydney Morning Herald, www.smh.com.au

Commercial Closet, www2.commercial.closet.org

Federation of Gay Games website, www.gaygames.org

Sydney 2002 Gay Games website, www.sydney/2002.org.au, accessed February 1998

16

Global Sport Sponsorship
What now? What's next?

T. Bettina Cornwell and John Amis

The investments made by transnational corporations in large-scale sport sponsorship agreements are well documented, not least in the pages of this text. While there are few truly global sport properties like the Olympics and World Cup, this is destined to change. Already, many sports while not achieving universal popularity do receive international media coverage in major markets and this in turn inspires international sponsorship. The sport sponsorship industry in many markets but particularly the United States and Europe is developing in sophistication as evidenced by specialized sports marketing firms, advanced training in sports and sponsorship marketing, and new specialty firms offering, for example, sponsor-sponsored matching services. Despite this, the practitioner and researcher view into the future is decidedly shortsighted due to the fluidity of the global context. We must constantly ask our selves: What now? What's next?

Sponsorship is a multifaceted phenomenon that changes depending on one's perspective. Businesses seeking to utilize corporate sponsorship as a marketing tool see it differently than do sports properties seeking financial support. Media markets, stock markets, and international markets; regulators, fans, employees, consumers and researchers all have their individual takes. There are, however, some issues that cut across several if not all interested parties, including: (1) the worldwide integration of sport and sponsorship with other forms of entertainment; (2) different approaches to the measurement and understanding of sponsorship effects; (3) enhanced consideration of employees and consumers in their varied roles; and (4) continued globalization of sponsorship. In this chapter, we provide a brief analysis of each of these four areas that, we contend, should form major foci of future research efforts.

Sports, Sponsorship, Entertainment and Communication

We have recently witnessed a definite blurring between what have previously been long-standing and comfortable distinctions: news and gossip (Dobbs, 2004), philanthropy and sponsorship (Mescon & Tilson, 1987), and entertainment and persuasion (Shrum, 2004). Within these debates, market-driven sponsorship has become part and parcel of a larger trend toward developing and "riding with" interesting information, entertainment and technology to reach consumers in their busy and increasingly international lifestyles. Sponsorship could indeed be viewed as one of the drivers of this integration by bringing together entertainment properties, such as sports, the media and corporate interests.

At the inaugural *Advertising Age* "Madison and Vine" conference (named to capture the intersection of the advertising and film industries) held in February of 2003, Steve Heyer, then president of Coca-Cola, informed the audience that if new business models are not developed, the old ones will simply collapse around us. This was a warning to advertising agencies and media suppliers that their traditional way of doing things would be brought to an end, in part, by the sway of firms seeking to integrate marketing and entertainment. One of the most important points in his address was that "brands are now portals" and that the Coca-Cola brand is a network larger than any twenty television networks combined, and that it is available to those with the right value propositions (Rothenberg, 2003). In a sense the tables are turned or at least turning. Heyer went so far as to suggest that Coca-Cola's network and power might be harnessed to help popularize a movie ... at a price (Heyer, 2003). That is to say that entertainment marketers (although not explicitly mentioned this would certainly apply to sports) would be charged a fee to associate with Coca-Cola. The logic is compelling, especially when one considers that there are few truly global media (with the possible exception of Microsoft and AOL/Time Warner) that could compare to the daily consumer contact that Coca-Cola has around the globe.

This proposition, that corporate sponsoring is at least one driver of the continued worldwide communication-entertainment integration, holds implications for both research and practice. Sponsorship, in part, gets around the boundaries of old media markets as sport, in particular, transcends international borders. Consumer interest in large part drives exposure – one could say that media content has a life of its own. Scholars must gain a more holistic understanding of sponsorship as an integrative and permeating force as much of our current research is overly micro in orientation, concerned with individual program outcomes.

Practitioners in this new world order should become "alliance managers" (Rothenberg, 2003; Farrelly & Quester, this volume). According to Rothenberg, the marketing and entertainment industries must find or make synergistic relationships for clients and create new forms of value in the demographic, psychographic and functional relationships found in their client base. For example, Samsung consumer electronics has held a sponsorship relationship with the International Olympic Committee since the 1998 Winter Olympics primarily to generate awareness. However, firm managers also had a desire to position Samsung as appealing to a younger audience, a strategy made manifest in the firm's sponsorship of the two *Matrix* film sequels to communicate a cool, young lifestyle image (Pesola, 2003). Thus, having generated awareness through these and other sponsorships, Samsung is now utilizing sponsorship to "achieve relevance and preference" (Pesola, 2003). For this reason, the firm sponsored the emotive torch relay at the start of the 2004 Olympic Games. Thus, the new alliance manager role suggests that sports marketing training must be multidisciplinary and international. While several universities currently include aspects of entertainment or international marketing in their sports marketing programs, many do not. Even the name "sports marketing" is subject to becoming a misnomer in years to come. Communications majors with little or no understanding of sports and international markets are no better off when the challenge is to create a seamless integrated marketing communications program at a global level. Furthermore, the realignment with entertainment is not the only possibility. Many sport sponsorships are also tied to charitable events and this suggests an even broader training base for the new practitioner. Consider the yellow bracelet LIVESTRONG campaign by Nike to support the Lance Armstrong Foundation for cancer research (Gard, 2004) where sports are integrated with charity but in a very delicate way so as not to offend a youth target market suspicious of commercialization. While perhaps intuitively obvious, it is worth emphasizing that this necessitates that sponsorship at the global level requires greater cultural and intergenerational sensitivity than has usually previously been apparent.

If this dramatic shift to "indirect marketing" (Cornwell, 2005) – where awareness and change in image are achieved through association rather than direct persuasive communication – continues, not only will we need to train our practitioners differently and more broadly, we will have to reconsider our communication objectives and goals. We will have to reconsider currently popular approaches to research and measurement of sponsorship effects. In the examination of sponsorship communication we have relied primarily on extending popular advertising and marketing paradigms and theories to sponsorship. While much of this research has been fruitful, it may have been too simplistic to account for an increasingly complex global sponsorship context.

Sponsorship Effects and their Measurement

Recently, social cognition researcher John Bargh (2002) criticized the field of consumer research for having missed out on major developments in his area. In particular, he noted that new evidence of unconscious information processing and the potential for social and self-related goal pursuits to influence basic reasoning processes. Researchers interested in sponsorship should also find his arguments interesting. Bargh (2002, p. 281), citing his own work, offers the following example: "if you present a subject with adjectives related to politeness, in the course of an ostensible language test in which she constructs grammatical sentences out of series of words presented in a scrambled order, and then give her a chance to behave in a polite manner (e.g., waiting patiently for the experimenter to end a conversation with another person), she will exhibit greater politeness (i.e., wait longer before interruption) than will participants in a control condition" (Bargh, Chen & Burrows, 1996). The point being made is that people cannot account for a good deal of what influences their behavior and judgment.

This suggests that many measures of sponsorship effectiveness, particularly recall and recognition, are too hard hitting. Moreover, many measures may be context and culturally dependent and therefore less useful in a global sponsorship setting. For sponsorship messages to be effective, there is no real need for a consumer to be able to identify a company as a sponsor of an event or vice versa to identify the event as something sponsored by the company. What *is* needed is behavioral change, behavioral change that the person may not be able to tie in any conscious way to their sponsorship experience. From the perspective of the fast moving consumer goods firm executive, the objective is in-store choice in favor of their brand – with or without the ability to reason why the choice seems right for them. From the perspective of the global charity, this is the positive feeling that motivates a person to donate. If we want to attempt to measure communication effects at this level, we must consider implicit memory measures that do not require the conscious retrieval of information.

Duke and Carlson (1993) reviewed implicit measures of advertising effectiveness and suggest several techniques that might be useful in an international sponsorship context. Word fragment completion, for example, asks individuals to complete the missing parts of words after some exposure to this word, or brand name (e.g. SP_I_E = SPRITE). Similarly, word stem completion asks individuals to complete a word by supplying its beginning or end (e.g. SPR_ _ _ = SPRITE). Another approach is perceptual identification where a word or logo is presented quickly without the opportunity for extensive processing. These techniques rely on either repetition priming, where the test word is one seen previously, or associate priming, where the test word is somehow related to previously presented information. These memory tests seem appropriate for sponsorship effectiveness measurement because the simple presentation of a brand name or logo in the sponsorship context may be all that is needed to prime memory.

The unconscious learning of sponsor–event relationships with the potential transfer of image from the event to the brand with repetition or associative priming is innocuous enough one might say, but goal priming seems far more sinister. It has been demonstrated that goal primes can be delivered both subliminally, with the person being unaware of the priming, or supraliminally, where the person is aware (Bargh, 2002, p. 282). Bargh cites as yet unpublished work by Spencer and Zanna demonstrating a subliminal prime for thirstiness that caused thirsty, but not non-thirsty, participants to drink more of a thirst-quenching drink ("SuperQuencher") than of any energy providing drink ("PowerPro"). Now the potential and the threat are clear. Sponsorship is in a strong position to both take advantage of and abuse non-conscious processing through the use of goal primes.

Further, in recent studies, consumers' post-advertising experience influenced the memory of their own experiences (Braun, 1999). Through reconstructive memory, advertising can influence the nature of what consumers remember. They may come to believe that the experiences they had were as the advertising suggests. The same could only hold true for sponsorship. Sponsorships have a strong image and experience producing potential and we know little about their ability to influence constructive memory for sponsors (an exception would be the work of Pham and Johar 2001 on constructive memory related to brand prominence) or experiences after the fact. Not only can communications after experience influence memories, it seems that memories can even be created. Braun, Ellis and Loftus (2002) showed that autobiographical referencing in advertising can make people believe that they had experiences that are mentioned in ads (e.g. shaking hands with a Disney character) when this was not the case.

It was argued in the opening of this chapter that the importance of global sponsorship effects and their measurement are important across the interested parties listed. It is maintained here that the potential power of sponsorship effects is deserving of additional researcher attention, particularly in countries without strong consumer protection. Just as international advertising has received criticism and encouraged debate regarding potential negative consequences in developing countries (Frazer, 1989), so will sponsorship. As evidenced here there is a need not only for practitioners to better understand their tools but for social science and public policy researchers to play an active role in understanding the potential effects of sponsorship in the consumer and social realm.

Employees and Consumers

Employees have long been argued as a central audience for sponsorship (Gardner & Shuman, 1988; Cornwell, 1995). However, little has been done in understanding the value of communication with this audience. The most we have established from case-study information is that employees, when left out of the firm's sponsorship decision-making and focus, feel disenfranchised by the oversight (Grimes & Meenaghan, 1998). What is the impact of customer focus but employee neglect?

Especially for organizations with large international workforces, employees are an important audience for their sponsorship programs. Furthermore, employee support for an organization's sponsorship program represents a potentially important source of additional value from sponsorship programs (Amis, Slack & Berrett, 1999). It has been argued that if employees are supported to identify with the firm's sponsorships that this will positively influence sponsorship-related citizenship behaviors such as spontaneously spreading positive messages to others regarding sponsored activities, and actively protecting and defending an organization's sponsorship program from attacks from internal and external critics (Cornwell & Coote, 2004a). Moreover, for multinational firms, sponsorship of the right sport can form a uniting bond that transcends country boundaries.

On the other hand, consumers as an audience of importance for sponsorship-linked communications have been the focus of applied as well as academic research from the earliest of studies. The role of the consumer has, however, been narrowly defined (actually assumed rather than defined) as passive, although potentially passionate, receivers of information. Thus, while the importance of loyal fans has not been missed, their role as co-producers has not been examined. Client or customer co-production of business solutions has been considered as perhaps particular to knowledge-intensive industries (Bettencourt, Ostrom, Brown & Roundtree, 2002) but aspects of this concept hold import for sports and other sponsorship-attracting events. One central idea with clear generalizability is that of proactively managing co-production behaviors. This suggests, for example, that consumer/fan advocacy and communication can be directed and supported to align with firm and property goals and objectives. While co-production principles have not been researched as yet, we can at least point to research that suggests that consumers are not passive communication consumers in the sport sponsorship context.

Thus, another perspective on consumers as co-producers in sponsorship stems from the meanings consumers develop during their sponsorship experience. Cornwell and Smith (2001) consider the personal meanings that event participants develop and take away from an event, some of which are not those intended by the event organizers or their corporate sponsors. For example, it appears that event participants make judgments about individuals perceived as invited or excluded from an event and then form attitudes related to these perceptions of exclusivity. In related research, Cornwell and Coote (2004b) find that a person's life experiences (for example, their experience with breast cancer) influences their level of organization identification with a sponsored event, which is in turn positively related to sponsorship-linked purchase commitment. Much more research effort could be devoted to understanding the consumer, not only as an audience for sponsorship but as an active participant in the creation of sponsorship communication meaning. Clearly emerging unintended event meanings (good or bad) are of concern to the sponsor and the property and the potential for unexpected meanings is multifold as sport sponsorships cross cultural boundaries.

Finally, we have yet to consider the impact of sponsorship on employee and customer relations beyond the hospitality marquees found at major events. What role does sponsorship play in fostering positive customer-employee interactions? While no empirical research is on offer, we can at least consider a case with potential in this area. Emirates Airlines sponsored the 2004 Melbourne Cup horse racing event, the one said to "stop the nation." On Cup day, business across Australia comes to a standstill and even those not in Melbourne dress for the event, make a bet and watch the race. Although one could see sponsorship of this race by Emirates as simply an extension of their other race sponsorships, such as the Dubai World Cup and the Singapore Derby (Middle East Company News, 2002), it has the synergistic advantage of resonating with both employees and consumers. Emirates Airlines has added sponsorships to its portfolio that parallel its international expansion (in this instance the opening of services in Australia and New Zealand) but at the same time has selected sponsorships that have high consumer and employee identification potential. They strike the balance between "furthering global ambitions and maintaining regional relevance" as suggested by Richard Gillis (*Marketing*, 2004). In the extensive consumer contact found in airline service, Emirates sponsorships provide common ground between Middle East culture and the cultures of other parts of the world.

Continued Globalization of Sponsorship

While each of the above topics, the integration of sports and entertainment, the importance of measurement, and the limited research on some aspects of employees and consumers within the sponsorship context, is potentially global in nature, there are some issues that spring specifically from the continuing globalization of sponsorship activities. We outline some of these issues and find them key areas for future research, although we do not proclaim them to be easily researched. Therefore, we advocate multidisciplinary and multi-paradigmatic research in every instance. These areas include: (1) internationalization of sport; (2) corporatizing of sport via sponsorship; and (3) differently politicizing sponsored sport.

Internationalization of Sport

Corporate sponsorships and sports have developed a reciprocal relationship; the two, at least at the professional level, having become integrated and in many respects, mutually dependent over the past twenty years. In part because of this relationship, there are, according to Mason (1999), four buyers of the sport product: fans that buy tickets and merchandise and follow their teams in the media, media companies that purchase broadcasting rights, communities that support sport infrastructure, and corporations that buy and sell teams or sponsor them. Mason suggests that these interested parties together will continue to support growth of professional leagues in the broader global entertainment industry. Moreover, Cohen and Prazmark (1999) have predicted that there will be a shift to corporate ownership of events. In times of escalating sponsorship fees, this will remove the fickle nature of sponsor-event negotiations that might leave a long-time sponsor without event participation. The new owner/equity paradigm will also speed the process of sports internationalization as sport is used in market entry strategy.

In addition to the global growth of leagues predicted by Mason, one could argue that there is a growing internationalization of sport overall. Some internationalization could be viewed as market entry in to previous "hold out" countries dominated by other sports (e.g. soccer in the United States) while other forms of internationalization are more diverse (e.g. the expansion of rugby). The internationalization of sport can also take the form of event creation – developing a sporting event where none existed. This is often supported if not led by corporate sponsorship. A prime example here would be the involvement of brands like Taco Bell and Mountain Dew with the X Games; the ESPN made-for-cable TV Extreme Games, featuring "new" sports such as mountain biking and snowboarding (see Gladden & McDonald in this volume). In order to better understand future globalization of sponsorship we must better understand the ongoing globalization and co-creation of sport.

Corporatizing of Sport via Sponsorship

We are only beginning to map the complex corporate relationships found in national and international sponsorship (Farrelly, Quester & Smolianov, 1998). However, there have been various discussions and examinations of the commercialization of sport in the business press and to a more limited extent in academic research. Commercialization, or the use of sponsorship for business-related purposes is perhaps becoming accepted. For example, one report published in *Marketing Week* (Singh & White, 2002), finds 73% of respondents recognizing that companies sponsor sport "to increase sales" (p. 30). While only 22% of respondents expressed a negative view of commercialization via sponsorship, 17% indicated that "sponsors have too much power." This is arguably, quite a different matter. The use of sponsorship by corporations can be viewed as positive, again, referring to the study published in *Marketing Week*, 63% of respondents agreed with the proposal that without sponsorship, there would perhaps be no event. When sponsors begin controlling the event or event outcomes, one has stepped beyond "simple" commercialization. Instead, we begin to witness a corporatization of certain commercially attractive sports characterized by a uniformity of players – particularly sponsors, broadcasters and leagues – organized to promote an entertainment experience with the ultimate purpose of profit maximization (Andrews, 1999).

Within the realms of sport sponsorship, corporate pressures can be covert, such as the allegations pertaining to the ways in which a sponsor may influence team selection (e.g. speculation that Nike pressured the Brazil coach Mario Zagallo and an unwell Ronaldo to play after the player was initially left out of the team to contest the 1998 World Cup Final (Fendrich, 1998)), or more overt, as with the perceived pressure on athletes to conform to particular desired physical and sexual norms (e.g. the well-publicized lack of interest from sponsors in Billie-Jean King and Martina Navratilova when their lesbianism became publicized (Kort, 2000)). The pressures might also be subtle but summative as in the case of National Association of Stock Car Auto Racing (NASCAR). With each corporate sponsor individually pressuring their drivers in speech, dress and manner, NASCAR drivers are becoming cookie-cutter similar, which, it has been contended, is making NASCAR boring (Macur, 1999). It is incumbent upon those involved in sport sponsorship to be more critically informed of such dynamics in order to understand their genesis and likely consequences.

Global Sports are Differently Politicized

Sports are played against a background of globalization and fragmentation. Even the most local of amateur events may see final scores posted to the World Wide Web. Globalization is composed of coexisting homogenizing, heterogenizing and hybridizing forces, and the tension between these forces is one of the key challenges in the cultural economy. Appadurai (1990) explores the order of this new cultural economy by developing a framework that incorporates dimensions of global cultural flow. He sees flows of people, technology, money, images and ideas moving around the globe and consolidating at particular points into national, regional and local structural formations. Sponsorship is an excellent conduit for such flows and major sport events, such as the FIFA World Cup and the Olympics constitute an interesting example of their consolidation (see, for example, Madrigal et al. in this volume).

It is argued that the scale, volume and speed of these flows have become so intense that the disjunctures between them affects the politics of global culture (Appadurai, 1990; Harvey, 1990; King, 1997). This is perhaps one of the reasons that global sporting events are often the staging grounds for global political events. This is not a new phenomenon but the targets are perhaps new. Because corporate interests are now as frequently represented in global sporting events as are national interests, the reasons for political action to be played out at these events is even more compelling. Just as the WTO meeting in Seattle became a "public screen" for a type of participatory democracy (DeLuca & Peeples, 2002), so may sponsored events increasingly become targets for staged "image events" that seek to shock.

Sponsorship has been shown to be a powerful multifaceted force in global society with both positive and negative, punctuating and cumulative effects. We must continue to critically examine sport, and the sponsorship of it, against a plethora of economic, cultural, political and social impacts. Business interests need not be in conflict with community and social interests but naturally there are those who will push the boundaries. The best path forward incorporates research and develops understanding that can be utilized to set policies and at the same time support business and cultural interests.

References

Amis, J., Slack, T. and Berrett, T. (1999) "Sport Sponsorship as Distinctive Competence," *European Journal of Marketing*, 33 (3/4): 250–272.

Andrews, D. L. (1999) "Dead and Alive? Sport History in the Late Capitalist Moment," *Sporting Traditions: Journal of the Australian Society for Sport History*, 16(1): 73–83.

Appadurai, A. (1990) "Disjuncture and Differences in the Global Cultural Economy," *Theory, Culture and Society*, 7: 295–310.

Bargh, J. A. (2002) "Losing Consciousness: Automatic Influences on Consumer Judgement, Behavior, and Motivation," *Journal of Consumer Research*, 29 (September): 280–285.

Bargh, J. A., Chen, M. and Burrows, L. (1996) "Automaticity of Social Behavior: Direct Effects of Trait Construct and Stereotype Priming on Action," *Journal of Personality and Social Psychology*, 71 (September): 230–244.

Bettencourt, L. A., Ostrom, A. L., Brown, S. W. and Roundtree, R. I. (2002) "Client Co-Production in Knowledge-Intensive Business Services," *California Management Review*, 44(4): 100–128.

Braun, K. A. (1999) "Postexperience Advertising Effects on Consumer Memory," *Journal of Consumer Research*, 25 (4): 319–352.

Braun, K. A., Ellis, R. and Loftus, E. F. (2002) "Make My Memory: How Advertising Can Change our Memories of the Past," *Psychology & Marketing*, 19 (1): 1–23.

Cohen, A. and Prazmark, R. (1999) "Future Speak," *Sales & Marketing Management*, 151 (8): 20.

Cornwell, T. B. (1995) "Sponsorship-linked Marketing Development," *Sport Marketing Quarterly*, 4 (4): 13–24.

Cornwell, T. B. (2005) "Indirect Marketing", Working paper, UQ Business School, The University of Queensland, Brisbane.

Cornwell, T. B. and Coote, L. V. (2004a) "Employee Identification with Sponsorship Programs: A Conceptual Framework of Antecedents and Outcomes," *2004 American Marketing Association Winter Educator's Conference Proceedings*, (eds), William Cron and George S. Low, 15: 305–306.

Cornwell, T. B. and Coote, L. V. (2004b) "Corporate Sponsorship of a Cause: The Role of Identification in Purchase Intent," *Journal of Business Research*, forthcoming.

Cornwell, T. B. and Smith, R. (2001) "The Communications Importance of Consumer Meaning in Cause-linked Events: Findings from a U.S. Event to Benefit Breast Cancer Research," *Journal of Marketing Communications*, 7 (4): 213–229.

DeLuca, K. M. and Peeples, J. (2002) "From Public Sphere to Public Screen: Democracy, Activism, and the "Violence" of Seattle," *Critical Studies in Media Communication*, 19 (2): 125–151.

Dobbs, L. (2004) "All the News that's Fit," *U.S. News & World Report*, March 1: 48.

Duke, C. R. and Carlson, L. (1993) "A Conceptual Approach to Alternative Memory Measures for Advertising Effectiveness," *Journal of Current Issues and Research in Advertising*, 15 (2): 1–14.

Farrelly, F., Quester, P. and Smolianov, P. (1998) "The Australian Cricket Board (ABC): Mapping Corporate Relations," *Corporate Communications: An International Journal*, 3 (4): 150–155.

Fenditch, H. (1998) "Nike Denies Influencing Brazil's Lineup," *Associated Press Newsviews*, July 14.

Frazer, C. F. (1989) "Issues and Evidence in International Advertising," *Current Issues & Research in Advertising*, 12 (1): 75–90.

Gard, L. (2004) "We're Good Guys, Buy From Us; Companies are Trying out Innovative Charity Drives to Burnish their Brands," *Business Week*, November 22: 72.

Gardner, M. P. and Shuman, P. (1988) "Sponsorships and Small Businesses," *Journal of Small Business Management,* 26 (4): 44–52.

Grimes, E. and Meenaghan, T. (1998) "Focusing Commercial Sponsorship on the Internal Corporate Audience," *International Journal of Advertising*, 17 (1): 51–74.

Harvey, D. (1990) *The Condition of Postmodernity: An Enquiry into the Origins of Cultural Change*, Oxford: Blackwell.

Heyer, S. J. (2003) "Steve Heyer's Manifesto for a New Age of Marketing: Madison and Vine Explained as Coca-Cola's Global Master Plan," AdAge.com (http://wwwladage.com/news.cms?newsId=37076).

King, A. D. (1997) *Culture, Globalization and the World System*. Minneapolis, MN: University of Minnesota Press.

Kort, M. (2000) "The Long Journey to Come Out Made Martina Navratilova a Special Champion – and Cleared the Court for All-out Competitor Amelie Mauresmo," *The

Advocate, August 15, http://articles.findarticles.com/p/articles/mi_m/589/is_2000_August_15/ai_63692905, accessed May 19, 2004.

Macur, J. (1999) "NASCAR is Shifting from Wild to Mild," *The Orlando Sentinel*, August 14: B1.

Marketing, (2004) "Sports Marketing: Global Deal, Local Glory," August 11: 36.

Mason, D. S. (1999) "What is the Sports Product and Who Buys it? The Marketing of Professional Sports Leagues," *European Journal of Marketing*, 33 (3/4): 402–419.

Mescon, T. S. and Tilson, D. J. (1987) "Corporate Philanthropy: A Strategic Approach to the Bottom Line," *California Management Review*, 29 (2): 49–61.

Middle East Company News (2002) "Emirates Airlines – New Official Event Partner of the FIFA World Youth Championship," December 15.

Pesola, M. (2003) "From Microwaves to the Matrix – consumer electronics – Samsung used to make Cheap Copies," *Financial Times*, September 11: 8.

Pham, M. T. and Gita Venkataramani Johar (2001) "Market Prominence Biases in Sponsor Identification: Processes and Consequentiality," *Psychology and Marketing*, 18 (2): 123–143.

Rothenberg, R. (2003) "What Steve Heyer's War Cry Means for Ad Agencies Now," *Advertising Age*, 47 (7): 20.

Shrum, L. J. (ed.) (2004) *The Psychology of Entertainment Media: Blurring the Lines between Entertainment and Persuasion*, Mahwah, NJ: Lawrence Erlbaum.

Singh, S. and White, A. (2002) "Proud to be Associated with ... *Marketing Week*," June 6: 30–31.

Index

Lightning Source UK Ltd.
Milton Keynes UK
21 December 2009

147802UK00001B/26/P